# The Anarchists of Casas Viejas

# The Anarchists of Casas Viejas

Jerome R. Mintz



Indiana University Press
Bloomington and Indianapolis

The paper used in this publication meets the minimum requirements of American National Standard for Information Sciences—Permanence of Paper for Printed Library Materials, ANSI Z39.48-1984.

Manufactured in the United States of America

**Library of Congress Cataloging-in-Publication Data**

Mintz, Jerome R.
The anarchists of Casas Viejas / by Jerome R. Mintz.
p. cm.
Includes bibliographical references and index.
ISBN 0-253-20854-8 (pbk. : alk. paper)
1. Anarchism—Spain—Casas Viejas—History. 2. Syndicalism—Spain—Casas Viejas—History. 3. Peasant uprisings—Spain—Casas Viejas—History. 4. Casas Viejas (Cádiz, Spain)—History.
I. Title.
HX928.C34M54 1994
335'.83'094688—dc20 93-2425

1 2 3 4 5 99 98 97 96 95 94

To the memory of my father, **Irving Mintz** (1898–1953)

and to my mother, **Mildred Mintz**

# Contents

# Preface

In the historical literature, the uprising in Casas Viejas is considered the classic example of anarchist rural rebellion. This book is about the development of the anarchist movement in the town of Casas Viejas in the period preceding the Spanish Civil War. It concerns the processes and the human dimensions of revolution and repression. This is a study in ethnohistory, and the circumstances and events examined are the means employed to interpret the lives of the Andalusian *campesinos* (the rural workers and peasants) at a moment when they were swept up by a new ideal.

The book is divided into three parts: the first describes the beginnings of anarchism in Casas Viejas in the year 1914, the merger of anarchist philosophy with the views of the indigenous campesinos, and the struggles of the early *obreros conscientes* (dedicated anarchists) against the landlords. The second part concerns the events of the tragic uprising in 1933 and the subsequent perceptions of the event within the town and throughout the nation. In the final section, the survivors recount their personal experiences during the troubled times that followed.

This study of anarchist rebellion is itself part of a revolution in historical research, one aspect of which is the re-examination of history, using data from those in a despised station—personal narratives and life histories of slaves and sharecroppers in the American South, for example, and in this instance, campesino accounts of circumstances in Andalusia. The new data are primarily oral; the narrators are uneducated, often illiterate. These oral versions challenge histories that have been based too often almost solely on the views of the educated and elitist classes. The introduction of these new sources in the study of social and political history can evoke a change in perception as radical as that stirred by the Impressionist movement in paint-

ing—now as then, the image of the world is bathed in fresh light, which lends to scenes a dimension and scope previously unrealized.

Since the history of anarchism in Andalusia is largely unwritten, this work is based primarily on field research. As Gerald Brenan observed, "the real history of the Anarchist movement is contained not in books, but in its daily press and in the memories of living anarchists."[1] In seeking these sources, I lived for a total of three years in Casas Viejas and came to know most of the surviving anarchists in the region. Beginning in 1965, I collected and studied the oral accounts of anarchists and other campesinos and townsmen, along with the reports of anarchist and local newspapers, church and court records, parliamentary debates and reports, and other documents that came into my hands, such as letters and journals. Each account, written or oral, was considered on its own merits and, whenever possible, was studied with the background of the writer or teller in mind. Quotations recorded during field research are identified by the name, pseudonym, or initial of the speaker.

Immediately after the uprising, Casas Viejas was visited by scores of reporters and writers and was subsequently studied by social historians. It will become evident, however, that despite the extensive material written about the town, the full story has not been told. Because of a number of factors discussed below, both contemporary and historical accounts distort or misinterpret what occurred at Casas Viejas. Various versions that generally followed class and political affiliation attained currency, and use of the insurrection for propaganda purposes took precedence over concern for truth. Equally striking is the fact that campesino perceptions of what occurred played a negligible role in fixing the historical record. My concern has been not only to provide an accurate narrative of what took place but also to explain the social implications of true as well as erroneous or misleading accounts. When the data that I collected contradicted standard descriptions of Spanish anarchism in general and the uprising at Casas Viejas in particular, it became necessary to demythologize the events, to re-examine some widely accepted concepts, and to consider the factors that led to misinterpretation.

Field research on anarchism and revolution undertaken during the period of Franco's dictatorship demanded caution and patience. Although winning the confidence of the campesinos over the course of time usually required little more than expressing my natural feelings and sympathies, it proved difficult to find some individuals involved (since some now lived far from the town), to win their acceptance, and then to interview and reinterview them. At first my own understanding was limited to previous written accounts, and the initial comments of townsmen who had been eyewitnesses of the Casas

1. *The Spanish Labyrinth*, p. 360.

Viejas uprising and were willing to speak about it were usually understandably evasive.

*J. M.:* How old were you then?
*Juan Moreno Vidal:* Sixteen.
*J. M.:* Do you remember a great deal?
*Juan Moreno:* Of course.
*J. M.:* Were you in the middle of things or on the sidelines?
*Juan Moreno:* I was only on the sidelines. I wasn't in anything. I was just looking. I didn't join anything.
*J. M.:* Who were the leaders?
*Juan Moreno:* At this time I don't know the names of these men.
*J. M.:* You don't remember?
*Juan Moreno:* I don't know.
*J. M.:* You don't wish to tell me?
*Juan Moreno:* That's not it. I just don't know their names—except Seisdedos.
*J. M.:* Could we speak of them using their nicknames?
*Juan Moreno:* Ah, their nicknames. I don't remember. I don't remember. Just Seisdedos. Seisdedos was here. [*Aside to Paco*] I won't give him their names.

It was often still more difficult to overcome the defensiveness of anarcho-syndicalists who had participated in the events. They had suffered under the repression, and they were wary. My principal guide and teacher in the ways of the *campo* and of rural anarchism was José Rodríguez Quirós, known by his nickname, Pepe Pareja.[2] Even though we became intimate friends, he was reluctant to tell me of his own involvement in the uprising. For a long time he denied being in town at that time, and it was only after I cross-checked his early accounts with others (including Antonia, his wife) that he finally admitted he had misled me:

It's right and natural that not knowing someone well, one would lie. One has to protect oneself. But rather than have you hear it from one of the many little rats that scurry around here who will tell a different story, I will tell you myself.

2. Nicknames are commonly used in small towns throughout Spain. Nicknames may derive from one's occupation, physical appearance, habits, or place of origin or current residence; or they may be inherited from one's forefathers, and their origin and meaning lost. Townsmen are usually better known by their nicknames than by their surnames; however, an individual is addressed by his Christian name. Nicknames do not translate readily into English, and in this work most are left in the original Spanish. For further discussion, see J. A. Pitt-Rivers, *The People of the Sierra*, pp. 160 ff.

On another occasion, he said,

> Nowadays we cannot do as we choose to. If we think of some idea, we have to think about it alone, without telling anyone. If we consult with anyone, we have to do it secretly. One has to be reserved—to keep one's thoughts to oneself. People see us together and they ask, "Why is this fellow here?" I say, "He is here to study the Spanish language." I don't have to tell them anything—if they don't merit trust.

My first conversation with Pepe Pilar (the nickname of José González Pérez) did not occur until after I returned to Casas Viejas in 1969, after a three-year absence. Early in December Pilar, a slight, small man, approached me on the street. He said that I wouldn't remember him, politely explaining that he had been sick when I had been in the town before. Actually he had been understandably suspicious and had slipped away whenever I approached. Now he said that he knew of my friendship with certain people and he wanted to talk to me—but not in the street. In time I learned that Pilar had been a member of Juventud Libertaria (Libertarian Youth) and that he was one of three men then alive who had been at the civil guard barracks on the day of the uprising. Because of his role in the events, Pilar was able to confirm or refute many of my own speculations.

There was some risk in sharing reports with me. On two occasions that I know of, people were called to the barracks of the civil guard and questioned about my activities. One received a visit from the guard at his home and was required to report to them each time that I came to his country cottage. Frightened but undeterred, he made an alternative plan: on the first of every month, he would arrive in town to collect his social security check; afterward, he would walk up the hill to Pepe Pareja's house, where I would be waiting.

On visits to anarchists in other towns, often either Pepe Pareja or Pepe Pilar would accompany me. To avoid being seen with me, they would leave the town through the fields. I would drive to the highway and pick them up when they climbed over the roadside fence. For my initial meeting with Manuel Llamas, I followed instructions and arrived in Medina Sidonia on a festival day, when the streets were crowded with out-of-town cars and the civil guards were expected to be too occupied to notice my arrival. On subsequent occasions, I would wait for him to appear at a friend's café.

Eventually I learned the indirect Andalusian style.[3] I had never met José Monroy, who spent most of each year with his sons in Valencia. He had been

3. Pitt-Rivers writes, "The Andalusians are the most accomplished liars I have ever encountered. I use the word *accomplished* literally, for it requires training and intelligence to distinguish rapidly when the truth is owed and when it is to be concealed, and to acquire conscious control over facial expression is an ability which takes practice from childhood" (p. xvi).

the leader of the local *sindicato* (revolutionary trade union) at the time of the uprising, and I was planning to drive to Valencia to try to see him. By that time he had probably heard of my interest. I must have learned in advance that he was coming to Casas Viejas for a visit, for one morning on Calle San Juan, among a group of men chatting on the street in front of a café, I noticed an unfamiliar figure leaning on a cane and knew immediately that it was Monroy. In this public situation we ignored each other. There were no salutes, no questions, no introductions. I walked past the group of men without stopping, went through the town, circled around, and came to Pepe Pareja's house from another direction. Within ten minutes José Monroy had struggled up the hill to meet me, and we embraced before a word was spoken.

Following Franco's death in 1975 and the introduction of democratic government in 1976, *los que tenían ideas* ("those who had ideas") cast fear aside and delighted in the pleasure of free expression. Many openly declared their views. During the election campaign of 1979 (boycotted by the anarchists), there was vigorous debate in the meeting halls and the streets. Posters and pamphlets were broadcast openly. José Suárez, in 1932 the first Socialist mayor of Casas Viejas, no longer glanced over his shoulder while conversing; he wrote his memoirs and was awaiting their publication. Some became willing to discuss the uprising for the first time; others, like Pepe Pareja, continued their daily routine, as steady under one regime as under another.

Until the attempted right-wing coup of February 1981, the political climate appeared to have changed sufficiently to dispense with the use of pseudonyms almost completely. Historical personages, national and local, are identified herein. Some of *los que tenían ideas* remain wary: one, whose manuscript I carried out of Spain several years ago and quote from in this study, did not wish his name to be used. A letter from Spain informs me that he has just passed away; out of respect for his wishes and his family, in this text his written and spoken words are labeled "Anónimo" (anonymous), as he requested.[4] In a few other instances pseudonyms or initials were suggested as a courtesy and a precaution. Offered this option, Juan Moreno Vidal insisted on having his matrilineal as well as his patrilineal name printed: "Given the time left to me in this life, I'm not afraid of anything."

Unfortunately, not all of those who aided this work during the Franco dictatorship have lived to see the end of those days. Pepe Pilar, so brave and so badly beaten; Juan Rodríguez (known as Sopas), accused of treachery;

4. Anónimo compiled a historical record of the period from 1910 to the present. Since the manuscript is handwritten and has not been published, there are no page references to quotations from the work.

José Monroy, who reluctantly became a leader; Juan Pinto, who believed his brother had been shot in his stead; and Manuel Llamas, who hid for seven years in the mountains—campesinos all marked by the anarchist rebellion—they are among those whose voices can be heard now only in the pages that follow.

# Acknowledgments

The periods of my field research were carried out with funds from the Ford Foundation (1965–66) and with a Guggenheim Fellowship (1969–70). A fellowship from the American Council of Learned Societies (1973–74) enabled me to devote that year to beginning a draft of the manuscript. Timely aid came also from the Littauer Foundation, the National Endowment for the Humanities, the American Philosophical Society, and from various offices of Indiana University. I am grateful to all of these organizations for their assistance.

Here I can thank as well the brigade of capable students at Indiana University who helped to collate, transcribe, and translate my tapes and notes: Carlos Polit, Henry Fernández, Carlos Cano, Judson Yearwood, Evelyn Kiatipoff Clark, Sandra Campaneri, Roberta Getman, Kay Villa-García, Jesús O. Cervantes, John Charles Thomas, and Moraima Maldonado-Mendez. Rita Brown, Mary Vaughn, Cathy Winkler, and Susan Diduk typed the several versions of the manuscript. Elena Fraboschi checked and clarified the translations of the Spanish materials that appear in the book and helped in innumerable ways to resolve problems, large and small. Trina Gay read the manuscript in its entirety and made many creative suggestions concerning style and clarity.

I thank Rudolf de Jong of the International Institute of Social History, Amsterdam, and Josefina Cedillo del Hierro of the Hemeroteca Municipal de Madrid for their aid. Gerald Brey kindly sent me copies of two articles difficult to obtain, and Ramón Salas Larrazábal located other elusive information. John M. Hollingsworth prepared the maps. Edwin Svigals, Davydd Greenwood, Michael Cahill, Jack Getman, Tomás R. Bennett, Rita Lichtenberg, and Alan Ritter commented on various parts of the manuscript. I am grateful to Julian A. Pitt-Rivers, Susan Tax Freeman, and Temma Kaplan for their careful reading of the manuscript and their constructive suggestions. Miguel Enguidanos frequently clarified obscure Spanish turns of phrase. My pleasure at completing the manuscript has been heightened by learning that Milton Glaser will design the jacket.

My wife Betty shared in the field investigation as well as in shaping the ideas formulated in this work. Carla my daughter and Aaron my son extended my knowledge of the village; Paul, who arrived later, helped in his own way to fashion this book.

My greatest debt goes to the campesino families of Casas Viejas. They were my teachers—courageous, generous, and open-hearted.

# Introduction

Anarchism seeks to recreate society, and the history of anarchism inevitably concerns dreams, struggle, and defeat. On January 8, 1933, anarchist uprisings began in Barcelona, Madrid, and Valencia. The insurrection was quickly beaten back; but three days later, on January 11, fighting unexpectedly broke out in the small Andalusian town of Casas Viejas. The workers paraded in the street, and *comunismo libertario* (libertarian communism) was declared. Then, in an exchange of shots at the barracks of the civil guards, two guards were mortally wounded. Reinforcements arrived to put down the uprising but were frustrated by stubborn resistance at the hut of a charcoal burner nicknamed Seisdedos ("Six Fingers"). On orders of their captain, the guards set the hut on fire, killing eight men and women. They then exacted a terrible vengeance on the town, rounding up and shooting twelve other men.

The incident at Casas Viejas symbolized the fury and the martyrdom of the landless workers of Andalusia. The town was seared by the massacre and the imprisonments that followed trials for insurrection. Virtually every family was touched, and local gossip assigning blame and responsibility created enmity that was to endure for decades.

The tragedy reverberated throughout every quarter of the nation. The anarchosyndicalist movement was in contention and disarray, and the uprising marked the final passage of leadership and power from moderates to a reckless militant minority. Public outrage over the costly strife and the subsequent cover-up of the massacre drove Prime Minister Azaña and his cabinet from office. At the same time, General Francisco Franco, roiled by the disconcerting hostilities, concluded that the Republic could not rule, and he moved closer to initiating a military coup.[1] The uprising at Casas Viejas became one of the stepping stones leading to the Civil War of 1936–39.

Anarchism was first brought to Spain in 1868. In September of that year, Michael Bakunin, the Russian aristocrat and revolutionary and the rival of Marx in the First International, formed the International Alliance of Socialist Democracy to propagate his "anti-authoritarian collectivism." In that same month, a military revolution in Spain drove Queen Isabella into exile. Bakunin reacted promptly to the news. He sent several of his disciples to Spain, among them the Italian revolutionary Giuseppe Fanelli, to win converts and to discover what advantage could be taken of this time of turmoil and uncertainty. Fanelli traveled by rail to Madrid, where in early November he addressed a group of young workers and craftsmen who were familiar with the works of Proudhon and the Catalonian federalist Pi y Margall. A few had just learned of the existence of the International and of the groups of workers in England, Germany, Switzerland, and Belgium who were organizing to destroy the exploitative capitalist system. With a nucleus of twenty-one converts, Fanelli established the Federación Regional Española of the First International. He then returned to Barcelona, where he repeated his triumph with a diverse group that included professional men; workers with organizational experience; and students, some of whom came from Seville, Cádiz, and Málaga.[2]

Spain is the only country in the world where anarchism developed into a major movement. Elsewhere the views of Marx triumphed over those of Bakunin. Marx's program of authoritarian socialism sought consolidation of state power and authority in the proletariat, at least as an interim measure. In contrast, Bakunin opposed all participation in the political process and preached the immediate destruction of the state. In his libertarian socialism,

1. In his radio address on July 18, 1936, the second day of the war, Franco declared that the nation was being destroyed by anarchy and revolutionary strikes. In the film "Franco, ese hombre," directed by José Luis Sáenz de Heredia and shown in 1973–74, the uprising at Casas Viejas was cited as one of the events that convinced General Franco to move against the Republic.

2. The story of Fanelli's success has become well known through the account of Anselmo Lorenzo, then a young printer, who was present at the first meeting. Although Fanelli spoke in Italian and French, languages not known to the workers he addressed, he made clear his anger against tyrants and the parasites who monopolized the riches and the productive capacity of the world. His identification with the exploited was understood and warmly received. In the days following, Fanelli gave three or four talks and then spoke with individuals during walks or in the cafés. He also provided newspapers and pamphlets explaining the program of the First International and Bakunin's International Alliance, statutes of workers' societies in Switzerland, and newspapers containing Bakunin's writings and lectures (see Anselmo Lorenzo, *El proletariado militante*, vol. 1, chap. 2). A number of Bakunin's French disciples, among them the ethnologist Elie Reclus, had arrived in Barcelona shortly before Fanelli in order to contact Republican Federalists. While Fanelli went on his historic trip to Madrid, they toured Valencia and Andalusia.

he sought the development of a federal organization of free communes. Marx proved to be the superior tactician, but Bakunin foresaw that revolutionary change would arise in peasant rather than in industrial societies. His views matched the Spanish temper—belief in local control and maximum individual freedom—and reflected the Spanish situation—that of an oppressed but potentially explosive rural population.

In their moments of greatest popularity, Spanish anarchists claimed more than a million adherents. Anarchist strength, however, was limited to particular regions: the rural areas in Andalusia and the Levant; the mining districts of Catalonia and Oviedo; and the urban areas of Barcelona, Valencia, and Madrid. Although Barcelona soon became the storm center of anarchism, until the turn of the century anarchist membership in rural Andalusia greatly outnumbered that in Catalonia. Anarchism had its greatest appeal among the landless workers of western Andalusia in Málaga, Seville, and Cádiz. The latter province is the locus of this study.

To anarchists, the evils afflicting mankind were the result of a corrupt social system and the oppressive authority of state and church. In contrast to church doctrine, they held that man was not born sinful.

*Pepe Pareja:* Egoism is created by the social order, for all beings have no egoism when they are born. Nor do they have any evil. The evil is picked up later, when the person is developing. He becomes bad because he picks up the impure environment of the social order.

Revolution and re-education were thought to be needed for a reversal of hearts and minds. The anarchists would establish a libertarian communism (as opposed to state communism) that would ensure individual freedom from authority. They would dissolve government (be it monarchical or republican) and the coercive institutions of the police, the judiciary, and the military. Once central authority had been destroyed, it would be replaced by local control and free associations. Rather than externally imposed order, spontaneous social action would prevail. In agriculture and industry, collective production and a federal system of exchange would come into being. Producers and consumers would be united; wage exploitation would cease; subsistence for workers and care for the young and disabled would be assured. Mankind would be revitalized by new forms of social behavior: competition would be replaced by cooperation, religious indoctrination by scientific education, armed frontiers by open borders, national patriotism by international fraternization, religious and civil marriage by "free love," and exclusive concern for individual welfare by a search for the common good.

Anarchism had all the requisites of a revitalization movement, containing features common to newly inspired political and religious groups that seek to effect change.[3] It promised to create a society based on the ideals of justice and brotherhood; it projected a way of life for individual growth and change; and it drew its strength from its dedicated local leaders and followers. Anarchist writers and orators, who attributed similarities among social movements throughout history to a creative tendency in mankind, were not averse to using religious imagery and developing a prophetic rhetorical style, often employing the apostolic message as a guide or a point of contrast.[4] At times in conversation the name of God might be invoked, but only to symbolize a common although incomprehensible creation and a shared heritage that calls for unity and equality among men. It was in this vein that José Vega, the obrero consciente of Paterna de Rivera, explained his beliefs:

> I believe that God created the light, created the water, created the earth and the air for all equally. Nobody should have the right to usurp a part of these things, these substances. If they are usurped by anyone, it is to the detriment of the rest.
>
> It is not known how universal matter was created, nor the form in which it subsists or exists in the universe. But it exists. And man, in his ignorance of and lack of penetration into why matter exists, creates religion. And that is why I have said God, because it's just that: the point at which man reaches and stumbles and can go forward no further. I don't know if it's because of lack of knowledge or lack of spiritual penetration.

The anarchosyndicalists wanted to reshape society into new modes, more humane and more just than those prevailing. But while they supposed that overthrowing the government would be relatively simple to carry off, they recognized that revitalizing society would require re-education and generations to accomplish. The society they sought to create was far from a supernatural millennium or a patent utopia. Anarchism promised toil and an enduring struggle for social perfection.

3. Anthony Wallace defines a revitalization movement as "a deliberate, organized, conscious effort by members of a society to construct a more satisfying culture." See Anthony Wallace, "Revitalization Movements," *American Anthropologist* 58 (April 1956): 265.

4. The reminiscences of so moderate an anarchist as Angel Pestaña, secretary of the CNT (Confederación Nacional del Trabajo), illustrate the attractions of the prophetic style: "I arrived in Barcelona with only the minimal essential knowledge of what a workers' organization was. I did not know how a sindicato should function or what its foundations should be or its reasons for existence. . . . Nevertheless, my entrance into the ranks of those who fight for social justice with only the mere knowledge of what the social struggle must be was not a difficult one for me. . . . The last one to arrive is always the first. The only thing he needs is to shout a lot or adopt a messianic tone. I didn't shout, but given my interpretation of the ideas of anarchism and of the social struggle, I was strongly immersed in the messianic tone that characterizes them. Besides this, helped by my temperament and lack of information, I was closer to mystical Christian solutions than those of reality, which demand study, preparation, energy, organization and capacity" (Angel Pestaña, *Lo que aprendí en la vida*, 2:35f.). Some anarchosyndicalists had had a religious education. Manuel Buenacasa, Pestaña's militant contemporary, for example, had spent five years in a seminary studying for the priesthood.

*Anonimo:* We wanted a terrestrial paradise, but not in the biblical sense: to live here—organized here. One man wouldn't be able to live off the work of another. It was the wish that each man work and not desire to live in luxury. One wouldn't be able to suck another's produce, and we would all eat. The world is work—intellectual and manual.

Despite the social purposes of anarchism and its antireligious and anticlerical bent, the model for conceptualizing anarchism became religion.[5] At first glance the religious model seems to make anarchism easier to understand, particularly in the absence of detailed observation and intimate contact. The model was, however, also used to serve the political ends of anarchism's opponents. Here use of the terms "religious" and "millenarian" stamp anarchist goals as unrealistic and unattainable.[6] Anarchism is thus dismissed as a viable solution to social ills.[7]

5. The use of religion as the key for conceptualizing anarchism was due largely to the influence of Juan Díaz del Moral, a lawyer and historian who was also a landowner and the notary of Bujalance in the province of Córdoba. Díaz del Moral's massive study, *Historia de las agitaciones campesinas andaluzas,* focused on campesino unrest in the province of Córdoba during 1903–5 and 1917–20. According to Díaz del Moral, the moral and passionate obreros conscientes absorbed in their pamphlets and newspapers were akin to frenzied believers in a new religion (*Historia,* pp. 187–92). English historians such as Gerald Brenan and, later, Eric Hobsbawm, Raymond Carr, and James Joll accepted Díaz del Moral's characterization and even identified an age and people whom they judged to be comparable—seventeenth-century England, with its Anabaptists and Fifth Monarchy men. They did their mentor one better: in their writings the relative resemblance, useful for comparative purposes to illustrate the passion and commitment of the anarchists, becomes absolute. Analogy becomes metaphor. In the intensity of the Civil War in 1937, Franz Borkenau, scanting comparisons, wrote, "Anarchism *is* a religious movement" (*The Spanish Cockpit,* p. 220). More recently, E. E. Malefakis has cautioned against overemphasizing religious analogies: "Díaz del Moral particularly favors such religious analogies with the result that his interpretations are occasionally overly romantic" (*Agrarian Reform and Peasant Revolution in Spain: Origins of the Civil War,* p. 137, n. 11; see also p. 138, n. 12).

In a pointed critique, Temma Kaplan has determined that "the millenarian theory is too mechanistic to explain the complex pattern of Andalusian anarchist activity. The millenarian argument, in portraying the Andalusian anarchists as fundamentally religious, overlooks their clear comprehension of the social sources of their oppression." She concludes that "the degree of organization, not the religiosity of workers and the community, accounts for mass mobilizations carried on by the Andalusian anarchists at the end of the nineteenth century" (*Anarchists of Andalusia, 1868–1903,* pp. 210–12). Kaplan notes that the religious comparison had been made earlier than by Díaz del Moral, particularly by Constancio Bernaldo de Quirós y Pérez (in his "Bandolerismo y delincuencia subversiva en la baja Andalucía"), who called anarchism a "secular religion" (pp. 207 ff.). Díaz del Moral's study, however, proved to be far more influential and appeared to validate the comparison.

6. Kaplan also argues, "In a secular age, the taint of religion is the taint of irrationality" (p. 211).

7. In his discussion of the distortions of anarchist activities by historians, Noam Chomsky warns that intellectuals may adopt the attitudes of their class in describing popular movements and the presumed need for elitist supervision ("Objectivity and Liberal Scholarship: II," *American Power and the New Mandarins,* pp. 62, 64). Writing forty-odd years earlier, Díaz del Moral ascribed to the campesinos racial and cultural stereotypes that were the common saws of his class. The sole cause for the waves of rural unrest, Díaz del Moral asserted, could be found in the psychology of the campesinos (*Historia,* pp. xix f.). He believed that the Andalusian field

The oversimplifications posited became serious distortions of anarchist belief and practice.[8] Gerald Brenan, Eric Hobsbawm, and Raymond Carr, for example, all maintained that there was a connection between anarchist strikes and sexual practices. Carr's description is the most recent:

> Austere puritans, they sought to impose vegetarianism, sexual abstinence, and atheism on one of the most backward peasantries of Europe. . . . Thus strikes were moments of exaltation as well as demands for better conditions; spontaneous and often disconnected they would bring, not only the abolition of piece-work, but "the day," so near at hand that sexual intercourse and alcohol were abandoned by enthusiasts till it should dawn.[9]

The level-headed anarchists were astonished by such descriptions of supposed Spanish puritanism by overenthusiastic historians.[10]

---

workers had inherited a Moorish tendency toward ecstasy and millenarianism that accounted for their attraction to anarchist treachings. Díaz del Moral was mystified by expressions of animosity directed toward him, but the workers considered him to be a señorito (see *Historia*, p. 372 n.), a landowner who does not labor and who is seen to live by his rents or the efforts of his foreman and laborers. From the workers' point of view, Díaz del Moral was the government official who prepared and guarded the hated land records. (See Borkenau's Civil War account of the anarchist execution of the notary of Seriñena and the burning of all his property records [p. 102].) Although he was both scholarly and sympathetic, Díaz del Moral could not comprehend the hunger and the desperation of the campesinos around him. Nor could he understand their rejection of the modest reforms proposed by middle-class intellectuals. He acknowledged that a gazpacho of bread and oil was the only food provided workers in the fields, but he observed that, though boring, it was plentiful and healthy and in any case better than what they could eat at home (pp. xiii, 230). Why protest? From his perspective, government repression of strikes was relatively mild: only a few men were kept imprisoned; the others were usually released on probation. Only illegal sindicatos were closed (p. 219). Why the sharp protest over such moderate action? He could not understand rejection of the proposals made by landowners, who, alarmed at the unrest, offered surplus lands that could be divided among some of the workers (pp. 375 f.). Nor could he comprehend their spurning the plans of well-meaning señoritos to educate and assist some to ascend to the middle class (pp. 211 f.). Why the need for radical and immediate change? How could the workers equate their agricultural tasks with intellectual endeavors (pp. 212, 377–78, and n. 1, 378)? Why should the workers lose heart simply because the government pressured and bribed their local leaders to move elsewhere (pp. 208 f.)? To Díaz del Moral, campesino ignorance, passion, ecstasy, illusion, and depression, not having a legitimate basis in reality, could be found only in the roots of their racial heritage.

8. Spanish anarchists have been classified as racially inferior Moorish fatalists on the one hand and as mystics and ineffectual utopians on the other. Brenan found that the "deeper layers of Spanish political thought and feeling are Oriental" (p. xviii). More recently, Carr reaffirmed Díaz del Moral's picture of the cycle of anarchist activity as "the sudden relapse into Moorish fatalism, apathy, and brute indifference" (*Spain, 1808–1939*, p. 445).

9. Carr, *Spain*, p. 444.

10. How could historians arrive at this view? Tracing the citations leads the reader back to Angel Marvaud, the French social historian, who observed that during the general strike of 1902 in Morón, marriages were postponed until the day of the *reparto*, the promised division of the lands. As a Frenchman, Marvaud undoubtedly assumed that everyone knew that a formal wedding ceremony did not necessarily govern the sexual relations of courting couples (*La*

*José Monroy:* Chaste? What do women have to do with a strike? Of course without any work the husband couldn't provide any food at dinnertime, and so they were angry at each other, and she wouldn't have anything to do with him. In that sense, yes, there were no sexual relations.

Could the dilemma of southern Spain, with its large landholdings and the marginal existence of its campesinos, have been settled by anarchosyndicalist plans? Writing at the time of the Civil War, Gerald Brenan, certainly no anarchist, argued that the intolerable conditions in Andalusia could have been resolved by communal ownership of the land.

The only reasonable solution through wide tracts of Spain is a collective one. . . . In many districts the peasants are themselves adverse to it, but the anarchist ideology in Andalusia has made it the favourite solution there and this is a factor which any sensible government would take advantage of.

For the advantages of communal ownership of the land are enormous. Under present conditions one has agricultural labourers dying of hunger on estates where large tracts of corn-growing land lie fallow because it does not pay to cultivate them. If the villagers could cultivate their land collectively, using modern machinery, they could feed themselves and sell the surplus. Hunger would disappear and, without injury to the State, their anarchist ideology, or all that matters to them of it, would be satisfied. . . . Only the incurable stupidity of the Spanish ruling classes and their governments and the ignorance of the traditionalist parties, who seem not to have the slightest notion of the conditions under which Spaniards really lived in the age which they profess to imitate, have prevented agrarian reform from being carried out long ago.[11]

The history of Casas Viejas has a tragic cast, revealing the conflict between two great ideals—democracy and anarchism. Anarchist opposition in a democratic society is morally complex, particularly in the case of the Spanish Republic, where the government intended reform but was considered to be ineffectual and unable to render justice.[12] Militant anarchists regarded de-

*Question sociale en Espagne,* p. 43): "La confiance dans le succès était si grande chez ces malheureux, qu'ils avaient convenu de différer les mariages projetés jusqu'au jour du partage." Misinterpreting Marvaud, Brenan noted, "Whilst strikes were in progress the workers gave up drink and tobacco, observed a strict chastity and did not play cards" (p. 175). See also E. J. Hobsbawm, *Primitive Rebels: Studies in Archaic Forms of Social Movements in the Nineteenth and Twentieth Centuries,* p. 84.

11. Brenan, pp. 123 f. Elsewhere Brenan noted, "Anyone who had known the Spanish poor will agree that by their kindly and generous feelings for one another and by the talent they have so often shown for cooperation they are perfectly fitted for playing their part in an 'anarchist commune' " (p. 195).

12. Casas Viejas was a fatal catalyst for the downfall of the government of Prime Minister Manuel Azaña, as Malefakis noted: "The atmosphere of insecurity created by CNT local uprisings helped turn countless votes against Azaña in the 1933 elections. Equally important, they

mocracy and moderate reform as undermining anarchist ideals, and the resulting social conflict proved to be mortally dangerous to democracy, without benefitting anarchism.

To most nonbelievers, anarchists striving to achieve their goals outside established political avenues have often appeared "naive to the point of self-destruction."[13] Even those sympathetic to anarchosyndicalism hesitate to support revolutionary solutions, conscious of the inherent dangers of power accruing to a small militant minority on the left or the right. It is, however, deceptively simple to renounce anarchism's revolutionary aspirations in favor of shallow political reform that may mask increasing inequality and class distance. It can be argued that a workers' movement that loses its ardor to restructure society may soon become conservative, neglecting or even opposing deep social change in favor of short-term benefits for a narrow group of union members. To anarchists, such circumstances assure the destruction of their ideals for humanity and make re-education and social revolution an impossibility.[14]

Fault may be found with anarchism's simple axioms and naive strategies; however, its revolutionary philosophy concerns basic injustices and essential truths. Who owns the land and its produce? Should not society be organized to provide for all and to ensure equity? Should not society attempt to do away with the causes of war and hatred? And as Pepe Pareja says, if civilization does not protest the coarse values that send a once useful horse, now old and

caused Azaña to adopt policies of stern repression which sometimes backfired—most notably at Casas Viejas, which probably damaged Azaña's position more effectively than all the other rural upheavals put together. In short, the Anarchosyndicalists, unable to carry out their type of revolution, prevented the Republicans from fully realizing their own revolutionary dreams. In the end the excesses that inevitably resulted from the 'dictatorial' policies that the CNT forced upon Azaña cost him even the support of many liberals who believed that 'democratic' methods could be applied at all times against all opponents" (pp. 305–6).

13. Raymond Carr, "All or Nothing," p. 22.

14. Today, as after each wave of repression in the past, the anarchists have re-emerged as a nascent revolutionary movement with their customary tenacity and lack of compromise. The CNT of the present day has been recreated as a mirror image of the past—a loose organization of *sindicatos* administered by committees, unpaid officers, and dedicated workers. The program of the anarchist congress held at Zaragoza in 1936 is still in force. Anarchists refuse to participate in elections, and, unlike the socialists, they have no political party that functions in government circles. They oppose the existence of the central government, the army, and the police. In each town the process of reorganization is underway: older men whose allegiance antedates the war unite with young workers and students. Newspapers and propaganda sheets arrive from Madrid and Barcelona. Posters announce regional meetings to be addressed by visiting speakers. The few slowly increase. *Centros* (meeting halls) are opened, contact is made between the towns, and regional and national organizations develop. The anarchists are no longer to be considered vanished dreamers from the past but active participants in the social struggle. Their numbers and organization, however, are woefully weak, and they have yet to recapture their earlier support.

blindfolded, to face the charge of the bull in the arena, what is civilization good for?

Neither revolution nor reform has offered anarchists more than a momentary vision of hope, followed by defeat and repression. This was the heart of the struggle in Spain in the 1930s, when political and social conflicts under the Republic reached a fatal intensity. The belief existed that comunismo libertario was within reach, and this illusion goaded anarchist militants to actions through which they were divided and defeated. For some defenders of a strong central government, any threat to social order, no matter how justified, warranted the severest repression.

# Part One

# One

# The Beginning of the Anarchist Sindicato in Casas Viejas, 1914

Deseo mi redención,
Vivir sin vividores
Que de los trabajadores
Hacen mil explotaciones.
Política y religión
Desaparezcan del mundo.
El fruto de su labor
Que en el abismo más profundo
Caigan violentamente
Papa, rey y presidente.
Que el pan que el obrero amasa
Lo coma con dicha cumplida,
Y que el derecho a la vida
Goce sin traba y sin tasa.
Que el albañil tenga casa,
Y el sombrerero, sombrero.
Que no se le robe al obrero
Ni por inquisidor,
Sacerdote, ni guerrero—
Como quiera que se llamen.
Sean libres para amarse,
Sin tener que humillarse
Ante un zángano haragán.
Deseo con gran afán
Llegue el venturoso día
Que hundiendo la tiranía
En la fosa del pasado,
Sea el amor libertado
Implantando la anarquía.

I long for my salvation,
To live without exploiters
Who feed off the workers
In a thousand ways.
Let politics and religion
Disappear from the world.
The fruit of his labor
Let popes, kings, and presidents
Fall violently
Into the deepest abyss.
Let the bread that the worker kneads
Be eaten by him with complete contentment,
And let him enjoy the right to live
Without troubles and taxes.
Let the mason have a house,
And the hat maker, a hat.
Let the worker not be robbed,
Neither by inquisitor,
Priest, nor soldier—
Whatever name they go by.
Let people be free to love each other,
Without having to humble themselves
Before an idle drone.
With great desire I await
The coming of that blessed day
When tyranny will be buried
In the graves of the past,
And love will be liberated
By the establishment of anarchy.

## José Olmo

Early in 1914 José Olmo García, a charcoal burner and the leader of the anarchist sindicato in the Andalusian town of Medina Sidonia, moved to the village of Casas Viejas, nineteen kilometers away. He was accompanied by his *compañera,* María Bollullo (called "María de los Santos"), and their three children, Palmiro ("Palmyra"), Paz ("Peace"), and Germinal ("Germination").[1] They carried their worldly goods on a *burra,* the same one that José normally used to transport the charcoal he cut and fired in the woods.

José Olmo was then thirty years of age and had won local fame as a fearless and convincing orator in the anarchist cause. As correspondent for the *centro obrero* (workers' center) of Medina Sidonia, he also received and circulated books, pamphlets, and newspapers sent from *Tierra y Libertad,* the anarchist newspaper published in Barcelona, and from José Sánchez Rosa, the anarchist writer and pamphleteer in Seville. José Olmo could read and write, but he often dictated his letters to someone who was more lettered than he. An ardent obrero consciente, José had refused to marry in the church or in a civil ceremony, and he would not baptize his children, scorning saints' names for those more political or poetic. In accordance with anarchist principles, he abstained from tobacco and wine.

At public meetings José Olmo had a fiery questioning manner. Manuel Llamas recalled that Olmo asked, "Why are the rich rich? Because they are legalized thieves. The bourgeoisie are wealthy, because they don't pay the worker a just wage. For every four parts, they pay one part to the worker and pocket the other three parts." Away from the speaker's platform, José appeared tranquil and self-possessed. He was tall and broad, but despite his strong presence and his youth, he was already marked by a debilitating illness common to the area—tuberculosis.

The move to Casas Viejas had been dictated by increasing persecution and misfortune. During the winter months, charcoal burners were customarily welcomed by the landowners and overseers of the forests: by clearing the woods of the low-lying brush—the mastic trees and holm oaks that knotted the mountainsides—they protected the valuable cork trees from forest fires and made the terrain accessible to livestock. Charcoal burners received no

1. Except for the name Paz (probably a shortening of "María de la Paz," one of the names of the Virgin Mary), the names chosen for José Olmo's children represented anarchist aspirations. "Peace" and "germination" are self-explanatory. Palmyra, an ancient center for the caravan trade in Syria, was idealized as a "free" city. Palmyra was a Roman terminus until 270, when an attempt was made to create an independent Palmyrene regime in western Asia Minor and Egypt. Palmyra was quickly retaken and plundered by Roman troops. The fate of the ancient city, seen as a symbol of freedom and independence, was well known to anarchists and socialists through a popular work by the Count of Volney, *Las ruinas de Palmira.*

wages for their work; for the right to clear brushwood and dig out the thick hardwood roots of venerable mastic trees, they provided the landowner or overseer, without cost, a portion of the charcoal they prepared.[2] But despite these valuable services, the landowners had singled out José for punishment in reprisal for his leadership in the anarchist sindicato and in local strikes. He was denied work in the nearby forests, and he was harassed and beaten by the civil guard. When he had no other work, José gathered and then sold to a fertilizer factory the bones of dead cows and burros that had fallen in the fields. Early in 1914, impoverished and eager for a change in fortune, José went to the great estate of Ahijón, fifteen kilometers from Medina Sidonia, where he received permission from the overseer of the forest to clear the brush from the wooded hillsides and to prepare charcoal.

The lands of Ahijón are typical of the great estates that had been retained by the nobility since the Middle Ages. A rolling estate of some 1,800 hectares, it contains rich soil for cultivation and grazing as well as hills ripe with cork and wild olive trees. Well watered, it is bounded by the rivers Barbate on the south and Álamo on the west. In past times the estate of Ahijón had been part of the holdings of the house of the duke of Medina Sidonia, once the richest family in the Spanish realm and masters of all Andalusia. The estate had since passed into the hands of the ducal houses of Medinaceli and Lerma, families intertwined by blood and marriage. Ahijón boasted a stately brick dwelling where the heirs could stay when they chanced to pass that way to visit their estates in the region, but it was rarely used. The absentee grandees who continued to own a large portion of the lands of Andalusia preferred to live in Madrid or Paris.

Although some estates were kept apart as private hunting preserves, the estates of the grandees were customarily rented to local entrepreneurs, who planted crops, grazed cattle, or subdivided the land into small plots to sublease at a higher price. It mattered little to the titled owners, who simply collected rent. On occasion the idle heirs of the great estates were forced to sell portions of their patrimony for ready cash; so it happened that Ahijón passed out of noble hands in 1905, when the duke of Lerma, who resided in Madrid, sold the estate to an untitled fellow *madrileño*. Although this signaled a change in the control of land in the area, the sale meant little to the two men. The rich but penurious duke of Lerma (who, his workers said, thought that a

2. Most charcoal burners made yearly agreements with landowners and overseers to clear the forest in return for a percentage of the charcoal for the house. The portion the house received depended on the quality of the wood the charcoal burner gathered. If the dead limbs of cork trees and wild olive trees were cleared from the *monte alto* (tree areas), the house received up to 50 percent of the charcoal made; if the brushwood of the *monte bajo* (brush area) was cleared, the house asked for 25–50 percent; and if roots such as those of the mastic tree were arduously dug out, the house was entitled to but 15 percent.

family of ten could live on one egg) continued to receive rents from his still vaster lands further south and in other areas; the new landowner, like the duke, remained in Madrid and collected his rents at a distance. For a time the new owner, who had not long to live and enjoy his estate even on paper, rented Ahijón to an enterprising doctor in the nearby village of Casas Viejas, Don Antonio Vela, who used it to graze his herds of cattle.

Since the village of Casas Viejas is only two kilometers from the boundary of Ahijón, José Olmo thought it best to move his family to Casas Viejas permanently. Aside from the opportunity to improve his own circumstances, José welcomed the move as a chance to further the anarchist cause. For some time a nucleus of workers in Casas Viejas had been asking the anarchists in Medina for help in forming a sindicato. José's move was applauded by the workers in both Medina and Casas Viejas. *Tierra y Libertad* listed in its column of membership news that compañero José Olmo García of Medina Sidonia notified "the compañeros, groups, and others who have corresponded or presently correspond with him to address their future correspondence to his new address, Calle Medina, Casas Viejas," and noted that anarchist pamphlets and almanacs had already been mailed to this new address.

## Casas Viejas

The town of Casas Viejas is set on an easily accessible slope that ends the long, low-lying plateau extending from Medina Sidonia. There are pasture lands for grazing on the sandy soil of the mesa above Casas Viejas; on the valley floor below is a narrow strip of spring-fed gardens whose groves contained orange, lemon, quince, pear, apple, plum, and nut trees. In the valley of the Barbate River, which winds across the valley floor a few kilometers away, the soil is sandy and fertile, with some patches of clay. At the farther edge of the valley, the rocky hillsides serve as pasturage for cattle and goats.

The name Casas Viejas ("Old Houses") referred to its cluster of *chozas*, the thatched huts and cottages of the campesinos that marked the town. The choza was a sign of poverty, for the campesino could afford to utilize only indigenous plants in the construction of his home. For beams the poor householder used the fallen limbs of wild olive trees and *pitones*, a long, straight-shafted plant. Cypress and cane cut from the nearby lagoon served as thatch and cross ties; cord woven from palm leaves lashed together the beams, cane, and cypress. The floor was dirt or stone; and if there were low base walls, they were made of mud mixed with rocks.

The ample water supply and the fertile gardens around Casas Viejas had always sustained a small number of families, but until late in the nineteenth century Casas Viejas consisted only of a cluster of chozas, a tavern set at the crossroads, and a rural hermitage that had been built in the sixteenth century.

The town's population swelled in the second half of the nineteenth century, when the common lands and the newly disentailed church lands near Casas Viejas were offered for sale. Church records were not kept in Casas Viejas until late in 1869; and the first full year registered in the church archive (1870) listed forty-eight births, including seven children born to *carabineros* (excise guards) and civil guards stationed in the village; six marriages; and sixteen deaths.

In 1914, when José Olmo arrived, the population of Casas Viejas was approximately 2,000.[3] The majority of the men of Casas Viejas were temporary day workers; a much smaller number had fixed posts on the estates as herdsmen or watchmen. Since the town is situated at the southwestern corner of the township of Medina Sidonia, nineteen kilometers from Medina, and at the edge of the boundaries of the townships of Alcalá de los Gazules and Vejer de la Frontera, the men of Casas Viejas have always furnished the work force for those estates too distant from the day workers of the other towns. The men were hired to prepare the lands for sowing; then they worked at weeding, cultivating, and reaping the harvests. Their employment was short-lived and subject to the weather. When the winter rains came, work halted; when the rains let up, the earth was often too muddy. For most campesinos, paid working days during the year averaged only 170 to 180 days, roughly six months of employment.

An individual worker could not purchase sufficient food for his family by his wages alone. In the winter plowing, the campesinos earned three *reales* (three-quarters of a *peseta*) per day; in the summer their wages doubled.[4] Some local foods were inexpensive in season: four to five oranges from the groves below the village could be had for five *céntimos* (one-quarter of a *real*);

3. Early official census data are only approximations, since until 1950 the population of Casas Viejas was not distinguished from the total population of the township of Medina Sidonia. The *Diario de Cádiz* of September 11, 1915, reported the population to be 3,000. Eighteen years later, however, *El Sol* (January 16, 1933) and the anarchist newspaper *La Tierra* (January 14, 1933) stated that Casas Viejas had a population of 1,200 (and *El Sol* added that there were 280 houses). At the same time José Suárez, the former deputy mayor, claimed that the official census totaled 3,000 persons. In a recent study, Gerard Brey and Jacques Maurice write that in 1930 the town had 1,843 inhabitants. These discrepancies may be due to whether only the nucleus of the town is considered or the population of the surrounding countryside, officially part of Medina Sidonia, is assumed to belong to Casas Viejas. In this regard, even today official census figures are difficult to use, since the political census units do not correspond to obvious geographical domains. In any event, it is clear that the overall population of the township of Medina Sidonia was stable during this period: the census for 1910 tallied a population of 11,846 (including Casas Viejas); the census for 1930 listed a loss of just ten persons, with a count of 11,836.

4. Malefakis (p. 100) computed the income of a field laborer in Andalusia and Extremadura in 1902 to be 1.5–1.75 pesetas (5 to 6 reales). Winter work during this period, however, paid only three reales. This daily wage was the equivalent of twenty-eight American pennies (at the exchange rate of 5.49 pesetas to the dollar). The national average for employed workers in 1914 was 4.7 pesetas a day, considerably above the wages paid to agricultural laborers.

sardines brought in from nearby Barbate could also be bought for five céntimos a plateful. However, a loaf of bread cost thirty-five céntimos, over half of a winter's daily wage; a liter of milk was fifteen to twenty céntimos; a liter of oil cost about fifty céntimos. Meat was far too expensive to be purchased.[5] During the rainy winter months, the workers would buy food on credit from the storekeepers and then begin to pay off their debts when work started again in the spring.

To survive the weeks and months of unemployment, one needed ingenuity, enterprise, and help from one's family. The village was fortunate in that the climate was relatively mild and the campo fruitful with wild vegetables, fruits, and game. From fall until the following summer, the cactus yielded wild prickly pears that could be eaten at the table or ground with grain husks and used to fatten a pig. In the winter months, men and boys would scour the campo for wild asparagus and wild chard and for land snails hidden under rocks and in plants. The excess of a family's find was often sold house to house, to stores and cafés, or to an enterprising merchant who would carry the country delicacies to the city for sale. José Monroy received his nickname of "Dancer" competing with other campesinos in gathering wild asparagus: once he found a fruitful patch he moved so rapidly, desperately pressing his foot on surrounding plants and snatching the asparagus, that to others hurrying toward the spot from a distance it seemed as if he were dancing.

Good hunters could add an occasional rabbit to the family diet. Others trapped birds for the table or for sale. The woods held larks and quail that had passed over the straits from Africa on favorable winds, as well as swallows and martins indigenous to the area. A prized catch was the brown thrush, which migrated from the north to feast on the fruit of the wild olive trees.[6] There were, however, territorial as well as seasonal sanctions on what the campo could provide. The estates were closed to hunting except by owners or renters. If a poacher was spied by watchmen or herdsmen, he would be

5. An advertisement in *El Guadalete* of Jerez (July 15, 1915) indicates prices of the period in the city. *Mortadela* (bologna sausage), *lomos* (ribs and loin), and *salchichón* (large sausage) sold for eight pesetas per kilo, the equivalent of a week's pay for a farm worker. Clothing was relatively expensive. Pepe Pareja once bought a pair of fine-looking shoes for strolling in the town, but to save on the price he walked to Chiclana, forty kilometers distant, where there was a shoe factory and prices were cheaper. His fine shoes cost thirty reales, the equivalent of ten days' labor.

6. Poachers would reach the woods with baskets containing 100 or more traps well before dawn, sometimes carrying lanterns to guide them in the darkness. The traps were simply made with wood and wound metal worked as a spring. A stick held the trap ready; a thread stripped from a palm leaf held a maggot to attract the prey. The traps were placed where the holly oak, hawthorn, and palm bushes grew in thick clusters and served as shelter for the birds. A bit of earth was scooped out and the trap set; then the trap was covered with dirt, leaving only the maggot exposed. As an additional snare, loops of wound horsehair were sometimes set in rows on the branches above. As dawn lightened the woods, the small wrens, wheatears, and finches would begin to stir and would spy the attractive lures set by the hungry poachers.

run off the land and lose his catch and traps. If a complaint was then filed or if the civil guard chanced on him, there would be a stiff fine to pay as well as a day lost going to the court in Medina. Despite the risks, poaching was an established way of bringing food and cash into the house during the weeks and months of unemployment.

Neither wages nor the gleanings of wild vegetables and game were sufficient to feed a family of five or six persons, buy cloth, and provide charcoal for cooking and for heat. A campesino struggling to feed his family inevitably became dependent on his children's aid for his own survival.

Children in the households of the campesinos began to work early in their lives, most often serving to guard livestock. Those forced by circumstances to work outside the family were more likely to be exploited, given onerous tasks, and overworked. There was no time to go to school, and children of campesinos rarely learned to read and write until they became old enough to join the anarchist centro.

*Manuel Llamas:* I was one of four children. I began to work when I was seven years old. One *duro* [five pesetas] each month. For food I had garlic soup with bread in the morning, a stew of chickpeas and fat at night, and I had a piece of bread in my pocket during the day. I never had milk, eggs, or coffee, which no one used then. I ate fat with a good deal of paprika to color it and to make it more savory. I worked for a small landowner who wanted to become a big landowner and was taking advantage of me and others. My uncle worked for him. Then I was promoted, as if I were in the army, and I earned two duros a month. I was very proud. I was eight years old. I learned to read when I was eighteen, in Jerez. I never went to school. I always hated the slavery. I learned to read, and I read history and natural history.

The daughters of campesinos were also required to help their families.[7] Young girls would be sent to serve wealthier families in the village or in the larger towns and cities. Since they slept and ate where they worked, it meant one less mouth to feed at home. As servants, their day's work was even longer than that of field hands. They cared for their employer's children, did the shopping, the washing, and the cleaning; they also helped the cook, usually an older servant, to prepare and serve the meals. Their tasks customarily ended at midnight, after the late supper dishes were washed.

The few céntimos older children earned by weeding, herding, or serving were pooled to help provide food for the family. As parents aged, the re-

7. In this region women did not do field labor until the 1950s, when cotton was widely sown. Some wives worked as seamstresses in their own homes. Others raised chickens and sold eggs. The earnings of serving girls were either contributed to their families or saved to buy linen for their own marriage.

sponsibility of children in aiding their family increased. The older campesino, worn out by work, could no longer endure the hard labor, and he would return to the tasks of his childhood, rejoining the youngsters at intermittent labor weeding in the fields.

The youngest children paid a bitter price in the struggle for survival. Of the fifty deaths that occurred in Casas Viejas in the year 1913, twenty-seven, more than 50 percent, were infants under the age of three. The causes of death were usually listed as enteritis, diphtheria, pneumonia, bronchitis, nephritis, meningitis, and generalized fevers. But lack of nutrition, as well as bad sanitation and poor medical care, contributed heavily to the high mortality among infants and children. Many of those who survived their first year were marked by rickets and tuberculosis.

Despite their common problems, there were differences in class allegiance among the workers. Some believed that their best interests lay in serving a *patrón* (landowner) or in maintaining good relationships with the landowners: not all the workers thought that social and economic change was possible, and there were others who feared the danger of reprisals.

*Pelele:* There was great fear then among the workers, derived from the time of slavery and the Inquisition. They trembled when the *señorito* appeared in the doorway.

The señoritos were not the only group feared by the campesinos. Facing the village plaza in Casas Viejas was a post of four civil guards, who patrolled the roads and the countryside for bandits, poachers, and trespassers and who kept a surveillance on "los que tenían ideas." There was also a barracks of a half-dozen carabineros, vigilant about smugglers bringing tobacco and other taxable goods from Gibraltar to the towns of the interior. Of less concern to the population was a municipal guard, a fellow townsman who patrolled the village streets at night to watch for unwelcome outsiders. Since there was no local crime within the town itself, the presence of these authorities was perceived as threatening rather than protective. The civil guard in particular denied the campesinos free access to the surrounding lands and prevented open discussion and organization. The guard was considered the authentic voice of the central government.

In every Spanish village and town, the church in the central plaza stood as a sentinel of the social order more formidable than the town hall of the government or the barracks of the civil guard. It was not the presence of the priest, a familiar figure in his long black cassock, that dominated the sensibilities of the people; it was, rather, that the church served as a rallying point for the ruling classes. During Holy Week the priest walked in a procession under a canopy carried by a civil guard on one side and a township official on the other. It was as much a demonstration of the triad of temporal power as a celebration of religious observance. As the procession came by, for the most part campesinos stood in silence on the sidewalk or remained in the cafés.

## Medina Sidonia

Casas Viejas, a relatively new town, is officially a *barrio* (quarter) of Medina Sidonia. It is without taxable lands of its own, and its chief administrator is a deputy mayor appointed by the mayor of the larger town. In contrast to Casas Viejas, Medina Sidonia is an ancient town, founded by the Phoenicians and later populated by Romans, Jews, and Moors. Set on a defensible hilltop, it had long been an important trade center in the pastoral lands between the sea and the plains. In the nineteenth century, the township of Medina Sidonia had held approximately 8,000 hectares of common land, part of the royal lure to repopulate the region after the reconquest, but these had been lost when the township lands and ecclesiastical holdings were disentailed and sold in mid-century. At that time Medina's eminence in cattle trading in western Andalusia was exceeded only by Seville and Jerez. To celebrate the annual fair held every May 4–6, 100 *fanegas* of land were set aside for the display of cows, horses, sheep, goats, and pigs; and buyers and sellers would come from as far south as Algeciras to trade.

At the time of the First World War, Medina Sidonia held a commanding position in the area. The township as a whole had a population of 11,835, approximately two-thirds of which were located in the town itself, with the remainder living in Casas Viejas and other rural settlements. Medina Sidonia was the judicial center for three townships, encompassing Medina, Alcalá de los Gazules, and Paterna de Rivera. As an indication of its legal activity, there were five licensed lawyers in the town, although only three of them were actually in practice. There were no banks in Medina, but a bank correspondent handled business affairs and arranged transfers of funds. There were ample medical facilities in the town: a hospital, Amor de Dios, where nuns cared for the sick, and four doctors—three assigned by the government to cover the large barrios, the fourth handling only private patients.

Medina was also rich in religious institutions. The ancient church, an imposing sixteenth-century Gothic structure set at the peak of the hill adjacent to the castle ruins, had been one of the seats of the Holy Inquisition. There were two other churches in Medina (one said to have been used once as a synagogue), and just below the town there was a shrine to the Virgin. There was a large number of priests and nuns by Andalusian standards: four priests served the two parishes, and a fifth was attached to one of the four orders of nuns. Medina boasted four convents: Las Hijas de la Caridad (The Daughters of Charity) cared for the sick at the hospital, and El Rebaño de María (The Flock of Mary) taught school. Two other orders, each with approximately eleven members, were Augustinian. These nuns, however, were cloistered. The sisters never left the buildings and grounds and could be glimpsed only when they approached the iron bars guarding a window at street level.

The hilltop town of Medina Sidonia was dependent on its ties to the outside, but lines of transport and communication were thin. Merchandise for the town was brought up the steep, winding hill in an open cart drawn by a line of three or four mules. Mail was carried in a one-horse shay between the towns. Travelers to Cádiz boarded a horse-drawn coach that left at 7:30 each morning for San Fernando, where they could catch a train to the capital. The coach, *La góndola,* completed the round trip at 8:00 at night, carried to the crest of the town by a fresh team of horses harnessed when they arrived at the foot of the hill. There was less demand for transportation away from the major cities, and the rough dirt roads and stone bridges, laid out in Roman times, were usually in poor condition from the winter rains. A one-horse carriage carried passengers to Alcalá, but there was no regular service at all (other than coaches for hire) between Medina and Casas Viejas.

In 1914 Medina Sidonia also had an anarchist centro, which, after a search frustrated by official harassment, was located in a modest house adjacent to the small Plaza Zapata. Unlike Casas Viejas, which still lacked a centro, Medina Sidonia had had an organized anarchist presence since 1872, just four years after anarchism was introduced into Spain. In September of that year a worker from Medina journeyed to Valencia to participate in the meetings of the Federación Regional Española. First admitted to the section of individual members, in a matter of weeks the new compañero was able to organize a section of twenty workers.[8]

8. The first section of the federación in Andalusia was founded in the city of Cádiz in 1870. A newspaper, *La Internacional,* appeared there, although publication ended after three numbers, when the editor was arrested. In the spring of 1872, Anselmo Lorenzo, the young printer who, after Fanelli's visit to Madrid, had become an anarchist propagandist and had attended meetings of the International in Valencia and Barcelona as well as in Lisbon and London, made a proselytizing visit to the south, where he found anarchist sections already established in Cádiz, Jerez, San Fernando, and Puerto Real, as well as in towns and cities in the provinces of Málaga and Seville. Within two years after its foundation, the total membership of the new federación counted between 20,000 and 30,000 members, and each week saw additional towns form sections. See Max Nettlau, *La Première Internationale en Espagne, 1868–88,* 1:120; and Anselmo Lorenzo, *El proletariado militante,* chap. 31 and p. 455, n. 101. See also Kaplan, pp. 52 ff. and 69–91; and Clara E. Lida, *Anarquismo y revolución en la España del XIX,* chap. 4. On September 24, 1872, the new compañero of Medina Sidonia, Diego Rodríguez Vargas, described to the general meeting "the precarious situation of the town, the victim of political fanaticism, as a result of which political factions composed of the most covetous had been able to exploit it for many years." He declared also that "the workers were going to free themselves from so many hypocrites," and he "hoped to have a section of various trades organized by the coming November." His success came even more quickly. Ten days later, the new compañero was able to inform the congress that he had united twenty workers to constitute a section. He requested a delay in the

Between 1874 and 1884, however, the number of organized workers in Medina grew only from twenty to forty-six. The focus of anarchist unrest in the region was the vineyard growing lands around Jerez, some thirty-five kilometers northwest of Medina Sidonia. Exploited, illiterate, and on the edge of starvation, the workers of Jerez protested their beggary with demonstrations and strikes. At times anger led to acts of sabotage in orchards and vineyards.[9] As the measure of protest and violence intensified, so too did local fear and government repression. Anarchist leaders were commonly arrested, tried on criminal charges, and given long prison terms or sent into

---

payment of dues until November 1, because they had been out of work for many weeks and even when employed earned only three reales a day and a gazpacho of bread and water. He asked for bylaws, pamphlets, and everything else that could be useful for propaganda. A month later, on November 5, Diego Rodríguez Vargas paid four reales for a subscription to the newspaper *La Razón* of Seville and asked for seventy copies of various pamphlets, including "What the International Is," "Social Organization," and "The Gospel of the Worker." He also contributed ten reales to aid striking workers (*Actas de los Consejos y Comisión Federal de la Región Española (1870–1874)*, 1:253, 264, 280, 325–26). The workers of Medina Sidonia had joined the international organization at the moment of significant change. At The Hague congress in September 1872, Marx had Bakunin and his followers expelled from the International. Shortly thereafter, the Bakunist minority met at Saint Imier, Switzerland, to form a new anti-authoritarian organization. The population base of the new organization was in southern Europe, and the two Spanish representatives at Saint Imier hastily convened a Congress in Córdoba to approve of the plan. One of the fifty-four delegates who went to Córdoba in December 1872 was Manuel Castillo Díaz, a carpenter from Medina Sidonia (*Actas*, 1:350). With Bakunin's death in 1876, younger leaders such as Peter Kropotkin, the Russian prince and geographer who escaped from a Tsarist prison that same year, and Enrico Malatesta, the Italian anarchist, became increasingly influential. Anarchist conceptions of a future society and the means to achieve it unfolded in new directions. Anarchocollectivists, following Bakunin, maintained that while property and the means of production would be held in common, the goods produced would belong to the independent trade unions responsible, with each union determining the distribution for its membership based on productivity. No others would share in these rewards. The concept of anarchocommunism, that the product as well as the means of production belonged to all of society, was an inevitable response to the ideological contradiction in anarchocollectivism. The new ideal, which was discussed simultaneously in several places, was clearly articulated in 1882 at the congress of Seville by Miguel Rubio and others, although at the time it was rejected by the majority at the meetings. By the end of the decade, however, through the writings of Kropotkin and Malatesta, anarchocommunism became the accepted ideal of anarchism. In a future anarchist society, the maxim would be "From each according to his ability; to each according to his needs." See Nettlau, *La Première Internationale*, pp. 397 ff.; Kaplan, pp. 135–43. By this time the Federación Regional Española (1868–81) had expired, and the Federación de Trabajadores de la Región Española (1881–88) provided the organizing structure. See José Álvarez Junco, *La ideología política de anarquismo español (1868–1910)*.

9. The conflict concerning violence as a tactic erupted at the Seville congress in 1882. A group of anarchocommunists from Arcos and Jerez advocated the use of violence against the large landowners. They were overruled and then expelled by the majority of anarchocollectivists, who feared that their fledgling labor unions would be closed and their modest gains lost. The dissidents then held secret meetings of their own, the Congreso de los Desheredados ("congress of the disinherited"), in 1883 and then again at the end of 1884. The exile of Los Desheredados from the federation lasted only four years, until 1886, and there is no evidence that they carried out any of their threats; however, their advocacy of violence and their secret organization served to support the worst fears of the bourgeoisie and landowning class.

exile. In the early 1880s the worker's protests were overshadowed by rumors of a secret organization called La Mano Negra ("The Black Hand") that allegedly plotted the murder of landlords and overseers and the destruction of crops and property. Any murder or serious crime against persons or property in the province of Cádiz was likely to be linked to this alleged conspiracy. Although the actual existence of La Mano Negra was in question, the authorities used it as the excuse for mass arrests in order to cripple the workers' federation. It is estimated that more than 5,000 workers in Cádiz and the neighboring region were arrested. Although membership in the federation throughout Andalusia fell from 30,000 to a scant core of 3,000, less than a decade later, in January 1892, hundreds of workers from the towns surrounding Jerez marched into the city armed with sickles and hoes. Aroused by the imprisonment of their compañeros, one group threw rocks at the door of the jail and cried to those inside, "Brothers, we have come for you!" One worker was seriously wounded in front of the jail, and there were other casualties in fights with police and in scuffles between the vineyard workers and city residents. In the fighting that took place in front of the city hall, there were shouts of "Long live anarchy!" and "Death to the bourgeoisie!" The aftermath was still more severe: a month following the event, four leaders of the march were garroted, and others received long prison terms.[10]

10. The name La Mano Negra purportedly derived from the toughened, dirt-stained hands of the workers (as opposed to the glove-protected hands of the bourgeoisie). In this regard, exaggerated tales spread among the upper and middle classes and are still recounted: "They [La Mano Negra] would stop people in the street and ask to see their hands. If they were white and soft, not black and calloused from working in the fields, they would stick a knife in you." Along with trials for a host of lesser crimes, there were three notorious murder trials linked to this presumed secret conspiracy. The most publicized case concerned the disappearance of a worker named Blanco de Benaocaz, who was allegedly murdered for leaving the society. Confessions, later repudiated, were beaten out of most of the sixteen accused, although the two men specifically charged with carrying out the murder never denied their innocence. After a lengthy trial and judicial appeals, all the men save one were found guilty. Seven men were sentenced to life imprisonment, and eight were garrotted in the city square of Jerez. Two of the accused committed suicide beforehand to avoid the final torturous eighteen minutes. As he was led to his execution, one of the defendants cried, "This is an inquisition!"

The charge that worker organizations conspired to murder landowners will concern events in Casas Viejas in 1915 and 1933, and so it is worthwhile to consider a key piece of evidence in the trial concerning Blanco de Benaocaz. A document of dubious authenticity, "Regulations of the Society of the Poor Against Their Thieves and Executioners," was introduced by the prosecutor to prove that the accused were linked to a conspiracy. The document, which purports to be the bylaws of the secret organization, had been in the possession of the police since 1878, five years prior to the commission of the crime being prosecuted, when it was allegedly "discovered" under a rock by an officer of the Civil Guard. The manufacture of false evidence by the authorities and other interested parties was part of an atmosphere of intimidation and repression. The internal evidence indicates that the document was a forgery, with ridiculous inventions and rules that smack more of the casinos of the rich than the centros of the workers. The regulations calling for seals, signed minutes, and initials written backward are absurdities, inconceivable in an organization whose members could not read or even write their initials forward. For the full text of the regulations (and the editor's assertion of their veracity), see Clara E. Lida, "Agrarian Anarchism in Andalusia: Documents on the Mano Negra." For more objective

As the anarchist movement matured, the membership became battle wise. Goals and tactics shifted as the anarchists sought to develop a mass movement. Individual acts of violence and vengeance were discredited and gave way to more widespread and carefully organized group action. There were attempts to organize strikes, demonstrations, and boycotts at more acceptable levels of protest.

Around the turn of the century, the workers of Medina joined the new anarchosyndicalist movement (revolutionary trade unionism) that had been developed in France. Anarchosyndicalism's arsenal of weapons included not only direct action such as sabotage and boycott but also the ordinary strike aimed at improving working conditions and the general strike whose goal was to topple the state.

Two stages of change were required to bring about an enduring social revolution. For the first stage, it was believed that overturning the economic and political structure could be accomplished instantaneously by a general strike that would lead to insurrection and thence to the destruction of central authority. The simplicity and directness of the plan had enormous appeal. Its efficacy seemed irrefutable, and it won acceptance among the campesinos of Andalusia.[11]

*José Vega:* It is very easy to transform the world. You abolish classes and change the social order. I forget who said it, but it's been said that when all the workers cross their arms and stop work, capitalism will be at an end. What is difficult is to have all the workers cross their arms at the same time—to agree to do it at the same time. The transformation itself is

---

evaluations of the existence of La Mano Negra, see Glen A. Waggoner, "The Black Hand Mystery: Rural Unrest and Social Violence in Southern Spain, 1881–1883"; and Kaplan, pp. 126–34. The workers of Medina Sidonia were spared the excesses of the repression, because the mayor and the judge in Medina protected their fellow townsmen against arbitrary imprisonment and deportation. The workers expressed their gratitude in *La crónica de los trabajadores de la región española*, 1:124 (session of May 23), cited by Gerard Brey and Jacques Maurice in "Casas Viejas: reformismo y anarquismo en Andalucía (1870–1933)," p. 24, n. 43. Concerning the Jerez uprising, some newspapers and historical accounts reported the workers' numbers as 4,000. See, e.g., Woodcock, *Anarchism*, p. 346. Kaplan estimates that 500–600 peasants were involved (p. 173). It is not known whether the marchers hoped to form a regional commune, if they were protesting the imprisonment of their fellow workers, or if they were responding to some other cause. See Kaplan's study for a full account of the circumstances of the march, pp. 168–85.

11. The principles favoring the strike were circulated widely in the anarchist press. They were affirmed at the Barcelona congress in 1910, at which the CNT was created: "Given a general strike, if all the workers fold their arms at a given moment, this will result in such a substantial upheaval in the history of the present society of exploited and exploiters, that it will inevitably cause an explosion, a clash between antagonistic forces that are struggling today for their survival; for just as Earth, if it stopped rotating on its own axis, would then crash into some other celestial body, if we were to stop working, we would likewise crash into all those who do not want us to escape the iron ring in which we are fixed" (Congreso Obrero Nacional, Barcelona, October 30–November 1, 1910; Session 5, Topic 7; reprinted in Díaz del Moral, *Historia*, app. 8, p. 544.

simple. When the workers are in accord, they can change the world at once.

The arduous task of reorganizing society, the second and more difficult stage of change, would mean the enduring revitalization of humanity.[12]

*José Monroy:* We thought that a general strike would triumph. We wanted to live without money, by the interchange of goods. Then it would be another battle. One had to form the organization and then arrange a system for the different organizations to cooperate with each other.

Beginning in 1902, a series of strikes electrified the countryside with hope of revolutionary change. Many of the campesinos who joined the organization then were inexperienced and naive, and they could scarcely find words to frame their demands.[13]

12. Bakunin's vision of the great change to take place included a succession of civil wars as the masses became aroused. According to Bakunin, even the creation of communes would bring about civil war. This contradicts the widely held view that the anarchists believed a utopian world would be created instantly. Bakunin wrote, "With the abolition of the State, the spontaneous self-organization of popular life, for centuries paralyzed and absorbed by the omnipotent power of the State, will revert to the communes. The development of each commune will take as its point of departure the actual condition of its civilization. And since the diversity between levels of civilization [culture, technology] in different communes of France, as in the rest of Europe, is very great, there will first be civil war between the communes themselves, inevitably followed by mutual agreement and equilibrium between them" ("Letters to a Frenchman on the Present Crisis" [1870], in *Bakunin on Anarchy,* p. 207).

13. Juan Díaz del Moral describes what took place in his town of Bujalance in the province of Córdoba from the point of view of a landowner. "Without previous notice, without making any petition, without any clue as to their motives, a general strike broke out on May 5 in Bujalance [1903]. On the appointed day, the workers stopped their work simultaneously, left hamlets and lands without custody, abandoned their livestock, and converged on the city. There was no violence: at a slight sign from the envoys from the centro, the workers stopped their tasks and followed the envoys; the domestic servants, coach drivers, errand boys, and other types of domestic servants joined the strike. The *ladies* had to carry out domestic tasks; the farm owners, helped by their friends and relatives, spread through the farms to take care of their herds. Since the strikers neither requested anything nor tried to parley, the authorities called the leaders over and tried to find out their purpose. Only then were some conditions made up in the workers' centro, which astonished the owners, little informed about the internal reasons for the strike. The wages they demanded were rather moderate. The novelty of the social phenomenon, seen in the town for the first time, and the fear of its consequences, would have made the owners accept the slight increase in wages without thinking. But the thing was that the conditions appeared to have been designed to be rejected. On the fifth, they were requesting seven and a half hours of rest per day; that is, they reduced working time to a ridiculous amount. Furthermore, the moment for declaring the strike appeared to have been deliberately chosen to ensure its failure. It was the time of the year when there are no urgent agricultural tasks; fifteen or twenty days later, putting off the harvest of lima beans would have caused serious damage; twenty or thirty days before, the omission of weeding would have damaged the seedlings. The strike did no harm to the owners other than having to take care of the cattle, whose feed on pasture lands was assured without much trouble. The conditions were not accepted. The strike took place in perfect order. The majority of workers remained home; some groups of

*José Monroy:* They asked for too much, because they lacked education. They thought they could reach the sky without a ladder. They still weren't professional. When I was young they were not professional, but they were beginning to learn. I was in the sindicato in Medina when someone arrived and said he had just seen a man seated in a chair on the street and that the chair should belong to us. He was simple and uneducated. There was good faith but lack of education. For that reason we would submit ideas to the assembly, and the bad ideas would be thrown out.

By the beginning of 1905, the revolutionary ardor had crested; and in the spring of the year, José Olmo, then only twenty-one, was one of the authors of an appeal to the workers of Medina to continue the struggle (*La Tribuna Obrera,* May 27, 1905):

And we the workers continue insensitive to our Calvary, and we go on humbly collecting the vile salary flung at us in exchange for twelve or fourteen hours of physical labor, having for sustenance a bit of bread of poor quality and a little oil that is still worse.

They urged the workers to unite against their exploiters on May 1.

Now is the hour, workers, for us to unite in a tightly bound sheaf. It is already time for us to join battle with those thieves of life and conscience, with these miserable exploiters, if we wish to be respected as men. Natural reason tells that we must unite for the common goal of a more just life, because if we do not, in the future our children will curse us.

Famine in 1905 doomed the strikes, and the death of their aspirations and the new hardship brought intense bitterness to daily life in Andalusia.

| | |
|---|---|
| Si el obrero pensara un día | If one day the worker would realize |
| Que sus hijos no pueden comer, | That his children cannot eat, |
| Con sus manos callosas le arrancara | With his calloused hands he would rip out |

three or four workers each circulated through the streets silently, with severe faces. In contrast to their usual custom, they did not speak or argue in loud voices; there was not a single confrontation. The taverns, constantly open, did not sell a drop of wine. The orders of the centro were being obeyed with marvelous unanimity. Overnight, moved by their new conviction, those men, full of faith in their ideals, had been transformed: they were controlling their instincts, their vehement desires, their vices, their most deep-seated habits. Days went by; hunger began to creep into the poorer homes; some of the strikers among those better off tried to help those in need. Twelve or fourteen days later, faced with the fact that the general strike (and the social revolution) was not bursting out throughout Andalusia, as could have been foreseen, given the courage and the presence of mind of the people of Bujalance, and since they did not want to lose the glory of having started it, the strike ceased as unexpectedly and quietly as it had started. The centro had been closed because of legal defects in its constitution; but the small number of men arrested were set free" (*Historia*, pp. 199–200).

| | |
|---|---|
| Las entrañas al perro burgués. | The entrails of the bourgeoisie dog. |

There was a profound gulf in commitment and understanding between the few obreros conscientes and the majority of the workers. The aftermath of failure was a prolonged period of wrangling and dissension. Conquered by hunger, the campesinos turned on the leaders who had demanded sacrifice but had failed to ensure victory. In 1908 the workers of Medina Sidonia were chastised in an open letter in *Tierra y Libertad* (October 15) for deserting their leaders:

Is it possible that you are the ones who in past years deserved the unanimous admiration of the neighboring towns because you knew how to protest social injustice and lent your valuable support to the movements to liberate our deprived class? . . . How do you justify your mistrust of a dozen men who work with you, who live with you, who have endured misfortunes and troubles in order to free you from the infamous capitalist yoke? And now, as a reward for their constant vigilance, you tarnish the ground on which they were working to the point of blaming them for the sad and regrettable situation through which you are passing, which is no more than the result of your wretched retreat.

The failure of the earlier strikes and other events such as the "Tragic Week" in 1909 in Barcelona prompted the formation of a more powerful trade union organization.[14] In 1910 delegates from all over Spain met in Barcelona and voted to form the broadly based CNT, the Confederación Nacional del Trabajo. This action required the cooperation of two diverse groups—anarchists and syndicalists—the former emphasizing libertarian ideas, spontaneity, and individual adventurous action, and the latter concerned with the development of a strong organization, carefully orchestrated group action, and tangible social gains. Future decades would prove the union of anarchists and syndicalists to be a stormy one, and in great measure the history of anarchosyndicalism concerns the struggle between the two groups for mastery of the direction of the revolutionary movement.[15]

The anarchosyndicalists of the CNT balanced two sets of objectives: the long-range anarchist aspiration to achieve a libertarian society; and the more

14. In 1909 protests against the recall of reservists for the war in Morocco led to the "Tragic Week"—200 dead, mass arrests, and the repression of the workers' centros. The influential anarchist educator Francisco Ferrer was executed as part of the campaign to destroy the movement. See Joan Connelly Ullman, *The Tragic Week: A Study of Anticlericalism in Spain, 1875–1912*.

15. The CNT was formally constituted in 1911. Its creation revived the lagging anarchosyndicalist movement, despite the fact that it was not legally recognized until 1914. Later in the year, the workers in Medina Sidonia met together in secret and reorganized. A notice subsequently appeared in *Tierra y Libertad* (April 10, 1912) that "in Medina Sidonia a group had been formed under the name Los Descontentos to aid in the continuation of the propaganda."

immediate syndicate demands for an eight-hour day, the abolition of piecework, higher wages, more hygenic conditions, and the elimination of child labor. The organization itself had to have the right to exist and function as the spokesman for the workers. For the first three years of its existence the CNT was illegal, but in 1914 the government recognized the right of the organization to function. In that same year the sindicato of Medina Sidonia won the right to open the door of its centro.

In the meetings José Olmo and one or two others served as guides and teachers for the others.

*José Monroy:* In Medina, Juan Martínez and José Olmo were equal. They would discuss matters between themselves and decide them. Juan Martínez was an orator and had a great deal of knowledge. Martínez was a field worker and charcoal burner. He was president at various times. He and Olmo were both organizers. Martínez was more bitter and difficult to take. He wasn't as communicative as Olmo. Olmo was more kindly. He talked to everyone.

Different ideas would come up at the meeting, but his [Olmo's] would always pass first. We had faith in him as a teacher. We saw him not as someone who would cure everything but, rather, as one who would educate the masses and organize them. In the beginning he taught the others, and they looked up to him. Naturally they followed the one who gave them their ideals.

José Olmo had gained a reputation for his eloquence and quick wit.

*Pepe Pareja:* José had the ability to express the rights that belong to a human being, and he was able to express them on his feet. Not everyone can do this—to think and express himself at the same time. He had arrived at that point of natural evolution.

His leadership, however, made him a target for the authorities and influential landowners.

*Anónimo:* In one of Olmo's stays in the [civil guard] headquarters, after prolonged and impertinent insults, a guard asked him his name. Realizing that this was mockery, for the guard knew his name well, Olmo answered, "My name is Fermín Salvochea."[16] In a moment the guards, leather boot

16. Fermín Salvochea, a revered leader in the region since the Republican insurrection in Cádiz in 1868, was sentenced to twelve years at hard labor for complicity in the workers' march on Jerez in 1892, even though he was in prison at the time of the march. He was then seventy-three years of age. Salvochea served not only as a symbol for José Olmo; he was also used as the model for the hero in Blasco Ibañez's *La Bodega;* see Brenan, p. 162, n. 2; Manuel Buenacasa, *El movimiento obrero español*, pp. 156–58; and José Sánchez Rosa, writing in *El Productor* (September 1919).

straps in their hands, hurled themselves upon him and struck him once and then again with satanic fury; they also slapped his face. But they were not able to humble him, and they ordered him to leave the headquarters. He left through the doors majestically, dauntless, his mind brightened with the light of reason, but his body aching from the blows of those hard-hearted ones who, with absurd cruelty, were trying to crush his spirit. His oppressors were left livid and dumbfounded, dejected, grim, downtrodden and withdrawn. Their torments could not succeed in bending that will of iron.

## Casas Viejas is organized

Anarchist ideals were introduced to Casas Viejas through various avenues. Some of the campesinos of Casas Viejas learned of anarchosyndicalism through contact with workers from other towns with whom they had labored on the large estates. Others had heard anarchist newspapers or pamphlets read aloud. Still others, like José Monroy, had been steeped in anarchism in the centro of Medina.

*José Monroy:* When I was thirteen years old, I went to the campo to weed, and my father put me in the organization so that I would have the right to work and no one would object. My father belonged to the organization, but he, like many, did not "have ideas." My father took me to the sindicato in Medina in 1905. We lived in Medina then. I was there every night. There I received my ideals and aspirations.

Some campesinos had developed personal philosophies akin to anarchism. Pepe Pareja had found his own thoughts echoed by anarchist teachings:

I was always working with the earth, and I always realized that one person alone can't set the table. United with others, one can do more. One can take advantage of the weather and the land. One can't do it alone. In groups, collectively, one can take advantage of the seasons, the lands.

Although Pepe Pareja customarily worked with his father and brothers sowing the land they had rented, on occasion he worked as a field hand in other townships, and on one such trip he learned how other towns were organized.

In 1913, when I was twenty-six, I went to Chipiona to harvest grapes. The people there were organized. At that time there were sindicatos in all or almost all the towns. Those who had sindicatos insisted that those who were not organized had no right to work. They had to show their sindicato card in order to get work. That small town was organized, and they had agreed that as long as there was one local man without work, no one could give work to anyone from outside. And if there was extra work, then those of the neighboring towns—Trebujena, Sanlúcar—had the first right to that work. Then, if there was still work available, those further away could work. Since these measures had been taken, I could do nothing but go back, because they wouldn't give me work. I was not organized. And if I had been organized, since the agreement was to give work to those from the neighboring towns and not to those from faraway towns like this one [Casas Viejas], I had no right to work and I had to come back. But I saw how they were organized.

The development of anarchism in Casas Viejas was given fresh impetus by the arrival of workers who belonged to the sindicato of Jerez, a city with a long history of tragic strikes. In 1913 the lands of Ahijón were leased to Diego Soto, known as Polaina ("Leggings"), an unlettered, self-made man from the mountain town of Ubrique, who with his three sons brought 100 teams of mules and oxen and thirty-odd workers from Jerez to sow wheat in the fertile pastures of Ahijón. During the day the workers from Jerez and Casas Viejas prepared the lands of Ahijón together, and since the days before the winter rains were short, after dark the workers would walk up to the town to talk in the cafés. The less sophisticated workers of Casas Viejas asked the workers of Jerez to orient them in the ways of anarchosyndicalism.

*Pepe Pareja:* It is just as if someone is in a dark room and the light is turned on. Then one can see clearly. This is what happened with the people who came here to give light, to organize us.

We met first to organize in the house of a friend. We had no meeting place yet. We had asked Corales, one of the workers who came to work for Polaina in Ahijón, to give a talk explaining the organization. He was very knowledgeable. We bought pass books for everyone. Each person would receive a pass book to show that he was a member and to list the dues that he paid. But a traitor informed the civil guard, who came and said that this was a clandestine meeting because there were more than nineteen present. They broke up the meeting.

The desire to form a sindicato was not dampened by the raid of the civil guard. Official sanction for the meeting could be obtained, but the major task was to find a leader to inspire the workers and to teach the principles of anarchism. The workers had to be taught both philosophy and tactics. The problems posed in Casas Viejas were being remedied in Medina Sidonia.

*José Monroy:* It was agreed between Medina and ourselves that we needed someone to organize us. We had to ask the permission of the governor to form a sindicato. Then José Olmo came here.

# Two
# Social Class

In earlier centuries the Moors had built a watch tower two kilometers from what would become the perimeter of the village of Casas Viejas. The squat tower commanded a strategic view of the valley leading to the mountains and the sea. To the southwest one could see the Laguna de la Janda, the inland marsh that supplied cane for tying the thatched roofs of the chozas.[1] The marsh attracted migratory birds to trap; it also nurtured malaria-carrying mosquitoes that infested the area. From the tower one could also see the vast undivided lands in the valley, typical of this region of *latifundios*. These large land holdings were owned by the noble descendants of the grandees rewarded after the reconquest, and by the lesser nobility and bourgeoisie who had purchased lands after the break-up of the common lands and church holdings in the mid-nineteenth century.[2] The number of these great landowners was small. In 1914 over half of the 54,000 hectares in the township of Medina Sidonia were owned by only twenty-two men, some of whom had extensive holdings elsewhere as well.

## The Marqués of Negrón

The most influential landowner in the township of Medina Sidonia was the marqués of Negrón, Don Salvador Hidalgo y Pardo de Figueroa. Don Salvador was the master of more than fifteen large estates and a score of smaller

1. The marsh (now drained for agricultural use by the marqués of Tamarón) is in the neighboring township of Vejer de la Frontera. In the year 711 it was the site of a crucial battle when the invading Berbers decisively defeated the Visigoths and began the Moorish occupation of the country.

2. For an account of the historical forces shaping the development of the latifundio system, see Malefakis, pp. 50–64; and Brenan, chap. 6.

land parcels, including pastures and groves at the foot of Casas Viejas. The family inheritance totaled over 10,000 hectares, approximately one-fifth of all the land in the township.[3] The marqués was the most powerful landowner in Medina Sidonia, the leader of the Conservative party, and considered the *cacique* of the town. He had little to do, however, with the management of his estates, leaving that responsibility to his local administrator, Alfonso Gómez. Like many other men of wealth and influence in the province, Don Salvador lived at some distance from his lands, in bustling Jerez. He owned a house in Medina Sidonia, which his servants kept in readiness for an occasional visit, made largely because of his interest in breeding fast horses. Don Salvador had studied in Belgium and held a degree in law, but his wealth made it unnecessary for him to practice his profession.

It was said that Don Salvador's granduncle, the marqués, had won the family's wealth by selling stolen horses and cattle to the French invaders during the Spanish War of Independence in 1808–14. With his profit he purchased land in Medina Sidonia, and in the mid-nineteenth century, after the division of the public lands, he bought a number of small lots (one lot, it was said, was traded for an old overcoat of his) in order to increase the dimensions of some estates and to form new ones. The wide cattle trails separating rows of lots, which had accommodated herds of cattle and sheep in transit, were swallowed up when the marqués purchased lots on both sides of a road and then closed it off. The marqués purchased other estates from the duke of Medina Sidonia, whose lands sharply diminished as each ducal generation sold a portion of its patrimony to meet current expenses. In 1910 the marqués's accumulated lands were inherited by Doña Josefa Pardo de Figueroa y de la Serna, the widow of the marqués's nephew, and her children. Doña Josefa was widely known as a charitable lady and patroness of the church, but she had little to do with managing her holdings. The administration of the family fortune was turned over to her son, Don Salvador, the new marqués of Negrón.

In his notebooks Anónimo had little good to say about the marqués:

Josefa Pardo was a charitable and generous lady. Her son was quite different. To him the poor were repulsive. He was absolutist, despotic, machia-

3. This represented an enormous property, particularly in Spain. Based on his study of the Inventory of Expropriable Property recorded in 1933 during the time of the Republic, Malefakis notes, "Most of the noblemen who held property were giant landowners . . . the possession of 250 hectares of arable land is enough to establish a person as a large owner by Spanish standards. If he holds more than 500 arable hectares, he enters a special category that probably includes less than one-tenth of one percent of the active agricultural population. Yet . . . more than three-quarters of the nobles listed in the Inventory for the six key latifundio provinces studied held more than 500 hectares in those provinces alone, without reference to their belongings in the rest of the nation" (pp. 69–71).

vellian, and highly unpopular. All his activities consisted of intrigues directed toward party politics. He had a hard conscience.

He stayed aloof from all contact with social and town life. If he talked with someone, which he very seldom did, it was with some administrators or people appointed to carry out agricultural business. He placed all his confidence in the servants of his household, and he never kept close vigilance over them. On certain occasions he said that they were like children of the household and that for no reason would they ever be sent away, although of course this statement was only meant for effect.

He gave the land completely over to the custody of his foremen. Years went by without his going to the campo, and when he did go, he was interested only in his possessions. He showed absolute indifference toward everything else.

The only thing he favored greatly were his Hispanic-Arabic horses. Concerning this we remember that he never came to the campo without seeing a gray mare called La Barranquera ["Surefooted"], on which he spent much time enjoying himself and repeating the phrase, "What a beautiful mare."

Anónimo's strongest criticisms concerned the marqués's machinations against the workers:

The marqués's action as chief of the Conservative party consisted of sly maneuvers directed toward the enforcement of absolutism. As he was despotic in character, we harbor bitter memories, since all his energies went to smashing the campesino worker's aspirations for the right to live. He did this by means of furious terrorist persecutions, calumnies, and lies about the most active leaders of the sindicato, whom he called ringleaders. As a result of his struggles with one of these leaders, José Olmo, the marqués received the nickname "The Tiger."

The actual management of the marqués's estates was in the hands of Alfonso Gómez, his administrator. Since Gómez, rather than the marqués, was present to make daily decisions concerning the estates, he had enormous power over the lives of the people employed there, as his son recalls:

Every day he would ride out on horseback to one estate or another, depending on what needed to be done. In the evening my father would return home and seat himself in a big armchair and receive petitions. One would come asking for firewood, another for straw; and he would make a decision about each petition. Then each estate had a foreman, and there were herdsmen and regularly employed workers and day workers. The warehouses in town were also under my father, but his brother was mostly in charge of the work there. My father was the administrator for fifty years.

Ignorant of the problems of land and work management, the marqués and his mother were dependent on the good judgment of Gómez, as the administrator's son recalls:

> The pay for the workers varied. Once it was five reales; later it went up to three pesetas. But they earned very little. Once the workers asked for one real more. A brother-in-law, Don Joaquín, and my father went to Doña Josefa and told her that the workers were asking for one more real. And she said, "What do you think, Alfonso?" "I think it's justified." "Well, then, give it to them."

The marqués's various estates were broad, unfenced stretches of pasture and tree-rich hills and mountains. (It was not until the 1920s that lands in the area were fenced.) There were natural geographic divisions of stream, arroyo, rock, and mountain, and pastures were often scattered some distance apart. As on most large estates in Andalusia, the land was not intensively worked, and some pastures were left untilled for as long as three or four years, used only to graze cattle on the natural growth. Nitrates were not used, and the fields were fertilized only by the droppings of the grazing animals.

Under Gómez's supervision, the arable land on each estate was divided according to the three-field system, as was the practice throughout Andalusia. One-third of the land remained in pasture. The second third, consisting of fields untilled for at least the previous growing season, were now planted with legumes, usually chickpeas but sometimes other crops, such as beans, oats, lentils, or sorghum. The soil bed for the legumes was plowed in January, and the seed was sown in February. The crop matured during the summer and provided nitrates for the soil for the next planting. The third portion of land, which had been planted in legumes the previous year, was now sown with wheat. Land prepared for the wheat was plowed some time between October and November, before or during the rainy season, according to the weather, and then sown during December and January. After the wheat harvest in the summer, the three-year cycle would be complete, and the land would be turned to pasture for the following year.

The lands of the marqués of Negrón were planted in wheat, corn, chickpeas, rye, and beans. The marqués was also rich in herds of cattle, pigs, sheep, and horses, and there were some goats as well. When rations were required to feed the campesinos in his employ, flour and chickpeas were drawn from his storehouses in Medina; fat for the chickpea stew came from pigs slaughtered on the estates; and just below Medina, on the marqués's estate of Pocosangre, his baker prepared bread to be carried to the workers on all the other estates. At the end of each harvest, the crop was carried up the long winding road to Medina by burros—the lead burro tagged with a copper bell to toll the way to the marqués's brimming storehouses.

## Don Antonio Vela

Casas Viejas could not boast of a resident titled family. The wealthiest landowners were Don Antonio Vela, the village doctor, and his sister Nicolasa, who together owned several hundred hectares of valuable pasture and rented thousands more. They had moved to Casas Viejas from Medina Sidonia and had built fine stone houses in the village. They also owned many of the other lesser village houses, including the old inn.

Like the marqués of Negrón, Don Antonio owed much of his fortune to the capture of plots of once public land offered for sale in the mid-nineteenth century. Francisco Vela, the father of Don Antonio, had begun buying lots of six and ten fanegas on the pasture lands of Las Yeguas and Benalup. He bought his first plot in 1864 for twenty pesetas and two years later purchased another. Buying and trading over the next few years, he gradually accumulated a number of adjacent plots. He bought the old inn, the first structure in Casas Viejas with a tile roof, for back taxes. His accumulated lands brought him a change in status: his first purchase recorded in the Registro de Propiedad in Medina identifies him as Francisco Vela, *agricultor* (farmer); another in 1866, when he was aged forty-four, refers to him as a *pelantrín* (small farmer); but later land deeds add the honorific *Don* to his name. Don Francisco was still acquiring lots as well as houses in Casas Viejas as late as 1882, when he was seventy years old. Prices for land had risen since his first purchase, and he paid 300 pesetas for a plot of land on his newly formed estate, Palmita. By the time of his death in 1884, Don Francisco had provided his son Antonio with a university education and a substantial inheritance.

When he was twenty-two, the year before his father's death, Don Antonio moved to Casas Viejas, where he celebrated his marriage to Luisa Morales, aged twenty-three. Don Antonio had graduated as a medical doctor; however, like the marqués of Negrón, he had little interest in his profession. Don Antonio concentrated his energies on managing the lands that he and Nicolasa had inherited. Nicolasa had married their first cousin, Francisco García Vela, a carpenter with the nickname Reinero, and they also lived in Casas Viejas. Together the two families formed a company to advance their fortunes. Beginning in 1884, they jointly purchased additional lands and houses. They rented the estates of the titled absentee landowners of the ducal houses of Medina Sidonia and Lerma to graze cattle or to subdivide into smaller lots that were then subleased at a higher rate. By subdividing one estate, they earned enough to pay the rent for the other estates. With their profits, they bought and sold cattle.

In 1901 Nicolasa's daughter married Don José Espina, a young doctor from Medina. Don José Espina was the son of a government engineer from Extremadura who had come to Medina to supervise the distribution of public lands and, having married a local girl, remained in Medina.

In one sense the marriage proved a boon to Don Antonio, since he promptly turned over his medical practice to Don José in order to devote all his attention to buying and selling cattle and to managing the lands. In the long run, however, the arrival of Don José reduced the amount of land controlled by Don Antonio. In a few short years the Espina family multiplied along with the riches, and foreseeable problems of management and inheritance argued for the dissolution of the joint company. In 1908 the two families wrote down on paper the names of their accumulated lands and houses, divided them into two approximately equal parts, and drew lots. It was a lottery without risk, and both sides came away abundantly wealthy in estates and houses.

An imposing figure with strong features and a thick mustache, Don Antonio Vela remained the most important landowner in the village. With the division of the estates, however, Don José Espina became important in his own right as the administrator of his in-law's lands, particularly since his father-in-law was said to love his "dark widow"—the wine bottle—too well. Like Don Antonio, Don José too preferred the role of administrator rather than medical doctor; and in 1909, a year after the dissolution of the joint company, he brought his sister's husband, Don Federico Ortiz, to Casas Viejas to take over his practice.

From the point of view of a working landowner, the rich made little active contribution to their own good fortune. José Suárez, whose family owned and worked land deep in the mountains, scoffed at claims of industry:

> Neither the grandees nor the rich worked. The grandees lived away. The rich rode their horses around the estates but did not work either with their hands or with their heads in the office—with the exception of Mora Figueroa [the marquis of Tamarón, of the township of Vejer], who was always a worker. Don Antonio and Espina both had medical degrees, but neither practiced medicine. In the north the rich Catalonians work. Here in Andalusia the rich do not work.

The two families had built grand, two-story stone and lime houses across from each other, each with a garden and patio. Although located in the village, the houses were arranged as spacious *cortijos*, or country estates. Family and servants' quarters were on the first floor. The upper story served as storage areas for the wheat, chickpeas, and rye. Additional storage rooms for lima beans and other crops were constructed adjacent to the house. There was also a room with tools and halters for the teams, where the workers congregated each morning before work and prepared coffee. Next to Nicolasa's house, which was newer and more spacious than Antonio's, were stables for six mules and eighteen oxen. In the sowing season each of the oxen would be yoked with a cow to form working teams. A foreman oversaw the lands and organized the work. There were herdsmen for the cattle, goats, and pigs; and three or four house servants lived in to do the cooking and to aid in the household tasks. Each year the storehouses that ran the length of the second stories of the houses were filled with wheat until the windows had to be closed to keep the grain from spilling out.

The families of the rich maintained a pattern of life entirely distinct from that of the villagers. They attended church and received the Eucharist regularly. They were the pillars of religion. Their children generally made friends with children in their own class or with others who were educated. In the small village they had acquaintances among the children of shopkeepers, artisans, and campesinos; but these contacts were intermittent, interrupted when the children of the well-to-do were sent away to the city to be educated. The bonds linking comrades were work, school, or leisure, as their fortunes dictated. Although the sons of the rich were not always the most brilliant of pupils, most received diplomas, either earned or purchased.

Although the wealth of the Velas and Espinas far surpassed that of any other family in the village, they avoided paying for anything, preferring to trade land use for services or to have a campesino sharecrop on their land. In order to have fig trees planted on one estate just above the village, Don Antonio divided the land into lots and allowed campesinos to sow a crop if they would provide fig tree clippings and then plant and tend them. When the trees were planted, the workers utilized the land around the trees for their own crops, thereby weeding and encouraging the growth of the trees. The estate came to be called La Ahorrativa ("The Saving"), because the fig trees were planted and cultivated without cost to the owner. Don Antonio admired such thrift, and like many of his class he saw the cause of poverty and misery among the workers as the result of squandering their meager earnings.

Antagonism between landowner and campesino was sharpened in Don Antonio's case by a morning ritual at Ricardo's bar. When Don Antonio would arrive at the bar each morning to have his coffee, he would face workers seated at the tables who were without funds to order anything.

*Juan Pinto:* When Antonio Vela would go in the bar in the morning, he would say, "You all must have already had your coffee. Now I'm going to have mine." He would not invite anyone to join him, and he would clap his hands and expect to be served first.

Don Antonio's ritual placed the tavern owner in a compromising position. As Juan Pinto described the situation,

this invariably upset Ricardo, who always served each one in his turn. He told him, "I don't make my living from you alone." Ricardo was always very reserved and serious with him, which accounts for the bar's popularity over the years. It is still the place where the workers are paid.

Once he [Don Antonio] came into Ricardo's bar where the men were having coffee and said they were throwing their money away. Ricardo told him to take coffee in his own home, because otherwise the workers would not come in. At that time it cost a *perra chica* [five céntimos] to have coffee.

Don José Espina was more of an enigma than Don Antonio, and town opinion about him was divided. Don José had a pleasant manner, and he often loaned tools to needy cultivators. To any request for money, however, he would respond that he was only the manager of the lands of his in-laws and could not afford it. Some believed him to be heartless; others found him amiable.

*José Suárez:* Espina was a very good man. He never gave money, but he did favors. If you were sick, he didn't charge.

The servant girls hired from among the campesino families of the town had a more intimate view of the penurious nature of some of the rich. Food was kept under lock and key.

*Carmen:* I was around ten or eleven when I began to work for the Espinas. I earned five pesetas a month. The wife of Espina, Sebastiana, was terrible. We ate and slept there. In the morning we would have coffee and milk and toasted bread. For the main meal at noon they would give us—there were three or four of us—white rice all stuck together and half-cooked potatoes—things I wouldn't ever eat today. If I only knew then what I know today! In the evening we had a stew of chickpeas and fat.

They gave us the putrid food that was left over. They used to make blood pudding with tomatoes, which is not an expensive meal, and after the left-over portion had been lying on the shelf for three or four days, they brought it to us. The cook said, "Who is that for?" "Why, for you."

When she left the room the cook threw it in the garbage. We never said anything to her. When they killed a pig, they would give us the old rancid lard. They never, never gave us any dessert—just white rice and half-cooked potatoes. Nothing else. Sebastiana's sister, Juanita, used to sneak in fruit and cheese under her dress for us—an orange, some figs. She knew we didn't have anything to eat. [An egg?] My God! We had milk for breakfast because they had cows. If I only knew then what I know now!

The doctors, Don Antonio, Don José, and Don Federico, were sensitive to the disease and dirt in the village, and their knowledge encouraged them to keep their distance from the villagers, many of whom suffered from tuberculosis. The gulf between the campesinos and the doctors would widen in 1918, when the world-wide influenza epidemic reached Spain. The epidemic touched Spain in June and by November had reached frightening proportions. In Casas Viejas the epidemic drove the death toll for the year to eighty-five, more than twice the usual number, and the doctors locked their doors, forbidding anyone to enter and denying their servants permission to leave. One of the untreated victims was Pepe Pareja's brother:

In 1918 my brother and I were planting wheat on land we had rented, and he said he felt ill. At that time people would fall sick with the grippe and be dead in twenty-four hours. So I said, "Get on the burra and go back to the pueblo." So he returned.

But the doctors weren't visiting anyone for fear of contracting the disease. They weren't walking in the street. They were locked in their houses. So the family went to Don Federico to ask what they could do for my brother, and he told them to put on leeches, which was a common method of curing then. The leeches were usually put on one's legs, and the blood circulated around and returned. But they put two leeches on either side of his chest by his neck, and he died, drowned in his blood. He died for lack of a doctor.

Despite the tensions and animosity that existed between the families of the rich and the workers, the social pattern of the village and the formal style of Spanish life contained the hostility, at least outwardly, on most occasions. Spanish workers could be fiercely independent and yet remain gracious in manner and speech. José Monroy, one of the leaders of the sindicato, observed, "I always addressed the rich in the same way [by their first names]. I have only one form of speech; but I took off my hat to those with degrees [*gente de carrera*], Don Antonio and Don José Espina."

## The middle-class landowners

In the eyes of the campesinos, the middle class included a wide range of townsmen: well-to-do landowners, small landowners, storekeepers, millers, tavern keepers, and even independent campesinos who rented small parcels of land each year to sow a crop. This broad category encompassed almost everyone except the rich at the one end of the social scale and day workers at the other. Since Casas Viejas was an agricultural village, the gradations of the social scale were usually dependent on land ownership.

The middle-class landowners were important sources of employment. Unlike the *latifundistas* (large estate owners), they could not afford to have their lands lie idle, and they worked every corner intensively. In the seasons of sowing and harvest they also hired the landless campesinos.

To provide bread for his family and have a modest surplus to purchase other necessities, a landowner had to possess at least forty to fifty hectares of unirrigated pasture land—anything less meant that he was at the mercy of the weather and happenstance. If the landowner were fortunate enough to possess irrigated land, then a *huerta* (garden) of even two or three hectares would provide him with a satisfactory livelihood.

Successful middle-class landowners living in town often had a variety of interests in town and in the campo. They lived in sturdy houses, were educated, and could have their children trained in a profession, skill, or trade. Although in continual contact with the campesinos, they were still set apart from them by economic interests, education, and social station.

The most prominent of these middle-class landowners were the brothers Antonio and Juan Pérez-Blanco. Each brother owned about sixty hectares of land, which they had inherited through the second marriage of their mother. Part of the land included water-rich groves and gardens below the village. The brothers managed a variety of enterprises: Antonio sowed his lands, raised cattle, and rented other lands as well, including his brother's; Juan kept the town's only general merchandise store in the first floor of his fine two-story house, which faced the plaza and the church. In time he also purchased a generator-powered mill in partnership with the local school teacher, Manuel Sánchez. The brothers were important to the town's economy, buying and selling in their commercial enterprises; they hired local townsmen as clerks, and paid campesinos to cultivate their groves and fields and to guard their cattle. Although they were better off than most, they shared many values common to the town and frequently served as leaders in community and church affairs.

Some middle-class landowners lived deep in the mountains and were independent of the town. A few owned considerable extensions of land, but much of it was mountainous, too rugged to sow a crop and useful primarily as rough grazing land. The family of José Suárez, the future major, owned lands in the mountains fifteen kilometers from the town. In 1900, the four Suárez brothers had inherited Las Algamitas, 2,200 fanegas of mountainous terrain at the boundary of Los Barrios and Alcalá de los Gazules, which they worked in common. Only 250 fanegas were arable, and so for the most part the brothers raised cattle, goats, and pigs. They were rarely seen in town except to sell their harvest or to purchase salt and oil.

Unlike the nobility or the local rich, middle-class landowners like the Suárez family both managed and worked their lands. They also furnished work for families who lived in the mountains nearby, with whom they claimed a closer relationship than usually existed between landowner and worker.

*José Suárez:* We had very few workers, about eight or ten families. We always gave meals to the workers. If they were sick, they were cared for. They were not abandoned. I didn't realize the calamities occurring outside.

Workers raised with the middle class knew how to do all agricultural tasks. Those on the large estates knew nothing. They didn't have to think of anything. We had a cattle herder for the animals; and in the summer, since we were in the mountains, we went to harvest the cork trees. The workers sowed, plowed, and threshed in the *era*. They knew how to harness the horses as well as to plow. They were better prepared and knew how to handle everything.

## Small-scale herders and renters

The small-scale renter and herder lived in an ambiguous position between the bourgeoisie and the workers. What distinguished them from other landless campesinos was their relative independence and enterprise. Rather than work for a wage, they risked their time and labor to raise a crop or manage a small herd of their own. They were skillful husbandmen and were generally more knowledgeable about animals, plants, and soils than day laborers accustomed to acting on orders in gang labor.

In former days the animals of landless herders would have grazed on common lands. At night the herdsmen would gather on the hill just above the town; and in the morning, when it became light, they would collect their herds. Since the public lands no longer existed, the herders had to rent land or graze their cattle, sheep, or goats on the old trails used to bring herds to market. Some of these trails had become more heavily trafficked highways linking the towns to the cities, but many of the wide, unpaved paths were still in use.

The good fortune of a small herder like José Monroy depended on his empathy with his animals and his success in fulfilling their needs. When the grass was burned out by the summer sun, he toasted the thick leaves of the cactus to remove their sharp spines and then fed the smooth leaves to his animals. When he had no other recourse, he would make clandestine night visits to pastures owned by others, running the risk of being caught by the owners, the watchmen, or the civil guard.

Pepe Pareja's father, Manuel Rodríguez, was a small-scale renter richer in sons than in land. He had eight sons, but he did not own a single hectare.

The sons could not attend school, but they were trained in all the agricultural tasks. As Pepe recalls,

> I guarded turkeys when I was little—six, seven, or eight years old—in my aunt's house. After that I guarded pigs. Later I guarded mares, sheep, and cows. When I was nine or ten years old, I would get up at five in the morning to care for the cows with which my father plowed the land. We had eight cows and their offspring, and during the day I would tend the ones that were not working, along with their calves. At night we would return home with all the cows. We would tie them with a rope to feed them so that they would be able to work the next day.
>
> When I was thirteen or fourteen my father said to me, "You're going to come with me to sow the land." Then I worked in the fields. I began to work with my father doing all the tasks of farming: plowing, sowing, weeding, cultivating, reaping, threshing, gathering the ripe grain, carrying it to the storehouse, delivering the portion due to the owners. In September, when all the harvest had been reaped, I cut firewood for cooking and heat for the winter. I liked it, because I had no other choice. I was the oldest, having seven young brothers. So I had to help my father in order for us to be able to eat.

Each year Manuel rented twenty to forty fanegas of land to sow wheat that was ground into flour to be used by the family throughout most of the year. The family had a hut in the village and another by the cattle trail through the campo, in the township of Alcalá.[4] Since animals could graze along the wide stretch of the trail, campesinos in town sometimes gave Manuel a cow to care for during the year. Under such an arrangement, the offspring of the cow belonged to the owner; however, Manuel could use the cow as a draft animal. The advantages to both parties were obvious: the owner did not have to care for the animal or provide it with feed, and he was able to secure a profit on the sale of the young. Manuel had a beast to draw his plow and still had no expense for feed.

Many small renters lacked a team, or seed, or tools, and so they were forced to mortgage a portion of their projected crop. Every step in the process reduced their yield. Some would borrow seed and then return the same amount of seed plus one-fifth of their harvest. Those without a cow or mule to draw a plow were forced to rent or borrow a team in order to sow their crop. Without draft animals, they were again obliged to arrange for a team to carry the crop to the threshing floor and to thresh it, paying one-quarter of a fanega of wheat for each cart load. To make matters worse, since the rights to the stubble had died with the sale of the common lands, the small

4. All that was required to build along the cattle trail was permission of the township government or the civil guard. For discussion of this practice, see Joaquín Costa Martínez, *Colectivismo agrario en España*, p. 264.

renter had rights to the land for only the growing season of the crop. Only the team used on the threshing floor was permitted to feed. If he had any livestock, he could not let them graze on the stubble of his crop, which now belonged to the original owner (or to the first lessee) of the land. These terms were in sharp contrast to the rights of the large-scale renter like Don Antonio Vela, who customarily rented an entire estate for a period of four or six years and had unrestricted use of the land throughout the entire period.

For the small renter, sowing a crop was a hazardous venture at best. Sometimes the rains came early and sometimes late. The small renter could almost always count on bad luck. As Manuel Rodríguez often said, "la siembra es oficio de arrepentido" ("Sowing is an occupation for repenters"). One was always repenting that too little seed had been sown or too much, that one had planted too early or too late. The crop harvested was usually insufficient to meet the needs of one's own family for the year, and one was forced to find other means to furnish additional food or cash. When their own tasks were ended, the men or their sons worked as day laborers or as reapers.

On the social level, the small-scale renters were considered workers; however, since they sometimes employed other campesinos to work for them, economically they clung to a position on the lower end of the middle class. Although they might work at times as day laborers themselves, when they plowed and harvested their own crop, their interests were identical with those of the landowners.

Some anarchosyndicalists found the small renters to be among the most intransigent foes of the sindicato. Since the small renters were heavily mortgaged, when they required help to sow or to harvest their crop, they could least afford to pay the decent wages sought by the workers. Pelele, one of the leaders of the sindicato in Medina Sidonia, considered the small renters more uncompromising than the landowners:

> The *perjuales* [small renters] had a team and would hire two or three men. They were the same as the landowner—or worse. When they met with the workers, they walked with them; then they walked with the others. They were two-faced.

The sharecropper who went half and half (*aparcería*) with a landowner was regarded still more warily. In this arrangement, the landowner customarily supplied the land and the seed, while the sharecropper contributed the team and the labor.

> *Pepe Pilar:* Here the problem was not with the small renters but with the *palomos* [doves], those who went in aparcería with the señorito. They were united with the señorito. Here we had many more of the middle

class, men like myself who rented twenty or forty fanegas from the larger landowners like Espina. We were with the anarchist movement.

Although relations among workers and small renters and sharecroppers were sometimes strained, in the larger perspective of the social struggle they experienced common woes and were united on most points. José Monroy, a small herder as well as an anarchosyndicalist, believed that there were no real antagonisms between the various elements of the middle class and the campesinos:

The rich have always been indifferent toward us. We got on better with the middle class—those who rented land and planted in aparcería. Then there was a large middle class, with many small renters. The middle class we considered workers.

# Three
# Campesinos

In country towns the agricultural cycle determined the calendar of activities. The agricultural year began on the day of San Miguel (September 29), and the initial plowing customarily took place after the first autumn rains. Until then the land was baked hard by the summer sun and could not be plowed with the light wooden Roman plow.

The vast majority of the men of Casas Viejas were campesinos. Most were employed as *eventuales,* workers hired for the day or for a given task. The working class in Casas Viejas included a small number of artisans and other skilled workers—carpenters, cabinetmakers, masons, shoemakers, barbers, blacksmiths, and bakers. These were the more favored skills that enabled a man to work the year around and earn wages higher than those paid to agricultural day workers.[1] A poor agricultural town, however, could support only a small number of skilled workers. Moreover, in order to learn a craft, one had to be an apprentice for many years, and there were few opportunities beyond what existed in one's own household. It was only a farsighted foreman, who earned a bit more than the field hands, who could afford to pay to have his son apprenticed to a craftsman such as a carpenter or a blacksmith.

*Juan Pinto:* I wanted to be a mason rather than a field hand, but I couldn't do it because I didn't know how. I was brought up by my father, and from the time I was ten or twelve years old I have had a plow in my hands, later a scythe, later I did planting, and later gathering the wheat grown for bread. It was this way until I married, and when I married we

1. Despite their relatively sparse number, skilled workers were in the forefront of organizing the sindicatos. They often served as representatives to the congresses. At the congress held at Córdoba in January 1873, for example, skilled workers such as weavers, carpenters, paper makers, masons, tanners, printers, and hatters far outnumbered the few farm laborers there. Of the fifty-one delegates present, only three were farm workers; see Max Nettlau, *La Première Internationale,* 1:62f.

continued in the same way, always working just the same—threshing the wheat, later killing rabbits with my shotgun because life was getting very bad one way or another. And that's the life of the poor.

Eventuales lived in the town. They went out to work on the land for the day, or a number of days, and then returned home.[2] Before dawn each day the eventuales would gather in the street by the plaza to be chosen by a landowner or foreman. Anónimo attributed the origin of this "shape up" by the plaza to the ancient slave market. The system continued to serve the landowners by helping to keep the campesinos submissive:

The custom of hiring in the plaza was very profitable for the latifundistas and their foremen or managers, because those who agreed to go to the fields always saw the great number of their compañeros who remained behind without work, and so those who had work were submissive and allowed themselves to be easily exploited. If someone who was discontented complained, the foreman or manager responded arrogantly, with great show: "There are men still waiting in the plaza! Take a walk!" The one who complained was dismissed immediately and would lose the chance to work.

Agricultural work spanned a wide range of knowledge and skills: harnessing the animals and plowing, broadcasting seeds, reaping with the short sickle and the long scythe, and cleaning and threshing the grains. Those engaged to work on the small irrigated huertas, the *hortelanos*, knew the season and characteristics of each plant they tended, the art of grafting the sweet orange onto the more sturdy bitter orange tree, and the method of irrigating uneven land so that all parts of the huerta would be watered equally. These were the ancient agricultural arts passed down from the time of the Moors. Because of their skills, and because they broke the ground with the heavy hoe rather than with the plow, hortelanos were paid a slightly higher wage than were field workers.

Work in the fields was governed by decades of carefully honed patterns that ensured dominance by the landowners and survival, albeit at a marginal level, for the campesinos. Tasks and corresponding pay were scaled at a bare subsistence level, according to import and energy expended. Field workers

2. The eventuales were divided into two categories: *jornaleros* and *peonistas*. The jornalero was customarily hired for a seasonal task such as sowing and cultivating the land or for the collection of grains, while the peonista would be hired for a day or days for a specific task. The busiest time for the peonista was in the spring, when he would be called on to help prepare the land in the huertas for planting. Later, in February, he would return to weed the plants. Jornaleros and peonistas usually worked apart, but peonistas occasionally worked alongside jornaleros to speed up the work and to take advantage of good weather. The jornaleros earned a smaller daily wage than the peonistas, because they were assured of more work days. Jornaleros were paid every ten days, but peonistas were paid the following morning when told if they were needed again.

earned three reales for the first plowing for wheat; the wage for the second cross-cut was one real higher (totaling one peseta), because more care was required when sowing the crop. Oxen, cows, and mules were used to lead the plow, but mule drivers earned one real more than ox drivers, because the mules moved more quickly and also plowed the final furrow. A sower was paid an additional real above the others because he bore the responsibility of ensuring that the seed was distributed properly, and because his work was the most tiring. The sower, working with four teams, carried a bag of seed weighing half a fanega (fifty-eight pounds); with the added weight, he often had to go barefoot in the heavy mud. Besides the extra real in wages, the sower received preferential treatment in the division of rations: he was given a larger portion of oil than the other workers, so that in the morning his bread was fried in oil—the slight addition of oil calculated to compensate for the extra strength and endurance required for his task.

## Gañanías

If the winter plowing and sowing were carried out on lands near the town, the men walked to the fields at dawn and back at dusk; but if the land to be worked was more remote, the men remained at work and slept in rude straw bunk houses called *gañanías,* which held some thirty men. They worked for stretches of ten days, going home on the afternoon of the tenth day for a change of clothing and returning to work late the following morning. In some locations, if a campesino worked twenty consecutive days, he would return to the village and enjoy one full paid day of liberty; but if he were discharged even as late as the nineteenth day, he would lose his free day. Few campesinos can recall having a paid day of liberty in those times.[3]

During the winter plowing, the men in the gañanías rose well before dawn, prepared coffee, and then went to harness the animals for the day's work. There was a break for a cigarette at 8:00 A.M., a *gazpacho* at 9:00, another meal at 1:00 P.M., two other short rest periods in the afternoon (at 3:30 and 4:30), and at 6:00 the men returned to the gañanía or to their homes. In the gañanías, the workers continued their tasks after dusk by the light of an oil lamp, weaving baskets from palm leaves to hold the threshed grain. At night they slept in rows on straw mattresses. Ventilation in the gañanía was poor;

3. According to common practice, if a campesino worked five days he was entitled to a half-day free and a half-day's pay and bread. If he worked up to four days and bad weather halted his work, he received only his bread for the day but no pay, and he was sent home. The free half-day and the half-day's pay were valid from the fifth day to the nineteenth day. Campesinos were entitled to a full day of liberty only if they worked through the twentieth day. The marqués of Negrón was said to be one of those landowners who did provide a free day after twenty consecutive days of work.

toilet facilities were on the ground outside. The workers were called *gañanes,* and they quipped, "That's because we're always *engañados* [deceived]."

Although the pay and the working conditions were oppressive in the gañanías, these were not usually centers of unrest and syndicalism. Even if the men had wished to discuss politics, there was too much danger of being overheard or denounced here. The only entertainment was the telling of folktales in the evening.

*Manuel Legupín:* In the gañanías we made baskets for the wheat. There was only an oil lamp. There was very little light. We didn't discuss ideas. We were a bunch of fools. The oldest told stories, fables. We would ask who was telling stories that night and we would go there.

Some of the tales, however, such as the story concerning the innocent daughter of a *marquesa,* expressed the underlying ferment of the time.

There was a marquesa who had a daughter. They hired gañanes and always gave them old, bad food. One day the daughter said, "I'd like to see a gañán. Bring me a gañán!" It was as if gañanes were some kind of animal, since the worst food was always given to them.

And she said, "Put it in the stable," thinking it was an animal. They brought in a man, and the girl said, "But this is a man, a human being like you and me. From now on they must eat the same food that we eat."

Versions of the tale vary slightly, but the essential meaning never changes: the campesinos were treated like animals, given rancid oil and food to eat and worked like beasts.

## The harvest

During the harvest, which took place during the months of June and July, teams of reapers moved from estate to estate. Because the nights were pleasant and there was no risk of rain, they slept in the fields rather than in gañanías, making their beds at the point where the work was halted at nightfall.

Reaping wheat was the most arduous agricultural task.

*Pepe Pareja:* The reapers would work a season of forty days. One cannot learn to reap in one day or even in one season. It takes three seasons to learn, working and sweating, working so hard you'd have to be taken home in a wheelbarrow. It takes three seasons—the hands covered, the body bent. Not everyone can do it or has the desire to learn to do it. I was the eldest and taught my brothers to reap.

Reaping was done by contract as piece work, an arrangement called *a destajo.* A price was set by the owner corresponding to the number of fanegas, and then a team of workers reaped the wheat as fast as they were able.[4] Working a destajo, a reaper could harvest a wheat field a fanega in size (1.6 acres) in two and one-half to three days, depending on the yield (from ten to fifteen fanegas of wheat for each fanega of land). The faster the work was accomplished, the sooner the reaper earned his pay and could go on to the next job.

*Juan Pinto:* We would start working before the sun came up and work until the sun set. Back then there was nothing but misery. One did not earn money. One was paid for what one cut, for we were not even day laborers.

Since working a destajo enabled campesinos to earn larger sums of money in a shorter time, many workers welcomed the opportunity. The organized workers, however, were bitterly opposed to the system. It meant not only maintaining an exhausting pace but also employing fewer men. Under the system of a destajo the men were set against each other. Only the strongest and fastest workers would be chosen by the *capataz* (foreman) to work in a team. The fewer men employed, the more each working reaper stood to gain.

The question of prohibiting work a destajo was often the central issue of agricultural strikes, but it was a cause that the workers never won.

*Pepe Pareja:* The owners set a fee and then remained tranquil. Out of greed for money, they ignored the moral right to rest that belonged to the workers. A worker could earn more a destajo in less time, but if the harvest normally took three days, what would he do on the third day? He was unemployed. It would be better to work a normal day. Meanwhile, the owner benefited because he supplied bread and oil fewer times and to fewer workers. Instead of working seven hours, one worked fourteen—double. There were only seven hours for reaping, because it was the most tiring work of all. Only the strongest could work a destajo. The owners remained tranquil about everything: food, the weather, and everything else. They robbed us. Relations between owner and worker were very bad.

The reapers customarily worked for seven days and then returned home for a change of clothing. Their stay in the fields varied according to the length

4. The prices for working a destajo varied according to the amount of land to be reaped and also according to the particular crop to be harvested. Each grain had its own peculiarities in reaping that caused variations in the price. In the hierarchy of difficulty in the reaper's art, wheat was ranked between two types of barley, *cebada avena* and *cebada blanca* (yellow barley and white barley). Wheat was easier to cut than cebada blanca, because the latter was slippery and required more tension in the left hand to grasp; cebada avena, on the other hand, was easier to reap than wheat because it was green when harvested, and it was possible to grip the stalks firmly. Canary seed (*alpiste*) was the easiest of all to cut. A small amount of canary seed was mixed with the wheat when it was sown: since the canary seed remained green longer than the wheat, it was used by the reapers to tie wheat into bundles.

of the task at hand and the intensity of the sun. There were no paid free days for the reapers, and whatever time off they took was at their own expense.

Working a destajo, men were often pushed beyond their endurance, while at the same time their diet remained short of the number of calories required for heavy labor. As a result, there was a common ailment among the workers which was called *el tercio*—the name given for exhaustion from hard labor and lack of nourishment. The worker would feel dizzy, and his legs would tremble. He could not go on and had to sit down.

*Juan Pinto:* When someone got el tercio, he would stop and grab some bread. In those days there was lots of tercio because there was so little to eat. It was not simply fatigue—the person was undone. He couldn't work.

When it came to nourishment, the impoverished worker had to reckon with his family's needs as well as his own. Juan Pinto said, "You went off in the morning with only a piece of bread, because you had to leave food for your family."

During the harvest the local workers had to face other threats to their livelihood. Every year starving Portuguese who would work for lower wages were brought in; competing teams of Andalusian reapers also came up from the provinces of Málaga and Granada, working their way northward as the crop ripened. The owners preferred outside reapers: they were cheaper, they thought less about free days, and they were too far from home to be distracted by family matters. The local campesinos, on the other hand, were concerned with maintaining at least their customary rate of pay in harvest time. Cheap labor undercut their wages at the only time of year when they were certain of earnings higher than normal. As Pepe Pareja said, "We wanted them to work at the same rate that we did. There was enough work for all."

## Rations

Rations for the working gangs were supplied by the landowners as part of their wages. Each day a crew of ten men received ten kilos of bread and one liter of oil; every ten days they were allotted one *medio* (two and one-half kilos) of chickpeas as well as vinegar and salt. The meal was almost always a gazpacho.

*Pepe Pilar:* In the winter there were two meals. There was a hot gazpacho in the morning. The bread was first cooked in water, that was then tossed out. The bread was then moistened with oil and put in a wooden bowl. At mid-day there was a fresh [cold] gazpacho. At night each one went to his own home. If one was at a gañanía, there would be a stew of chickpeas at night.

In the summer there were four meals: a hot gazpacho at 9:00, a fresh gazpacho at mid-day, another fresh gazpacho at 4:00 of softened bread, oil, onions, and cucumbers, and a hot gazpacho at night.

The food was shared by the workers from a single large wooden bowl Twenty or thirty men ate from the same bowl, and each worker had a spoon to dip into the oil-soaked bread. The men would stand around the bowl of gazpacho, each taking his turn.

The quality of the rations was often dubious:

*Anónimo:* The bread was made by the latifundistas. The grain was almost whole. They left almost all the bran in the flour, and it was poorly mixed and many times badly baked. Worst of all, they cheated on the weight of the bread, so great was the miserable avarice of these large property owners.

In measuring the oil, they placed a false wooden bottom inside the container in order to make it hold less oil. Concerning this we recall some verses composed about a landowner that go,

| | |
|---|---|
| Conocemos a un señor | We know a gentleman |
| Que viste de negro liso; | Who dresses in black; |
| A las panillas les pone | He puts in his oil measures |
| Primero y segundo piso. | A first and second floor. |

The oil was bad. We can say it was actually the residue of oil. In winter it so hardened in the containers that it had to be heated in order to be utilized.

Some workers in Casas Viejas maintained that Don Antonio and his wife, Luisa Morales, kept two vats of oil in their storehouse—one for their family and one for the campesinos—and the workers received rancid oil and moldy rations.

*Pepe Pareja:* We were reaping wheat in Los Barrios [where Don Antonio rented land], and then we came to the [nearby] estate of Palmita. They brought food down for us to eat: oil, vinegar, and salt. We paid for the bread ourselves, but according to custom, the rest was paid for by the house. When we arrived we asked for oil. We had a jug of vinegar. Someone brought down a jug of oil. When it came we made gazpacho. We put in the tomatoes, vinegar, and garlic, and then we added the oil. But after we put in the oil, we couldn't eat it. The next day we said to the foreman, "Tell Luisa Morales, the wife of Don Antonio, that the oil is bad, and if she has no other, give us the money and we will buy oil from the aunt of María Flores" [a storekeeper].

When Luisa Morales was told this, she said, "We all eat this oil. The reapers must be saints made of another type of wood." However, she gave us the money, and we bought oil from the aunt of María Flores.

She was a victim of her money. We have a short stay here on earth. I've been poor all my life, but I'm not really poor because in my spirit I'm not poor.

If an individual campesino tried to protest against conditions, he ran the risk of swift retribution. But even before they were organized and had the protection of a sindicato, some Andalusian campesinos could be uncommonly independent. When Pepe Pareja worked alongside the workers of Jerez plowing the pasture lands of Ahijón, he had differences of opinion with overseer and boss concerning the rations and pay:

Polaina gave us meals—bread, chickpeas, and fat. I ate the first spoonful and said, "What am I chewing?" I spit it out. It was a cockroach. I didn't eat another mouthful. Later I said to the cook, "It would be better to increase the gazpacho with bread instead of cockroaches." So what did they do? The foreman dismissed me. Then I said to him, "I'm not leaving because I don't want to." And I kept on working, and at the end of the eight or ten days they paid me, and I continued working. They had no right to fire me. I was right. What right did he have? Because he was in charge?

The campesino, however, could not be permitted to have the last word.

The day before, I had been plowing with a team and oxen. Francisco Polaina Romero, one of the sons, said to me, "Rodríguez, leave the team there and take a hoe and go with those men to level out the banks of the arroyo so that the teams can cross over."

"Francisco," I said, "working with the hoe, I'm entitled to a higher wage than working with a team."

That afternoon he said to me, "Tomorrow you go with those weeding." This had happened before the previous other incident, and so when the cook complained, they said to themselves, "Let's get rid of this fellow." I had to go to weed for a lower wage.

Workers sought to be responsible for their own meals so that they could vary their diet and improve the quality of the food they ate. Yet although they were united in their dissatisfaction, they disagreed among themselves as to the best solution.Some feared that the owners would not fully compensate them in wages for the actual cost of the food and they would be worse off. Opinion was divided among the landowners as well as to the advantages of providing rations: it was clearly a monetary saving to do so if the alternative was to pay a cash compensation. The landowners had flour and chickpeas on hand from their own fields and lard from their droves of pigs. In this way nothing that they raised was wasted, and often the only commodities they had to purchase were oil and salt. It had always been the custom to supply rations; they did not know what to expect if the custom changed.

Years later, long after this system had been discontinued nearer the cities, the practice of supplying rations survived on the estates near Casas Viejas.

When it was finally abandoned, the landowners found to their pleasure that they had rid themselves of a troublesome obligation.

## Fijos

While the eventuales lived in town, walking to the fields to work and then returning home in the evening, each estate also had a small number of *fijos*, fixed permanent workers who customarily lived on the estates the year around. Fijos constituted only a small percentage of the total work force, but they were the backbone of the estates.

The hierarchy on the estates usually ran as follows: the señorito, the owner of the estate who lived in the city and came only for occasional visits or not at all; the *administrador* in charge of all the estates; the *aperador* (resident manager) of the individual cortijo; the *manijeros* (foremen), who headed groups of men assigned to particular tasks; the *pagador* (paymaster), who kept the books and paid the men their wages. Below these were the workers, the most important of whom was the *boyero mayor* (head ox drover), under whom were the plowmen and cattle guards. In addition, there was a *conocedor* (expert) to care for each type of animal: a *ganadero* (herdsman) for the cattle, a *yegüero* for the breeding mares, a *porquero* (swineherd), a *pastor* (shepherd), a *cabrero* (goatherd). The cortijo would have a *casero* (cook), who prepared the meals, made the bread, and fed the chickens, as well as an assistant to help the cook. In the sowing and reaping seasons there was also a *gazpachero*, a man or boy who carried supplies to the men living in the gañanías and to the reapers in the fields. The wages and benefits each received corresponded to their station and importance on the cortijo, with the administrator earning a daily wage three to four times higher than that of the workers. He too was provided food if he chose to eat with the men in the morning and at mid-day.

The boyero mayor had the responsibility of feeding and caring for the oxen the year around, and of organizing the work during the planting season when the labor force was increased. Since the campo was largely unfenced, fields of wheat, stubble, and pasture often were separated only by narrow paths. When the wheat was growing, the head drover and the other cattle guards had to keep the oxen and cattle from straying and ruining the crop. In the sowing season the head ox drover might have eight or more men to help him; afterward, half that many would remain to finish the work, and then he would carry out his responsibilities alone until the following spring.

Herdsmen and their families often lived isolated lives distant even from the cortijo. Their huts were located in rough, broken land used for forage.

There was no chance for education and few opportunities for socializing. The herdsman kept the animals in his care well watered and protected from sun and wind. He guarded them against wild dogs. The goatherd was expected to milk the herd and to turn the milk into cheese for sale. A skillful herdsman could increase his herd by careful attention to the breeding animals and to orphaned or rejected offspring. If he was fortunate, he could pasture a small number of his own animals, whose offspring could be sold for cash.

The fijo was employed on the basis of a verbal agreement from one year to the next which was marked by the anniversary of San Miguel. He worked for a lower wage than did day workers, but on the other hand, his employment was guaranteed. Since workers were always balanced on the sharp edge of hunger, this was an important consideration. To compensate for his meager wage, the fijo also received monthly rations of flour, chickpeas, oil, salt, and vinegar. Customarily he was permitted to raise a few turkeys and chickens, and perhaps a pig or a goat—all important incentives for men with large families and no other means to provide meat or prepare lard. Usually each cortijo had a large garden nearby, fenced in by prickly cactus to protect the vegetables from the cattle. In the summer months the fijos had cucumbers, green peppers, and tomatoes. On occasion there was a bonus. Managers and foremen received yearly gratuities, and if the patrón was generous, even the workers and herders and their families might receive a gift when a visit was made to the estate—two kilos or so of chickpeas, some lard, and possibly one duro (worth five pesetas).

At the same time, besides working for a lower wage than that of day laborers, the fijo had no days off and had to ask for permission to go into town. Because he lived on the cortijo, he was at the beck and call of his patrón or foreman. Every aspect of his life—including his attendance at mass, if his patrón was a worshiper or if the cortijo was visited by a priest—was under scrutiny, and his livelihood depended on his good conduct.

## Fijos and eventuales

Circumstances of employment created a gulf between eventuales and fijos. The security and dependency enjoyed by the fijos contrasted with the uncertainties of employment suffered by the eventuales, whose work was always short-lived and uncertain, subject to the whims of the weather, the crop, and the landowner. Eventuales lacked security and the loyalty that generally accompanied it. The tension was increased because the fijos enjoyed only a relative security. While the ties between fijo and landowner were akin to those of medieval serf and master, the fijo was contracted for the year only. At the end of that period he could leave or be discharged. But during the year's employment, the fijo had constructed a hut, raised some chickens and turkeys, and perhaps sold eggs to earn extra cash. His security lay in the stability of life on the estate and in the good health and goodwill of the patrón and his administrators. Worker unrest loomed as a threat to the fijo, because it demanded that he take actions that would compromise his ties to the patrón. Fijos therefore could not be counted on to jeopardize their positions voluntarily; on the contrary, they often identified with the landowners and the cortijo. If conditions on the estate were relatively relaxed and the food decent, many fijos saw little to complain about.

Anónimo, despite his contemptuous portrait of the marqués of Negrón, noted the fijo's loyalty to his patrón:

> In later years, in the house of the marqués of Negrón the bread was good and complete. Furthermore, the campesinos were permitted more animals for themselves, even pigs, which formerly had not been allowed anywhere. And in this way the fijo campesinos lived well, serving and praising their masters unconditionally, earning very stingy salaries, buried in frightening misery, their consciences brutalized, with a mentality almost primitive—savage and uncultured. Only at times were they able to achieve even rudimentary levels of education. With respect to these conditions, we remember especially the campesinos of the marqués of Negrón for being the most fanatic and servile. Some of these would have preferred that a misfortune occur to their child rather than to an animal of the [patrón's] herd. They could not express themselves except in the most savage manner. Some of them boasted that if anyone tried to get them to join in a strike, they would empty their shotguns at him.

## José Sánchez Rosa

José Sánchez Rosa, the anarchist pamphleteer in Seville, expressed the cross-currents of loyalties among the workers in the imaginary dialogues that he wrote. In his *En el campo*,[5] a worker crossing the field of an estate in order to ask for work is stopped by a watchman, who tells him that he is trespassing and that he must enter by the road.

> *Watchman:* Well, the sign says very clearly, "Passing is prohibited."
> *Worker:* How many prohibitions have we poor in this life! We're even prohibited from eating. For what do we eat even when we are working? Bread of poor quality cooked in water and very little oil, or bread uncooked and soaked in a broth of water and vinegar. We are prohibited from clothing ourselves, for what do we dress ourselves with?—Rags! We're prohibited all the pleasures of life! And this we call life!

5. A pamphlet published in Seville in 1911. As a youth José Sánchez Rosa had participated in the march on Jerez in 1892. He learned to read and write while in prison. Sánchez Rosa corresponded with scores of sindicatos and promulgated the anarchist cause in person, debating with other speakers and urging workers to educate themselves and their children (see *Tierra y Libertad,* August 21, 1912).

When the worker calls the watchman a wage slave, the watchman reacts indignantly:

*Watchman:* What do you mean by slave, my friend? Be careful with what you say. I am no slave nor does my *amo* [boss or master] consider me one! If you could see how he speaks to me when he calls to give me some order or when we happen to meet one another. If it pleases him, well, he speaks to me in a manner very——very——well, how can I explain it to you. You will see, it's as if he were my father. "Look, José," he tells me, "I esteem you highly because you are one of the best servants I have, and as long as you continue faithful and obedient to my commands you will never want for bread in my house." I tell you, he speaks to me in a manner that I wish you could see and hear.
*Worker:* It's as if I were seeing and hearing him. I know the tone he uses to speak to you. And he will also give you some cigarettes.
*Watchman:* Yes, he gives them to me and it pleases me very much because the cigarettes the señorito smokes are very good.
*Worker:* Of course they are good. They had better be good! Whatever they keep for themselves is good indeed, the very best, since the bad, the worst of everything that remains, is for us.
*Watchman:* Of course. Should they give us the best and keep the worst of everything for themselves? Now you are dumb!
*Worker:* Me dumb? Let's just say that the amos don't deserve what's bad—they don't even deserve the worst. What do they do in the world to deserve anything? They exploit people, make others work for them, suck their blood, destroy them!
*Watchman:* Don't speak this way of the amos, at least not about mine, because they are among the best! They never cease doing charitable works. A poor person never arrives at their door without receiving some alms.
*Worker:* With this are the disinherited satisfied—with alms! That is what they give us as a salary, when in freezing cold and soaked to our bones in water we plow the land! We plant in it the seeds that germinate, and each grain reproduces 100 or more than 100 percent! That is what they give us—alms—for taking care of these fields and weeding them! That is what they give us when, suffocating under the burning rays of the summer sun, we cut the golden spikes of grain ready for reaping! That is what they give us—alms—for doing whatever tasks are necessary until we carry the clean grain to the granaries of those who are called los amos. Los amos! They don't break the new land, or sow it, weed it, reap it, or cart the wheat to the threshing floor, thresh it, winnow it, and sift it. How much redounds to the bosses from our hard labor in battle against all the elements—the land, the cold, the water, and the heat. When the harvest is finished they have it all, and we—look at me!

The arguments of the worker are new to the watchman, and the worker continues:

*Worker:* . . . Those who are called amos are in possession of the riches that belong to all men. They usurp, retain, and exploit treasures that are not theirs. Still worse, they rob the rest of mankind of their natural and social rights. And I say that lands and other treasures do not belong to them because the land should not be the exclusive property of anyone. It was not made by anyone. It is a natural element and ought to be for the common benefit of all the children of nature, just as we have the benefit of the air when we breathe in the free countryside and the heat of the sun. And when someone appropriates to himself what belongs to everyone—although secular laws and customs favor him—he will be condemned by natural law, each time louder and louder.

The two men separate, the watchman unconvinced, only to meet again in two years. Experience, not words, has reshaped the watchman's view of the world, and he now joins the worker. In the years that have passed, his daughter has been dishonored by the señorito and then abandoned and forced to become a prostitute; his son was taken into the army and sent to Morocco where he has been killed; and his wife has died of grief. In the pamphlet, worker and watchman are united. But like the faithful and gullible watchman portrayed by Sánchez Rosa, the campesino fijo had to be convinced by experience that his best interests were with his fellow workers.

## Doves (Palomos)

There were few posts for fixed workers, but fijos sometimes voluntarily cut their ties to the cortijo. Not everyone wanted to live under the eye of the foreman and landowner. There were greater risks in town, and more hunger, but there were advantages as well. There was more freedom of choice, greater ambience; an enterprising man could sow a crop; there were more opportunities for one's children to find work and to meet other young people and to marry.

There was also a compelling economic reason to leave the cortijo. The worker viewed the harvest time as his prime opportunity to accumulate cash by working a destajo. It was the period of greatest temptation for the fijo to leave the security of the cortijo in search of temporary higher-paying work.

The landowner, however, also saw the harvest as the most critical period of the year. He needed experienced hands to reap and thresh the wheat and bring it swiftly and safely to his storehouses. From his point of view, higher wages were undesirable, because they reduced his net cash profit. The fijos ensured the presence of a sufficient work force to bring in the crops at the lowest cost. But the landowner saw that something was needed to keep the fijo on the land through the harvest. Since he would not raise wages, an alternative solution was to share a token amount of untilled land with the worker. Because it was expected that the campesino would work with more vigor when sharecropping, the results would benefit the landowner as well as the worker.

Around the years 1909–12, some landowners provided this added inducement to their fijos: those workers who did not take any days off could harvest for themselves one-half the yield of a fanega of land. In a good year a fanega could yield ten to fifteen fanegas of wheat (sixteen to twenty-four bushels). The offer was a temptation for a worker whose family was close to hunger. However, it created sharp conflicts among the campesinos, for if there was protest and a strike, the campesino fijo could not participate, or else he would lose the wheat he had sown and cared for. These fijos were also obligated to participate in the rituals and activities of a Catholic brotherhood. The campesinos who accepted these conditions were called palomos ("doves"), referring to the phoenix chosen by an insurance company as a symbol of security and painted on all its vans. In the eyes of the other campesinos, they had enslaved themselves and sold their birthright for half the yield of a fanega of land.

*Manuel Legupín:* The marqués of Negrón had [the estate of] Las Yeguadas, and he had twenty palomos on the land. The number of day workers varied. Sometimes there were 100. At harvest time they would bring in men from Granada, and they brought in many Portuguese. The jornaleros could strike, but the palomos could not. If the jornaleros were in a bar drinking and a palomo came in, they would leave. Once three of us, two from Casas Viejas and a third from Medina, were taking cart-loads to be threshed, and a palomo joined us as a partner—there were two on each cart. And the man from Medina said, "Stick it up your ass. I won't work with any palomo." And he left to cut cane in the Laguna de la Janda.

Palomos were ostracized by the workers in town and were publicly scorned in the songs sung at Carnaval.

*Manuel Legupín:* Around 1910, 1911, 1912, there was a *murga* [singing group] in the Carnaval in Medina. The name of the *maestro* was el Loco, and they had a song about the palomos:

| | |
|---|---|
| Un obrero que lloraba | A worker cried |
| Con sentimiento y con pena | With feeling and pain |
| Porque a su padre lo echaban | Because they put his father |
| A trabajar con cadena. | To work with chains. |
| Su madre le aconsejaba: | His mother counselled him: |
| "Ve ganando 3 reales | "Go and earn 3 reales |
| Y media fanega de tierra." | And a half of fanega of land." |

They carried placards with palomos painted on them.[6]

6. Another Carnaval song described how the dispute carried over among the women who met at sewing:

| | |
|---|---|
| Estando en el Zaguán | One day some five or six girls |
| Estaban cosiendo un día | Were sewing in the front room, |

The system of using palomos soon broke down. Even the reward of half the wheat from a fanega of land could not always diminish the lure of piecework in the wheat fields at harvest time. Nor could it outweigh the social pressure exerted against the palomos and their families, and the loyalty demanded of the men by their fellow workers.

| | |
|---|---|
| El obrero que sigue a un tirano | A worker who follows a tyrant |
| Un verdugo se suele volver, | Becomes a hangman himself |
| Que no mira pariente ni hermano | Who does not recognize his brothers |
| Ni su padre que le ha dado el ser. | Nor his father who gave him life. |

Deep divisions continued among the workers concerning their best interests and courses of action. Disagreement between fijos and eventuales would sharpen in the strikes still to come. But all shared the enduring problems of lack of work, hunger, and exploitation. In the campo each worker had his own spoon, but he ate from a single bowl with his fellow workers.

Campesino observations of cooperative efforts in nature—the anthill and the beehive—reinforced the anarchist axiom: survival depended on their working together.

*Pepe Pareja:* For the land to produce, what is needed is collectivization—that is, a joint effort of all the people. Each one should employ his own mental and manual faculties. He who is weak by nature can be employed in something simpler, and he who is stronger will be placed where his strength is needed. They will treat each other as brothers. Selfishness will not exist. Everything will be done with faith and with a will to produce what is needed for nutrition.

---

| | |
|---|---|
| Unas cinco o seis muchachas, | |
| Y en disputa se ponían. | And they got into an argument. |
| Se dice una a la otra, | And one said to the other, |
| "Sola llevo la razón | "I am the only one who is right here, |
| Que mi novio está parado, | For my boyfriend doesn't have a job, |
| Porque el tuyo es un bribón." | Because yours is a villain." |
| Y terció la otra, | And the other one answered, |
| "Sin ser esclavo | "He isn't a slave |
| Siempre se ha trabajado | But has always worked aparcería |
| Aparcería con el patrono." | With the patrón." |
| Nunca se ha recuperado | She never recovered |
| De aquella riña. | From that quarrel. |
| Entre compañeras, | Between us, compañeras, |
| Les diré el resultado. | I'll tell you the outcome. |
| De puntapiés que le dieron | They kicked her so bad |
| Llevaba ella | They left her |
| Su vientre hinchado. | With her belly swollen. |

# Four
# The Church in Casas Viejas

## The campesino and the church

By the turn of the century, Casas Viejas had grown into a small town. It was a town of predominantly poor men, the hillside dominated by chozas. By now, however, there were a few two-story houses with tile roofs. There was a central plaza by the church, and Calle San Juan, the short main street, was set with paving stones. The gentry of Casas Viejas and Medina Sidonia next had plans to construct a new church and do away with the old rural hermitage, whose walls were badly in need of repair.

The old hermitage had been founded by a cleric in about 1555. In 1680 the bishop of Cádiz instituted a rural chaplaincy to serve the people living in the area. During a visit to Medina, the bishop stipulated that "mass be said every holiday; and there should always be, except when impeded, a confessor maintained there from the Sabbath of Palm Sunday until the close of Holy Thursday and from the Holy Sabbath until Whitsunday, to administer the sacraments to the many people in the nearby cortijos."[1] The bishop ordered the Holy Gospel to be preached during Lent and the sacraments of penitence and the Eucharist to be administered. It was a modest chapel, and the appearance of the priest, even at the few times designated, was subject to the disposition of the weather and the condition of the muddy highways.

This chaplaincy continued until the second half of the nineteenth century, when the sale of the common lands brought in new landowners and workers, swelling the population. Until 1869 baptisms, marriages, and deaths in Casas Viejas had been entered in the church records in Medina Sidonia, but in November 1869 the growing village began to keep its own accounts. In 1878

1. Francisco Martínez y Delgado, *Historia de la ciudad de Medina Sidonia*, pp. 202–3.

the first resident priest, under orders to Medina Sidonia, came to Casas Viejas. Religious life thereafter was a continuing and stable presence in the village.

It is impossible to describe with absolute certainty the beliefs of those who first settled at the crossroads and built the cluster of huts called Casas Viejas. On the surface, social pressure to conform to Catholicism tended to make belief and practice appear uniform. Throughout Andalusia, however, the relationship of the campesinos to official Catholic doctrine was always somewhat ambiguous. While the sons of the middle and upper classes could afford to attend school and learn the received wisdom, the poor remained illiterate and relatively ignorant of doctrine. They knew little of the Old Testament, and they normally had access to the Gospel only through the priest.[2] Most priests, however, provided the sacraments and little more. The mass was in Latin, a language many priests could not read well themselves, and only certain scriptural passages were read, usually dealing with rites that were repeated year after year. Many campesinos clung to beliefs older than the church itself. Their social ideas were derived largely from their oral tradition and experience.

There are a number of distinct strands to consider concerning this religious belief system: folk tradition, church rituals; and skepticism—the denial of supernatural power and canon law.

## The shrines

In the nearby towns of Alcalá, Vejer, Medina, and Conil, towns centuries older than Casas Viejas, there were shrines where in earlier times the Virgin had been seen by at least one of her faithful. Each shrine had its attendant brotherhood of believers, who cared for the shrine, celebrated a yearly festival, and did charitable works in the name of the Virgin. Townsmen took pride in their local Virgin and recounted the miracles performed by her. In some shrines paintings were hung as testimonies to the host of wonders. Miraculous cure after grave illness was the dominant theme of the paintings, but a range of other miracles was depicted, including dramatic escapes from bandits or soldiers, salvation from drowning, and recovery from accidents and from encounters with brave bulls.[3]

The paintings were often inscribed with simple details of the miracle wrought:

2. Beginning in the early nineteenth century, there were Protestant translations of the Gospel circulating in Spain; however, few such texts were available. In any event, Bible study and education were not encouraged; see George Borrow, *The Bible in Spain*.

3. See Jerome Mintz, "Comfortable Old Shrines, Divisive New Visions." For examples of shrines in northern Spain, see William A. Christian, Jr., *Person and God in a Spanish Valley*.

José García Berdolico, found to be seriously mentally ill, was commended by his wife to Our Lady of the Saints and was cured in the year 1860.

Yves Gautier, gravely ill, was commended to Our Lady of the Saints by his wife and his mother and became well. 1878.

Pilgrimages brought out believers who came to honor the Virgin and to pray for help with present or anticipated needs. They were eager to show their devotion by following in the train of worshipers, or by helping to carry the figure of the Virgin on its heavy platform the painful kilometers from the shrine into the town. The pilgrimage was an important social occasion as well as a religious rite. It attracted numerous people indifferent to faith, drawn by a sense of loyalty to their town; others found appeal simply in the excitement, the festive air, and the display of finery.

Although Casas Viejas had no shrine, the local population was not immune to the lure of miracles and sympathetic magic. When there was drought and divine intervention seemed to be needed, Don Diego, the priest, would have the statue of La Dolorosa, Our Lady of Sorrows, leading a procession of villagers and children from the church down to the Barbate River. The followers would immerse themselves, toss water into the air to simulate a downpour, and pray for rain.

*José Monroy:* We went to the river with the statue of the saint to ask for water, and I immersed myself in the water too. And sometimes it rained on the way back to town, and sometimes it rained a few days later.

Even skeptics agreed on the positive results of these autumnal pilgrimages; but they also observed that the priest waited until clouds appeared from the direction of the sea before leading the appeal for divine assistance. In addition, the skeptics had a considerable body of lore to counter the tales of miracles for each saint and each shrine that dotted the countryside.

*José Suárez:* Once a worker had a fruit tree that did not give fruit, and so he cut it down, and it was carved into a saint. The worker went to church, saw it there, and said,

| | |
|---|---|
| En mi huerto te criaste. | I raised you in my garden. |
| De tu fruto no comí. | You never gave me any fruit. |
| Los milagros que tú hagas | The miracles that you make |
| Que me los claven aquí. | They can nail to my forehead. |

Often belief eroded under the cumulative effects of experience and observation; sometimes there was a sharp break due to sudden disillusionment.

Life in the campo, with its uncertainties and hardships, could turn the most devout feelings into stinging despair:

*José Suárez:* I never went to church. Oh, I went in to see what was done there, to see a mass, but I never went to pray. My mother believed. She wanted to hit me when I didn't pray. To me it was always foolishness. Then when my sister was twenty-two, she had peritonitis. My mother had three or four saints' images and pictures in the house. She put candles in front of them when my sister was sick. My sister was sick for six or eight days, and then she died. We had taken her to the doctor in the town, but he said he couldn't do anything. Then my mother broke all the saints' images in the house. "Useless," she said.

José Suárez, a thoughtful man of the countryside who would become the local socialist leader, developed a reverent view of the universe, but one that was outside the Catholic credo:

Man, the sun, the seas are mysteries. I believe in a God that is above all things—that made the world, the sun, whatever you wish. But this God who puts people in hell and who talks—that I don't believe in. There is something great I don't understand, something undefinable—a great thing we call God. I can't define it. But the one who sends people to hell and who walks behind us, that I can't believe.

## Jesus

To most believers and nonbelievers, Jesus remained in a separate station. Less interwoven with local shrines and folk belief than the saints and the Virgin, Jesus was at once more remote and, at the same time, more human. Although church ritual generally tended to make Jesus appear awesome and mysterious, during Holy Week, when the statue of Jesus was taken down from its position in the church and paraded through the crowded streets, everyone was touched by his vulnerability. In this return to a village community, Jesus was resurrected as a man once again. Held by townsmen, his body close enough to touch and his terrible wounds more visible, the crucified Jesus appeared as a stricken neighbor. He evoked not awe but pity. Isabel Vidal asked, "Why would anyone do such a terrible thing to this man?"

The anarchists cited the life of Christ and his teachings to point out the hypocrisies of the church.[4]

4. Anarchist writers and orators could express enthusiastic agreement with the ideals of early Christianity, but they saw these as having been quickly sacrificed. "Christianity makes all men equal before God. None of the modern demagogues has gone further than the early Christian fathers with regard to their radicalism. They are well known for their eloquent attacks against the most powerful on earth, against property, against privilege, against the law itself. Little

*José Monroy:* The anarchist orators, and not the priest, explained what happened to Christ. The orators would not tell the story of Christ, but they would make references to it. What I know of Christianity I know from them, not from the priests.

*Pepe Pareja:* The orators used the words of Jesus Christ. Who killed Jesus? The capitalists. How many Jesus Christs have been killed since then? Those who wanted to do good for humanity.

Jesus was seen as one of the exploited—martyred by the priests, the army, and the government lackeys whose modern counterparts now paraded under his banner. Asked Manuel Llamas, "What was he but one more victim?"

## The church

In a small town the shadow of the church touched every house. Catholic ritual and canon were interwoven into daily life: the day's greeting, *Dios te guarde* ("God protect you"); the calendar; the masses; and myriad social customs paying homage to God, the church, and the priest. The church controlled education. It established rules of conscience and conduct. It ordered the rituals and kept the records of birth, marriage, and death. Attendance at mass and attitudes toward the church were signs of class allegiance and measures of social conformity.

In the past the Inquisition had dealt severely with heresy, and the wooden benches where the inquisitors had sat in solemn judgment still remained in place in the church in Medina Sidonia. Deviance from the established norms continued to attract public attention, fear, and potential harassment. Conformity held sweeter rewards. The local clergy wielded power and patronage: a recommendation from the priest could bring the chance for employment or the opportunity for one's son to go to school; in a moment of difficulty, the priest's word could mean clearance with the civil guard or with the district court judge. For the fijos, church attendance was often a condition for a place on the cortijo or a position of responsibility.

In a small town where each step was noted, a thoughtful man had to balance fear and social conscience. An articulate and intelligent man like Juan Vidal, the shoemaker, had "ideas" but for the most part kept his opinions to himself. The son of a civil guard, Juan exercised caution concerning authority. Rather than affront the official powers, he had his children baptized in the church. "Everything within the law," he would say to his family. It was better to guard his fame as a musician than to risk notoriety as a rebel

by little that great spirit is lost; humble men rise and become more powerful than other men; those who were forsaken become masters" (*Tierra y Libertad,* January 3, 1907).

or social agitator. Vidal had mastered the guitar, the *bandurria*, and the concertina; and on festival days he would play in the plaza in front of the church, where celebrants would dance *jotas, sevillanas,* and *manchegas*. But while he did not join any association or speak openly, his accommodation to authority did not lead him to attend mass himself. Like many in Andalusia, although he was lively in the plaza, in his heart and in his house, his views were bitter. Isabel Vidal, Juan's daughter, recalled the saying,

| | |
|---|---|
| Todo lo que hay | Everything |
| En este mundo es mentira. | In this world is a lie. |
| No hay más verdad que la muerte. | The only truth is death. |
| No hay quien me lo contradiga. | No one can convince me otherwise. |

Self-protection and self-interest usually required public conformity:

*Isabel Vidal:* On the street you never say the truth. On the street you tell people what they want to hear. I would wear a medallion so that a dead mosquito wouldn't bite me. That's how much good I believe it would do.

## The mass and the sacraments

Worship at the town church attracted a somewhat different congregation from those drawn to the shrine. There was of course some overlap; however, religious observance in town was sharply circumscribed. The masses said on Saturday night and Sunday morning were attended by men and women of the upper and middle classes (landowners, town officials, and many middle-class shop owners), by those dependent on them (foremen from nearby cortijos and storeclerks), and by the defenders of the social order (the civil guard and the carabineros).

Few campesinos ever attended mass.[5] The church was hospitable to the middle and upper classes; campesinos felt excluded. It was their custom to congregate in the café, not in the church.

The church was a social magnet that attracted women and the young. The daily lives of women were more sharply circumscribed than those of the men, and mass was the one certain time other than shopping that women had reason to leave the house and patio. Since literacy was rare, the church served as a major source of drama, ritual, and entertainment. It also provided the opportunity for a stroll in the promenade in front of the church and the chance to hear an interesting tale or share a bit of information. As a social

5. P. Francisco Peiró describes the declining church attendance throughout Spain and notes that in some villages the priest said mass alone (*El problema religioso-social de España*, p. 13; see Brenan, p. 53).

occasion which required fine clothing, it particularly drew women of the middle and upper classes. A middle-class landowner recalls the conflict in his home:

*Manuel:* My grandmother used to go to the church, but not my grandfather. She used to say, "I go to church because if I don't my friends will wonder why not."

Now one day he came home drunk, and she scowled at him; and he responded, "I'm coming from the café so that *my* friends can't say that I don't go."

The church attracted women among the campesino families as well. Many members of the sindicato had been raised by their mothers in an atmosphere of faith that gradually eroded as they grew to manhood.

*José Monroy:* At that time there was belief instead of education. When I was small, I had faith in the saints. My mother taught me those things. When I went to sleep, I had to say the "Our Father," and I couldn't go to sleep until I recited it. With this education, I learned to believe. I lost my faith when I gained a little knowledge and when I entered the organization and listened to the arguments. My father had some faith, but he did not tell me to pray. Faith belonged to the women.

Campesino women with children, however, were usually too occupied to attend mass regularly, even if they wished to. In addition, they thought themselves too poorly dressed to appear in public. Many kept a small image of the Virgin at home—some out of custom, others because of a profound faith in the Virgin's miraculous powers.

The confessional was rarely visited by campesino men or women. The priest sat alone waiting for penitents who did not appear. The rite of confession was unacceptable to people, even if they were believers, who practiced gossip and deception as art forms and who fought for every vestige of privacy in a crowded environment. Besides, they were suspicious of the clergy and demanded to be treated equally with any other man or woman.

The rites of marriage and baptism were scarcely more compelling to the campesino than were mass and confession. The campesino often avoided the formal rites of marriage while more pressing social and personal obligations were met. To new couples, the most essential matter was to establish a household—to construct a choza and to buy linen and furniture. Parish records show that almost one-third of the brides were pregnant or had had children months and in many cases years before they married. Apparently the concerns of church ritual were often ignored until the couple could afford the fee or until they came in contact with the priest. In many instances this was accomplished when the priest took the initiative to visit the houses in the countryside and completed the formal church requirements on the spot.

There was usually greater concern about baptizing one's children, and with good reason. Infant mortality was high. Of 248 deaths in the village between 1910 and 1916, 117 were infants under the age of three, or over 47 percent of all deaths; of these, 22 percent died during the first six months of life.

It was not fear of purgatory that prompted most campesinos to baptize their children. The concept of a purgatory where infants could be sent was irreconcilable with commonly held notions of humanity: As José Suárez put it, "no father is going to make a devil and an inferno to burn his own children. No good father does that—when they're bad, to burn them? No good father does that."

Nor was baptism thought to be a guard against illness. Rather, it was protection against the sanctions of the church concerning burial. The cemetery, like the rest of the village, was divided by class and custom: the rich could afford to be interred in a niche in the cemetery wall; the poor were buried in the ground.[6] Unbaptized children, however, were buried in unconsecrated ground in a plot set aside for them and for suicides. Respectability and appearance were important to the villagers. To be set apart from the other dead of the village beneath ground on which the public walked represented a cruel blow to the family, a source of shame and gossip. As a result, mothers with newborn babes rarely took them into the street before they were baptized, for fear that if the child died *moro* (unbaptized), it would be denied a proper burial.

In spite of the general acceptance of religious and social custom, however, some children remained unbaptized for months or even years. Those who lived in the campo were not subject to the same pressures as those in the village. Some families could not afford the fee; others were diffident about the matter. A few took this means to express their opposition to the church.

Some independent-minded townsmen, like Juan Vidal, would not enter the church for any reason whatsoever. In 1915, when Juan was fifty-two, on the occasion of the marriage of his daughter, he returned on foot from Medina Sidonia where he was working and said that he was too tired to attend the ceremony at the church. The priest, Don Diego Fuentes, was forced to race up to his house to receive Juan's permission for his daughter to wed and then

6. See David Gilmore's description of a cemetery in "Class, Cognition, and Space in a Spanish Town," pp. 444–46.

hurry down again to perform the marriage ceremony. Juan would use any excuse not to enter the church. Nor would he accept clerical supervision of the burial of his ten-year-old daughter. When the child died, Juan took the key to the cemetery and interred her himself in the middle of the night. He would not have a priest present to read a mass over her grave.

## Campesino and clergy

Both skeptics and believers made a distinction between clerical authority and religious faith. Even among believers there was widespread anticlerical sentiment, ranging from cynicism to contempt. The campesinos knew that the clergy were no better than other men, subject to the same passions, and often a good deal worse. Too many of the clergy were seen as wastrels, fornicators, and sluggards. The campesino compared the cleric to the cuckoo who deposits its eggs in the nests of other birds to be raised. Tales and jokes often made the priests the butt of their humor—the sexually indulgent corrupter finally brought to heel by the poor campesino, or the well-chosen victim of a bandit who robs from the rich to give to the poor. The priest was always the perfect foil:

*Pepe Pareja:* The atheist who was on the point of death called for a priest and a lawyer to be at his side. They were happy, since they assumed that he wanted to confess and make out his will. But when they came in, he said, "I don't want to confess or make out my will. I just want to die as Christ did, between two thieves."

Although the people might pray to saints, and perhaps even think kindly of a local priest, the collective image of the clergy was that of idle, self-indulgent men. Pelele said of his mother, "My mother was religious, but at least she had this virtue: she was against priests."

The antagonism between campesinos and the clergy did not mean that open hostility or ill will prevailed on a personal level. The relationship between the local priest and the townspeople of Casas Viejas was always friendly and cordial. From 1897 until 1918, Don Diego Fuentes served as the priest of Casas Viejas. A native of the nearby town of Conil, Don Diego was a country priest on intimate terms with the life of the campesino. He enjoyed hunting partridges and often went shooting with the village barber. Don Diego would bring a caged partridge, whose cries would attract other birds. He was a very sharp hunter. Not a rich man, Don Diego was dependent on marriage and baptismal fees to supplement the small salary he received from the state. He himself also plowed the land behind the chapel and sowed wheat there. An upright man concerned with church rituals, Don Diego was familiar with townspeople of every generation, and he was on good terms with everyone.[7]

Don Diego's plowing notwithstanding, the campesinos observed that the duties of the church were carried out by a large corps of priests, monks, and nuns who, like the grandees and the rich, for the most part did no labor.

*Juan Pinto:* I won't say whether the church is a lie or the truth. All I can say is that there must be a spirit in the world that has brought us to life here. But from this it doesn't follow that God keeps us alive. God did not make the church or anything. The church was made by a mason. The saints have been made by someone who knows how to make them. Now I believe that there has to be control in everything in order to restrain bad thoughts. But if priests went to work, instead of just being priests and not doing anything, it would be better. They should go to work just like everyone else. They're in the church for only two hours. The rest of the time they should have a job. But they don't have anything to do. If there were fewer priests it would also be better. Isn't that right?

Anarchist attitudes toward the clergy paralleled the views commonly held throughout Andalusia. A keen observer of the natural as well as the social world, the campesino "with ideas" perceived that nature had a remedy for socially detrimental behavior:

*Pepe Pareja:* In April, according to the season, many male drones leave the hive because they do not wish to work. And afterward they like to eat the honey of the worker bees. But the queen bee—their own mother—leaves with them and kills them because they do not wish to work. This is an interesting example. If one produces, one can eat. One has the right to consume, but only if one produces.

The number of clerics in Andalusia was far below that in the northern and central regions of Spain,[8] but in the south as well as elsewhere in Spain

7. Relations between priest and townspeople continued to be positive after Don Diego's tenure ended. From 1918 to 1925, Don Manuel Barberá Zaborido was priest of the town. As Isabel Vidal described it, "everything was all right in his eyes. The second day of Carnaval he would say, 'Let's make a chorus.' Cortabarra was the leader. The priest was not in the chorus, but he followed behind. He would write the verses, but the others did not have enough time to learn the words, so they always sang the same verse. The music they played was 'La Cucaracha.' They sang, and the priest followed. When they reached a bar, they would close the door, and he would take off his cassock and dance. He would say, 'Very well done. We've been practicing for a whole year.' Actually they practiced one day. He used to go into the mountains and baptize the children with water from the river. Once, here in the pueblo, he went to baptize a child. He put a cassock on one of his friends, Florito, and both went dressed as priests to the christening. There was no bad priest here."

8. On the unequal distribution of priests, see P. Francisco Peiró, pp. 28–31. For parts of Cádiz he notes that there were approximately 2,400 persons to each priest.

the role of cleric offered middle-class parents the promise of a respectable profession for their sons.[9] Some of the poor also thought of the church as an opportunity for their children to find a livelihood away from the fields. It held attractions similar to the post of civil guard or carabinero—security and shorter working hours.[10]

*José Monroy:* Some thought that the church was a business, like a tavern or some other commercial business. After all, thousands of priests made their living from it. They didn't produce anything but sicknesses to inject into humanity.

The gulf that usually existed between campesino and clergy was widened by the social struggle in the fields. Religious brotherhoods competed with the anarchist sindicatos for the workers' loyalty.[11] Landowners required the palomos in their employ to participate in the religious brotherhood of Los Hermanos Marianistas.

The partisan actions of some priests on behalf of landlords lent support to the image of interlocking capitalistic and clerical interests. During the strike of 1912, the priest of the town of Paterna de Rivera, a few kilometers north of Medina, was accused of recruiting strike breakers.

9. However, there were innumerable accounts of men who could not accommodate themselves to the obligations and limitations peculiar to the clergy. According to José Suárez, "when I was ten we had a very good teacher [in the campo]. He was the son of a rich man in Algeciras. He had studied to be a doctor but found he didn't have the stomach for operations, and so he became a priest. Then he got a servant girl in his father's house pregnant, and he left the priesthood and married her. He was my teacher. And he was a good teacher, because he had two professions. Unfortunately, he lost them both. His father threw him out of the house for marrying the servant girl, and so he went to his father-in-law's house. His father-in-law was cutting charcoal for us, and he asked my father if he could serve as a schoolteacher. So my father built him a little house, and he was with us for five or six years. He was a fine man, and his wife was a wonderful woman. She had a noble character, and what a worker! He was then about thirty-eight or forty years of age. No one thought anything the worse for what had happened. That was the way with the sons of the rich—they had to have a profession."

10. Angel Pestaña, the noted anarchist leader, described the attitude of his hard-working but impoverished father: "He was a practical man and thus wanted 'that his son not become a beast of work as he himself had been'—these were his words—and so he got the idea of educating me for the priesthood. It is true that my father was a deist, of course, as were all true Spaniards of his time; but he did not believe in priests, in the church, or in the rites imposed by the latter. He was a perfect 'Voltairian.' He did indeed want me to study, but only because, as he used to say, to be a priest was an occupation, just like being a miner, a mason, or a carpenter. But quite a bit more lucrative. 'I work twelve or thirteen hours to earn fourteen reales,' he used to say, 'and a priest, by just wielding his benediction and saying a few words that nobody understands, earns five duros. That's all there is to it' " (1:9).

11. Concerning Catholic labor activities and the attitudes of workers toward religious orders, see Ullman, pp. 37 ff.; and Carr, *Spain*, pp. 455 ff.

*Anónimo:* If this move against the unity of the workers by some of the clergy, brazenly collaborating with the capitalists, was not sacrilege, we do not believe there could be anything closer to it. . . . God does not pardon those who oppress the poor or those who defraud the workers of their wages.

Although the future was not yet within their grasp, the anarchists conceived of symbolic changes to demonstrate their beliefs and their hopes for better days to come.

*Pelele:* I remember the centro obrero [in Medina Sidonia] from when I was five or six [in 1901]. I walked like a cat behind my father. He was against religion. There was a group of men, and he told me when I saw this group not to say "adiós." It was then the custom to say "Dios te guarde" and for the other to respond, "Vaya con Dios." Instead, I was to say, "Buenos días" or "Buenas tardes." And when I said "Buenos días" to them, they embraced me and said, "This one is a revolutionary of tomorrow."

Even some clerics, in their mature years, found themselves part of an institution whose teachings they could neither endure nor change.

*Pelele:* My father was the herdsman for the cows of a priest [in Medina Sidonia]. He had eight to ten Swiss cows on a small estate called The Sanctuary. One night the priest asked my father, "Francisco, do you believe in God?"

My father answered him honestly: "I? No."

Then the cleric commented on what my father said. "Nothing exists except living beings, land, sun, moon, and vital stars. We [priests] are like riders checking a horse by the reins. We are nothing more than a brake on humanity."

After they had spoken, he said to my father, "About what I have said . . . ," and he made a motion with his hands to his lips. He had the position of a priest, it was his living; but afterward they talked every night.

## The Barefoot Carmelite monks

The divisions between the classes in the Andalusian countryside created two contradictory historical accounts concerning religion: the written histories of the well born and the oral traditions of the campesinos. A case in point involves the varying accounts of the Barefoot Carmelite monks who, during the eighteenth and nineteenth centuries, constructed a monastery in a remote area two leagues (eight to nine kilometers) from Casas Viejas. Today the monastery lies in ruins, and these ruins and the nearby caves, where hermit monks once spent long silent days, shelter herds of goats and a few cattle. From 1715 to 1835, however, this was a moderately busy center of Carmelite activity.

In 1715 the order of the Barefoot Carmelite monks received 610 fanegas of pasture and mountain land for which they had petitioned the township of Medina Sidonia in order to build a monastery in the rugged area known as The Wilderness of the Raven. An ample stone monastery was constructed, and the monks began work on a stone staircase leading down to a spring on the valley floor. A five-foot image of Elijah the Prophet was carved from the green and still soft wood of a muricated oak tree and set up in the chapel.

According to written accounts of the Carmelites, the monks elected to go to this new wilderness area in order to endure greater hardships than they had experienced in previous assignments. They lived as worker and hermit monks, maintaining perpetual silence and speaking only when it was a practical necessity. The broken countryside surrounding the monastery was used primarily for grazing. To help to support the monastery, the Carmelites had been given the right to tithe the campesinos and herders on the land 10 percent of the produce from their crops and the offspring of their herds.

In time the thirty-six nearby springs surrounding the monastery became famed for their power to cure a variety of ills, including scurvy, cachexia, jaundice, excessive gas, menstrual ills, tumors, and other intestinal disorders; and visitors from Gibraltar, Algeciras, Tarifa, and Medina Sidonia came to bathe in the healing waters. At the height of its limited luster, around 1770, the monastery was visited by the doctor of Medina Sidonia, Don Francisco Martínez Delgado, who described the spacious cloisters and the comfortable lodgings available. The doctor noted too how the monks, who offered the rites of confession and communion, "give spiritual nourishment to the many families that inhabit the mountains working and herding."[12]

While the monastery was considered to be a beneficent institution by the clergy and pious visitors, among the campesinos it acquired fame of a different sort. Rather than housing monks who had elected to work there, the monastery was said to hold only the worst monks—"all those to be punished"—sent there to do penance. Otherwise, why come to a region better suited for goats than a company of men? According to José Suárez, "the monks stayed in hermitages during the day and at night came out to rob chickens."

Instead of considering the monks providers of "spiritual nourishment," the campesinos saw them as oppressors forcing their will on a hostage population. José Suárez said: "The monks made it obligatory for everyone on the land to go to the monastery for mass. They sapped the campesinos'

12. See P. Silverio de Santa Teresa, O.C.D., *Historia del Carmen descalzo en España, Portugal, y América*, 111:715–17; and Martínez y Delgado, p. 226.

meager resources and took advantage of the labor of others. "If they wanted a cow or a goat, the people had to give it to them."

Their demands were said to have exceeded clerical law.

*Silvestre:* They would knock on any door. The person inside would ask, "Who is it?" And they would answer, "The Holy Inquisition." Since there was so much fear, the people would open up right away, and they would take from the house anything that they wanted—the woman, the girl, or wheat, or bread, or whatever they wanted.

The monks were said to have taken young maidens to the monastery where they were tortured until they surrendered themselves.

*José Suárez:* There was one couple—the man was thirty-eight, and his wife was a little younger. She was very beautiful. When the monks saw her at mass, they wanted her. They killed the man. They put him in a pit and tortured him to death with a pole set with several blades. They put the woman in an opening in the wall and tortured her. One of the ways they tortured her was by dropping water on her head. But she would not submit to them. They killed her too. As proof they killed the man, when the monastery was abandoned the people found his remains—his bones and his coveralls.

The end of the monastery came quickly in the eighteenth century, but again religious and campesino accounts differ. According to the written records of the Carmelites, the monastery was first badly shocked by the attack of a French patrol during the War of Independence. In mid-winter of 1810, French soldiers took the monastery's sentinels by surprise and shot them. Alarmed by the noise, the monks fled and hid in the brush, although one aged, deaf monk, unable to hear the tumult in time, was captured and abused by the soldiers until their commander rescued him. The French soon left the area, however, and the frightened monks were able to return to their monastery.[13]

Two final fatal blows came not from the French but from the Cortes, the Spanish parliament, which sought to make sweeping religious and land reforms. In 1820 the Cortes decreed that monasteries with fewer than twenty-eight ordained monks should be closed. With its meager resources and gifts, the Monastery of the Raven had difficulty maintaining the twenty to twenty-five monks who lived there. Although the law of 1820 was not carried out, it foreshadowed future events. When church lands were disentailed in 1835, the lands of the Wilderness of the Raven were returned to the township of Medina Sidonia and subsequently sold.

13. Silverio de Santa Teresa 12:765–66.

According to campesino tradition, however, the end of the monastery came not from the French or from the Cortes but from the lust and rivalry of the monks themselves.

*José Suárez:* There were two heads there. The two leaders fought over a woman. One lunged forward and thrust a blade through the other's chest, and at the same moment the second slashed the other so that his intestines fell out. He put his hands on his belly to hold them in, and then he put his bloody hands on the wall. I saw the fingerprints myself on the wall near the staircase.

Finally the irate shepherd families battled the monks. According to Juan Pinto,

The last monks were killed at Sierra Blanquilla. At that time they chased them from the convent and they killed them with sticks, bullets, or in any way that they could, with whatever weapons they had. They killed them because they hated them. They were ones who used to grab someone's daughter, or take a man and then kill him. They were in control. The people said, "This breed of men has to be eliminated."

All agree on the final fate of the monastery, if not on the actions of the monks who had lived there. When the order's lands were disentailed, the monastery was abandoned and slowly fell to ruin. After more than fifty years of labor, work on the long stone staircase extending down the hill was halted, and the cut stones were left lying on their sides. The wooden statue of Elijah, the oak now hard as steel, was carried by ox cart from the monastery to its new home in the chapel in Casas Viejas.

# Five

# The Centro Is Organized

## Local practices

When José Olmo arrived in Casas Viejas in 1914, he found that conditions made the campesinos receptive to his arguments and his oratory.

*Legupín:* In those days there was no work. The workers had nothing to eat but wild asparagus and chard. They were all idle in the plaza. Landowners wouldn't cultivate their estates. They raised cattle. José organized us. He brought in books and pamphlets. Syndicated, united, we were strong. To be isolated was worthless.

Grievances were based in part on the legacy of a broken social contract. The campesinos believed that they had fulfilled their part of the old feudal bargain: they had loyally provided the landowner with their strength and energy from sunrise until dark. The landowners, however, had failed to carry out their reciprocal responsibilities. The wages paid workers were too low for them to sustain themselves and their families. Most important, the land was not cultivated intensively and did not provide the campesinos with sufficient work days. The workers and their families were starving. Manuel Llamas recalled that José Olmo said, "Those people who exploit the worker have to provide work."

To help in his struggle to unite and educate the campesinos, José Olmo turned to the anarchist press. In these newspapers and pamphlets, José had an army of great teachers to provide the most advanced libertarian thought of the age. The newspapers *Tierra y Libertad* and *La Voz del Campesino* ("The voice of the peasant") contained syndicalist news: strikes in Spain and abroad, aspirations to the eight-hour day, and demands to end contract labor. There were also discussions of public health and science, including articles pointing out Darwin's fundamental error—that mankind had survived and mastered all other creatures not by battling each other for survival but, rather, through cooperation.[1] Great literary works were reprinted in *Tierra y Libertad* during this period: Ibsen's *Enemy of the People* was serialized from July 16, 1913, until February 25, 1914; Anselmo Lorenzo's *Proletariado militante* and Kropotkin's *Gran revolución* also appeared. In addition to this great range of literature, history, and science, letters submitted by readers provided news of the social struggle from the smallest towns and gave courage to the membership to imitate the daring actions reported: the formation of a new youth group, the establishment of a bond of free love, or the inauguration of a strike.

The vast majority of the workers, however, including their leaders, had never been to school and could not read. The newspapers and pamphlets were read aloud by the more learned.

*Legupín:* We paid one *perra chica* for a [reading] lesson at night. During the day we were working or guarding the flocks. I could read a bit when the sindicato started, but I learned more there. I remember *El Botón de Fuego* very well. Pepín, who has a truck now, was fourteen or fifteen then, and we would give him books and pamphlets and go into the plaza, and he would read them to us. He wasn't an anarchist, but he could read well.

Anarchosyndicalist principles matched campesino notions of cooperation and the exchange of labor and goods. Gang labor on the great estates made the idea of cooperative labor seem feasible, and local history and common practice recalled earlier cooperative use of the land.

In an earlier age property had been the concern of the tribe and the family, not the individual. Before the Christian era, Celtiberian tribes had shared work and harvest yields; and hereditary family plots were redistributed to attain equity in agriculture. During the Middle Ages the townships formed in the territories reconquered from the Moors received communal benefits to encourage new settlers who were needed to repopulate the region. The anarchists asserted that a wide network of cooperation and exchange then existed linking the townships together in a primitive form of federalism.

*Manuel Llamas:* In 1400 private property of the land didn't exist. The towns were the owners of the land. They organized an interchange between themselves. They lived freely. It was an ancient federalism. There were free towns. They had control of the crop, and there was a federal administration. They exchanged the surplus with other towns.

1. Rafael Rueda López, November 3, 1915. This argument had been advanced earlier in Kropotkin's articles and subsequent book on the theme; see *Mutual Aid: A Factor of Evolution.*

Then land was ceded to the grandees. That was the beginning of private property. Then began the division between the slaves and the rich.

Each township still retained communal systems concerning land and work: seed, pasture lands, hunting and trapping rights, the storehouse, the water for mills and for irrigation—these were shared by the townspeople. Sometimes workdays were set aside to provide for the general welfare, and plots of land were periodically rotated by lottery. The setting determined the system: in coastal towns the fishing catch was divided by the crew; in mountain villages the townsmen cut timber and divided the profit; in the plains reapers worked in teams and shared the harvest or the wages earned.[2]

In Casas Viejas the water that flowed through the village was shared by the millers and hortelanos. It was used first by the mills to power their grinding wheels. It then passed below the village to a section of the huertas, where it was available for irrigation for specific periods. When his turn came, the hortelano removed the rocks in the irrigation ditch leading to his huerta and placed them in the stream bed to block the main course. When his time period ended, he replaced the rocks to permit the water to continue its course. The schedule ran over a three week cycle, alternating days and nights, so that each grove could have a long pull at the water. When huertas were sold, the water rights were retained with the land; when they were subdivided through inheritance, the time allowed to divert the main stream was subdivided as well.

The nineteenth century marked a watershed for traditional rights and practices. At that time the common lands of the townships and the land held in entail by the church were tempting targets for the monied middle and upper classes, who wanted to expand their holdings.[3] Their sale, it was argued, would help pay the national debt, stimulate agricultural production, and encourage the growth of a prosperous peasantry. As a remedy for social ills, however, the redistribution of land in the mid-nineteenth century proved to be a disastrous failure. In Medina Sidonia the common lands were divided into plots of six and nine fanegas and offered for sale in lotteries open to heads of households. But instead of being purchased by peasants and landless workers, the lots were bought by speculators and the well-to-do. Although the small lots sold for only a few pesetas, landless laborers were in no position to take advantage of the opportunity to buy them. Workers did not have

2. Historical examples of collectives and cooperative efforts in Spain, particularly in the north, are legion. See Costa Martínez, *Colectivismo;* and Gabriel Jackson, "The Origins of Spanish Anarchism," pp. 135–43; see also Michael Kenny, *A Spanish Tapestry,* pp. 14–21.

3. The passage of disentailment legislation in the Cortes in 1835 did away with the right of religious orders to own land, and the following year church lands were ordered to be sold. In 1855 all common lands not declared for the use of the townships were also considered for sale, and in subsequent years the townships rapidly divested themselves of their holdings.

surplus cash, and there was no credit available to purchase land, tools, and animals. As a result, those who won the right to a lot often found the land useless to them. It was said that one lot was traded for a guitar, another for a bottle of wine. In a short time the small lots were in the hands of the wealthy or the more astute, becoming absorbed into already existing ducal estates or consolidated by the rich bourgeois into new estates. In addition, the loss of the common lands meant that the campesinos were locked out of areas that previously had provided them with pasture for cattle, land to till, game for the table, and wood for charcoal.

In the nineteenth century the township of Medina had owned approximately 8,000 hectares of land that were utilized by the townsmen. After the sale of the lands in the following century, the small agricultor was forced to turn to the large landowner or large-scale renter rather than to the township to rent land to sow a small crop, and he found that the terms of land use had suddenly stiffened: after 1853 small rented lots had to be vacated after the harvest, and the small tenant thereby lost the right to pasture his animals in the stubble. Whatever stubble remained from the harvest now belonged to the owner or to the large-scale lessor, and not to the small renter who had sowed the crop.

In most townships only fragments of the communal holdings remained. In nearby Vejer de la Frontera, however, substantial communal land survived into the twentieth century. The common lands of Vejer were divided into 365 plots of twenty-five fanegas each. Since the number of families now outnumbered the plots available, a lottery was used as a means of periodically redistributing the plots. Only the heads of households in town could participate in the lottery, with the lucky winners earning the rights to the land for four years.[4] Rather than a model worthy of being followed, however, the lottery in Vejer and elsewhere simply provided proof that the campesinos had been deceived and robbed of a greater patrimony.

From the vantage point of the campesino, the central government had countermanded campesino custom and had brought about a reign of disorder and injustice. The government sustained the idle, unproductive rich and protected them in their exploitation of the workers. Successive governments had repressed worker protest and betrayed peasant and worker: they had sold off the public lands; their police patrolled the private preserves and kept the hungry campesinos from hunting. Both state and church were used by

4. In practice, since taking possession of the land meant relocating, the custom was to collect rent from the family already cultivating the plot. For a history of Vejer de la Frontera, see Antonio Morillo Crespo, *Vejer de la Frontera y su comarca: aportaciones a su historia*. The lottery, popular with many peasants as a model for a still greater *reparto* (division), was not highly regarded by the collective-minded anarchists, who held that the land had to be worked in common.

the rich to dominate and intimidate the workers. Both abused the social codes of the local community. Worse still, the government conscripted the young to be mutilated and killed in foreign wars.

Clearly, peasant values and nature itself were more moral and more just. Were not cooperative social and economic relationships at the heart of Andalusian life? Were not goods exchanged and sometimes shared? Money, always scarce, played a limited role in campesino relationships. A day's labor or the loan of animals or tools could be repaid by work in kind or by a meal, a gift of eggs or fruit or game, or a special favor.

In daily life, a poor family ate from a single bowl, and it was a moral and practical imperative for the children to share gracefully at the table. Pepe Pareja said, "If a child has two pieces of bread, he must be told to put one down and not hold one in each hand. This is *egoísmo*" (selfishness). These values were carried into adulthood in the fields, where twenty or thirty men stood in a circle and ate gazpacho from one large bowl set on the ground. As José Monroy observed, "in the campo there is one bowl for everyone. If for each spoon you take, he takes three—he eats more bread—it is egoísmo."

Social controls in rural Andalusia were achieved not through government regulation and police surveillance but, rather, through social sanctions that were enforced by gossip and by various forms of criticism and public censure. At Carnaval, questionable conduct was trumpeted to the public in song.

Already anarchistic in spirit, the campesinos needed little encouragement to embrace Bakunin's anarchism. Pepe Pareja said, "We wanted a life of liberty. No one has the right to dominate his fellow creatures." The workers were convinced not only by anarchist arguments but by the courage of José Olmo:

*Pepe Pilar:* He was an orator, the fiercest there was. Once in the plaza, looking down toward the civil guard, who were there and could hear him, he said, "This force, the civil guard—assassins, murderers, cowards." One couldn't resist his oratory.

José Olmo carried his faith with him everywhere. His first son, Palmiro, often accompanied him to the campo:

I remember well that when my father and I went to work, he always carried a book by Anselmo Lorenzo under his arm. When I was young I rode on the donkeys and he would sing. And my father would say, "Palmiro, listen to this. The sun rises in the morning lighting up the whole world. We want liberty for the worker to shine like the sun."

I said, "I don't understand."

He sang to me, "If we want to free the workers in Spain, in Italy, and in Turkey, we must have the idea of anarchy. Believe in it."

"I don't know what to learn."
"Learn everything that I tell you. Learn, and you will arrive."

On June 8, 1914, the first sindicato of Casas Viejas was inaugurated. The day was a signal victory for José Olmo. At dawn workers began coming in from the campo to join. Miguel Barrio of Medina Sidonia addressed the crowd on the dangers of alcohol and card playing, which dulled their senses, and he urged the workers to abandon them for the newspaper, the book, and the pamphlet at the workers' centro. The good news of the opening of the centro was later reported in *La Voz del Campesino* (June 28, 1914), which made special mention of José Olmo.

Throughout the meeting the young battler José Olmo developed the theme of "the origin of human misery and the means to end it." He attacked private property and the elements of authority, striking well-aimed blows against them and against religion and politics. To relate in detail everything worthwhile that he said would be an interminable task, and we do not have sufficient space in our newspaper. At the end of his summation, our compañero received a unanimous ovation, ending the ceremony at 1:00 in the morning with a "Long live the union and the fraternity of the workers!"

Bernardo Cortabarra, a campesino, was elected president for six months until the end of 1914. Bernardo was considered very *simpático* (congenial), and he was moderate rather than militant. He was not the real leader of the sindicato, but he could read and write, which was a great advantage to a league of illiterate men. Cortabarra sometimes led an impromptu chorus during Carnaval and was well known for his skill at mimicry.

*Pepe Pareja:* He could read very well. He could laugh or cry and change his voice when need be to that of a woman. He could express all emotions. But if you asked him what he had read, he couldn't explain it. But he could read very well, and I had the impression that he enjoyed listening to himself read as well.

The second secretary was Juan Estudillo, a shoemaker with a taste for learning and a reputation for saintliness. He was a great reader of popular novels, and he practiced vegetarianism under the influence of one of the local customs guards, who wrote articles on naturalism under a pseudonym, Duende de la Pena ("Spirit of Sorrow"). Estudillo, who was thirty years old in 1914, spoke little in public, but he was always called on to aid in correspondence with the newspapers and in requests for books and pamphlets.

Although José Olmo was the organizer and leader of the sindicato, he held no official position. This was in keeping with the organization's practice of protecting the outstanding leaders. In moments of conflict, the authorities would be most likely to arrest the centro's officers, leaving the sindicato leaderless. It was therefore the wiser course to try to shield José Olmo from harm.

## Anarchist ideals and practices for the individual

The organization of the sindicato was only a beginning. The individual had to be educated to live in harmony with his fellow men. Anarchism was not only a goal but a way of life. It enumerated both positive and negative precepts to uplift the worker and enable him to contribute to the common cause. Campesinos were encouraged to adopt higher standards of morality and to reject the self-defeating values of the street—alcohol, card playing, and the brothel. New customs and habits were required to usher in the coming age. Foremost in this self-reformation was the need to learn to read and write. The anarchist first primer, *Cartilla filológica española,* argued that literacy marked a primary division among men.

Mankind can be divided into the good and the bad. The good and the bad can be subdivided into the literate and the illiterate. Any other division is artificial, false, ridiculous, or stupid. The subdivision between literate and illiterate, purely accidental, should not be a reason for vanity among those more fortunate or the cause of shame among those who have not had the good luck or the opportunity to learn. The bad are almost never so by nature but, rather, almost always as a result of social pressure, injustice, or the influence of bad examples, which circumstances they cannot alter.[5]

For the campesinos, literacy was even more elemental: it divided men from animals. By learning to read and write at the sindicato, men could become more than beasts of the field. Then the great change would begin.

*Pepe Pareja:* I was already a man and did not even know how to make a round *O* with a quill. And I was ashamed to be a man and not even know the letter *A*. I said, "This cannot be," because not knowing how to read, one cannot work with words. Nor can one converse with people, or anything like that. I had to learn, even if it was only a little—and by sacrifice or whatever was needed. And for this reason I learned the little I know. For example, one might have a mind to keep account of something; and not knowing how to write a number, how can one put down the number 20 or 30 or 200? So this is why I also wanted to learn. And since, of course, one needs numbers and one needs letters to express what the numbers say, then I had to learn something about letters and numbers. I

5. *Cartilla filológica española: primer libro de lectura,* p. 59.

didn't know how to read and write, and then I learned something: sprinklings here and there. That means that today someone gave me lessons, tomorrow someone else. Thus I learned the whole of the primer, the first letters—without a teacher, by sprinklings. One person taught me a lesson, and then perhaps two or three days went by and no one gave me a lesson. The most beautiful thing in the world is to learn. Education is the principal base for everything.

Alcoholism was responsible for much of the social malaise among many workers, and it was a major target of anarchist reformers. Excessive drinking robbed the worker of his senses and deprived his family of food. Anarchist newspapers and pamphlets hammered out the evil of this vice:

> Workers, do not drink! . . . How many workers, wretched heads of the family and worse husbands, forget the most sacred duties and waste away in alcoholic libations and in games a half or a third of the already scanty wages that they earn, leaving children and wife without bread, forced to starve, and subject to all the afflictions of life! How many prefer to leave their children naked, barefoot, illiterate, animalized, rather than give up the Sunday partying to feed and educate them a little better?
>
> That a glass of wine may occasionally be necessary to revive the working machine and to quench the sadness of melancholic thoughts in the sort of rapture that it produces—this we understand too. But to resort daily to intoxication and to become a habitual drunkard, to go to the tavern to waste the few céntimos earned after so much sweat, rather than bringing home the bread necessary for the nourishment of the children—no, we do not understand it, because it is the depths of brutality and cunning.
>
> Workers, do not drink![6]

The evils of alcoholism had been preached at the inaugural meeting of the sindicato in Casas Viejas, and when the centro was opened, the only drink allowed was *mosto,* unfermented grape juice. Card playing, the usual pastime in the cafés, also had no place in the centro, where learning and discussion were the guiding rules of conduct.

*José Monroy:* We were opposed to cards because they prevent people from developing themselves. Instead of studying to improve their lot, their minds are on the king and the jack, to see which will fall. Anarchism was always opposed to card playing. It took time from learning to read and write. No one was forced, but one was advised to read and to study.

The bullfight was also opposed by anarchists. A remnant of medieval cruelty, the bullfight was thought to desensitize people to suffering and to distract them from the task of educating themselves.

6. *Tierra y Libertad,* April 1, 1909.

*Pepe Pareja:* Bullfighting stemmed from the time of the Inquisition, the age when the feudal lords had slaves. When a slave did something wrong, he was put in a circus, like the ones with wild beasts that exist today for the recreation of capitalists. Its feudal origins are enough to make intelligent and idealistic persons hate bullfighting. There was much discussion and protest about this. Bullfighting was hated even more when it was observed that in a bull ring it is inhumane to ride a blindfolded horse in order to prick the bull, so it will advance against the horse and by the force of its horns will leave the horse dragging its guts on the ground. A person who has a sensitive heart should not look at this spectacle. I, for one, no matter how skilled a bullfighter may be, cannot go to see it. To me it is repulsive. To kill a blindfolded animal after it has given its service and its youth should not be allowed by mankind. This is how I understand it. I believe that civilization should protest against these things, for if not, what is civilization good for?

Proscriptions were not of a puritanical order. As José Monroy put it, "coffee and tobacco were not prohibited, but one was advised against using them. Men were warned against going to a brothel. It was not a matter of morality but of hygiene."

Everyone could enlist in the sindicato, but only a minority could achieve the insight and determination required to reshape personal habit and custom. The obrero consciente, the dedicated anarchist, symbolized the devotion and knowledge necessary to revitalize humanity. He represented an ideal unattainable by the majority. He drank wine in moderation or not at all, did not attend mass, baptize his children, or use God's name in his forms of salutation. Nor was he to be seen at the brothels that existed in the larger towns and cities. Card playing in the bar was shunned in favor of reading at the centro. After learning to read, the obrero consciente steeped himself in the teachings of anarchism and in the sayings and songs supporting his cause. Once his faith was established, he might be asked to serve on the strike committee or the committee to aid political prisoners, and he could be elected secretary, treasurer, or correspondent of the sindicato. Yet although he might win the admiration of his fellow workers, the dedicated anarchist rarely felt himself able to live up to his own image. No matter how deep his knowledge or rich his language, the obrero consciente almost always felt himself a novice aspiring to master a new order of knowledge and understanding.[7]

A few enthusiasts extended their views to diet and became naturalists or vegetarians on the premise that man becomes what he eats. Vegetable foods promised a nobility denied to carnivores. The principal difference between vegetarians and naturalists was that the latter ate only uncooked foods.

7. See Díaz del Moral's description of the obrero consciente in *Historia*, pp. 225 ff.

*Pepe Pareja:* The naturalist says that everything that goes through the [cooking] fire loses its ingredients. It is dead. The naturalist, who obtains his nutrition purely from raw vegetables, is more noble than the carnivore, who feeds himself by sacrificing animals. Therefore the distinctiveness of a person depends on the food which he takes in, which creates his uniqueness.

Naturalism and vegetarianism, however, attracted few adherents, even among the obreros conscientes. As often as not, these regimens were followed for reasons of health or from a desire for longevity rather than moral principles. There were only two vegetarians among the campesinos in Casas Viejas: Juan Estudillo, who also eschewed the use of salt, and Pepe Pareja, who had adopted his diet following a serious intestinal illness. There were no vegetarians in Medina Sidonia and only one, José Vega, in Paterna de Rivera.

Some anarchosyndicalists regarded matters of diet scornfully: Anónimo said, "A few followed [naturalism], and those who did had no more strength than a pansy. It wasn't worth anything for battle." Contrary to exaggerated accounts of anarchist zeal, most thoughtful obreros conscientes believed in moderation, not abstinence.

*José Monroy:* One could drink a bit, a glass of wine with one's meal, but not drink to excess, not to get drunk. Anarchism opposed drunkenness. It was against nature and bad for the pocket. But in general it was "Do as I say, and not as I do."

The practical needs of daily life moderated the behavior of even aspiring obreros conscientes. Fervent belief could not grant immunity to retribution by landowners and the civil guard. The outstanding anarchists were kept under surveillance and harassed. They found it difficult to work, and they were the first to be imprisoned in times of labor strife.

*Pepe Pareja:* These things were according to the ambience that existed. The clergy and the landowners would know you and point you out if you used words like "salud" instead of "adiós." "That one." "That one" meant "We have to eliminate him."

The range of behavior was determined by circumstances and by personal choice. José Olmo, the leading anarchist in Medina Sidonia and Casas Viejas, refused to baptize his children or give them saints' names. He did not smoke, but he drank wine moderately, and he ate meat when he could. His courage and sacrifice were better measures of his devotion to the anarchist cause than his diet.

## Membership

Not every worker in the town and countryside rushed to join the centro, but in time workers who failed to hold a card and pay dues were considered traitors. Workers who argued against the need to join were rebuked in one way or another.

*Pepe Pareja:* They say that once a man went over to a mule who was grazing free in the pasture. Now the mule is a mixed animal—the offspring of a burro and a mare. And one day this man went over to this mule grazing in the pasture and said to it, "I'm going to put the yoke on you so that we can work the land. I'll plant watermelons and cantaloupes. And I will put aside the rinds for you as a fine gift."

Since this is a fable, in which animals can speak, the mule answered, "I don't think that I will accept the yoke. I'm quite content with the grass I have."

And now the farmer who was going to work the land answered him. "But your father was not like this. Your father worked fourteen or sixteen hours every day and was content."

Then the mule answered, "Yes, what you tell me is true. But one must not forget that my father was an ass."

The creation of the sindicato jarred the equilibrium of the town. By the end of the year, there were 170 dues-paying members,[8] and a letter was sent to *Tierra y Libertad* (June 20, 1915) announcing the formation in Casas Viejas of a new youth group that had taken the name "Youth for Justice." With the rapid growth of the sindicato, old habits of submission and deference seemed to be shattered, and some rejoiced and some regretted the shifting of the social balance.

8. *La Voz del Campesino,* December 15, 1914. The following year a correspondent for *Tierra y Libertad* made a more generous estimate, reporting that after two or three months José Olmo had organized 500 workers in Casas Viejas (July 21, 1915).

# Six

# Free Love

## The concept of free love

In the free society, men and women will not be united by judge or priest, because [the latter] will not exist; nor will any human being have any say about these couples freely united; nor will there be any ties other than love; and if later on they deem separation to be beneficial to their happiness because of disagreement or incompatibility of character, they will separate without any more trouble, and each will again be able to join another person who best suits his (or her) liking.[1]

In rural Andalusia, the practice of free love was often the most daring personal commitment to the anarchist ideal by an obrero consciente and his compañera. It was a direct affront to state and church representatives.

Free love was the fulfillment of equality between the sexes. It demanded purity and fidelity without clerical or governmental interference and control. The couple remained together because of mutual love and need, and not because of arbitrary law or canonical decree. The free union could be dissolved by mutual consent if their love should erode. Inevitably, however, the term "free love" was taken by those outside the movement to signify promiscuity, the reverse of the anarchist ideal.[2]

*Pepe Pareja:* Free love does not mean having different women, having different lovers. Free love means that a woman has the same rights as a man. But to have free love one must be educated, one must have intellectuality. If a woman offers herself to a man out of her passion for him, well, today a man simply takes advantage of her and then leaves her bereft of her vir-

1. *El Proletario* (Cádiz), July 1, 1902.
2. "How harmful it is to abuse free love, that is, to commit libertine actions in the name of free love" ("El amor libre," *Tierra y Libertad*, April 28, 1915).

ginity. If one does not have equal passion, one must not take advantage of a woman. One has to have this determination.

The concept of free love stands in sharp contrast to the overworked notion of male superiority usually attributed to Andalusians. Although campesino men and women were separated vocationally and socially, there was a sense of equality between them. Women were not chattels but independent personalities. Free choice, mutual respect, and deeply felt passions characterized Andalusian relationships. Men were protective of women not only for their honor but, during the course of their marriage, because of their shared experiences and the hardships of life they endured together.

In many ways the concept of free love articulated virtues, somewhat idealized, that had long been recognized in the village. The social and sexual code stressed faithfulness, virginity, and monogamy. Village mores insisted that a girl be faithful to one *novio* (boyfriend). Although there might be initial competition for a desirable girl, once a match was settled, other suitors maintained a respectful distance.

*Pepe Pareja:* I was going with a girl, and after a while we stopped seeing each other. While she was seeing someone else, she sent a message for me to come down on Sunday. I came down instead on a Monday. While I was talking at the window, the new boy friend came along. He said, "Do you have a lot to say? If not, I'll wait and go in and talk to the parents."

I said, "No, I'm leaving." She asked me what I wanted to do, implying that she would give up the other fellow for me. I said I would think about it. But I didn't go back to her.

Later, when she was married, I would see her occasionally at the fountain, and she would blush; but she never spoke to me nor I to her. I respected her husband, because he was a good fellow. He deserved respect. She didn't speak to me until the end of the war, when we met on the roadside. And then we never spoke again.

Prudishness was as rare as promiscuity. Once a match was made, it was assumed that during the extended courtship the couple would circumvent the defensive strategy of the woman's family. After a sufficient time, a courting couple established intimate ties and represented a future family of their own. They saved to construct a cottage and to buy furniture and linen in order to prepare a proper household. These provisions established the young woman as a homemaker, and they signaled as well the man's good intentions. There was no hurry to go to the church; pesetas needed for the ceremony could be put to better use. Those living in the campo a day's journey from town could wait until the dry season, when the roads were passable, to have their union sanctified, or until the priest happened by on his burro, or until such time as their offspring were baptized.

*Juan Pinto:* Father Barberá would go through the mountains, and if he ran into a child, he would baptize him by the side of the road, which was his duty as a priest. For him the water of the river was just as good as the water in the church. And that was it. Father Barberá married me. We were on the way to church, and he met us on the road. He liked wine a good deal. Then he said to us, "You can go back. You're already married." He married us right then and there and sent us home. And once there, we had our fill of wine, which was what he wanted.

A marriage ceremony and a baptismal certificate are, after all, commemorations of facts. Many married and baptized a child on the same date. Yet children described in parish records as born both out of wedlock and of unknown parentage were exceedingly rare. Children listed as born out of wedlock were almost always born to an established household in which one parent could not formally be identified because of a previous marriage.

In Catholic Spain marriage was considered a sacred rite by the church, and divorce was impossible; but social bonds, though less rigid, had tensile and enduring strength. Some couples lived together and raised a family for many years without benefit of ceremony, obtaining religious sanction when it proved to be necessary or convenient, when they possessed the necessary pesetas, or when they bowed before familial or clerical pressure.

Pepe Pilar had put off going to the priest to formalize his common law marriage because of his anarchist beliefs. His father-in-law was deceased, but there was persistent pressure from his wife and his mother-in-law to legalize the marriage, and he slowly gave way to their desires. In time Pilar agreed to record the marriage with the civil authorities in Medina, but it was not until after the birth of their fourth child that he agreed to see Don Francisco, the priest.

At that time I had four kids, and my wife and I weren't married. My wife didn't have my convictions, and it bothered her that we weren't married, and she was always after me to get married. So because of the ignorant ideas that she had, since it always disturbed her, and since she was a good woman, I decided to satisfy her and marry her. I didn't want to see her suffer. So I went to the priest. I told him that I wasn't married and I wanted to get married.

"Do you have children?"

"Yes, four."

"Four! But why haven't you married before now?"

"Because there's no need of it; but my wife is suffering from not being married, and so we will marry."

"But don't you know that the four children are not legitimate? Now it will cost you twenty-two pesetas to arrange for the papers."

"Well, when I have twenty-two pesetas, I'll return and get married." And I started to go.

"Wait! If you don't have the twenty-two pesetas at one time, you can pay two or three or one peseta. I'll put down the payments for you."

"No. When I have the twenty-two pesetas, I'll return." And I left.

About a year later, I met the priest on the road near the cemetery. He was in the shade reading a book, and I passed, mounted on a burro. We said good day, but he was very involved in the book he was reading. Then he hailed me: "Hey, aren't you the fellow who came to me a year ago to be married, and you needed twenty-two pesetas?"

"That's right. But I didn't have the twenty-two pesetas, and I left. I have to give food to my children."

"Well, come to my house tonight and we'll discuss it."

So I went to his house and he said, "You come and I'll marry you at once. I don't care if you have the money. I don't care. When can the novia come?" He called her the novia.

"Whenever you care."

"Tomorrow."

"All right, I'll come. But don't you start up with me, asking me questions or lecturing me. Just marry me and nothing else. Otherwise I won't do it."

"Don't worry; I won't bother you. Just come. Come tomorrow after 8:00, after Mass."

"No. You must marry me earlier, because I have to go to work. I can't miss a day of work."

He said all right. We went there, and he didn't say anything to me, but he said to my wife, "Your husband is an anarchist, isn't that so?"

And my wife replied, "Father, I never heard that word before. I don't know what it means."

And he said to her, "Yes, your husband is an anarchist."

Village mores did not insist on legalisms. Affection, love, and children, as well as gossip and reputation, effectively ensured the stability of most relationships. Nevertheless, it was one thing to slide into a relationship that temporarily ignored clerical and secular law, and quite another to challenge the official authorities.

## José Olmo and María Bollullo

For a time José Olmo and María Bollullo were the only couple in Casas Viejas who lived in declared free union. Before their union in Medina Sidonia, José, just one year older than María, had been a friend of the family and had come to the house frequently. María was strikingly handsome. She was petite, with a clear intelligent face and shining black hair. At first each had a different admirer. They would encounter each other in the plaza while strolling with their novios, and María would say to him jokingly, "You come to my house and say you want to marry me, and here you are with someone else." They said it was all in jest, but José's novia became annoyed at the jokes, and they split up. Subsequently José and María began to walk together.

The birth of José Olmo's first son came in 1910. It was inscribed in the civil register, but the boy was not baptized, nor was he given a traditional saint's name. Instead, the birth was announced in *Tierra y Libertad* (April 7, 1910):

> A beautiful boy with the delightful name of Palmiro has been brought to the civil register of Medina Sidonia as the son of compañeros María de los Santos Bollullo and José Olmo, the first offspring of their free union. Our sincere congratulations to these compañeros for the strength of their convictions in removing themselves from the bureaucratic procedures used by the black-clothed priests.

Although the couple lived together without clerical or civil sanction, José continued to be on good terms with María's family. When they moved to Casas Viejas, María's father joined them to work with José in the forest preparing charcoal. By all the standards of village life, José was a good provider and respectful son-in-law: he was steadfast, strong, and *formal*—that is, he kept his word and was a man of honor.

When José and María arrived in Casas Viejas, they already had three children. In 1915 another daughter was born. Her birth was announced in *Tierra y Libertad* under the notice "Fruits of a Free Union."

> The home of our compañeros María Bollullo and José Olmo, of Casas Viejas, has expanded with a baby girl who has been named Acracia ["Anarchy"]. In such a home, formed by the free union of said compañeros, one may breathe the air of those freed from all prejudice with their children, Porvenir [Palmiro], Paz, Germinal, and Acracia.[3]

## Pepe Pareja and Antonia Márquez

The first free union of a local couple in Casas Viejas was that of Pepe Pareja and his compañera, Antonia Márquez Mateo.

3. November 3, 1915. The personal notes printed in the anarchist press demonstrated that the bonds of free love were stronger than clerical sanctions; they made it clear that courageous individuals were expressing their beliefs by positive action. The notices were a source of inspiration to those willing to test their strength and will. One could not pay mere lip service to ideals: free love was one step on the pathway to the free society. A congratulatory announcement appeared in the anarchist press whenever that step was taken.

*Pepe Pareja:* In Medina there were several who did not marry. Here I was the only one. For a time José Olmo was here, and he lived with his compañera, but my ideas came not from him but from my reading.

*Antonia Márquez Mateo:* I began to go with Pepe when I was twelve. He was nineteen. He taught me the ideas of free love.

*Pepe Pareja:* There were others in the town who were unmarried, but they had gotten into their situation unintentionally. The girl became pregnant and they were forced to set up house. They didn't marry and continued in this way. Some possibly couldn't pay for inscription in the church register, although it wasn't much. If the priest saw a couple who wasn't married and had children, he went to them and asked them to marry. Later the church married them for free.

The motives impelling the few faithful like Pepe and Antonia to declare a free union were complex. They not only proclaimed the ideals of love; they also protested against the sham of swearing oaths dictated by detested institutions:

*Pepe Pareja:* Why should I want to pass before these false orations and have to confess and receive the Host? Why should one submit oneself to the church and the state? The state has more right than the church, but what does the state do but erect borders between nations, causing enmity and raising armies, when there should be brotherhood and all should live in harmony?

There was another compelling reason to circumvent the laws of state and church: marriage and baptism meant certain identification for obligatory service to the state.

*Pepe Pareja:* The motive for not registering with the state is that if a recently married couple has sons and they are registered, and a situation arises when the state needs them when they reach the age of twenty years, they put them in the army to be killed. But if it is not written down anywhere, they do not know where you live. They don't know who you are. This is a protest that they should not be machine-gunned after they have been raised. When it's your time to die, well, you die—but not by machine gun fire. At twenty years of age they send your sons to protect the frontier. What frontier? There are no frontiers. They send your son to kill other sons.

The families of Pepe and Antonia had accepted the match when they thought it would result in a legal marriage.

*Antonia:* Pepe's mother was content with me because I could sew. But my mother said, "Watch out; he'll turn out like his father," who had a reputation for liking women. My father said, "That's not important. Men are free. He's a good fellow."

When Pepe made his offer of companionship in free love, however, Antonia's father, who was a goatherd in the employ of Francisco Vela, reacted sharply.

*Pepe:* Her father was a member of the sindicato, but he didn't want his daughter to be the first to live in free union. I spoke with him. He agreed with the idea, but not for his daughter. It's always comfortable to agree when it involves someone else. I went to her father and told him that I wanted to marry his daughter in free union, and he rejected me at once.

*Antonia:* My father didn't want me to marry Pepe [in free union], because I would be the first of my friends to marry this way. My father said, his daughter, his first daughter—no.

The celebration of the free union of Pepe and Antonia was planned for early September 1914. Antonia's father had been away from the village guarding Paco Vela's herd and his own few goats. But he returned home on a holiday to sleep in his own bed. When he rose in the morning he confronted Antonia.

*Antonia:* That morning my father got up—the day before had been a fiesta—and he said, "Little girl, get up, I want to talk to you. This lazy one doesn't move! I'm going to have to smack this girl. Antonita, get up. I want to talk to you."

"Ay, my God!" But I didn't get up.

He tells me, "You, look here, you'd better let that man go."

I kept quiet.

"Answer me, lazy. Are you going to leave this man?"

I didn't answer him. If I had said yes, he would not have done anything; but since I didn't answer him, he started to beat me. There were some shoes hanging there, and he seized them and started to beat me black and blue. My sister grabbed my father by the legs, but he kept beating me. He hit me such a hard blow on the head that he could have killed me. I ran out and went up to the vegetable patch on the slope. I had to run around a tree, and when I turned around—my father was behind me, running. I reached the house of a neighbor. When my father got to the neighbor's small patio, he had to stop. He couldn't enter.

I was saying, "Ay, my God!" The neighbor sent her little girl to look for Pepe, and he came to where I was. And he said to me, "What's the matter?" I told him what had happened. And I stayed there for five days until my house with Pepe was fixed up.

*Pepe:* Everything was all prepared. I had bought the furniture, the same bed that we have now.

*Antonia:* I said, "Why is it that my parents are disappointed?" Of course I couldn't talk to them, because they weren't pleased. They were the ones who were annoyed.

The party for the free union of Pepe and Antonia was celebrated on September 16, 1914.

*Antonia:* I couldn't go home, and so I was married in the clothes I had. Pepe was well dressed. First we had a celebration in the house. My brother-in-law, Paulo, Pepe's sister's husband, played the guitar. There were some refreshments—food, a bit of wine, and other things. Then about 1:00, we were invited to have dinner with José Olmo. They had stewed a turkey, which they had bought. They didn't have any turkeys of their own, and it was a sacrifice for them because it was very expensive. And we had wine, fruit, and coffee with milk.

*Pepe:* My father and brothers and friends accompanied us—Juan Vidal, Juan Antonio, the family of Paco Estudillo. José Olmo was our best man.

*Antonia:* Olmo's father-in-law was there, and two or three of their friends from Medina. They wanted us to stay longer and have the evening meal with them as well. We had arrived at 1:00. But we said, "No, we have to leave."

There were many girls who had said they wanted to marry this way, but after they saw what happened to me, they backed off.

We stayed in Casas Viejas for six days, at the house Pepe's parents had in the village, and then we went to live with them in the campo. We stayed with them for sixteen years. It had been much easier at home, where I did not have to tend the animals or do the work of the campo. Life was much harder there.

*Pepe:* It was all out of fear of what people would say. Afterward I would meet [Antonia's father] in the town or on the roadway, and I would always greet him, but he wouldn't answer me.

Eventually there was another confrontation between father and daughter.

*Antonia:* My father-in-law had a male goat, and my father used to tend his herd of goats. And there was a river that one had to cross. And when I saw my father coming close to the river, I said, "Ay, my father!" I didn't even think that I had to avoid him or anything else, but I saw that it was my father—"Ay, my father!" And I went to see him.

And when I got close to him, face to face, he says, "Get away! Get out of my sight! I don't want to see you. Get out of my sight, for I don't want to see you!"

"Ay, God, I no longer have a father or a mother!" And so I cried, because I had neither a father nor a mother. I used to cry a lot when I was young. "Ay, I don't have a father or a mother. I don't have a father or a mother!"

So Pepe's sister-in-law, who was there watching this, says, "Ay, why did you leave your parents? Why did you leave? Why did you leave?" And by this time my father had gone by. I didn't fear him any longer; I didn't have any fear that he wanted to kill me.

One of our neighbors learned about this meeting by the river, and she went to my mother's place, crying, "Ay, Doña Manuela, look at your Antonia with her father. The poor dear little one! What things have happened to her! Poor little dear! Look, look at the poor little one!"

And there was my father, and so my mother said this to my father: "Listen, have you seen the girl today—I mean Antonita?"

He said, "Yes, I've seen her."

"And did she come to you?"

And he said, "Yes."

And my mother then started to cry very much, and so did the neighbor. And the neighbor told my mother about the whole thing.

And so my father said, "Well, the girl, you've got to go after the girl." My mother had to go to the house after me. And my mother came, and a sister of mine, because my father cried a great deal, after having done what he did.

So, this one [Pepe] says, "OK, I'll go with you."

I said, "No. If my father beats me, he'll do it to me, but you won't see it."

When I arrived home, my father saw me. "Come!" crying, and "Come!" screaming, and "Come!" hugging me, the poor dear man! My father was a very affectionate man.

I had not taken any clothes from my home. The neighbors had loaned me linen for the bed. My trunk was still at home. Two days later my father, and my husband with him, decided that nothing would be lacking except for the church.

*Pepe:* Ten months after our wedding, he took sick and died. He called me in to him and asked my forgiveness.

Not long after the union of Pepe and Antonia, another couple, Juan Pino and Salvadora Estudillo, celebrated a free union. They were older than Pepe and Antonia and had been novios for some time. Several years afterward, in a late marriage, Juan Estudillo established a free union with a widow. But there was no stampede to declare oneself bound only by the ties of free love. Living in free union required a special kind of heroism. Even the dedicated often preferred to follow local custom and simply create a household without bothering to notify the priest.

Pepe and Antonia's marriage in free love has lasted more than sixty-five years. Their relationship, however, continued to be an affront to local authorities, who dealt with them after the Civil War, as we shall see.

# Seven
# The End of the Workers' Centro

## The strike of 1914

A strike began in the district of Jerez on June 10, 1914. It was timed to coincide with the harvest, when workers were needed and any delay would place the crop in jeopardy. The workers' demands were reported in *Solidaridad Obrera* (June 25, 1914): a contract stipulating wages and hours during the following year, a minimum wage of two pesetas, sanitary living conditions in the gañanías, respect for the workers' organization, and an eight-hour day.

*José Monroy:* Our work was from sunrise, 6:00 in the morning, until sunset, 9:00 at night. We didn't win the eight-hour day until the time of the Republic. We wanted to get rid of working a destajo. Then there were no fixed hours of work. It's better to work for a wage. Otherwise they put in fewer workers; it costs them less to feed them. The workers could have earned more, but we were too many. We wanted to get rid of a destajo in order to provide more work.

The conservative newspaper *El Guadalete* of Jerez responded to the workers' accusations with indignation:

It is a lie that the campesino works sixteen hours a day. It is a lie that we put them up in filthy housing. It is false, patently false, that we landowners are intransigent (June 26, 1914).

To establish their argument, the newspaper cited the wages of three and one-half pesetas paid to the *sabañeros,* who did the heavy labor of carrying the straw up a ladder to its storage place. Of course each step in the threshing process had its own pay scale, and the sabañeros were the highest-paid workers. The editor asserted that no one worked more than seven hours, but that the landowners could not accept a straight eight-hour day, with specified and unvarying hours, because of the nature of agricultural labor. Work on the threshing floor, for example, depended on the wind—the calm at daybreak, when the straw was carried to the haystack, and the sea breeze later in the afternoon, which allowed the winnowing to begin.

In this type of work, how can we accept an eight-hour day? If the eight-hour work day is in the morning, what will we do when the wind blows up in the afternoon? And if the work is for the afternoon, how can we take advantage of the morning calm—unless we pay overtime or double daily wages? We would accept the eight-hour day if during this time the worker would always produce, as does the city worker, carpenter, locksmith, mason, or cooper.

The campesinos, however, no longer wanted to bear alone the burden of uncertain wind and weather. The strike continued. In order to break the deadlock, the landowners brought in workers from Málaga, who were told only that there was a shortage of labor in the province. The strikers then had the difficult task of convincing these men that they too must abandon their work. The workers of Jerez also responded with a weapon of their own—a boycott of those using strikebreakers. The most notable boycotts were against landowners near Jerez who also had commercial establishments in the city. The workers and their wives refused to buy there, and the women stationed themselves nearby to discourage other shoppers.

The anarchosyndicalists had no strike funds, no paid employees, no treasury, and consequently no choice but to keep expenses to a minimum and rely on short, punishing strikes. To help the workers of Jerez, the centros in the villages and towns collected small sums from their members, which they sent to the central office. The campesinos of Casas Viejas contributed forty pesetas, and those of Medina Sidonia sent fifty pesetas; a larger sum, 233 pesetas, came from the sindicatos of Barcelona.[1]

The sindicato of Casas Viejas was also one of those in the province that voted to join the strike in a show of support for the workers of Jerez. This

1. The expenses of the sindicato in Jerez during the period of the strike of 1914 illuminate the minuscule scale on which the workers had to fight. Expenditures totaled 2,818 pesetas and 85 céntimos ($513 at the 1914 exchange rate of 5.49 pesetas to the dollar). Money received during the strike period came to 2,768.78, leaving a deficit of 50.07 ($9.22). The expenses were as follows: forty-three telegrams and telephone calls (56.75), 255 letters sent and 153 received (45.40), tobacco for prisoners (36.25), 2,000 sheets of paper, 5,000 manifestos, 2,000 convocations (54), and official stamps (1.20). The largest amounts were the charity vouchers for strikers (2,431.50) and charity in hard currency (171.25). See *El Guadalete,* July 14, 1914. The editor of *El Guadalete,* undoubtedly reflecting the opinion of many others in Jerez, expressed disbelief that this sparse list represented the expenditures of the sindicato and called it a fabrication.

decision presented serious difficulties for the small sindicato, whose number included many newly inducted and naive campesinos. To be effective, the strike demanded organization, energy, and persuasive powers. At the same time, the leaders had to avoid direct confrontation with foremen and landowners or face reprisals later. Grievances would be remembered in the town for years afterward and could deprive a man of his livelihood or set his neighbors against him.

*Pepe Pareja:* I had to inform some people to help us—but I did it indirectly. I had a burra, and I used the excuse that I was gathering food for her to go to see them. It was in front of the very bosses themselves. I used the burra as a pretext. And I said, "You're working, and others are making petitions. You're being a traitor."

A major obstacle in winning the strike was the faithfulness of the fijos, who felt bound to the estates and to their patrones.

*Pepe Pilar:* There were many strikebreakers. They were mostly the older workers who had been raised in the house, and their fathers had been raised in the house as well. In 1914, my brother, who was a few years older than me, went to the goatherd of the Espina household and said, "Don't go down to milk the goats tomorrow. We're going out on strike."

The goatherd was an old worker, and he said, "I'm going."

My brother said to him, "If you go there, we'll drag you back."

The next morning the goatherd left before us to go down, and we went, three of us, my brother and I and another, to catch up with him at El Tesorillo [just below the village]. I was only fourteen at the time; my brother was twenty-three. I don't remember who the other fellow was. Everyone in the village was waiting above.

"Where are you going?" my brother asked.

"I'm going down to milk the goats."

"No, you're not. We're out on strike."

"The only way I'll go back is if you chop me up and take me back in a basket."

"Then we'll take you back in a basket."

At that moment the corporal and a carabinero arrived and asked what was going on. They said to the goatherd, "You do us a favor now, and listen to us. Forget about milking the goats today. Don't go there this afternoon."

So he went back. They brought the goats up from the campo, and there was an old servant woman in the house who milked them.

The strikebreakers were the oldest workers. They had been raised in the house, and their fathers were raised there, and they knew nothing more than to betray their fellow workers.

The *pegujaleros*, the small renters, were split in their sympathies concerning the strike. Social beliefs and self-interest divided some families.

*Pepe Pareja:* My father planted white barley, and it was time to harvest. It was a dangerous time for the plant, for if the wind came from the straits, the grains would fall. But how could we, four brothers, go to pick them when the sindicato was on strike? We couldn't go. He wanted us to go. We recognized that we were obligated to observe the petitions. We had to observe them. One has to suck on one teat; one cannot suck on two. If we work for our father and the other workers gain, can we take advantage of what they won? I had many disagreements with my father. He had one type of understanding, and I had another.

The strike dragged on through the month of June and the first part of July. After weeks of bitter dispute, the governor of the province was welcomed as arbitrator by both sides. The sindicatos could not endure a protracted battle, and the landowners were anxious to harvest their crops. The governor regarded the resolution of the strike as a personal triumph: wages were slightly increased for winter work; the owners also agreed to improve the conditions of the gañanías. The settlement was, however, largely a defeat for the workers, since most work in the harvest would continue to be done as contract labor. Still, a significant change was made concerning rations.[2]

The new contract stipulated that in winter the campesinos would work *a seco,* without rations. Although many workers applauded the change, others regretted having to arrange for their own food. It seemed of little importance at that moment, since food was inexpensive and prices stable. Individual workers pooling their money spent only two *gordas* (twenty céntimos) each day for bread and oil. The improvement in quality was worth the effort it cost them. It was not until the price of grain and other foods soared after the First World War broke out in August 1914 that the cost of food became as critical as wages. The landowners were able to take advantage of the high prices the shortages created, but the workers became its victims. Away from the vicinity of Jerez, however, many patrones ignored the contract agreement concerning food. The more distant estates continued to provide a hot gazpacho as part of the wage, as usual. It had always been done that way, and they were not about to change; and far from towns and cities it was difficult for the workers to protest or bring pressure on the patrones.

2. Minimum wages for winter work were established at six and a half reales (1.52 pesetas). Summer wages for threshing remained about the same as was then customary. Since the workers near Jerez used machinery in the harvest, the 2.75 pesetas paid to machine operators was the keystone of the agreement. Campesinos who carried the grain to the threshing floor were to receive 2.50 pesetas; those who worked on the threshing floor, 2.25 pesetas; and those who gathered up the grains that fell to the floor, 1.25 pesetas. Wages were again higher for those who did more demanding tasks: the sabañero earned 3.50 pesetas, and the sifters earned as much as the machine operator, 2.75 pesetas, if there were two workers, or as much as the sabañero, if one worked alone. *El Guadalete,* July 10, 1914.

As for the landowners' promise to improve hygienic conditions, there was little that could be done to force the issue, short of burning down the gañanías. In a very few instances, some improvements were made—such as adding an adjacent eating room—but in most cases nothing was changed, and with the strike ended there was no impetus to effect improvements.

After observing the strikes carried out in Medina Sidonia, Anónimo placed the blame for their failure on the militant leaders, who had arbitrarily neglected to give the campesinos participation in the decision to strike. Lack of planning and organization resulted in the imprisonment of the leaders, thereby depriving the sindicato of direction. In Anónimo's view, the leaders also failed to educate the campesinos *inconscientes* who, innocent but suspicious, believed that their small dues went into the pockets of the leadership. Whatever mistrust existed, it was due to frustration over the negligible results of the struggle.

There had been conflict and antagonism in Casas Viejas before, but the strike of 1914 marked a new level in the struggle between landowner and campesino. Even faithful members of the centro would look back with some nostalgia to earlier days: "Before the strikes, there were no conflicts. Everyone lived badly but in tranquility. We went off to work singing" (Legupín).

The strike of 1914 had settled none of the larger issues nor any of the nagging social complaints. The question of contract labor was unresolved. Rising prices intensified the plight of the campesinos, and the hard winter of 1914–15 stirred worker unrest throughout the province. There was a serious rate of unemployment in the towns around Jerez. In February 1915 the mayor of Medina Sidonia reported that aid had been given to 800 unemployed workers. As the plowing of 1915 ended and spring approached, a new contract had to be negotiated, and another strike threatened. Although the strike of 1914 had gained little for the workers of Casas Viejas, the organization of the local sindicato had caused alarm among landowners and the civil guard. They worried about the new power of the workers and the demands the sindicato would make for the harvest of 1915.[3]

Subsequently *Tierra y Libertad* observed (July 21, 1915),

> Within two or three months our compañero [José Olmo] had organized more than 500 workers who, in concert with those of Medina, constituted two powerful worker organizations of such strength that the bourgeoisie felt terrorized. Since pride predominates among those exploiters, each day the desire for conquest grew in them. They were furious, since through the action of reason and justice the village had escaped from their claws.

3. *Diario de Cádiz,* February 15 and 16, 1915.

## Gaspar Zumaquero Vera

In January 1915 the six-month term of Bernardo Cortabarra, the first president of the centro obrero of Casas Viejas, ended, and an election was held. The new president was Gaspar Zumaquero Vera, a forty-year-old mason. He had less education than Cortabarra, but he was a skilled artisan and a sensitive man of good will, with a lively personality. Zumaquero was short and broad; he was a happy man, pleased to converse and exchange jokes. His graceful wife, Isabel Montiano, somewhat taller than her husband, was equally *simpática*. They had two active young sons who promised to look just like their father.

As summer approached, a strike was called for the district, and the compañeros of the centro of Casas Viejas voted to join the strike. In May, however, Gaspar Zumaquero was summoned to the barracks by Corporal Pedro Pozo Gómez and Don Luis Guinea, the deputy mayor, a retired civil guard who now owned a store in the village. The conversations were secret, but it was evident that Zumaquero was under pressure. At one point he confided to Juan Estudillo that

> he was unable to sell out the sindicato because of a slander designed to damage the best compañeros, and then he asked the secretary [Estudillo], "Would you be able to do that, Juan?" And when Juan asked why he brought up such an idea, Zumaquero answered that he believed that Guinea, the corporal, and others of the bourgeoisie were plotting against the sindicato (*Tierra y Libertad,* August 18, 1915).

The local officials involved then announced that Zumaquero had signed a statement canceling a scheduled centro meeting concerning the strike. The other members of the centro, ignorant of what had taken place, initially accused Zumaquero of being a traitor. It is not known how much Zumaquero was able to reveal to his compañeros in his own defense, but he did inform his wife and his *compadre* how he had been fooled: called by Guinea and Pozo to the barracks, he was asked to sign his name several times to prove that he could read and write. He had signed a blank piece of paper, to which a compromising text was then added. Under threat of imprisonment, he was forced to keep silent about the matter. No one else had been present at the meetings of Zumaquero, the corporal, and the deputy mayor; and his story could not be corroborated. The fear of being imprisoned, the pressure to turn traitor, and the suspicion expressed by his fellow workers help to explain Zumaquero's tortured state of mind at the time.

On May 29 Gaspar Zumaquero, accompanied by his brother Manuel, set out on a journey for which he alone knew the purpose.

*Pepe Pareja:* Zumaquero said to his brother: "I'm going to Algeciras, and I want you to come with me."

"Why?"

"Just come with me."

When they got to Alinoso [twelve kilometers from the village], he told his brother he had to move his bowels, and he went off a bit. Then he knelt down and cut his stomach open. Manuel raced to him, only to see his brother take the knife and cut his own throat.

Zumaquero's suicide stunned the town, and the unexplained circumstances surrounding his death led to the fabrication of serious charges against other members of the sindicato. Two weeks later (June 14, 1915), the director of the *Diario de Cádiz,* R. del Río, published an interview with two unidentified friends from Medina Sidonia and Casas Viejas, who reported that Zumaquero's death was tied to a plot against the landowners of the region. The anonymous informants accused José Olmo of being the chief plotter, and they linked all the local anarchist leaders to the conspiracy. The alleged scheme was similar to La Mano Negra (one of the *Diario's* headlines read, "An offshoot of La Mano Negra?"). In both there was said to be a plan to ransack the estates, burn the crops, and murder certain landowners, in this instance the marqués of Negrón and Don Antonio Vela, among others. The members of the centro of Casas Viejas were accused of having held a lottery to determine who would carry out the murders, with Gaspar Zumaquero allegedly drawing the task of killing the marqués of Negrón. Unable to commit the murder, Zumaquero was said to have asked the advice of corporal Pedro Pozo, who took him under his protection; however, Zumaquero reportedly either lost his courage and committed suicide or was killed for failing to carry out his oath to murder the marqués.

The leaders of the centro—José Olmo, Juan Estudillo, Bernardo Cortabarra, and Manuel Zumaquero—along with four men from Medina Sidonia, were imprisoned in Medina while the case was being investigated.[4] Witnesses were summoned to make depositions prior to a trial. Gaspar Zumaquero's brother, Manuel, was under special strain, and his friends blamed his eventual breakdown on his repeated summonses to court and his subsequent arrest. Manuel died insane nine years later.

The centro was officially closed. For a time this action appeared to be unnecessary. Gaspar Zumaquero's death and the arrest of the other leaders seemed to demoralize the membership. In one swoop the sindicatos of Casas Viejas and Medina Sidonia had been rendered immobile for the duration of the strike.

4. Other charges accumulated. Additional arrests were made in late June, when it was alleged that an insurrection designed to free the imprisoned men had been uncovered (*Diario de Cádiz,* June 29, 1915).

At the end of the summer, however, a fearless public statement, signed by twelve women and eleven men of the town, appeared in *Tierra y Libertad* (August 18, 1915) to defend the accused men. The statement publicly declared the motives for Zumaquero's suicide—fear of imprisonment and pressure to turn informer. It accused Deputy Mayor Guinea and Corporal Pozo of forcing Zumaquero to his death by their threats of sending him to prison. The arrests and charges against José Olmo and the others were denounced as slanderous inventions.

When the accused asked to confront the witnesses, the civil guard used the pretext that this was a confidential matter. The one who declared that the suicide said, "Olmo, you have ruined me!" is unable to appear.

The corporal, the letter writers protested, was continuing to harass witnesses and even Zumaquero's widow.

When the corporal was informed that the widow was going to make a statement in Medina, he came personally to her home and told her that the prisoners were the ones who had caused her husband's suicide. She answered him that the ones he alluded to were innocent and that she blamed no one, but she asked him please to stay out of her house because on seeing him she felt ill, since he was the one who had frightened her lost husband by calling him so often to the post.

The compañeros particularly defended José Olmo, since he had been singled out by the civil guard as ringleader.

We come to say that if the weight of the law wishes to fall on the head of compañero José Olmo, since his conduct among us has been irreproachable, our consciences are aroused, and we cannot be accomplices with our silence. We raise our voices in his defense to protest against those who damn him without justification.

A still more impassioned protest was prepared in prison by José Olmo. It appeared in *Tierra y Libertad* some months later (January 19, 1916), under the heading "I Accuse":

Not being a judge able to try without just cause, nor a prosecutor able to condemn the innocent, I have vigilantly and relentlessly dug into the roots of the conspiracy, to investigate whether the hands that forged it were black from labor in the fields and browned by the rays of the sun, or if they were the gloved white hands of the bourgeoisie and the bemedaled ones of the military. I have preserved the trustworthy facts in a notebook so that they can be made known and spearhead a campaign. . . .

Today three months have passed, perhaps because the prosecutor did not wish to condemn those truly responsible for the suicide, or the inventors and intriguers of the imaginary conspiracy, because they belong to his class—the bourgeoisie and the authorities. It is time for the prosecutor to ask for further proof concerning the motive of the suicide. . . .

They begin the proceedings again, and every day the witnesses travel to the court in Medina. And now, after having endured three months of imprisonment through the perfidy of our enemies, if we regain our liberty through the true statements of the witnesses, we carry away the physical attrition of what we have endured morally during the sad days and worse nights in damp cells.

Tuberculosis has taken its hold on me, on my children, and on my beloved compañera. My house is undone, threatened, and besieged by hunger. I bear a living wound made persistent and aching from abuse and injustice. But I shall not rest on the hope that the Federación de los Campesinos and the lawyer Barriobero will succeed in our defense at the trial. . . .

Today things are the same as in the past. They select a victim in order to dignify themselves and cover their embarrassment, even though they have had to resort to false statements. I cannot be an accomplice to this with my silence (since they want to saddle me with the dead body [of Zumaquero]), and I will face all iniquities, vigilant about my liberty and that of my compañeros. I ask of the prosecutor more proof, greater justice, and further inquiry. And I ask him: Are you not satisfied to do justice concerning the suicide with the declarations taken from various witnesses, in particular those of the apprentice of the suicide, the widow, and his compadre? From them it has become evident that the suicide blamed the corporal of the civil guard and Señor Guinea, saying that they were driving him crazy by having him sign his signature so many times without knowing what he signed, and threatening him that if he did not sign they would imprison him. Though he believed his actions to be wrong, he did as they said, because he did not want his children to see him go to jail (at least I have examined the apprentice, and so he declared to me).

Does it not seem strange to the prosecutor that three months have passed, and others have not supported these truths? Since in this world everything is odd, it does not seem strange to me, because I know that some have not done so for convenience, others because they do not wish to harm anyone, and others because of their limitations and ignorance. But it is strange to me that the newspaperman Río, director of the *Diario de Cádiz*, has not been interviewed, since he ought to know the identity of those two gentlemen who set out from Medina Sidonia and Casas Viejas and told him whatever they knew, so that he could make a deposition for them. . . . I state publicly that the deposition and accusations of the corporal are false (as can be proved), just as it is false to say that the sindicato approved only of whatever Olmo said and wanted, when in truth whatever was decided was by all of the members.

The declaration of Señor Guinea is false when he claims that the suicide told him that Olmo compelled him to call the meeting of the centro. It is a lie in every detail, because as an enemy of all abusive authority and coercion, Olmo always left the president free to carry out his duties. And it is false, it is slander, for the corporal to say that Olmo made the workers revolutionaries. Harmony has always been my theme.

José Olmo and the other imprisoned workers were eventually set free without a trial. None of the accused officials were brought to trial or punished.

While the leaders of the centros of Casas Viejas and Medina were imprisoned, sindicato leaders in Jerez had negotiated a new contract with the landowners' association and the governor. Because of the rising cost of living, the workers had set as their goal a minimum base of five pesetas a day, an eight-hour working day, an extra peseta a day to be set aside for pay during periods of unemployment, accident insurance similar to that covering industrial workers, and most significantly, the development of public lands under the control of the sindicatos.[5] In the end, the workers settled for far less: a bonus of one real per day over the previous year's contract *for those who worked through the harvest.* The landowners considered the bonus their insurance for a successful harvest.[6] The workers failed to win any of the benefits they had asked for.

## The new church

At the close of the summer of 1915, José Olmo was released from prison. At approximately the same time, a committee was named to enlist subscribers to aid in the building of the new church in Casas Viejas. The construction was evidence of the growth of the town and the influence of the new gentry; however, major support came from outside the community. The committee was headed by Don Rafael Bernal, the doctor of Medina Sidonia; the most important of the subscribers were Doña Josefa Pardo de Figueroa and her son, Don Salvador Hidalgo y Pardo de Figueroa, marqués of Negrón. The local population was represented by Don Antonio Vela as vice-chairman and Juan Pérez-Blanco as administrator of the collection.

Religious enthusiasm was less significant than social position in the community:

*José Monroy:* Juan Pérez-Blanco was a good man, responsible. He had a shop. He never would go inside the church. If there was a funeral, he would join the group as they went past his house on the way to the cemetery. Since he was one of the elders here for a long time, they made him head of the group to raise the subscription for the church, but it had nothing to do with his going to church. He didn't go to mass. He just tried to do the best that he could for the *pueblo.* He was mayor several times.

5. *Tierra y Libertad,* June 22, 1915.
6. *Diario de Cádiz,* June 22, 1915.

In mid-September the first stone of the church was laid, in a ceremony hosted by Don Antonio Vela and attended by the bishop of Cádiz and the marqués of Negrón, various other guests, the civil guard, the royal guard, and a large number of townspeople. It was a festive occasion, replete with speeches and toasts by the visiting dignitaries. Six altar boys carrying a crucifix and candles in holders preceded the bishop, who gave a brief talk before the laying of the first stone. The bishop, dressed in a white cloak and cape, pointed out to the honored guests and to the impoverished townspeople asembled at the outer circle that the church represented a sanctuary light:

Our mother the church loves all her children in the same manner. In her there are no class differences, there are no monarchs or needy. All are sons of a common father and are beloved brothers who are nourished with the bread of angels, a bread more nourishing than any earthly food.

After the holy litany, a shovelful of cement was thrown into the ditch, and the first block was slowly set down by a winch. In his talk afterward, the marqués of Negrón applauded the development of the village, which now could boast of solid buildings, streets, and a plaza. He assured the townspeople that they would soon have a bridge across the Barbate River and locomotives crossing the valley. The final guest speaker, Señor Bernal, then asserted his disbelief that there were any there "who shared the thoughts of a popular writer, Victor Hugo, who said that the church was a backward school and that when the church began, civilization halted."[7]

Following the ceremony and prayers, a lunch of fine wine, cakes, sausage, and ham was served at Don Antonio Vela's house. Afterward the marqués and the bishop set off together to the hill of Medina, where the bishop turned left for Cádiz and the marqués circled the hill to the right and continued on toward Jerez.

To construct the high new church, experienced masons were brought in from Seville and elsewhere. Local workers were employed in more menial tasks. For a time, even José Olmo was hired to cart stone with his burro.

*Pelele:* José Olmo told us not to bother about the church. He said, "The church will fall by itself when the new world comes into existence. The church is hypocritical. Now it exists because the way of life is hypocritical. When work is assured, when man can live from his work, the church will fall."

7. *Diario de Cádiz*, September 17, 1915.

# Eight
# The Death of José Olmo

## Medina Sidonia

Medina Sidonia was a more worldly town than Casas Viejas. Its social diversions were greater for every class. The workers congregated at the cafés and at the centro, while the señoritos took their coffee and wine at the casino, a private club for the affluent, where only members were allowed. The first floor of the casino was a bar; upstairs there were newspapers, a billiard table, and card tables for those who played *tresillo* or other games. Members came to socialize, to exchange impressions, and sometimes to transact business. Women were allowed in only during the fair, when the yearly dance was held. The casino was the logical place for the town gentry as well as notable visitors to congregate. The marqués of Negrón would visit there when he came to town for the day in his coach, or when he spent the night at his house on Calle Álamo.

Of more compelling social attraction were Medina's two houses of prostitution. As in all other business and social affairs, the houses and their patrons could be distinguished roughly by class. The women in the house on Calle Cilla, available for the price of one duro, drew a clientele with coin, including the señoritos from the casino. The madam was La Ninfa Tuerta ("The One-eyed Beauty"), who was considered a "hot" prize in spite of one eye with a whitish cast. Herself the mistress of an official of the *juzgado* (court), she was no longer available to customers. The house was divided into three or four small rooms, and one room was used as a salon for serving drinks. Her girls were young and usually well dressed. There were no sanitary facilities in the house, however, and the girls invariably had venereal disease. They all came from outside the town, and they usually remained three or four months before moving on. The changes had little effect on local hygiene. The danger of contamination seemed less of a deterrent after two or three drinks, and it was common for the bourgeoisie as well as the workers to prime themselves at the bar of Pepe Núñez, or one of the other cafés, before a visit to the house. Once there, another drink or two, and lights would go out. A visiting jurist, taken to the house of La Ninfa Tuerta for an evening's entertainment, complained that its occupants were so foul that he showed evidence of the clap by morning.

There was a second house above, next to the castle ruins. There, in a battered choza, María la Rubia ("Maria the Blonde") presided over four middle-aged women in her service. The choza was partitioned into three separate rooms, with an additional center room where drinks were sold. When curious youngsters gaped in at the window, one of the women, La Montañesa, would lift her skirts for a single cigarette. The men with more serious intentions paid a fee of two pesetas, their wages for more than two hard days in the fields. Those who would bargain for less could visit other women of the streets. Some years later, one of these, Chana la Zapatera (Chana the Shoemaker), would gain local fame for taking on a *cuadrilla* (team) of reapers from the province of Málaga for the cut-rate price of one peseta each plus a tip from the foreman.

The brothels were the mark of a complex order of civilization: a smaller, simpler town such as Casas Viejas had no such entertainment. The men from Casas Viejas would sometimes visit the houses in Medina, often with disastrous results. N.'s brother and brother-in-law went there one evening, and both returned with venereal disease. N.'s brother died of the disease, and his brother-in-law perished from the cure. The long-range effects of such visits could be seen in the high incidence of syphilitic children born in the town.

## The strike of 1917

Although Spain was neutral and country towns like Medina Sidonia were far from the battlefields of France and Germany, by 1917 three years of war had brought widespread hardship even to remote areas of Andalusia. Trade was curtailed, and scarcities of food and goods had sent prices soaring.[1] The Spanish government had lost prestige because of its failure to protest against German attacks upon shipping. The number of strikes in cities and countryside doubled during the year. In the cities, unrest was continual. In the countryside, protest flared at harvest time, the only season of year when the united strength of the campesinos could present a threat against the landlords.

1. Between 1914 and 1920, the cost of living more than doubled, with most of the increase taking place after the start of 1917. See Malefakis, p. 145.

A strike was declared in Medina Sidonia on June 1, 1917. As in every agricultural strike, its success depended largely on whether or not the fijos would quit their responsibilities and join the day workers. The landlords and government authorities took countermeasures. A strike committee sent to the campo to call out the fijos was arrested and jailed. The following day, a second group sent out to continue the campaign was also arrested. Word reached town that the group was being brought back in the custody of the civil guard. The workers' comrades and their families, José Olmo at their head, raced to intercept the march to prevent the men from being taken to jail. At the entrance to the town, Anónimo reported,

> José Olmo, taking the lead, climbed on one of the benches off the path and addressed the multitude standing on the level ground between the hut of the excise tax guard and the dung heap of Los Carros [the cliff over which garbage was dumped]. That man of action and rebellious spirit counseled calm and absolute order, and urged them to continue the march united up to the town hall, in order to demand the release of the prisoners. . . .
>
> The freedom of the prisoners was immediately obtained. These men, with their thin mattresses, blankets, and pillows on their backs, embraced their companions. And with shouts of "Long live the strike and the union of the workers!" this great scene came to a close without a single incident.
>
> The strike was ended satisfactorily with the triumph of the campesinos, demonstrating the great power of unity. The spirit to struggle was reinforced and invigorated.

In order to earn a livelihood after his return to Medina, José Olmo had again sought work with his burros transporting charcoal from the forests to town, collecting the bones of dead cattle from the campo, and delivering water from the spring below Medina to the houses above in the town.

> *Palmiro:* My father had a pack of donkeys and mules. We would go into the countryside. I was very little. We went into the fields and gathered chips where the charcoal was made, and he sold them. I accompanied him to fill bundles of hay. I had to lead a burra. Once I remember walking tied behind a burra when we went to sell the hay in Chiclana. He sold the hay and bought salt.

Olmo was once more in the center of the workers' movement in Medina Sidonia, alongside compañeros Rufino Gil and José García, nicknamed "Cabeza Cántaro" ("Big Head").

*Palmiro:* In Medina there were demonstrations then. He called the priests and the military "parasites." He said the workers wanted to live and work for themselves, and not for the parasites. I saw that he always had to pay for what happened and had to hide. One civil guard, called Caranico, who was friendly to me, told me, "In the barracks they put a pistol to his head and threatened to shoot him." He said, "I've never seen a guy with more balls than your father."

The major area of confrontation was to the north, in Barcelona, where regionalists, bourgeois capitalists, and anarchosyndicalists pressed their respective demands. The campesinos of Andalusia were spared the terrorism that took place in Barcelona between the years 1917 and 1923, when hundreds of persons were assassinated by *pistoleros* (gunmen) in the employ of both the sindicatos and the employers' federation. In Andalusia the struggle between landowners and campesinos would become bitter, but it would not descend to the bloodletting of the northern city.[2]

## The fall of José Olmo

In the closely contested elections of February 1918, Liberal politicians in Medina Sidonia sought a political alliance with a few anarchosyndicalist leaders. They pressed for the endorsement of José Olmo and one or two others in the hope of winning the votes of their followers. There were, of course, no anarchist candidates.

Anarchist policy had long considered politics and elections bourgeois snares, and there was particularly good reason to disdain elections in Spain. Despite the passage of the law of universal suffrage in 1890, elections were no guarantee of fair representation. Candidates were chosen by party leaders in Madrid, who favored politicians resident in the capital. These men, certain of being elected, ignored the needs of the majority of the population, who lived in rural areas. In the local towns, the cacique saw to it that the expected

2. In July 1917, Prime Minister Eduardo Dato, then in office but one month, ordered a tight censorship and suspended constitutional rights. In the Andalusian countryside the authorities could act with even greater impunity. In the region of Jerez and Medina Sidonia, following the orders of the minister of the interior, General Guerra, the outstanding anarchosyndicalists were called to the posts of the civil guard in the middle of the night. Twenty-eight men from Jerez, including Diego Martínez and Sebastián Oliva; and eleven from Medina, among them Rufino Gil and José García, reported to the guard. (José Olmo was one of the few to escape the net.) Once there, the men were arrested, their wrists shackled, and they were tied to each other by a rope. Then they were marched hurriedly toward the sea, where a ship waited to take them into exile in the African territories. However, although the march was made under the cover of night, they were observed, and the news was carried back to Medina. The members of the sindicato instantly organized a protest strike. The following day the news of the arrests and the strike aroused the mayor of Medina, who hurried to the capital to complain of the detentions to the governor. The men were ordered returned to their homes.

vote tallies for his district were returned. To control the results, common practice included manipulating the lists of eligible voters (subtracting and adding names to ensure a majority), paying voters to cast favorable ballots, and intimidating opposition voters to keep them from the polls. It was common for impoverished campesinos inconscientes to accept the small sums offered for their votes. Obreros conscientes never deigned to vote.

In the election of February 1918, José Olmo and other local anarchist leaders made common cause with representatives of the Liberal party, in order to help them defeat the candidates of the Conservative party. Olmo returned to Casas Viejas once more, this time in the company of José Núñez, to win votes for the Liberal politicians.

It was commonly believed that the motives for Olmo's actions were personal as well as political. Those who had aided in the cause of the Liberal party received modest rewards. José Olmo was offered steady work tending bar in the tavern owned by José Núñez, while his compañero Rufino Gil became a municipal gardener and watchman. Although the jobs were short-lived, they had disastrous social consequences for the men. José Olmo's identification with politics and his willingness to serve intoxicating drinks were antithetical to the goals of anarchosyndicalism. His actions seemed a betrayal of his own suffering. Gossip reported that he had been paid off and had opened the tavern with his own capital.

*José Monroy:* José Olmo lost the prestige that he had before he opened a tavern. The workers ran from him. They didn't see him as they'd seen him before. A tavern was the idea of a señorito. Pepe Núñez had various taverns. He provided a place to sell wine, coffee. I don't know what the conditions were, but Olmo was the proprietor. Olmo never spoke in the organization after that. We spoke to him, but in a guarded way.

The moral standards of the anarchist cause were now used to judge Olmo.

*Manuel Llamas:* José Olmo was a victim of circumstances. We respected him for what he had done. He was noble. But we no longer had *confianza* [confidence] in him, because of the economic question. He had taken money. Those of the Liberal group in town had provided him with money to buy a bar, and this was contrary to the principles of our organization. Because he had prostituted himself in this way, the rest of us no longer had confianza in him. At the end, he was losing his friends. Who knows what he thought? Whether he was losing his faith? But because of his disregard [of anarchist principles], the organization would not accept this awkward predicament. But he accepted the situation and therefore prostituted himself.

Bartending did not suit Olmo, and he soon returned to transporting charcoal. Still, he was unable to regain his reputation, his position of leadership in the centro, and the esteem of fellow anarchists. Ironically, José Olmo's fall coincided with the resurgence of the anarchosyndicalist movement in Andalusia.[3] The anarchists had been electrified by the Bolshevik revolution of October 1917 and the overthrow of the Kerensky government in Russia. Although the anarchosyndicalists would come to have small regard for authoritarian Soviet Communism, they initially deluded themselves into thinking that the revolution in Russia had been anarchistic and that the events would inevitably be repeated in Spain. CNT leader Ángel Pestaña's visit to the Soviet Union in 1921 and his reports of the massacre of the Kronstadt sailors would make it impossible for cooperation to continue between the CNT and the Communist Third International, but for over three years the anarchists looked to the Russian situation as an example of their own aspirations.[4]

3. Juan Díaz del Moral has left a powerful description of the events then taking place in the countryside: "Those who witnessed that time in 1918–19 will never forget that astonishing scene. In the campo, in shelters and settlements, wherever campesinos got together, wherever they met to chat about one thing or another, they always returned to one theme that they treated with seriousness and fervor: the social question. In their work breaks during the day (*los cigarros*) and at night after the evening meal, the most educated would read aloud pamphlets and newspapers, to which the others would listen attentively. What had been read was followed by corroborating perorations and endless praise. Not everything was understood: there were unknown words; some interpretations were childish, others were malicious, according to the character of the person who expressed them; but ultimately everyone agreed. It could not be any other way! It was the truth that they had felt all their lives, although they had never been able to express it. They read continually; their curiosity and their desire to learn were insatiable. Even on the road, mounted on horseback, with the reins or halters loose, campesinos could be seen reading; there was always some pamphlet in the saddlebag with their food. The number of copies of newspapers that were distributed is incalculable; each person wanted to have his own. It is true that 70–80 percent of them could not read; but this was not an insurmountable obstacle. The dedicated illiterate bought his own newspaper, gave it to a compañero to read to him, and then marked the articles that pleased him most. Later he would ask another comrade to read the article marked, and after a few readings he had committed it to memory and would recite it to those who did not know it. It was unbelievable! Although the favorites were *Tierra y Libertad, El Corsario, El Rebelde, La Anarquía y El Productor,* they sought and received copies of all the Spanish press opposed to authority, and some of the American. They read books and pamphlets of the founders of anarchism: Bakunin, Kropotkin, Reclus, Malato, Malatesta, Faure, Grave, Most, Mirbeau; and the Spaniards Anselmo Lorenzo, Federico Urales, Soledad Gustavo, Ricardo Mella, Leopoldo Bonafulla, José Prat, J. López Montenegro were and are familiar names to many campesinos; and there are sufficient numbers who have read writings of all of them. There was a book available in the province, as in almost all of Spain, that had a singular success: *The Conquest of Bread,* by Kropotkin. There was not an obrero consciente, even among socialists, who did not know it." (*Historia,* pp. 191f.)

4. Malefakis cites the statistics of the institute of social reforms concerning the number of strikes in Spain during this period. Although the data are far from complete, the overall picture is revealing: "From 1914 to 1917 an annual average of 231 strikes of all kinds were reported, 32 of which were in agriculture. The total number of strikes reported rose to 465 in 1918, to 895 in 1919, and finally, to 1,060 in 1920. The pattern was the same for agricultural strikes:

During 1919–20, as the CNT swelled in number and strength, José Olmo's fortunes fell to their nadir. Local gossip told of José carousing with José Núñez and other local political leaders. It was said that after a few fortifying drinks at José Núñez' bar, after laughter and loud talk, a few bourgeois companions would stroll with José up to the house on Calle Cilla, where they would be welcomed by La Ninfa Tuerta. A few more glasses of wine, and the lights would go out in the small partitioned rooms. It was rumored that José had contracted a social disease in one of these escapades.

Some of José Olmo's closest friends from Casas Viejas, however, never lost their faith in him.

*Pepe Pareja:* They meant to seduce him from his ideals, because he was a true anarchist. They used to take him to a house of prostitution. They did this to degrade him, to lower him, to change his ideals, and to get him ill with venereal disease. They wouldn't force him to go, but they induced him to in order to rid him of his ideas. He fell sick because of this. But he always kept the same ideas.

The final blow to Olmo's health, however, came in 1920 from a beating administered not by the civil guard but by the sons of a campesino family seeking vengeance:

*Anónimo:* José Olmo devoted himself during a certain time of the year to going out into the campo with his little donkey to carry out the tasks involved in making charcoal and later selling it, so that with his earnings he could alleviate the needs of his wretched home. It was during these occasions that he often visited a *rancho* [small cottage in the campo] inhabited by a family with whom he came to have a sincere friendship. In this family there was a young girl, a minor, who gave many indications of letting herself be dominated by her sexual appetites, in the face of which she was very weak. This young girl, in order to shield her lewdness, blamed Olmo for being lustful with her. She told this to her parents, and consequently two or three of her brothers waylaid him in the place called La Cañada de la Jari in the pasture lands of Pozo del Lobo.

Without asking for an explanation, they surprised him and gave him a brutal and bestial beating. Worn out, they left him helpless, stretched out on the ground. These cowardly aggressors fled quickly because of the panic that the criminal action produced in them. Everywhere the specter of calumny followed them. Years afterward this young girl married, and then later abandoned her home, husband and children, and went to establish herself in the brothels. The lie was brought out into the open.

---

these also doubled in each of the first two years of the *trienio* and increased still further in 1920. In 1918 agricultural strikes numbered 68, in 1919 the Institute reported 188, and in 1920 it listed 194" (p. 147).

After the beating José Olmo took to his bed. His tubercular condition became acute. His breathing faltered. Palmiro recalled that, "they said it was pneumonia. My father was never sick. He was stronger than an oak. I learned later that some of his own companions had beaten him."

At 1:00 in the afternoon on May 10, 1920, at the age of thirty-six, José Olmo died of pulmonary tuberculosis. At noontime a priest hurried to the house to marry him to his compañera, María Bollullo. Whether he was conscious or not in his final hours is not known. The church and civil records of Medina Sidonia show only that José Olmo was married and died on the same day one hour apart. Presumably the ceremony was carried out to protect his compañera and their children. One of the witnesses to the marriage was José Núñez. The week after José's death, Palmiro, Paz, Germinal, Salud, and Acracia were baptized and given Christian names.

*Palmiro:* They married him when he was dying. It was Pepe Núñez and some other scoundrels that had a priest marry him. He didn't confess. No, I don't think so. I don't know. I wasn't there when he was dying. When my father died, this man Núñez, the one who had the store, changed my name. Eight or nine days later, we went to the main church to be baptized. I remember that I was on a stool. They gave me salt. It tasted bad, and I spit it out.

Olmo's opponents thought that his death and supposed repentance signified the final defeat for anarchism in the area.

*G.:* All the anarchists were there around his house, to protect their leader, because he was the leader of them all. But when the priest went in and he confessed and was married, they left, and that was the end of anarchism in Medina Sidonia until the time of the Republic.

The anarchists themselves, however, saw in Olmo's death not the end of their organization but more proof of the capitalists' conspiracy against mankind. Manuel Llamas said, "He was a victim, a sacrifice for free ideas, one victim more, just like Christ."

The Olmo family soon left Medina Sidonia for the last time.

*Palmiro:* My mother sold the burras, and she opened a store; but after four, five, or six months, we went to Cádiz, and we stayed there, with all of the five brothers and sisters. My mother didn't know what to do. She was working. I couldn't work because I was very little. I liked school, and playing soccer.

Two years after the family arrived in Cádiz, Salud died of pneumonia. The family was reduced to desperate poverty.

*Palmiro:* Mother was working washing floors when I was at the school, the Colegio de la Viña. I left to earn four duros every month. My poor mother didn't have enough to pay the school. I went to work as a bellboy in a hotel, and at night I went to the priest at the church, who didn't teach me anything that I didn't already know by heart. When I reached fourteen, I said that I wasn't going back.

We were five brothers and sisters: Palmiro, "Flor de la Tierra" ["Flower of the Earth"], that's me; the second was Paz; the third, Germinal; the fourth, Salud; and Acracia. My father told me that Palmyra were ruins in a country that had been very anarchistic and was razed by the capitalists.[5] I believe that the ruins are in Greece. They were destroyed because the people there preferred destruction to humiliation. Everyone in Palmyra preferred to die rather than live under capitalism. The ruins of Palmyra. And that's the reason for my name, Palmiro, Flor de la Tierra.

When she was forty, in 1926, six years after her husband's death, María Bollullo had her photo taken. The portrait shows a strikingly handsome woman, with an intelligent face and brilliant black hair. She placed the photo side by side with the tattered portrait of her husband, José Olmo, taken years before. His photo shows a clear-eyed, broad-faced young man. For the portrait José had stood behind a cardboard model of a well-dressed man with a watch fob. The workclothes and rough hands of a charcoal maker are not visible behind the cardboard image.

The anarchist movement itself soon seemed to slip away. In 1924, the year after the installation of Primo de Rivera as dictator, anarchist activities were outlawed. The CNT was dissolved, and the centros were closed. Anarchist leaders were arrested, and anarchist newspapers and periodicals were shut down. From 1924 until the end of the dictatorship in 1930, the anarcho-syndicalists remained silent, although the core of the membership continued to meet and plan in secret.

5. See chap. 1, n. 1.

# Part Two

# Nine

# In the Time of the Republic

## Impending change

In October 1926, Don Francisco Gallardo, then the resident priest of Casas Viejas, sent a letter to the mayor of Medina Sidonia, requesting that the name of the hamlet of Casas Viejas be changed to the more dignified Benalup de Sidonia. The first half of the proposed new name was taken from the tower of Benalup, located two kilometers southeast of the village; the second half signified the town's incorporation within the township of Medina Sidonia. The request for the change had been brewing for some time. To the local gentry, the name Casas Viejas ("Old Houses") brought to mind a heap of impoverished chozas. In contrast, Benalup was associated with a romantic past—a line of watch towers manned to alert the inhabitants to danger.

In the thirteenth century, the Moorish defenders of the tower of Benalup had surrendered to the troops of Alfonso the Wise, and the tower had passed to Christian soldiers and then into the hands of Christian landlords.[1] In time a cortijo and a mill were located there, to take advantage of the nearby spring. The tower, however, had languished in a dell of relative quiet. The site of the village became the crossroads where there was traffic, an inn, an even richer supply of water, and a cluster of thatched huts, casas viejas.

The mayor of Medina Sidonia brought Don Francisco's request to the town council, and no objections being voiced during the thirty days required for hearing any, Casas Viejas became officially Benalup de Sidonia. The new

1. In 1271 Alfonso the Wise ceded the tower and the surrounding lands, including the site of the present town of Casas Viejas, to the first bishop of Cádiz, Fray Juan Martínez, and to the Franciscan order to which he belonged. In 1422 the estate was divided and sold: half went to the ecclesiastical community of Cádiz; the bishop sold the other half to Seville for 400 *doblas* of Moorish gold. A subsequent sale, in 1434, at more than twice the previous price, brought the lands to the city of Medina. In 1855 the lands were disentailed.

name, however, was rarely used by the local campesinos, who continued to refer to the hamlet as Casas Viejas. Maps of the area also carried the older name. Outsiders scarcely heard mention of the new name. Even the bishop of Cádiz, on a rare visit to the town in November 1934, almost a decade after the change, recorded in the book of baptisms that he had visited Casas Viejas.

In the same year that the town's name was changed, Don Antonio Vela's son, José Vela, known as *El Tuerto* ("One-eye"), had an imposing generator-powered flour mill built in the center of the town. The new mill soon supplanted the five water-powered mills in the village and others on nearby estates.[2] Since the new generator was powerful enough to provide electricity beyond its own needs, the kerosene lamps lighting the main street were discarded as well. A few electric light bulbs were strung at the main intersection. They cast a feeble light from dusk until midnight, when the power was cut.

If the new name of Benalup beckoned backward toward the past, the new generator, housed within massive, whitewashed walls, was a signal of another sort. The pale street lights it powered were a sign that modern ways were coming to the remotest corners of the country. Spain was struggling to accommodate its historical traditions to the modern world; and as electricity was generated in rural towns, the need to modernize the country's administrative machinery became clearer. A move was begun to shed the nation's heavy trappings of royalty and military orders, to cut its dependence on the central authority of Castile, and to distribute power and responsibility more widely and evenly.

The need for change throughout the country focused on the seat of authority in Madrid. In January 1930, in the face of growing economic problems, General Miguel Primo de Rivera was forced to resign his power to King Alfonso XIII. A year later, in April 1931, municipal elections in the major cities proved that support for the monarchy had since eroded. The elections mandated republican rule, and the king, unable to muster military support for his reign, went into exile. The Republic was declared.

The change was welcomed with great exhilaration throughout Spain.

*Anónimo:* With the advent of the new regime, there were demonstrations with flags and music, new national anthems to celebrate the great event. Exhilarated crowds invaded everything. There were continual shouts of "Hurrah for the Republic!" Speakers spontaneously took strategic places

2. A smaller generator-powered mill had been in use for ten years, but it produced only a modest electrical output and had had little effect on the town. Two years after the new mill was built, José Vela sold it at a profit to Juan Pérez-Blanco, the landowner and shopkeeper, and Manuel Sánchez, the schoolteacher. José Vela had lost the sight of one eye in a childhood accident when his sister damaged the cornea with a pair of scissors.

> and gave fiery speeches to the crowds that gathered around. They referred to the old monarchical regime with loathing phrases and insults, condemning its spiteful activities. . . . The names of streets were changed to others associated with the new regime. There was nothing but jubilation and praise! . . . All state organisms at the service of the humble classes! It seemed at first sight that everything had been transformed, that a social revolution had taken place as if by magic, and that capitalism had lost its enormous cruel and despotic power.

The new government faced a wide range of social, religious, and political questions. Agrarian problems varied from region to region and defied a single remedy. The small landowners and renters of northern and central Spain were troubled by the meager size of their land holdings, by population density, variable soils and rainfall, and lack of credit. In Andalusia landless day laborers rather than small proprietors made up the bulk of the population. Undercultivation on the large estates made unemployment and want endemic. The impoverished and impatient workers posed the most terrible example of injustice and the greatest threat to the stability of the new government. As a result, the major focus of agrarian reform was upon Andalusia.

Between April 14, 1931, when the Republic was declared, and July 14, when the members elected to the Cortes were seated, a caretaker government met in San Sebastián and assumed control of the country. The coalition, composed largely of bourgeois moderates, intellectuals, and working-class Socialists, pledged agrarian reform and moved to resolve the nagging issues of the countryside. In the first month they required landowners to employ workers in their own township before any others could be hired. When recalcitrant landowners withdrew lands from production, the provisional government, frightened at the possibility of agricultural paralysis, ordered landowners to continue farming in accordance with customary practices or face having their lands turned over to workers' societies. Then, in quick succession, agricultural workers were promised benefits already common in the industrial sector: the extension of the industrial accident law; "mixed juries" to arbitrate contract disputes; and the long-sought eight-hour day. The results of these endeavors raised wages and reduced hours; they also stirred hopes that even more audacious changes were still to come.

## José Suárez Orellana, first Socialist mayor of Casas Viejas

The proclamation of the Republic on April 14, 1931, and the creation of a provisional government prompted a series of swift entrances and exits in the local government of Medina Sidonia.[3] On June 5 the new local administration was settled. The newly elected councilmen chose one of their number, Don Ángel Butrón, to be the mayor of Medina Sidonia. Don Ángel in turn selected three council representatives from Casas Viejas, one of whom, José Suárez Orellana, he named deputy mayor of the smaller town.

In 1931 José Suárez was thirty-seven years of age and had lived in Casas Viejas for only one year. He was well known, however, since he had grown up in the mountainous region nearby, and had visited the town many times in the past to buy provisions. He had married a village girl and was widely respected for his intelligence and goodwill.

*José Suárez:* In the mountains it was a tranquil life. We didn't have newspapers, nor did we listen to the radio. We didn't have cars. It was a primitive life—work, eat, sleep. First cousins married each other because there were no other women. For fifteen years I was with my family in the campo. Then I began to go out into the world, and I began to see its calamities. My father would never leave the *finca* [farm], and I'd go to the town to buy things and then return. I was the eldest. I went to town to bring back flour and other goods. My father gave me all the authority I wanted, but he didn't want me to leave and settle in town. My father was old-fashioned. He didn't want me to go to town and be perverted, to catch a venereal disease from loose women. All the vices—wasting money, drinking. My mother felt even stronger about it. She wouldn't hear of it. The creatures of the forest—foxes, genets, badgers, and mountain cats—defend their young until death.

I wanted a profession, but they wouldn't allow it, and I didn't know much of the world. I thought that if I left the mountains, I would come to nothing and would have to return a failure, humiliated. I had no books or anything until I married and could buy them—not until I went to the lowlands. I came to live in the town in 1930 because I had married [in 1922], and had to earn money. When I arrived in the pueblo, I spoke with people in the cafés. I liked the social life. I had more capacity than the others. In the land of the blind, the one-eyed man is king.

José Suárez was honored but not awed by his selection as deputy mayor. He knew the needs of the town, which he described in the newspaper *El Pueblo* (August 26, 1932):

3. Don Andrés Núñez Suárez resigned as mayor on April 20, after only five days in office; his successor, fellow councilman D. José Núñez, was in the post two days. Then on April 22, Don Ángel Butrón was authorized by the central government to form an administrative committee for Medina Sidonia. To serve as deputy mayor in Casas Viejas, D. Ángel chose D. Antonio Alcántar Serrano, whose brother Baltazar had been deputy mayor for many years during the monarchy. Times were different, however, and Antonio held his post but one month until the municipal elections.

Upon being appointed mayor, I find myself saddled with a run-down holy cemetery adjacent to the town that gives off a foul smell and makes life difficult for the inhabitants of Casas Viejas. For in this cemetery there is not even the poorest shelter and autoposies must be performed right there on the ground. Most of the streets are unpaved and sewage water runs through them. The townspeople empty their garbage on the street, which is highly dangerous to public health and gives the town the look of a dump. There is no market place, garbage collection, or slaughterhouse. Slaughtering is carried out right there in the middle of the street, the same as a moroccan tribe might do. . . . There is only one physician for all the townspeople; there is no pharmacy. There are two national schools that have the capacity to accommodate twenty children but take in sixty. In spite of such overcrowding, which is unhealthy and detrimental, many other children are left without any instruction at all. As for the urban police, there are two town guards: one doubles up as a telephone operator, and the other is over eighty and should have retired, given his age and his inability to perform any service that requires agility. Stores must cater to the public at all hours of the day, in spite of the law. There is no town court, and in order to pay taxes one must go to Medina Sidonia, a trip that costs some people more than what they owe in taxes. This is of course unfair to taxpayers, most of whom are not wealthy.

As for social services, the monthly budget [for the entire town] provides twenty pesetas for milk and stew, and fifty pesetas for drugs.

Believing that Casas Viejas was being ignored, the new deputy mayor asked the mayor of Medina Sidonia for a larger share of township benefits—funds for a school, a market, lights, and street repairs. José Suárez now entered the world of politics and social ideas.

When they made me mayor and the people supported me, I began to study how to help them. It seemed to me that the Socialist party was the one that was going to do something for the workers. They were involved with social questions. I liked all that I read of their program. My father never knew anything other than work. But ever since I was young, I always felt the suffering of others as if it were happening to me; and when I came to town and saw my fellow human beings suffering misfortune and hunger, I became involved. There were people without food and clothing.

In Casas Viejas the Socialists had between thirty and forty members. I organized them and was the president. We had the most educated and intelligent people in the pueblo. The CNT had those who couldn't read or write.

## Juan Rodíguez ("Sopas")

Two other men from Casas Viejas were chosen to be councilmen: Juan Bascuñana, a well-liked shoemaker, and Juan Rodríguez, known by his nickname "Sopas," who had recently opened a small food store. Until the previous year, Sopas had been a campesino. A man of great endurance and strength, he was considered to be the fastest reaper in the town. No one could match him. When the teams of reapers would begin their work in lanes, he would soon be far out in front of the rest. In 1930, however, when he was thirty-two, Sopas realized that even the swiftest field worker could not keep pace with his debtors—the landowners and the storekeepers. "I made up my mind not to work in the fields any more. It wasn't worth it. I began to buy and sell. I saved a little and opened a store—bread, lard, potatoes."

In politics too Sopas seemed far in the lead. He had learned to read while he was in the armed services in 1918, and his opinions were respected. Soon, however, he would have a falling out with his fellow Socialists and would move his allegiance to the anarchosyndicalists.

## The workers and government programs

In the first days of the Republic, the landless laborers of Medina Sidonia and Casas Viejas were buoyed by the new reforms:

*Antonio:* In 1930 under the monarchy, we earned one and one-half pesetas or two pesetas. In 1931 under the Republic, wages jumped to four or five pesetas a day. In 1930 we worked from 7:00 A.M. to 7:00 or 8:00 or 9:00 P.M., according to the season, since from March to October the days are longer. In 1931 during the time of the Republic, we worked eight hours, apart from rest periods, in such tasks as plowing and winnowing. Reaping, we worked seven hours a day for ten pesetas.

During this period other rudimentary rights were resolved to the workers' satisfaction. Landowners in the township of Medina Sidonia finally honored a stipulation that workers would provide their own food rather than be supplied by the house. This had been the practice near Jerez ever since the strike of 1914.

*Manuel Llamas:* In this part of the province, workers supplying their own food did not come until the Republic. Before the Republic, they would put ten or fifteen or twenty or more men to one bowl. Now they would put out a wooden bowl and an additional clay bowl or two.

Under the eight-hour work rule, contract labor was greatly reduced, although some landowners anxious for a rapid harvest and some workers eager for a quick profit continued to perpetuate the system.

*Pepe Pareja:* Contract labor was prohibited under the Republic. Reaping was stipulated as a fanega of land in four days, working seven hours a day. Working by contract, it took three days or two and one-half days for a fanega. When the eight-hour day came in, contract labor was wiped out. But some always worked by contract out of selfishness. The worker, through ignorance or egoísmo, did not respect the rights of his fellow workers. In order to gain a few extra pesetas, he put himself in jeopardy. For a few pesetas he did harm to himself.

Workers eagerly awaited other far-reaching reforms. In the province of Cádiz in 1930, the cadastre showed that only 500 persons controlled 74 percent of the land. Many of these same 500 persons also owned estates in other provinces. In Cádiz the contrast between large and small landowners was extreme: ten large estates extended over some 55,000 hectares, but more than 40,000 small landowners owned fincas each covering less than ten hectares. In the township of Medina Sidonia, which included the village of Casas Viejas, eleven estates took over roughly one-fifth of the township lands, or about 10,000 hectares.

A vigorous program of land reform seemed assured when the national elections of June 28, 1931, brought the Republicans to power with a formidable mandate.[4] The possibility of reform, however, provoked a landowner reaction that placed the existing agricultural system in peril. In the face of an uncertain future, lands were withdrawn from production. Some large landowners, fearing that confiscation was imminent, tried to sell out; some avoided risk by pasturing cattle rather than sowing a crop; others kept their land in fallow to protest against the decisions of the "mixed juries" that often proved favorable to the workers. Little investment in crops and wages could be foreseen until the plans for land reform were clarified.

Small renters were badly affected by the uncertain conditions in the countryside. As lands were placed on the market or taken from production, the small renter had no land on which to sow a crop. Pepe Pareja's father was forced to sublet fifty fanegas in the township of Tarifa from another renter.

With the decline of the fortunes of the small renters, conditions worsened for the landless worker as well.[5] Even if land became available, for most

4. The election results gave an unrealistic picture of Republican unity and strength, since they were aided by a new election law that awarded the winning party 75 percent of the seats in each district regardless of the margin of victory. The anarchists had refused to participate in the elections, with the result that their views were not represented in the parliament; the conservative wing had not yet organized to mount strong opposition. Without rapid concrete results, the illusion of overwhelming Republican support soon vanished.

5. Even legislation earlier praised by the workers proved to have mixed effects. The decree enforcing municipal boundaries in hiring had strengthened local worker organizations, since it became more difficult to hire outsiders at lower wages or to import blackleg labor to break strikes. However, the decree also worked a hardship on migrant laborers from poorer regions and from barren mountain towns, who depended on seasonal work.

small renters the new wage levels were prohibitively high, and they could not hire workers as they had done formerly. Pepe Pareja's father had mature sons to aid him in sowing and harvesting, but others were less fortunate. Since the small holdings had been worked more intensively than the large estates, a major source of employment was lost. Instead of providing work for landless workers, small renters now joined the ranks of the field hands waiting by the plaza to be chosen for the few remaining tasks.

In the absence of a dramatic land-reform program, government attempts to alleviate hunger and unemployment turned back to the temporary and insufficient measures that had been favored by the monarchy and the dictatorship. Township officials were forced to provide a dole for the unemployed. The mayor of Medinia would send an allotment of 150 pesetas to Casas Viejas for distribution to the heads of households in the form of bread or money.[6]

## Forced allotment

Republican mayors had one other method to cope with excessive unemployment: they assigned workers to estates whether they were needed or not. It was commonly held that those who owned land had a moral imperative to provide work for those who did not, and so men were sent to various estates whether the land was sown, fallow, or used as pasture. If the land was not under cultivation, the men cleared the fields of rocks and did other odd jobs. Wages were one peseta.

*José Suárez:* If it rains fifteen or twenty days and a man is not working, he can't wait to ask the government for help. We had to look for the quickest way to help him. The mayors had power to find a solution to the problem. I would write down the number of men to go to each finca.

From the landowners' point of view, the assignments were deliberately provocative. Since the workers were not needed, they were not welcome.

6. Anónimo described the procedure used in Medina Sidonia: "[When] persistent bad weather and rain prevented the workers from going out to the campo, bread alms were established for families, just as in the time of the monarchy. This 'calamity charity,' as it was popularly known, consisted of two and a half *libras* [pounds] of bread per person. In order to receive this, the campesinos would form a long line according to a roster of their names and would pick up vouchers at the office of the municipalities. These vouchers were apportioned to all bakeries and were then exchanged for bread. These alms eventually had to be suspended—the bakery owners refused to cooperate, because the municipality would not pay them adequately. Subsequently, the workers were each given six reales."

*José Suárez:* Once I wrote down sixteen for Don Antonio Vela. He was above on the slope. "Is that agreeable?"
"No!" he yelled.
"Then we'll write another number. Thirty-two," I wrote. "Is that agreeable? If not, we'll write another number."
"Yes. That's agreeable."

Nicolasa Vela, Don Antonio's daughter, bitterly recalled,

The Republic was impossible. There was a great deal of unemployment. People went hungry. They didn't eat. The children were barefoot. And the Republic municipal governments expected us to bear the expenses. They'd send men to the finca to work or be paid. It was an unbearable expense. How could we do it? It would have been our ruin. How could we feed twenty men who weren't working?

The system was frustrating to the worker as well as to the landowner. The worker had to endure a humiliating situation, in which his presence was despised and he was either ignored or given onerous or useless chores.

## Landowners in Casas Viejas

Time had brought about few changes in land ownership in the township since 1914. The marqués of Negrón had remained the dominant landowner, with fifteen estates totaling roughly 10,000 hectares. His holdings comprised one-fifth of the township lands. Some of his estates lay between Medina Sidonia and Casas Viejas, and his lesser holdings included some of the irrigated huertas near the smaller town. In Casas Viejas the two most influential local families continued to be the Velas and the Espinas, but in the years since 1914 responsibilities in the family hierarchy had shifted. Don José Espina still managed the estate of his in-laws and so remained directly involved in local affairs. Don Antonio Vela, however, had a much diminished role. During the dictatorship Don Antonio had been considered the cacique of Casas Viejas; however, by 1931 he took much less interest in the personal management of his lands. Don Antonio was seventy-one years old and a widower. After the death of his wife, he gradually spent more time with one of his married daughters in Seville and finally lived there most of the year. His estate, however, remained intact, since he left his lands in the charge of an overseer instead of turning them over to his children.

Don Antonio's sons, Juan and José, both with large families of their own, managed their own affairs rather than their father's. José Vela, El Tuerto, rented lands and bought and sold cattle. Juan Vela had married well and managed the lands of his in-laws after his father-in-law died, only a few weeks after the marriage. Juan's wife, Ana Barca Romero, was popular in town for her charity to the poor. Although the two brothers lacked their father's wealth, in his absence they assumed additional importance in the village, and José Vela, in particular, was feared and disliked because of his dominating personality and his power. José Suárez considered him the principal agent of oppression in the town, and during Suárez's tenure as mayor, he fought to have the fees José Vela charged to small renters reduced.

The duke of Medina Sidonia rented his three fincas, Pedregocillo, Peñuella, and Herradura, to José Vela. José Vela paid four duros a fanega and in turn charged smaller renters twenty duros for each fanega. I said, "Send the duke a summons and tell him to come to Medina."

They said, "Are you crazy?" The duke is in Paris. He's not going to come because of our summons in Medina."

I said, "Do it."

And sure enough, the duke showed up. I said, "Will you allow this situation to continue? You rent for four duros, and Vela rents it for twenty. Why not rent to us directly?"

And he said, "Of course." José Vela was a demon.

## Juan Sopas and José Suárez

The inauguration of the Republic had opened government councils to men of varying classes and interests. Those who sought swift reform, however, found themselves in an impenetrable thicket of delay and disagreement. At first Juan Sopas and José Suárez worked together, but there was a falling out, and Sopas was removed from the council.[7] His name appears in the records of only one council meeting in Medina when he voted on an appropriation

7. In the elections of 1931, Sopas organized a protest vote at the polls. "To oppose the candidates that were named, I advised the people to vote for Ramón Franco [the brother of General Francisco Franco]. In 1929 Ramón had wanted to end the monarchy and start the Republic. To oppose the Republic, I said we would vote for Ramón Franco. And people followed me. We all voted for him. But they burned the votes." Sopas's strategy was little understood by the campesinos who followed his advice. Juan Pinto said, "In the election Sopas told the people to write in Ramón Franco's name. Franco had come to Cádiz to stir things up. My brother said to him, 'How are you going to do that when there's no place for it on the ballot?' The result was the the votes were thrown out." The campesinos had not realized that they had spent their votes solely in protest. They had voted as a bloc and were amazed to discover that their candidate had not received a single tally. A group of workers protested in front of the mayor's office, and the civil guard posted in the town arrived to restore order. For a few minutes, there was the threat of a violent confrontation until Father Gallardo arrived. Juan Pinto continued, "The people saw that there was no one on the left because of the deception that had taken place. This was when the town rebelled and wanted to move on Suárez. The whole street was filled. It was like an ant colony. Since Suárez was mayor, and the mayor had to be protected if the people move against him, the civil guard confronted the people, hitting several with their rifle butts. After two or three blows, the civil guard was ready to fire on them. But then Father Gallardo, who was in a café, came out on the street, asking, 'What's happening? What's

of a few pesetas to repair the instruments for the town band. Deeply offended by his dismissal, he shifted his allegiance sharply to the left:

When the Republic came in, I was put on the council, but then I became opposed to the group in power—Suárez and the rest—and then they were all against me. I was for the worker. They kicked me off the council. I saw that they weren't for the people. They were against everything. Then I opposed them and went over to the CNT. I moved to the anarchists.

In 1932 there were about 300 members of the CNT and about twenty to twenty-five in the Socialist party. The rich landowners were monarchists. There must have been fifty Socialists, but they weren't organized as such. When I moved from the Socialists to the CNT, the workers moved with me. They didn't have confidence in Suárez.

After Sopas left the Socialist party and the town council, he quickly acquired prominence in the anarchist ranks. Intelligent and articulate, he was appointed to the defense committee. Sopas soon became anathema to the Republicans. He had been one of them; now he seemed to want to sow discord and confusion.

José Suárez too soon found himself disenchanted with the failure of the mayor and the council of Medina to bring about change. Control over local affairs resided in Medina and not in Casas Viejas. By the end of August, Suárez resigned as deputy mayor, although he kept his seat on the council:

I had an illusion of life that was different from reality. I thought life was good and generous. But when I entered the world of social conflict, I found the world to be different. How perverse life is, how treacherous! How many there are to deceive you and to trick you! The ones who tricked me most were the ones I had depended on. There were so many quarrels.

There was a novel called *Tierra baja* ("Lowlands"), about a young man who comes down from the mountain. He is noble and simple. How many cars there are! How many trains! Look at the electric lights! This is paradise. But he's betrayed by a girl who leaves him without any money, and they want to put him in jail. How evil are the lowlands! It's an inferno. And he returns to the highlands once again.

Unlike the hero in the novel, however, Suárez remained in town and became the leader of the Socialist party in the area. In subsequent years he

---

happening?' And he told the civil guard, "That's it. Don't hit them. The people don't know anything. That's all. Show respect for me, and nothing will happen. Nothing will happen here.' Then the people controlled themselves; they moved back, and everyone went home. And that's the way things remained. It was Father Gallardo who controlled the situation." Violence was forestalled. The balloting, however, had raised suspicion about the Republic and the local Socialist leadership. Later people would recall Sopas's role in initiating the events.

would play an important role in the local agrarian cooperatives begun under the Republic. In addition to continuing as councilman in Medina, Suárez often acted unofficially as village spokesman when there was a difficult situation to be resolved.[8]

As 1931 came to a close, it was evident that the government lacked a clear, workable plan of action to alleviate injustice in the campo. In the coming months, attacks from the left and the right would reveal that the government offered scant leadership in the parliament and in the countryside. Hunger and unemployment would sharpen the issue of land use, while land reform seemed a forgotten promise.

8. When ten chozas burned to the ground later in the year, José Suárez wrote to the marqués of Negrón, asking for aid in rebuilding them. The marqués sent eight carts of cypress and additional poles. Suárez was later called on to return the favor to the marqués by resolving a dispute. "The mayor of Medina sent seventy men to work for the marqués of Negrón. The marqués didn't have tools for them; it was agreed that they would use their own tools, and if any broke he would pay for the repairs. After the work was over, he was presented with a bill for 2,000 pesetas. He called me out to see him and said, 'All these old tools aren't worth even twenty duros, and they give me a bill for 2,000 pesetas.' I said to him, 'Look, you have many cows. If a cow died, you would have lost 2,000 pesetas and wouldn't think anything of it. Just think to yourself that a cow died. I know that it isn't just, but you're confronted with seventy men.' He said, 'Suárez, you reason like a saint. Here's the 2,000 pesetas.' I said, 'Don't give it to me. Give it to the mayor.' "

# Ten

# The Split within Anarchosyndicalism

| | |
|---|---|
| La política es veneno | Politics is poison |
| Para el hombre productor. | To him who works the land. |
| Cañete del vividor. | It is the sponger's tool. |
| No contiene nada bueno | It contains nothing good. |
| Comer del trabajo ajeno, | To eat from someone else's labor. |
| Es su objeto principal | Is its main object. |
| Defender el capital | To defend capital |
| Con refinadas malicias, | With complete malice |
| Falseando la justicia, | Thwarts justice |
| Eternizando así el mal. | And perpetuates evil. |

## The CNT and FAI

After seven years of clandestine activity during the dictatorship (1923–29), the anarchosyndicalists could once again organize freely, with the increased possibility of achieving their revolutionary goals. The membership, however, rapidly polarized into its two principal constituencies—*cenetistas,* the relatively moderate members of the CNT, and *faístas,* the more militant revolutionaries of the FAI (Federación Anarquista Ibérica). The latter held dual membership in both the CNT and in their own secret organization.

The CNT, founded in 1910, had hoped to develop as a powerful trade union capable of dealing as an equal with industry and with government. As immediate goals they sought to improve wages and working conditions and to uplift the level of education. In contrast, the FAI, which came to life in a secret congress in Valencia in July 1927 during the time of the dictatorship, vowed to maintain Bakunist revolutionary and antipolitical traditions within the CNT. To guard their membership and their revolutionary temper, the FAI was organized in small, like-minded secret cadres (*grupos de afinidad*).

There was at least one such group within almost every CNT sindicato, and multiple *grupos* existed in the larger sindicatos.

Being a small town, Casas Viejas had only one faísta group, which was attached to the Federación de la Juventud Libertaria (Federation of Libertarian Youth), the youth organization of the FAI. In Medina Sidonia, however, there were three FAI grupos de afinidad. In the 1930s the most outstanding faísta in Medina was Manuel Llamas:

> I was thirteen when I joined the CNT, and when I was eighteen or nineteen I became a member of the FAI. It was all secret, to keep out the uninformed. We would talk to each other to see if we had the same idea. After four or five words one can see if there's an affinity, if one has trust. It's like love between a man and a woman—they meet, and after only a few words they know. Each group had ten or fewer members. When the number reached ten, another group was formed. The essence of the FAI was the idea of liberty. We were to propagate anarchism in order to emancipate the worker. We would propagandize among the youth—books, newspapers, talks—sowing education.

The attitudes of the CNT and the FAI toward the Republic were in sharp contrast. The cenetistas were inclined to give the new government the opportunity to fulfill its promises; the faístas, however, would not tolerate a reform-minded, bourgeois, democratic regime.[1] The effects of the struggle between the two wings centered in Barcelona, but they reverberated throughout every sindicato in Spain.

Cenetistas and faístas could often be divided by generation: the militant faístas who sought swift action were frequently young idealists, impatient for change and eager to arouse the membership to battle; the cenetistas were

1. In June 1931, the month of the general elections, the CNT held its first general congress since 1919. The meetings brought together spokesmen for the 511 sindicatos, representing more than half a million members. The congress, delicately balanced between moderates and militants, was opened by Ángel Pestaña, the secretary of the CNT, a trade unionist and moderate. The keynote address, however, was made by Rudolph Rocker, the Austrian anarchist theoretician. Rocker, whose talk was translated into Spanish, warned workers against being misled from their hatred of capitalism and the state by false promises and by Republican measures to improve their conditions. "The greatest danger confronting the CNT in Spain today is the democratic danger," warned Rocker (*Memoria del congreso extraordinario celebrado en Madrid los días 11 al 16 de junio de 1931*, pp. 24–25). The views of the moderates were expressed in subsequent debate by Galo Díez, who spoke of more than two decades of repression and frustration: "When we go before the people—those of us who speak in the forum, who write in the press—what do we speak of to the people? We don't speak of their desires, their needs, their misery, their rights. We speak always of the revolution. Is anyone encountering a revolution on the corner? For twenty-five years I have dreamed of revolution. Twenty-five years have passed, and I still cannot wake myself. . . . If we compare what the Republic gives us with what we desire, the Republic gives us very little; but if we compare it with what the dictator gave us, it is sufficient. It is a great deal" (p. 191).

generally older campaigners, skeptical of the results of a lightning engagement at the barricades. They were suspicious of the secret, elite leadership of the FAI and concerned over the possible carnage that their policies would bring. Having endured a long siege of repression, the cenetistas wanted to witness some progress toward economic equality and social justice in their lifetime. They feared that violence in the streets would encourage a right-wing takeover of the government and plunge them once more into silence and apathy.

The loose organization of the CNT enabled it to contain its diverse membership but also made it vulnerable to confusion and to control by a well-placed minority. The policies and actions of the CNT were conducted primarily by administrative juntas, beginning with the sindicato, whose junta consisted of a president, secretary, treasurer, and council members. At each step in the confederation, a representative was sent to participate at the next organizational level—from the sindicato to the district to the regional confederation, then to the national confederation.[2] In addition to the juntas, however, there were two major committee systems established as adjuncts to the juntas that had developed some autonomy: the *comités pro presos,* or committees for political prisoners, which worked for the release of prisoners and raised money for the relief of their families; and the *comités de defensa,* or defense committees, whose tasks were to stockpile weapons for the coming battle and to organize the shock troops who would bear the brunt of the fighting. There was confusion and conflicting authority between the administrative juntas and the defense committees as well as between the local and national organizations. Control of the organization's stocks of weapons and explosives, however, gave the defense committees the unique ability to initiate actions of their own.

2. In agricultural towns such as Casas Viejas, all the workers belonged to a single sindicato. The sindicato of Casas Viejas was united with those of Medina Sidonia, Paterna de Rivera, and other nearby towns in a *comarcal* (district) federation, whose seat was in Jerez de la Frontera. The various comarcals were then allied in a regional confederation, whose administrative center for western Andalusia was Seville. The regionals were tied to the national confederation. At each step in the confederation, the ruling body was an administrative committee composed of representatives from the preceding level. At the top level, the regional committees reported to the national committee of the national confederation. In the cities, the system was necessarily more complex. Looking at the organization from the bottom up the smallest units were the groups of workers of a single craft in individual shops and factories. These workers were represented within their establishment by a shop delegate. The succeeding unit, the section, was composed of workers from various factories who were in the same craft. Each major industry had sections comprising the various crafts. The sections were part of a sindicato that represented all the workers of a single industry. These industrial sindicatos (*los sindicatos únicos*) were the major units of the system. The sindicatos were united in a local federation, which was tied to a comarcal and then to the regional and national federations. This description of the CNT and the FAI is drawn in great measure from Alexander Schapiro, *Rapport sur l'activité de la Confederation Nationale du Travail d'Espagne, 16 décembre 1932–26 février 1933*, pp. 224–27. See also John Brademas, *Anarcosindicalismo y revolución en España (1930–37)*, chap. 1; and Gerald H. Meaker, *The Revolutionary Left in Spain, 1914–1923*, pp. 149 f.

Because of the decentralized structure of the CNT, it was relatively easy for faístas to extend their influence. A single FAI group might ultimately have its way throughout the entire organization. Undoubtedly the most influential FAI group was "Los Indomables" (the indomitable ones), in Barcelona, since it included Juan García Oliver, the strike organizer and street fighter, and Buenaventura Durruti and Francisco Ascaso Budría, who were strike leaders, bank robbers, and strong-arm men for the organization. Their influence extended beyond the city to the smallest country village where the split between the old guard and the new militants was mirrored.

To gain undisputed command of the CNT, the faístas purged the anarchosyndicalist movement of its moderate leadership. The paramount struggle had begun in the sindicatos of Barcelona, where faístas insisted that CNT committees be composed of members of both the FAI and the CNT. The faístas took aim at the secretaryships of those committees. They also fought for editorial positions on national and regional publications. In addition to assuming these positions of leadership, the young, uncompromising adherents of the FAI played the most active roles in organizing strikes and in the ensuing street fighting, where they gained the respect of their fellow workers. From their point of view, they were saving the parent organization from the weakening forces of reformism. They believed they were keeping alive the volatile spirit of revolution. By initiating strikes and insurrection, they hoped to ignite the masses and bring on the great revolution. In Barcelona, the strident tone of the FAI's *Tierra y Libertad* made *Solidaridad Obrera*, the regional newspaper of the CNT, and its editor Juan Peiró, appear conservative by comparison. In the growing argument the moderate cenetistas were characterized as *bomberos* (those who pump water to put out a fire), *traidores* (traitors), *vendidos* (turncoats), and *enchufistas* (opportunists). Faístas in turn were called *inconscientes* (irresponsible), *imbéciles* (imbeciles), *atracadores* (thugs).[3]

In the months following the congress of June 1931, as the power and direction of the movement passed into the hands of the militants of the FAI, the membership of the CNT found itself drawn into sudden, violent strikes that seemed to erupt without plan or forethought. Audacity rather than organization, it was believed, would bring the masses into action, destroy the government, and hasten the great day of revolution. In July, faístas organized an armed attack on the central telephone offices in Madrid. A crippling strike hit the Barcelona docks, and there were strikes by barbers, bricklayers, and taxi drivers. Throughout the remainder of the summer, other

3. Schapiro, pp. 26–27. The character assassination became so intense that at the Madrid congress in 1931 it was decided that any member of the CNT who insulted a compañero and could not provide proof would be expelled from the confederation.

waves of strikes brought out miners, fishermen, and metalworkers, among others. In the fall another general strike was called in Barcelona, where barricades were thrown up in the streets and shots were exchanged between workers and the police. In Andalusia as well as in the industrial north, strikes increased in number and intensity during the summer. On July 18 a strike was called in Seville, and a worker was killed in a fight with strikebreakers. Two days later, at his funeral, there was a pitched battle in the streets, during which three civil guards and four workers were killed, and hundreds were wounded. A general strike throughout the province was declared, and the governor responded by instituting martial law. The sindicatos were closed, and the threat of *ley de fugas* (shot while trying to escape) was imposed.

The moderates protested the awakening of hopes that could not be fulfilled, and they deplored the use of tactics that could doom the social reforms they had gained. But the FAI newspapers beat a drum call to action. By September 1, 1931, the increasing tempo of violent, uncoordinated strikes drew a statement of conscience from the moderates of the CNT. The *Declaración Treintista,* so-called because it was signed by thirty members, protested against revolution sparked by an audacious minority rather than by the great mass of the working class. They argued that a minority revolution, even if successful, would result in dictatorship. The thirty signers also deplored the use of violence for the sake of violence. The day following the publication of the *Declaración Treintista, Solidaridad Obrera* continued to attack the excesses of the faístas: "It's very simple to throw the masses into the street to receive blows from clubs and machine guns . . . but whoever does so, rather than a revolutionary, is a moral assassin."[4] The protest of the moderate treintistas, however, was drowned out by the uproar in the streets of Barcelona. Instead of reversing the trend toward violence, the treintista protest became the excuse for the expulsion of the signatories from posts of influence within the organization.[5]

The sporadic anarchist strikes, not yet strong enough to overthrow the Republic, had created an atmosphere of fear and uncertainty. Now the government responded to the growing disorder. In the summer of 1931 it formed a new force called *Guardias de asalto* (assault guards). Well trained and lightly armed, they were to take the place of the despised civil guard in problems

4. "Proceso de formación," *Solidaridad Obrera*, September 2, 1931. For discussion of these and subsequent conflicts between the CNT and the FAI, see Brademas, chap. 5.

5. Within six months Ángel Pestaña was dismissed as secretary of the CNT (and in December 1932 he was even expelled from the metallurgy sindicato), and Manuel Rivas, a faísta, was named in his place as secretary. In October 1932, Juan Peiró resigned his post as editor of *Solidaridad Obrera*. The struggle within the CNT would continue, but with these and other key posts in faísta hands, power tipped in favor of the FAI. The treintistas eventually published their own newspaper, *Cultura Libertaria*, and in subsequent months the war of words and deeds intensified.

involving social disorder. In October 1931, the Law for the Defense of the Republic was passed, giving the government, in the person of the prime minister, extraordinary police powers to act against those who defamed or attacked the Republic. Under the law the prime minister could repress the constitutional rights of vaguely defined enemies, deport persons to Spain's African possessions, and suspend publication of newspapers. Arguing for the law, Manuel Azaña, the newly appointed prime minister, asserted that it was necessary "to inform the nation that a Republic with authority, peace, and public order is possible."[6] Both left and right protested against the government's new dictatorial powers, and the turn of the year brought fresh violence and new assaults on public order.[7]

On January 18, 1932, there was a serious anarchist attempt to overturn the government. An uprising inspired by the FAI began in the mining district of the Llobregat valley in Catalonia. The uprising was not well coordinated with the national committee of the CNT, who said they were not informed of the plans. By the time a general strike was mounted, the uprising had been defeated. Its failure was the cause of bitter recrimination, and faístas accused Ángel Pestaña, the moderate leader, of undermining the strike. The government, meanwhile, turned to the Law for the Defense of the Republic. There were mass arrests, and more than 100 Anarchist leaders were slated to be deported without trial, among them Buenaventura Durruti and Francisco Ascaso, the leading militants and pistoleros of Barcelona.[8]

6. Manuel Azaña, *Obras completas*, vol. 2, *Defensa de la República (Sesión de Cortes del 20 de octubre de 1931)*, p. 67. See also José Peirats, *La CNT en la revolución española*, 1:51 ff.

7. Some of the most publicized violence had nothing to do with anarchosyndicalism, but the events revealed the deep social wounds of Spanish rural life. On December 31 in the town of Castilblanco, Extremadura, a demonstration by campesinos belonging to the Socialist Federation of Land Workers was confronted by four civil guards. When a group of women sought to enter the town's centro, one of the guards fired a shot. The enraged campesinos attacked the guards with their hoes and shovels and killed them. A week later, in the Castilian town of Arnedo, the civil guard fired into a group of striking workers and their families, killing six and wounding sixteen.

8. Before the ship on which he was imprisoned left for West Africa, Francisco Ascaso wrote a farewell message to his comrades: "Poor bourgeoisie that needs to resort to these means in order to survive. It shouldn't surprise us. They are in combat with us, and it is natural that they should defend themselves, that they should martyr us, deport us, kill us. No one dies without showing their claws. Beasts and men are alike in this regard. It is unfortunate that their claws should find victims, especially when those who fall are our brothers. But it is an inevitable law, and we must accept it. Let us hope the agony [of the bourgeoisie] will be brief. Metal doors cannot imprison our joy when we think about it, because we know that our sufferings are the beginning of the end. Something is breaking down and dying. Its death is our life, our liberation. To suffer in this way is not to suffer. On the contrary it is to live a dream that we have cherished for a long time, to assist in the development and realization of an idea that has nourished our spirit and has filled the emptiness of our lives. To leave, then, is to live! Here is our salute; we do not say goodbye but, rather, until a little while!" (José Peirats, *La CNT en la Revolución española*, 1:65.)

The government, however, soon yielded up some of its prisoners. Deportation without trial was too reminiscent of actions during the dictatorship. The resulting agitation as well as the threats against the lives of government ministers hastened the release of a few of the anarchists. At the end of November 1932, Durruti and Ascaso were back in Barcelona to join with García Oliver in hatching new plans.

## Anarchist agrarian plans

| | |
|---|---|
| ¿Dónde vas con paquetes tan listo<br>Que de prisa te veo correr? | Where do you go, bags and all,<br>In such haste that I see you running? |
| Al congreso de los anarquistas<br>Para hablar y hacerme entender. | To the congress of the anarchists<br>To speak and make myself understood. |
| El anarquista, ¿qué quiere decir? | What does the anarchist wish to say? |
| La gran falange obrera<br>Que reclama el derecho a vivir:<br>Rojo pendón, hay que vencer | The great phalanx of workers<br>Reclaims its right to live:<br>Under the red flag, we must overcome |
| A la explotación. | Exploitation. |

With the rise of the Republic and the growth of the CNT, anarchist dreams were reformulated. The exact form of agricultural collectivization had been slow to take shape. Initially, collectivization had been tied to the ancient commune, and plans consisted of reiterating general principles. As the sindicatos developed following the creation of the CNT in 1910, it became clear that these trade unions could provide the mechanism for a federated organization of collectives.[9]

Such a system would be in harmony with local customs of exchanging labor, services, and goods. It would eliminate the profit system so favorable to large landowners, middlemen, and merchants. It would bypass the campesinos' oppressors and creditors; and it would end the need for hard cur-

9. Brenan found that "the policy of collectivizing the land, which during the Republic was the Anarchist solution for all agrarian questions, seems to have been first adopted at a Regional Congress of the C.N.T. at Córdoba in July 1923. A resolution was then passed to the effect that parceling the land was a mistake and that the large estates at all events should be handed over to *sindicatos de agricultores*. This was the solution desired by the Catholic syndicates as well" (p. 181 n.).

rency, which was always in short supply among the poorly paid and debt-ridden workers.

*Pepe Pareja:* All the evil of this world is in money. If there were no money, there would be no war or any of this. How many crimes would not have been committed? As a part of social development, it will be discovered that people do not need money. There can be exchanges between nations of article for article—each valued for what it is worth. I believe that in this manner not only a single nation but the whole world can get along.

The new age introduced by anarchosyndicalism would implement the natural cultural laws that the government, the church, and their minions had subverted. The community would no longer fulfill the will of a distant and arbitrary government. The civil guard, now used to protect the property and goods of the exploitative class, would be obsolete. There would be no strange troops or police quartered in the town; no orders mandated by a land-rich cacique; none of the young inducted into the army to be mutilated in foreign wars. Workers with common needs would link arms across frontiers and end the folly of war.

The destruction of authority and of constrictive institutions like private property and the use of money would have immediate reverberations within the character of society. It would affect basic social units such as the family, where the tyranny of the male mirrored the authoritarian rule of the state. The end of arbitrary government would also introduce a new era of individual liberty. Personal liberty, however, would be under the guiding control of the collective. Freedom from state and church meant the enforcement of village codes and strict local control. Since the commune and the social code would be one, the natural social rules for the benefit of all would prevail. In the future collectivist society, conformity to law would come not from the armed might of the state but, rather, from community pressure. As Anónimo described it, "in the collective there is order. If someone does something wrong or harmful, he has to appear before everyone, before the community. That has great weight."

## The meetings in Jerez

In mid-January 1932, thirty-one delegates from the sindicatos attended meetings in Jerez de la Frontera to consider future plans and the ongoing situation of agricultural workers in the district of Cádiz.[10] They had to deal with a number of pressing problems. A minimum wage was needed to maintain a decent standard of living and to equalize the work force throughout the province. At harvest time, workers from the poorer mountain towns emigrated to the richer lands of the valley and plains and caused wages to drop. The delegates from Málaga complained that Portuguese migrant workers also undercut wage levels and that *manijeros* (hiring bosses) were exploiting migrant workers, charging them interest rates of 20 percent for loans. Impoverished migrants wandering the highways between jobs required aid from the compañeros, and means had to be devised to distinguish true workers from slackers, who would deplete their meager reserves. A drive for new members was essential, but although the meeting proposed to send two representatives to make a round of the towns, it was observed that the simple days of "saddlebag propaganda" by burro had passed. The resources of the sindicatos were too thin to meet the range of problems confronting them: even a modest program of rationalist education for children was beyond their means.

> Over three months ago it was agreed to open a center [in Paterna de Rivera] and to create the schools. The teacher was also selected; however, up to now they have not been able to open. It is precisely because we lack the economic means for the inauguration.
>
> We are experiencing a severe crisis in employment—as everywhere else—together with the constant cry for help coming from the jailed or the sick, and we have no choice but to attend to these matters with a gesture of solidarity and leave aside the original question of education for better days.[11]

The issues revealed the limits of their real social power; however, hopeful that the future was close at hand, the group also considered steps to be taken following a successful revolution. The sixth theme of the meeting was "Once the private ownership of land is abolished, how should agricultural production be organized?" The prime movers of anarchism, Bakunin and Kropotkin, had laid down basic principles concerning the land, and now the Spanish rural proletariat was eager to speak for itself:

10. *Memoria del primer congreso comarcal celebrado por la Federación de Trabajadores Agrícolas de la comarca de Cádiz, en los días 17 y 18 de enero de 1932, en Jerez de la Frontera.* Twenty-two of the delegates represented fourteen sindicatos in the province of Cádiz, with a reported total membership of 17,572. Nine other persons attended, including a representative from the district of Cádiz and another from the regional confederation of Andalusia and Extremadura. Six delegates, primarily concerned with local reactions to migrant labor, came from the neighboring province of Málaga.

11. Ibid., pp. 13–14.

We are in a position to know that these are things that will inevitably come up at the beginning of revolutionary victory and that we must face. . . . and resolve. [p. 21]

The author of the report on future agricultural organization, and first secretary of the Jerez congress, was Miguel Pérez Cordón. A promising young writer and orator, he was the son of Juan Pérez Mena, himself an ardent propagandist. Pérez Mena, a small independent wine merchant, bought wine from distilleries and then sold it to bars and cafés in towns throughout the region. The family had lived in Casas Viejas during the reign of Primo de Rivera (1923–29) but then moved to Paterna de Rivera, ten kilometers north of Medina Sidonia.[12]

Miguel Pérez Cordón worked as a campesino, but as his compañero José Vega Ortese recalls, he was intent on educating himself: "During rest periods at work, he would read instead of resting or playing cards or other kinds of nonsense. There were men like him who lifted themselves a bit more over the rest in their knowledge."

By the time of the Jerez congress, Pérez Cordón had gained attention as a writer and spokesman for the anarchist cause, publishing in *La Voz del Campesino* and *Solidaridad Proletaria* of Seville. During 1932 he was at work on a novella, *Amor y tragedia.*[13] Pérez Cordón was then twenty-three years old and personally quite attractive.

*José Vega:* He was short, slightly blond. He had blue eyes. He was slender, nice looking, attractive. Women liked him. He was egotistical, like all of us a little bit. He had a nervous temperament.

José Vega, however, saw one inevitable flaw in Pérez Cordón:

Cordón was a good lad. He was good, an idealist, very fine, very pure. In Cordón I saw a beautiful person. What happens to these people—and it is one thing that I detest and, since that is the way I feel, I will say it—when they are praised and admired by the rest, well, they become godlike, as we say here. One's vanity grows, and in a young man as he was, well, it is all the more natural, right? He thought himself godlike. His vanity grew greatly, and he thought himself superior to what he was in reality. That was what happened to Cordón. He was very good, very good, and intelligent. He had all the good qualities of a good person and a cultured man. But it was just as with Napoleon. Everybody created an idol and set him on a pedestal. In his vanity he believed himself a god. This is what hap-

12. Earlier, the family had lived in Algar (Cádiz), where Miguel was born.

13. *Amor y tragedia* was published as no. 330 in the series *La novela ideal,* November 30, 1932.

pened to Cordón. Nothing more. But apart from all that, he was very kind and a good man.

The plan that Miguel Pérez Cordón presented to the congress matched the collectives at the scale of the Andalusian latifundio.

> The tendency would be toward continuously expanding production. In contrast to present circumstances, with the campo subdivided into ranchos or cortijos, settlements would be established, each encompassing 4,000–10,000 aranzadas.[14]

Each of the rural settlements would be run by an elected junta of campesinos. The junta would report to the local council of production, which would oversee every type of agricultural enterprise.

There would be three types of land use: individual (family) farms, communes (small groups of like-minded individuals), and sindicatos. Thus, while the plan focused on the utilization of existing large estates, other types of small, independent holdings more common in the northern and central regions were not ignored. Small properties would not be confiscated after the revolution, and they would be incorporated into the overall plan.

> Doubtless an individual will appear who wants to work alone or with his sons without having to deal with anyone regarding the system of production.
>
> There will also be those with temperamental or ideological ties who by mutual agreement settle on a farm, whatever type of crop there may be, and work it communally.
>
> And we will also have the large majority of those who would work in the local agricultural sindicato, which would organize the work and also the distribution of the produce.[15]

The notion of community diversity after the revolution was supported by anarchist conceptions of individual liberty. "Practically speaking," noted Cordón, "it is possible to achieve perfect harmony among them all, with no need to hinder the freedom of the individual" (p. 20). Independent farmers and communes would frame their own organizations, and a representative from each, along with one from the collective, would attend an annual assembly called by the local council of agricultural production. The local council would include technical personnel with advanced knowledge of crops and soils, so that problems common to all agriculturalists could be resolved.

14. *Memoria del primer congreso*, p. 20. An *aranzada* is an ancient land measure of approximately five hectares. The settlements would each comprise roughly 2,000–5,000 hectares.

15. Ibid., p. 19.

Further up the ladder would be a zonal council and, finally, a national congress. The organization would parallel that of the free townships that would appoint representatives to the syndical organizations. Issues affecting widespread areas, such as the location of a processing plant, would be settled at the zonal and national congresses.

The largess extended to the small property holder had its practical and political side. In the Andalusian provinces of Cádiz and Seville, landless laborers composed the largest social class, more than 50 percent of the rural men, with small landowners making up but 10 percent of the rural male population. In many northern and central provinces, in parts of Galicia, Catalonia, Old and New Castile, Levante, and Biscay Coast, the situation was exactly reversed: the number of small peasant proprietors exceeded 50 percent of all rural men.[16] These small landowners were identified socially and economically with the lower classes. Many had joined the anarchist ranks, and their interests could not be threatened or ignored. At the first session in Jerez, it was noted that "even though each region may approach the problem in a different light, they all have the common desire to have the land available to all who produce from it."[17] While this excluded parasitic absentee landowners and profit-conscious entrepreneurs, small landowners could continue on their independent course.

The development of large collective settlements would not immediately eliminate other types of land use, but it was clear to some campesino theorists that the sindicatos would outproduce independent farmers and that the latter would become obsolete. The sindicatos could afford better equipment to cultivate the land, and a system of cooperative effort in production and distribution among them would greatly increase their capacity. As soon as the advantages became evident, it was thought that the small independent landowner and those in communes would be won over.[18]

There was no representative from Casas Viejas present at the Jerez meetings, and in fact Casas Viejas and Medina Sidonia were cited among those needing organization, towns "where the people were anesthetized to politics" (p. 9). The township of Medina Sidonia, with a reported membership of 500

16. See Malefakis, pp. 96 ff.

17. *Memoria del primer congreso,* p. 9.

18. "Each branch of production and each form of organization of agricultural work would compile its statistics, so that at the end of the year one would be able to evaluate whether the individual, the communal, or the collective form of production yielded better results. As the organization of large collectives, with their tractors and machines of every kind, would undoubtedly yield better results, everyone would soon join in this form of production" (ibid., p. 20). Cordón added one caveat in describing the complicated relationships: the collective would willingly aid an individual family or a commune, but the work performed must later be paid back in kind.

workers, was, however, represented by Manuel Llamas, who would carry back the results of the meetings:

It was our idea that once we gained control, we would reorganize the fincas. In each finca we would put one of our men as foreman to be in charge of the collective. We would decide how many men each needed. The produce would be put in a central granary, and individuals would take what they needed.

Before 1932 it was always our ideal to work collectively. The tendency was always the same from the beginning, from Bakunin and Kropotkin and the rest. We were not able to look for the means, because we were not near the realization. It was not necessary to do so. But we always looked toward the end. If the circumstances had merited it, we would have looked to the means. Only 10 percent of the workers wanted to work alone. We knew it was very difficult to change mankind, but we had this idea. One can never reach one's goals at the very beginning.[19]

Within a month, the report of the congress at Jerez was printed, and copies were circulated to newspapers and sindicatos throughout the country. The plans became the common themes of discussion in the centros obreros. There were myriad social problems to be anticipated.

*José Monroy:* If we had won, we would have made collectives. Each finca would be a collective. One would take what one needed for the day, and in this way we would get rid of egoísmo. If one had all one needed, why would anyone want more? Each day one would get bread and the other necessities of life. One would have what one needed for each day from a common store. Since this is a small town, everyone knew everyone else's needs. The rich could keep their selfish grasping for money. They could have it. We wanted only the land. We had no intention to take their houses. That was theirs. Each had his own house.

*Pepe Pilar* [*excited*]*:* No! Only what they needed. If they had extra rooms, take them. You here. You there.

*José Monroy* [*tranquil*]*:* Each person had his house. We were interested in the land.

*Pepe Pilar* [*angry*]*:* If one had too large a house, we would use the rooms.

*José Monroy:* But this situation never occurred. The land would be taken. No, we would not pay for the land. One is born without land. Only the

19. Díaz del Moral maintained that the Cordoban campesinos were heavily in favor of individual ownership: "Not just the masses but almost all their leadership think that the problem of the land is simply a matter of its division; very few trust the aptitude and preparation of these peasants for collective property. . . . If a referendum were possible, 999 out of 1,000 would choose land distribution: to each his hoe, to free himself from wages and not to serve anyone else" (*Historia,* p. 377). Brenan noted that a regional distinction should be made: "Except perhaps in some parts of Lower Andalusia, 90 per cent of the field laborers continued to prefer parcellation" (p. 181 n.). The evidence indicates that in Andalusia there was a wide range of belief, and the degree of support for collectivization depended on a variety of factors, including local organization and prevailing political and social conditions.

land of the large landowners, those with vast estates that lie unproductive, would be confiscated. We would not bother the small landowners; only if one had 4,000 or 5,000 fanegas.

The currents of philosophical and practical disagreements sometimes ran deep. Anarchists had always foreseen that the revolution was only a prelude to a more significant struggle requiring vast social change.

## *La Voz del Campesino*

Despite the unity expressed in the Jerez congress regarding the future reorganization of society, there was continual dispute between the moderates of the CNT and the militants of the FAI concerning tactics to achieve the revolution. As the membership discussed the shining future of collectivism, struggle for the mastery of the organization had already taken shape at meetings held the previous day concerning the regional newspaper, *La Voz del Campesino*. As in the confrontations in Barcelona, the faístas of Cádiz sought secretaryships of committees and editorial positions. Demanding greater enthusiasm and citing the need for galvanizing the masses, they attacked moderation as a sign of weakness.

The editor of *La Voz del Campesino* was Sebastián Oliva Jiménez, considered a moderate by all parties. A police report filed on Oliva the following year provides an appraisal of his character.

Sebastián Oliva Jiménez, aged fifty-two . . . is a person of good habits. In his beliefs he is opposed to all authority. At present he has lost the influence he had over the working masses in the campo because of his sympathy with the ideas of the treintistas. . . . He is a very active man dedicated to educating the sons of campesinos. He writes for some newspapers and had the responsibility of directing *La Voz del Campesino*, which was distinguished by the acquisition of his ideas. In his private life he enjoys a good reputation among those close to him with whom he cultivates friendship.[20]

The dispute concerning the editorship of the newspaper began innocently. The committee on the press reported that it agreed with the current goals of the newspaper and with its director, and suggested that he be given an assistant editor. The report also proposed that *La Voz del Campesino* be expanded to six pages, even though this would mean a deficit that would have to be paid for by the organization. At the outset of the discussion, Sebastián Oliva relinquished the chair "to make certain that the newspaper

20. *Dirección general de seguridad* (Cádiz: Jefatura de Policía de Jerez, 1933). Archivos de la Audiencia Provincial de Cádiz, sumario 6, no. XI, octubre de 1933.

issue is considered with absolute freedom," little realizing that the discussion would take a drastic turn.

The floor was then taken by Miguel Pérez Cordón, author of the agricultural report. An idealistic faísta increasingly impatient for the revolution, Pérez Cordón could express only dismay at the newspaper's lack of zeal:

Cordón, from Paterna, shows great surprise at the fact that the majority opinion should agree with the orientation of the newspaper, for he has visited several towns and found none in agreement with its ideology, because it does not conform to the norms of the CNT. He believes the current director should leave the directorship of the newspaper.

Saborido, from Arcos, in favor of the majority opinion, states that he has not heard a bad word about the ideology of the newspaper, and that all he has heard is that the paper is too small, that it should be enlarged, and that this is the consensus of the organization which he represents.

Cordón, from Paterna, again shows surprise that Arcos should favor the ideology of the paper, for several towns that he has visited do not think this way; he points out that the paper has not covered the abuses inflicted upon the working class in the last few days and states that the paper should have a more inflammatory style, to inject [a feeling of] revolutionary power among the workers.

Tejero, from Jerez, says that the ideology of the paper is all right and that even though the director's style is moderate, it is still revolutionary, and he does not believe that excitability is a must for a revolutionary; so he agrees with the direction of the periodical.[21]

Even as the chairman urged calm, Sebastián Oliva had decided on his course of action. Protesting that the paper was being evaluated on the basis of a single article, he said that he was submitting his resignation in order to end the debate. José Rodríguez Zaragoza, the delegate from the regional federation, acknowledging the underlying implications of a change in editors, assured the membership that the militants had no wish to take charge of the sindicatos or the newspaper. Adding that the newspaper could not publish articles to incite the masses if no one wrote them, he agreed that if a compañero more capable than Oliva were available, he should be appointed. In response, the representative from Grazalema argued that the workers, not the newspaper, would make the revolution. He returned to the original point that the newspaper should be enlarged so that additional articles could be added. At this Pérez Cordón bridled once more before the session came to a close:

Cordón states that he does not wish to talk about the periodical any longer, but that he does wish to reply to the delegate from Grazalema, and he says that we are headed for failure if the workers are not educated and

21. *Memoria del primer congreso*, p. 16.

incited toward revolution, because the Republic has not solved the most compelling problems of life at the national level. The workers are sick and tired of the Republic. A small fire burns out when one pours water on it, and one has to throw wood in the fire in order to brighten it. [P. 17]

The debate spilled over into the next session, when Pérez Cordón asked to correct the minutes of the preceding meeting, claiming that "he had not censured the administration of the newspaper—rather, what he had censured was its overall tone. He denies having anathemized Oliva as a person" (p. 19).

Deeply offended by the characterizations of himself and his work, Sebastián Oliva addressed to his compañeros some farewell comments as editor:

He states that he is worth little, but he also asserts that he has always devoted himself to the cause of the workers, and still does so. . . . He says he will print the newspaper until the new director takes charge of it. He continues saying that Galileo, Bruno, Servet, and many others were persecuted by their contemporaries for stating the truth and that he finds himself in a similar situation for the same offense. "Thus," he says, "I shall continue walking on the edge of the road, yielding the right of way to all others. [P. 19]

Chagrined, or perhaps unable to comprehend the wounds he had inflicted, Pérez Cordón remained the devout revolutionary in his response: "Cordón manifests surprise that Oliva should adopt an aloof attitude, and feels that he should of course continue in charge of the newspaper until the new director takes over" (p. 19).

Finding a new editor, however, proved more difficult than had been imagined. On the following day, the members were dismayed to learn that the next designee declined to accept the post, protesting that he lacked the ability. Galán, the delegate from Trebujena, created a new furor when he fiercely observed,

All we wanted was to add to the fire. Now, instead, we've succeeded in putting it out.

Girón, from Arcos, says that all this should have been said before, when the agreement was reached, and not now.

Galán replies, "I talk bluntly when it damn well pleases me."

GG. AA. [Guerrero] [says], "Once again this matter has taken on a personal note, and this change of direction is far from a personal matter, for this is not a question of blaming the conduct of individuals, but rather an ethical question, concerning only ideological orientation." [P. 25]

Finally, Cordón himself was offered the post, but he too refused, declaring that he was not qualified and that he had already been delegated to begin a propaganda mission. The damage to *La Voz del Campesino* was irremediable, and its publication would end in a year's time. The pool of literate talent was not so large that it could sustain internal warfare between militants and moderates. But the pattern was familiar. The moderate cenetistas stepped back or were forced out, and the militant faístas captured the dominant positions in the organization.

With somewhat less acrimony, the meeting accepted a suggestion by Pérez Cordón that two persons be named to undertake a proselytizing mission in nearby towns. Those designated would hold meetings and distribute literature. After others had declined, Pérez Cordón agreed to make the journey with another compañero.

Pérez Cordón was the natural choice for the task of propagating the anarchist cause. He was admired for his intelligence and, despite the ill feeling he had caused at the congress, was considered very simpático.

Some months later, far from the acrimonious disputes of the meetings, Pérez Cordón was at ease again in the world of ideals. Reflecting on the sights of the journey he had taken, he issued a challenge to the people of Arcos de la Frontera, an ancient town perched high atop a breathtaking cliff.

> Become worthy of these heights, breathing the enlivening and vital air of pure emancipatory ideas. Erase from your minds and from your behavior those thoughts and actions that belong to the past. They are a weight that prevents the brain from perceiving what is attainable—a libertarian Communist life—and that prevents you from feeling in your hearts all the anger and pain that fill us when we contemplate the present life of the proletariat. Yet all that anger and pain are necessary to attack with superhuman drive a society based on legalized hypocrisy, treason, hunger, and crime.
>
> Where are we going? From the past to the present we have come through centuries of struggles and bloody fanaticism! Now we are going from the present to the future—to a future that in the evolutionary order can never end. This future depends on us, on the efforts we make in order to shape it, on the love and faith we employ in building it. Our liberty, our peace, and our victory depend on the selflessness and idealism with which we begin.
>
> Let us coordinate our actions, and give them all the seriousness and resolution the future deserves and the present requires in order to eliminate [oppression]. Let us soak up the spirit of revolt apparent everywhere, and let us discuss with high minds the new economic and social structure of the future. In this dazzling period in the revolution and evolution of the hispanic soil, minutes will shape years, perhaps centuries.
>
> Let us fly high up, like the eagles, above all baseness, above all those behaving like frogs, cicadas, and toads, and become impregnated, saturated by our most sacred ideas, for they will be the guiding light in our road toward our libertarian future.[22]

22. Miguel Pérez Cordón, "Como las águilas," *La Voz del Campesino*, October 29, 1932.

# Eleven
# The Year 1932

## The new sindicato

During the years of the monarchy and the dictatorship, a small group of obreros conscientes in Casas Viejas had continued to meet secretly in the campo. The meetings, though infrequent, kept the small core together and in contact with their compañeros in other towns. When the Republic was declared, their discussions and meetings became open.

Some of the campesinos who had helped José Olmo form the first sindicato eighteen years earlier were still active—José Monroy, Juan Estudillo, Pepe Pareja—they provided continuity, experience, and a tie to the struggles of the past. There was no one, however, with José Olmo's commanding presence and his gift of oratory. Leadership and responsibility were divided among the older leaders.

*José Monroy:* After Olmo, after our struggles, came light, and instead of one there were twenty or thirty. We didn't have the same faith as those who followed Olmo, because there was no one here with the same amount of knowledge. There were some who were informed, but it wasn't worthwhile because they were neutral. They didn't act in the organization. Pepe Blanco, the tavern owner, was one such person. He had the faith, but he didn't manifest it with anyone. Juan Estudillo the shoemaker had great faith, but little knowledge. He didn't have the development, and he didn't express himself.

Since the beginning of the Republic, few formal moves to reorganize a sindicato in Casas Viejas had been made, but within weeks of the district meetings held in Jerez in January 1932, anarchist orators came to town to hold meetings and arouse the less committed workers. Pérez Cordón, who had been raised in Casas Viejas, was one of those who came to speak, as he reported later in the newspaper *CNT* (January 18, 1933).

With what joy the orators were received whenever a meeting was held. Tomás Torrejón and I went and gave the first meeting to constitute the sindicato in March of last year [1932]. Women, men, children—everybody came, perhaps principally to see me, because it was there that I had grown up. I left there with an intellectual battle concerning my beliefs—the profoundly religious ones, and the anarchist theories—new to me—that rapidly did away with all of the preoccupations that had seeped into my brain, negating my true temperament.

We spoke that night about everything: of the ruling inequality of the regime and of how one had a right to life without selfishness, hatred, without wars and suffering. We were called on another occasion and a crowd gathered larger than the first time. That's how the pueblo started to evolve, fighting with the present regime to win something by which they could sustain themselves, and dreaming of the day when it would be possible to create that society that some depict in books, others by word of mouth. Avid for learning, they read everything, debated, discussed, and chatted about the different modes of perfect social existence.

It was generally agreed that José Monroy, the goatherd, had the greatest experience in syndicalist matters, and he was chosen as the first president of the new sindicato. Monroy was then forty-two years old:

I couldn't read or write much: not then or now; but I had more experience than others in the sindicato. I had belonged to the organization in Medina and in Jerez, and I knew the ways of the organization. To open the sindicato, we had to write to the governor for permission and at that time name a temporary junta. Then there was an assembly to choose the officers—to confirm the provisional officers and to choose new ones. I went with Juan Martínez of Medina and Diego Balboza of Chiclana, who, though he was a man of the campo, wrote short novels. To secure the permission of the governor, we went to Cádiz for his signature. This was in July of 1932. Then we had an assembly, and I was named president. There was a secretary, a treasurer, and eight committee members.

José Monroy was well liked, and he was respected for his intelligence. He could explain sindicato matters, but he was not an orator like José Olmo. Nor did Monroy seek to establish overwhelming personal authority:

When I said something, they did it, but it was in the name of the organization. I couldn't do anything as an individual. I always brought everything to the assembly. It was not as though I were a dictator. People had to assume responsibility.

As expected, Juan Estudillo was named to a position of responsibility. Estudillo was then forty-eight, but he appeared older. His posture was stooped from years bent over, sewing shoes. A vegetarian, gentle and humble in manner, he was considered a pious saint of anarchism. Juan Estudillo maintained a steady correspondence with the anarchist press, ordering the latest pamphlets and novels, on occasion submitting newsworthy items to *La Voz del Campesino.*[1]

The ranks of the initiated were thin, however, and not everyone named to the central committee was familiar with syndicalist affairs. A young new recruit named José Villarubia Gutiérrez was designated secretary.

*Villarubia:* I was away, and when I arrived in Casas Viejas, they told me I had been named secretary of the centro. I was the first and only secretary. I was exactly twenty years old. I had always been a campesino. I had no experience in syndicalism either before then or at the time. I had no ideas. They had to name someone, just as they had to name Monroy president, and just as they had to name Juan Estudillo treasurer. There were also three committee members: one of the sons of Seisdedos, and two others. I didn't know anything.

The sindicato imitated the structure employed in Medina and Jerez. As José Monroy explained, "we had a defense committee, because Medina had one, and we copied them."

The officers had only limited goals and did not initiate any actions on their own authority.

*José Monroy:* We never called any strikes here. We were too small and without power. We always worked with Medina and Jerez. The strikes were called by the district office in Jerez, and we would go out for solidarity so that they couldn't shift workers from here to work there as scabs. We would not be traitors. Strikes always began in Jerez and Medina. We never thought of beginning a strike here.

An estimated 300 men joined the new sindicato. Most were campesinos, but workers of every craft participated, including a dozen or so shoemakers and an equal number of masons. Once the workers were united, they moved

1. One such brief note, entitled "Excessive Zeal," described a recent outrage perpetrated by the civil guard: "A youngster died in this village—the age is unimportant—and the father told a carpenter to make a black and red coffin, bearing the initials "C.L.": "comunismo libertario." The carpenter made the coffin and took it to the home of the dead youngster. Twenty-four hours later, the carpenter was called by the sergeant of the civil guard, the chief of the post, and a deposition was taken. Immediately afterward the father of the dead youngster was called in, and a deposition was taken. He was sent to jail, and there he has remained since the seventeenth of the last month" (*La Voz del Campesino,* July 2, 1932).

quickly to protect the general wage levels established for the district. If someone was not paying the wage listed in the sindicatos, he was boycotted until he agreed to the terms.

The centro, a large room located across from the market and just up the street from the plaza and the church, was in the heart of town. Its furnishings were spare: there were wooden benches and chairs and a large study table piled with newspapers and pamphlets. On one wall was a portrait of Bakunin, and, on the opposite side, one of Captain Fermín Galán, executed in 1930 for having declared an independent republic in Jaca, Aragón. The only other prominent decoration was the red and black banner of anarchism.

Normally the bars and street corners beckoned the workers from their overcrowded chozas. Now the centro became the gathering place to discuss social issues and to dream and plan for the future. Those who aspired to learn to read and write would sit around the large table studying. For those who had mastered the letters, there were books by Bakunin, Reclus, Kropotkin, Lorenzo, and Tolstoy; a copy of López Montenegro's *Botón de fuego* was worn with use. When meetings were called the elected officers would sit at the table facing the assembled workers. No wine was permitted inside the centro, but one could order a glass of mosto from the tavern next door.

It was common throughout Spain for sindicatos to take symbolic names for themselves. Those of the centro of Casas Viejas took the name Los Invencibles—"The Invincibles."

## Juventud Libertaria

Despite these signs of enthusiasm, even among the obreros conscientes themselves there was sharp disagreement concerning aspirations and tactics. These differences were often tied to a break between the generations. José Monroy observed "the old-timers thought one had to work and organize slowly. One had to form the organization and then arrange a system for the different organizations to cooperate with each other."

The younger members tended to be more militant, less patient about a cure to remedy the inequalities in land and wealth. They were the heirs of past failures to change the misery of field labor. Some were secret members of the Federación de la Juventud Libertaria, an organization formed by the FAI to enlist the youth in their cause. The FAI had gained a certain mystique due to their exploits and their faith, which even the older generation had to acknowledge. José Monroy put it this way: "Those in the FAI were more reliable. If you gave them a job, they did it. There was one FAI group here with about twenty members. The FAI was more secretive and demanded more confidence. They were action groups set up to defend the organization."

The one Juventud Libertaria group in Casas Viejas included Pepe Pilar, Manuel Quijada, and Antonio Cabañas Salvador, called Gallinito ("Cockerel"), a nickname common to the descendants of his mother's family. Gallinito was also known as "El Rubio de Cadizone" ("The Redhead from Cádiz"), because in his youth he had spent some years with family members living in the capital city. The introduction of both Gallinito and Pepe Pilar to the Juventud Libertaria came through their contacts in Cádiz, where both had belonged to the same group.

In 1932 Gallinito was twenty-seven years of age. Since he had been raised partly in the city, he had more schooling than the other campesinos, and he could read and write. However, he knew less about the agricultural tasks of the campo, and he usually worked as a peón in construction. In bad weather, he went to the campo searching for wild asparagus.

In stature, he was not an imposing figure. As José Vega described him, "Gallinito was short, frail, and homely. He had a fiery tongue, but physically he was frail."

Gallinito stood out from his companions, however, because of his revolutionary fervor. He was considered to be the leading militant in the town.

*Pepe Pareja:* Gallinito wanted things accomplished overnight—everything in his hands at once. There were several like that. He was ready to lose his life for humanity if it were necessary. Gallinito was an obrero consciente."

He was eager to embrace all the virtues of the obrero consciente, including vegetarianism, and so he went to talk to Pepe Pareja.

Pareja's belief in the anarchist cause was as great as ever. He shunned positions of leadership, however, preferring to remain independent and without official responsibilities. His work also took him away from town for long periods of time. Although he was now forty-four, Pepe had lost none of his strength and vigor and he was always sought after by those forming teams of reapers. For the most part, he followed the pattern established by his father—renting a few fanegas each year to sow a crop, so that he rarely sought work as a day laborer. When his crops were sown, he would set traps for birds, disdaining the gun for looped horsehair snares, which he strung along the branches where birds were likely to light. In his diet, like Juan Estudillo, he remained a vegetarian:

I was practicing vegetarianism, and Gallinito spoke with me about it. He wanted to come to our house to eat with us and to pay for what he ate. At that time there was a sergeant of the civil guard here and he said to me, "Come here. What's that fellow doing at your house?"

I said, "He comes to my house to eat. Since I'm a vegetarian, he wants to eat with me and be a vegetarian. There's no payment involved." I had to say something without casting suspicion on Gallinito.

The sergeant said, "Stop hanging around with him. He'll get you into trouble." He said it without malice, to warn me. He was trying to help me out. If I associated with Gallinito, I'd get into trouble. Afterward Gallinito didn't come again.

Gallinito kept away from Pepe's home, but he continued to follow Pepe's difficult regime, even to the extent of experimenting with naturalism and eating only uncooked foods. He collected and read a number of volumes on vegetarianism and naturalism.

Although Gallinito made every effort to become a true obrero consciente, there was some resentment toward him.

*José Monroy:* Gallinito wanted to do more than the others. He had been in Cádiz, and so he knew something. He had the faith and the intellectual capacity, but we didn't share our confidence with him. He wanted to know more, and he knew less. He was a pedant.

Although Gallinito was not popular with the older leaders, he served as mentor of a group of ten or so young women, to whom he taught the principles of anarchy. Gallinito was the novio of one of the most attractive girls in the group, seventeen-year-old María Silva Cruz, known as La Libertaria. María had earned her nickname because of the black and red neckerchief that she wore—to the consternation of the sergeant of the civil guard, who was responsible for order in the town. This flaunting of anarchist colors prompted the sergeant to take action, as Gallinito reported in *La Voz del Campesino* (July 2, 1932):

A young girl strolled in the street wearing a scarf around her neck in the distinctive colors of the CNT. The sergeant of the civil guard, chief of the post, tried to intimidate her into removing it, and when she did not agree, this "gentleman" at once snatched off the distinctive badge, showing no respect to the young girl or to the numerous persons who witnessed the act.

The incident did not intimidate the young women, whose number included María's sister Catalina, her first cousin Catalina, and her close friend Manolita Lago. They continued their activities, and at the end of the year the following notice was published in *Tierra y Libertad* (December 22, 1932):

A group of young women in the village of Casas Viejas have formed themselves into a group with the name of Amor y Armonía ["Love and Harmony"]. The group desires relations with all other groups of men and women. At the same time, it sends a strong salute to the political prisoners.

Others in María Silva's family were involved in the sindicato. María's father, Juan Silva González, and her uncle, Jerónimo (both known by the family nickname Zorrito—"Little Fox"), were affiliated; the latter was particularly known for his zeal. Raw and unschooled, Jerónimo Silva aspired nonetheless to be an obrero consciente, and he was named secretary of the committee to free political prisoners. Juan Pinto said, "Jerónimo Silva was rough and unpolished, but he had a great deal of faith in anarchosyndicalist beliefs."

María's family on her mother's side was also active in sindicato affairs. Juan and Jerónimo Silva had married two sisters, whose bachelor brothers, Pedro Cruz (known as Perico sin Hueso—"Boneless Perico") and Francisco ("Paco") were members of the centro. Perico, more vocal than his quiet-mannered brother, was a committeeman in the junta.

The four men, brothers and brothers-in-law, were also tied together by occupation. For years they had labored together as charcoal burners with María's grandfather, Francisco Cruz Gutiérrez, better known by his nickname Seisdedos ("Six Fingers").[2] Seisdedos and his family were known to be hard workers as well as sympathetic and generous people.

*Silvestre:* Seisdedos and his sons would go to the campo, cut wood, and make charcoal. He had a hut he had built there. When the river rose and the people could not cross to come to town and buy supplies, he would give them what food he had. Once a woman fell ill in the mountains, and her husband abandoned her. The family of Seisdedos took her in and cared for her until she died there in the mountains.

Seisdedos, almost seventy-two years old and a widower, no longer tried to keep up with the younger men. He rarely went to the campo, and he took little interest in sindicato affairs.

2. Gabriel Jackson speculated erroneously that Seisdedos might have earned "a sobriquet frequently attached to alleged thieves" (*The Spanish Republic and the Civil War, 1931–1939,* p. 101). In fact Seisdedos had a vestigial finger on his thumb, as do some of his descendants today. Rather than being considered thieves, Seisdedos and his family are universally praised by townspeople for their virtue, honesty, and generosity. One well-known tale of Seisdedos concerns how he caught a thief stealing the year's charcoal he had prepared. He held the man at gunpoint but then simply ordered him away rather than turn him over to the civil guard.

*José Monroy:* Seisdedos had always been in the woods making charcoal. When they returned to town, he came on occasion to the sindicato, but it was very seldom. He was a good man, reliable, but ordinary. He had no knowledge of the organization. Jerónimo Silva came more often and was more intelligent, as was Perico, Seisdedos's son.

## The general membership

The sindicato had quickly claimed the allegiance of the overwhelming majority of workers in Casas Viejas, but its membership was far from single-minded. Only a small percentage of the men aspired to be obreros conscientes. There was a sharp division between the men "with ideas" and the other members concerning commitment to the anarchosyndicalist cause. Although they had common problems and concerns, there was a wide gap between those who played cards in the bars and joined the sindicato as a social necessity and those who went to the centro to study and to participate in planning social action.

*Juan Pinto:* The people who were preparing themselves for politics—Monroy, Juan Estudillo—all those lived in a different way from ours. They did not get together with us, because they had different ideals. They were outside. They lived apart. They did not care for our kind of conversation, because they had very different ideas.

I belonged to the CNT because they were the majority group. But I didn't know anything. How could I have had any ideas?

*Cristóbal:* I belonged to the organization, but what did I know? I couldn't read or write. I was interested, and besides, one couldn't get work otherwise. But how should I know what changes there were going to be? They said things would be better. We would have our necessities without using money. Since all the villages and the cities were involved, we expected a change of government, a change in the system. What the exact system would be I'm not too sure.

Some who were members in good standing refused to become deeply committed to sindicato affairs.

*Carito:* I was a member of the sindicato, but not one of the junta. They said if one didn't sign with the sindicato, one could not work. I was asked to join the junta, but I said, "If you put my name down, I'm walking out that door and not returning."

"OK," they said, "we won't force anyone."

Comunismo! Nonsense. If you have a finca, do you want me to take it from you?

Other members were often passive during critical times.

*Andrés:* I was in the sindicato. There was no help for it. There were plenty of strikes before the uprising of 1933. They put me in the commission to call the men in from the fields. But I never went. I wasn't going to call anyone from work. I stayed in my house.

While everyone could recognize the injustices and the inequality they suffered, many had never thought of larger social issues, and some who had were skeptical that any action by the CNT could better conditions. For others, the sindicato was another external force directing their actions. As Silvestre said, "Everyone belonged, because you had to in order to get work."

At times the leadership found it necessary to act against those who refused to join but tried to take advantage of the cooperative operations the sindicato had established:

*Encarnación Ruiz:* Alejandro and someone else had collected asparagus and wanted to sell them to a collection point, but Pepe Pilar and another man said they couldn't sell them there, because they weren't members of the sindicato.

While those less involved in sindicato affairs preferred not to disturb established social relationships in town, some of the militants, such as Pepe Pilar, were implacable and impatient foes of the status quo. Pepe's small, slight frame belied his fearlessness. During the monarchy he ran the risk of carrying messages between groups of anarchists, and he was preparing a small cache of weapons for future use. In the town he was not afraid to voice his objections to representatives of the social order. On one occasion, when he was one of a group of nine men helping to repair several chozas that had burned down, he crossed swords with the priest himself, Don Francisco Gallardo.

*Pepe Pilar:* The priest sent to Las Lomas and to Espartina to obtain the cane and thatch, and we did the work. Afterward, when we were in the last house, the priest said to me, "Let's get a half *arroba* of wine and a lamb to inaugurate the houses that are finished."

But then the priest and I had a discussion. I told him, "I don't believe that Jesus Christ was the son of God. I believe that he was a good man. But they killed him because it didn't suit their interests to have a man with such ideas around—just like today." I told him of our sufferings and our bitterness.

He said, "We're not at fault. Capital is at fault."

I said, "You're defending capital."

He said, "I don't have to work wearing this cloth. I have my own money."

"Exactly. You're with the capitalists. You're defending not the church but capital. You're not for the poor man. You work for your own kind.

How is it that you have the right to everything and we have nothing? Why do you have money and I have none?" I asked him how much money he earned, and he said sixteen duros a day. And he went off.

We didn't have the wine or the meat. The rest of the men were mad at me. It was my fault. But I didn't want his meat or wine.

## Strike

In the agricultural provinces, spring always brought the threat of strikes. The season was the prelude to the struggle between workers and landowners to protect their respective interests in the year's harvest.

On March 28, 1932, the construction workers of Jerez went out on strike. Five days later in Chipiona a workers' assault on the carabinero barracks left two workers dead and several others wounded. That same week there were sympathy strikes by workers in Jerez and in Cádiz, Sanlúcar, Arcos, Villamartín, and other cities and towns. The campesinos of Medina Sidonia and Casas Viejas also joined the strike. In the campo of the Medina township, ganaderos left their cattle unattended. The landowners then protested to the provincial governor, who "declared that abandoning cattle in the campo would be considered an act of sabotage, and the authors of such an act would be detained."[3] He had the sindicato of Medina closed and ordered some arrests.

For their part, the campesinos made a distinction between beef cattle and milking animals. They were herdsmen first and strikers second.

*Pepe Pareja:* I remember a worker asked me, "Can I go to milk the goats?"

I said, "Why not? Milking the animals is necessary in order to save the animals, and the milk is needed for the children and the aged. Yes, milk them. But cattle? Let the owners guard them themselves. Don't give them water or food."

Pepe Pareja's attitude was fairly widespread, and elsewhere in the campo goatherds milked the animals in their care to prevent harm from coming to the herds. They were duly applauded in the local press for avoiding damage to the economy of the area.[4] By April 8 the strike was over, and those workers who had been detained were set at liberty.

It appeared that there would be peace in the campo through the harvest. A good harvest was beneficial to both worker and landowner. It was the season when the worker could pay off the debts he had accumulated during

3. *El Guadalete* (Jerez), April 5, 1932; see also the issue of March 29, 1932.
4. Ibid., April 7, 1932.

the winter; it was also the landowner's opportunity to take in his profit for the year.

However, in the following month of May 1932, a new crisis flared in the countryside, when landowners petitioned to enlist Portuguese workers for the harvest. The desperate Portuguese reapers would work for lower wages than the Andalusian campesinos. The governor, acting under the new law of *términos municipales* (township boundaries), which prohibited the importation of outside workers until all local workers had been employed, decreed that landowners could not act on their own: "In order to utilize Portuguese workers, owners and [local] workers must agree that they are needed."[5] In a telegram sent earlier to the minister of agriculture, Diego Martínez, secretary of the Jerez CNT, had already refused to enter into such an agreement: "Because of the permanent crisis of unemployment, Portuguese workers should not be permitted entrance at harvest time."[6]

The dispute continued through May, with opposing regional newspapers carrying on the duel. *La Voz del Campesino* reported that 10,195 workers were ready for the harvest in the area, while the conservative paper *El Guadalete* asserted that there was no guarantee that sufficient workers were available, adding that even if there were local workers unemployed, they lacked the skills necessary to harvest the crops (May 10, 1932).

The conflict widened at the end of May, when workers went on strike in fourteen towns in the province. There were boycotts and lockouts in the cities and the campo, and some random acts of violence occurred. In Cádiz a bomb exploded in the window of the town hall. The strike spread to the smallest towns. Pepe Pilar said, "To show our unity and solidarity, we went out too. We struck in Casas Viejas and in Medina to give them more force."

As usual, when a strike was declared in the campo, the major problem was to enlist the fijos on the estates to join the walkout. Pepe Pilar, who as a teenager in the 1914 strike had followed his brother to the campo to drag recalcitrant workers back from the fields, now fell heir to the same task:

When there was a strike, the younger group would go to the campo and talk to those who were working.

"What are you doing here? We're striking for all of us. You're hurting our cause."

The older ones among us would reason with them, but the younger ones would say, "If you won't come, we'll drag you back." And they would put their hands on people. It happened various times.

"If you won't walk back, we'll drag you back."

5. Ibid., May 19, 1932.
6. Ibid., April 20, 1932.

Confrontations between strikers and the civil guards were now likely to result in bloodshed. The memory of Castilblanco in Extremadura, where four civil guards had been beaten to death at the turn of the year, was still fresh. The workers were frustrated and angry, and the guards were taut and primed for action. In San Roque several workers were wounded when government forces disrupted a demonstration and fired into a crowd. By June 2 the provincial government had succeeded in dampening most of the disturbances. On June 3, however, there was a serious incident at Medina Sidonia.

*Pepe Pilar:* In Medina they sent a committee of ten to twelve men to convince those on the cortijos reluctant to strike to join us. They went out to the finca of Pocasangre [owned by the marqués of Negrón]. Knowing that the guards were waiting for the committee, the rest of the pueblo went down to welcome them. The civil guards were up above by the castle. When the men went to meet the committee, the guards shot into the crowd. They killed one and wounded two more. People fled in all directions.

The action was unprovoked. There had been no confrontation, and the civil guards, some distance away, were in no danger. As Pelele described it, "there was a pair of guards in the mayor's house, and they got drunk. Then during the demonstration they shot a couple of workers. I was one of those wounded."

Blame for the tragedy fell not only on the civil guards and the town's Republican mayor but also on the national politicians who had armed the Republic with the Law for the Defense of the Republic, which gave the government exceptional police powers. Some anarchosyndicalists also criticized the militant faístas for their part in the poorly planned events. Anónimo protested that in calling the strike, the militants had acted completely on their own and had not consulted the membership.

The following February at Carnaval there was a song about the tragedy. It is said that the song was forbidden, but it was sung everywhere secretly.

| | |
|---|---|
| Pueblo de Medina, | Town of Medina, |
| Tierra donde he nacido, | Land of my birth, |
| Aunque muy lejos | Although I'm far away |
| Nunca te olvido. | I never forget you. |
| Hoy te recuerdo | Today I remember you. |
| Con pena y dolor— | With pain and sorrow, |
| El tres de junio | On the third of June |
| Del treinta y dos. | Of the '32. |

| | |
|---|---|
| Un día de luto | A day of mourning |
| Que sufrimos los obreros | When we workers remember |
| Por las almas perdidas | The souls of those |
| De aquéllos que han asesinado, | Who were assassinated, |
| Que murieron a traición | The ones treacherously killed |
| Por las balas despedidas | By the shots discharged |
| Por aquellos fusiles | By those rifles |
| Que fueron disparados | That were fired |
| Por la reacción. | By the reactionary forces. |
| La multitud se desplegaba | The multitude fled |
| Y los heridos decían, | And the wounded were saying: |
| Que en el mundo todo se paga, | In this world everyone pays (for his crimes) |
| Que el castigo les vendrá un día. | And they'll get their punishment one day. |

## Andrés Vera, the new priest

On June 1, 1932, Don Francisco Gallardo, who had been the priest of Casas Viejas since 1925, left the parish for a new assignment. Don Gallardo had been a popular figure. He enjoyed tobacco, wine, and hunting. He was well liked by those who shared his tastes. Even those contrary to the church were included among his friends. After the campesinos' ballots had been discounted in the 1931 elections, Don Gallardo—not a timid man—had been able to stop the ensuing confrontation with the civil guard. It would have been well to have a man of his temperament in the village during the difficult months ahead.

Three weeks after Don Gallardo's departure, his successor, Don Andrés Vera, arrived. Don Andrés was a quiet, shy man, at home with church rituals and uncomfortable in his encounters with the workers:

I came to Casas Viejas as a young priest in my second assignment, from a parish in the region of Gibraltar. That's where I was raised. The difference was startling. In Gibraltar there was plenty; in Casas Viejas, there was poverty and misery. There were only three or four who had land around Casas Viejas, and of course when the land is badly distributed, there is more misery. The syndicalists didn't bother me, but when I walked down Calle San Juan, there would be whistles. There was no other street, and one had to pass there. Some of them would not go to church for burial but would inter the dead without me—not many, but a few. And they would not allow themselves to be entered in the church records. They tried to influence people to stay away from the church. I didn't know the syndicalists. They were in a different environment, and I was there only a short time. I was involved in spiritual matters.

When asked how the men found work—did they shape up in the plaza?—he answered, "I don't know. I was in the church and in my office, so I didn't see those things."

Almost symbolically, as the clerical office changed hands, so did the civil guard. The sergeant who had kept such careful watch over the members of the sindicato and had confiscated La Libertaria's neckerchief was transferred elsewhere. Another officer was posted to the town, Sergeant Manuel Alvarez García, who had just been promoted to his present rank in June. Sergeant Álvarez was the son of a retired sergeant of the civil guard. He was forty-five years old, and he had been a guard since the age of eighteen. The change was a welcome one for the town. The new sergeant was less authoritarian than his predecessor. He occasionally sat in on a card game with townsmen, and he quickly became well liked.

In mid-June, shortly after Don Andrés arrived, a group from Cádiz came to burn down the church. They had brought along cans of gasoline, and they urged the townspeople to join them in leveling the church. There were also raucus opinions expressed concerning the priest. Isabel Vidal recalled that some women said, "Let's beat up the priest!" And she had objected, "The poor fellow—he's just arrived." Isabel's son, Juan Moreno Vidal, added: "Someone suggested castrating the priest and afterward converting the church into a schoolhouse. Since it was so high, they could add a second tier and have one floor for boys and one for girls."

But the villagers, syndicalist or not, could not be driven to harm the church or the priest, and they prevented the outsiders from carrying out their threats. Juan Vidal, no friend of the church, was one of those who spoke out against lack of reason. His daughter Isabel reported, "My father was never a member of the sindicato. When they came to burn the church and the saints, he said, "Fight against whomever you have to, but it's cowardly to destroy the saints."

The leadership of the sindicato felt nothing would be gained by the proposed attack. As José Monroy put it, "we had no interest in the church at that moment. [After the revolution] we could use the church for a central institution, as a granary or a school—something beneficial."

Even the more militant members had no taste for pillaging the church in their own town.

*Pepe Pilar:* Eight or nine came from Cádiz, all steamed up to cause us trouble. This was during the Republic, before the uprising took place. They were from the Communist party, from Russia. They spoke to Suárez since he had proposed agrarian reforms and those things. They asked Suárez if there was an organization here with sufficient spirit to follow this movement. Their intention was to burn the church. They painted the hammer and sickle on doors and on the pavement. They accused us of being fairies—not capable of doing anything, because we didn't respond to their call to go and burn the church. They wanted to organize us, but Suárez told the boys, "You don't have to do anything. These people have come here to create a conflict, and we shouldn't do it." And it wasn't done, nor were they listened to, nor did anyone join them or take part in anything.

## The duke of Medina Sidonia

The financial affairs of the ducal house of Medina Sidonia had reached the end of a long decline. Beyond the palace in Sanlúcar de Barrameda, little remained of the family's once unsurpassed riches. The palace itself belied the condition of the duke's dwindling purse: it was in extraordinary condition, and its polished marble steps were virtually unworn. But of course no one lived there. The duke resided in Madrid, not in Sanlúcar, and the palace merely housed the vast archive dealing with the administrative history of Andalusia, once the principal domain of the dukedom. Sanlúcar had earlier been an active port in the flow of ships between Spain and the New World. The parrot that accompanied Columbus on his third voyage in 1498, now stuffed, perched in full plumage in a richly appointed room of the palace, a frozen memory of past glory. Little else remained to the duke other than the palace, the mementos, and his illustrious title.

The family's property had been divided and subdivided through generations of inheritance. The Napoleonic Code, which ensured that at least one-third of the inheritance would be divided equally among the heirs, served to diminish the inheritance of the titleholder in each generation. Spendthrift habits and indolence hastened the loss of wealth. The palace in Madrid had been sold and the duke lived in a hotel. The ducal lands were nibbled away, turned into cash, and the estates fell one by one into the hands of newly rich entrepreneurs. To meet expenses in 1925 and in 1930, the duke sold off some holdings in the township of Medina Sidonia. By the time of the Republic, he was left with less than 1,000 hectares in all of Spain, roughly half of them situated in the province of Cádiz.[7] The inheritance continued to shrink. In May 1931, the duke sold a small tract of forty-eight hectares near Casas Viejas to Don Antonio Vela. By that time the duke was forced into the embarrassing position of asking Don Antonio's sons, Juan and José Vela, for advance rent on two of his remaining estates, Cantarrana and Peñuela.

Late in the summer of 1932, the duke sold still another estate near Casas Viejas to Don Antonio Vela, who was then living in Seville with his daughter. This last transaction, however, had more to do with the duke's meddling in national politics than with his reduced means. On August 10, 1932, General

7. Malefakis, p. 68.

José Sanjurjo, the marqués of Rif, formerly head of the civil guard, had led a right-wing revolt against the Republican government. The monarchist plot was badly bungled, and its supporters were easily defeated. There was no popular wave of support for the general, contrary to what the plotters had expected; when General Sanjurjo declared martial law in Seville, where he was headquartered, the workers went out on strike. Sanjurjo attempted a hasty escape to Portugal but was arrested en route. It would soon become known that a number of grandees, among them the duke of Medina Sidonia, had been enlisted in the plot to overthrow the Republic. Upon General Sanjurjo's arrest, the plotters suddenly found themselves in jeopardy. Some, like the duke, rushed to convert their properties into cash to carry into exile until a more successful revolution could tumble the Republicans from power.

*Sebastiana Vela:* The duke and his brother, the marqués of Molino, came to see my father. The duke was a short, very slight man. The marqués of Molino was just his opposite—tall, elegant, and heavy. The duke wanted to sell the estate of El Asiento del Duque ["The Duke's Chair"] before leaving. He sold the estate hurriedly, because he needed the money, and fled to Paris. He didn't return until the time of Franco.

## Land reform

Paradoxically, the right-wing revolt had a decisive impact on land reform. After the initial reforms by the provisional government, land reform had languished. For a year and a half the Cortes had debated fruitlessly on the depth and extent of reform needed, the compensation required for expropriated land, and plans for subsequent settlement. The Agrarian Reform Bill finally proposed had been bottled up in the Cortes for four months, under attack by all sides. The monarchist revolt brought the deadlock to an end and goaded the delegates to action. Unfortunately, the final bill reflected the tortuous compromises made by contending interests. It was a complex law, difficult to administer and often misdirected in its effects.[8]

A major defect of the bill was that it did not distinguish sufficiently between problems in the northern and southern sections of the country and, as a

8. There were four types of land to be confiscated: land left uncultivated, land continuously leased for twelve consecutive years (except in the case of widows and others unable to work the land); land left unirrigated, where irrigation was available; and, in great measure as a result of the Sanjuro revolt, the *señorío-jurisdiccional* lands of the great nobility (which in feudal times had been under the authority of the nobility without being their legal property, and which they had expropriated after 1811). The law regulated the amount of land that could be owned in accordance with land use. Those who cultivated their lands directly could keep a greater percentage in excess of established limits approved for vineyard, orchard, and grain fields. The bill promised to have great effect on the *ruedo* lands—those lands within two kilometers of a village. See Malefakis, p. 184.

result, between the effects of the law on large and small landowners. The confiscatory provisions had the effect of frightening and alienating landowners with small and medium-size holdings in areas where legislation enabling confiscation was actually lacking. Unfortunately, the bill also followed the accepted practice of determining land wealth in each township rather than calculating it on a national scale, with the result that holdings diversified in various townships could escape proper assessment in the reform program.

The Republic began the process of reform by cataloging land holdings for the first time in 1933, with the Inventory of Expropriable Property; however, expropriating land and organizing agrarian settlements required more time and greater determination than currently existed. The proposed agricultural settlements came under attack locally from landowners whose estates would be confiscated. The plans were criticized by the workers as well. Many campesinos, whether steeped in anarchist ideals or in the principle of private property, objected to the proposed wage system of the new settlements and to the edict that ownership of the land on which they would live and labor would always belong to the state. Nor would anarchists lend their support to a palliative measure that would tend to serve the state by pacifying only some of the working class.

In all, the law proved so complicated and unwieldy, and the government so sluggish in carrying it out, that it became to everyone little more than a source of bitter disappointment.[9]

## The Espinas' new house

On June 24, the campesinos of Jerez de la Frontera went out on strike, and a week later they were joined by construction workers. At the same time, the campesinos of Casas Viejas struck, because some landowners refused to agree to contract terms and tried to hire workers outside of the labor exchange. Despite these conflicts, there was relatively little labor trouble during the summer of 1932, and the men reaped the most abundant harvest in many years. Ironically, the bumper crop aggravated the difficulties in the countryside. Earlier estimates had forecast a wheat shortage; and with rising prices driving up the cost of bread, the government had ordered the importation of a quarter-million tons of wheat. The glut of foreign wheat and the high local yield caused wheat prices to drop dramatically. Lands were withdrawn from production to drive the price up, with the result that unemployment increased. The workers were concerned with survival rather than profit, and they could not survive without work. Manuel Llamas recalled, "there was

9. See Jackson, *The Spanish Republic*, pp. 84 f; and Malefakis, pp. 358–61.

no work at all in 1932. In those days there was only unemployment, misery, and punishment."

Throughout Andalusia there were rumors of plots to discredit the left and to throw doubt on the Republic's ability to keep order. In the late summer and autumn, it was believed that fires had been deliberately set in the dry pasture land to create turmoil in the region.[10]

*José Monroy:* Occasionally there are fires in the campo, but you can see that they are rare. Fires were *set* in 1932. The campo was insured, and the landowners set the fires themselves or paid people to set the fires. If the crop was bad, they could collect from the insurance company. But the aim was also to make the Republic look bad. They said the fires were the fault of the sindicatos, and as a result they threw many people into prison.

In the autumn of 1932, the land was dry. As usual, no rain had fallen during the summer months, and the autumn rains were late. The soil was baked and cracked, and what vegetation remained was brown and crumbled underfoot. In the past at such times of crisis, the statue of the Virgin would be carried from the church to the road overlooking the fields and then down to the Barbate River, where the people would pray for rain. The inauguration of the Republic, however, had unleashed a current of anticlerical and antireligious sentiment, and now the tension between worker and landlord made a pilgrimage appear unwise.

*José Suárez:* They didn't want to take out the Virgin for fear of someone doing her harm. So in Espina's house they took down an image of the Virgin, a small image, and put two candles in front of her, together with a glass of water and a stalk of wheat, to show her that rain was needed.

Although times were bad for most, the Espinas had decided to construct a spacious new house. It was to be located directly on the plaza, adjacent to the church. One side wall would be just across the street from the civil guard barracks. The property was narrow, without room for a garden, but living in such close proximity to the church was a sign of prestige. Since the front door opened onto the plaza, it would be possible for the women of the household to attend mass without having to go into the street itself. The Espinas intended to keep their other home as well, just twenty-five meters down a nearby street. The older house was set on a much larger land area, as befits a cortijo, with an ample center garden and adjoining stables and storage houses. The Espina family would continue to live in their first home during the week, but on Saturday nights they planned to sleep in their new

10. See *Tierra y Libertad,* June 24 and July 1, 1932.

house. When they arose on Sunday mornings, they would have the luxury of walking a few short steps across the plaza del Socorro and into the church.

By the end of December 1932, the lower foundation walls facing the barracks of the civil guard had been constructed. The thick new wall, head-high, gave the appearance of a battle breastwork.

1. José Olmo
(posed behind a cardboard frame of a suit)

2. María Bollullo, wife of José Olmo

3. Assault guards and a civil guard walking through Casas Viejas

4. A civil guard and an assault guard in a house-to-house search in Casas Viejas

5. An assault guard on the destroyed mud wall of the choza of Seisdedos (ABC/Serrano)

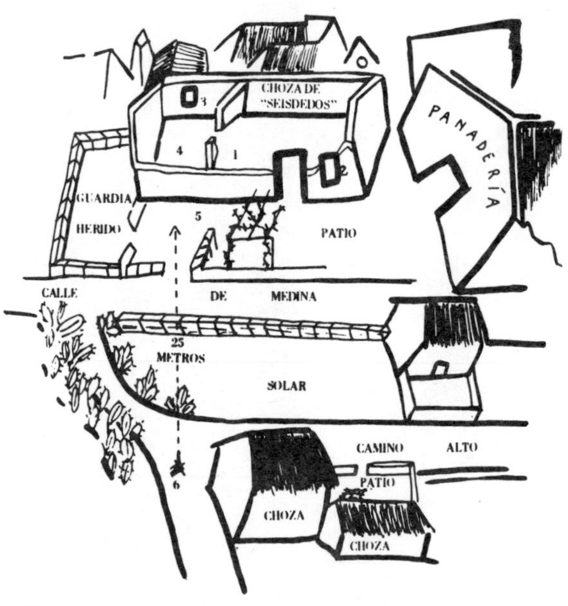


6. Plan showing the location of the choza of Seisdedos (CNT, February 22, 1933)

7. María Silva, *La Libertaria* (ABC/Serrano)

8. Lieutenant Artal of the assault guards
(*on the left*)

9. Captain Manuel Rojas Feijespán

10. The victims of Casas Viejas

11. The Espina house (1966)

12. Campesinos (1966)

13. Juan Pinto (1966)

14. Hortelano (Gallinito's brother)

15. Young campesinos weeding the fields (1971)

16. Sharing the gazpacho at work (1971)

17. Calle San Juan, Casas Viejas (1970)

18. Hortelanos (1971)

19. Shepherd and son (1970)

20. Bowlmaker (1970)

21. Campesinos preparing to pedal to work (1966)

22. Young boy after a day weeding in the fields (1966)

23. Young boy after work (1966)

24. Women watching a class of children (1966)

25. Neighbors (1978)

26. Mother and child (1970)

27. Young woman (1970)

28. Grandchild (1970)

29. José Rodríguez Quirós (Pepe Pareja) and Antonia Márques

# Twelve
# Insurrection

## Barcelona

In the fall of 1932, the Republic faced a new test. Having survived General Sanjurjo's uprising from the Right, it was now confronted by the possibility of an anarchist revolutionary strike. This danger promised far more serious consequences than the abortive monarchist rebellion.

The crisis began in November, with the threat of a railway strike. Underpaid railway workers, who earned between three and one-half and four and one-half pesetas a day, wanted a minimum wage of eight pesetas. In addition, they asked for full pay after retirement, accident security, and an eight-hour day. The railway companies refused to meet the workers' demands, arguing that unfavorable economic conditions made it impossible for them to pay higher wages or to provide additional benefits. They offered the workers a raise of only fifty céntimos a day. The gap between the two sides was enormous, and both workers and management refused to yield. The railway workers threatened to strike and turned to the CNT for support.

At that time the most militant faísta cell in Spain, Los Indomables, the Barcelona group that included Juan García Oliver, Francisco Ascaso Budría, and Buenaventura Durruti, met to consider this new development. What caught their attention was not the economic disruption that would result from a railway strike. More intriguing, as Juan García Oliver pointed out to his compañeros, were the strategic opportunities of a transportation paralysis. When they launched their revolution, the major battles would be fought in Barcelona and a few other urban centers. It would be essential to prevent government reinforcements from reaching these areas. This meant that elsewhere the civil guards and army troops would have to be pinned down by local uprisings. A transportation strike would weaken further the government's ability to move its forces to respond to the insurrection. With the army immobilized, the aroused populace would join the battle. The day would be won once the soldiers, already propagandized by anarchist literature and oratory, came over to their cause. García Oliver proposed that the railway strike be their long awaited moment to rise.[1]

Los Indomables presented their heady dream of revolution to the regional committee of Catalonia and won its approval. The date of the rising was to be determined by the forthcoming railway strike. The revolution was only weeks away.

Aside from the feasibility of revolution at that time, was the expected railway strike a realistic possibility? Railway workers were represented by two competing unions—the Sindicato Nacional Ferroviario of the UGT (Unión General de Trabajadores), and the CNT-affiliated FNIF (Federación Nacional de Industria Ferroviaria). The UGT, which controlled the large majority of the workers, had virtually ruled out a strike, and there was little hope that they would walk out in sympathy with the FNIF. Trifón Gómez, secretary of the UGT union, did not believe it possible to mobilize the workers, few of whom had revolutionary aspirations, in the more than eighty different companies that composed the rail system.[2] Besides, if the FNIF declared a walkout on its own, it could command only a minority of the railway workers. And the membership of the FNIF itself was divided and uncertain of striking. It was clear from the outset that a general railway strike was unlikely.[3] During the month of December, however, the CNT pressed the FNIF to strike, and as the possibility waxed and waned, faístas envisioned the tantalizing idea of toppling the government. Ignoring the uncertainty of the situation, they hurried their preparations through faísta-dominated committees. Acting on instructions from the national committee of the CNT, the national defense committee and the Catalonian defense committee stockpiled arms, bombs, and ammunition. The local *cuadros de defensa*, the small groups

1. A. G. Gilabert, *Un héroe del Pueblo: Durruti;* see also José Peirats, *Los anarquistas*, p. 88. My account of the inner workings of the CNT and FAI at the time of the revolt relies on Alexander Schapiro's confidential report on the CNT for the International Association of Workers. Schapiro, a highly esteemed Russian anarchist, arrived in Barcelona in December 1932, with the aim of organizing the Iberian Secretariat of the International Association of Workers. His intent, however, quickly changed. "From the first day of my arrival in Barcelona on December 16, I realized at once that the national committee of the CNT was embarking on a movement of far-reaching breadth and that all considerations of internal organization would have to be subordinated to the events that were underway" (p. 4). Schapiro decided to concentrate on the functioning of the organization and the disturbing factionalism in the CNT; but before he could begin his study, the insurrection of January 8 began. His goal then was "to provide what is most pressing—to search for the causes of the events, to fix responsibility, and to draw conclusions that have implications for the movement in general" (ibid.). For an analysis of the circumstances in Barcelona that led to the January uprising, see Brademas, chap. 7.

2. *El Sol*, December 31, 1932.

3. Schapiro, pp. 6–7.

of shock troops under García Oliver's leadership, were alerted to the coming battle.

Few doubts about the possibility of the railway strike were expressed in the anarchist press, and to readers it appeared that a walkout was inevitable. The weekly *Tierra y Libertad,* once a major source of educational, literary, and doctrinal works to educate the workers, was now the strident voice of the FAI. A new newspaper, the daily *CNT,* organ of the national organization, appeared on November 14, 1932, just as the railway strike came to public attention, and it supplied a drum roll for the faístas. In the following weeks, it attacked the legitimacy of the Republic and trumpeted the cause of direct action.

"One must defend the Republic." A lie! Hypocrisy! Must one defend privilege? The latifundios? Exploitation? The sacred right of property? Must one defend the capitalist regime in danger? Must one halt the advance of the social revolution? . . . This is the hour of the workers. Neither anything nor anyone can delay their march toward complete liberation. [November 22, 1932]

With great enthusiasm, all of Spain applauds the actions of the railway workers. The FNIF will triumph with their strike. [December 16, 1932]

Railway workers! Now more than ever, we must go to battle. The Confederación Nacional del Trabajo is at your side. [December 17, 1932]

On December 19 there were screaming headlines:

There is a complete Socialist dictatorship. The counterrevolutionaries of the Casa del Pueblo [Socialist Union headquarters] prohibit all social action. Meetings of railway workers are not authorized. Our newspaper has been denounced, confiscated, hidden, and fined. The Socialists have declared war on the working class. The fascist repression begins.

Nor did the newspaper ignore the crisis in the countryside. There were series of articles on the landless campesinos, the failure of the agrarian reform program of the Republic, and the need to arrive at an immediate remedy for long-standing problems. Running concurrently with the rising clamor concerning the impending railway strike, the articles on the landless campesinos cataloged the evils perpetrated in the countryside: "The campesino is always depreciated, always ridiculed. For him there is eternal injustice, deception, and thoughtlessness. And there is hunger—for him who produces bread for everyone. Campesino of Andalusia, think of this" (December 6, 1932).

As the day of the revolt loomed closer, an exhortation to the campesinos was set in bold type above the headlines:

**Workers: Bear in mind that the instruments of production are invincible weapons. A sickle can be used for something other than to reap, and a hoe can serve to dig the grave for all that has outlived its time** (January 2, 1933).

The revolutionary rhetoric underscored the danger to the Republic, and the government made clear its intention to respond to an insurrection with determination and force. Railway workers would be placed under martial law, and the sindicatos would be dealt with severely. The railway companies also pledged to fire workers who struck.

The members of the national committee of the CNT now reached a critical point in their planning. Since the CNT was a confederation whose members were bound only by voluntary agreements, the power of national officers was restricted, and the potential for unified action was sharply limited. Since August 1931 it was recognized that regional autonomy stood in the way of unity. The national commmittee, desperate for the uprising to sweep the country, decided on an extraordinary ruling totally out of keeping with their anarchist beliefs.

Regional and local independence separated anarchism from other political movements. The right of each unit to determine its measure of participation had been secure since the Córdoba congress of 1872. It assured that strike action would come from independent decisions of sindicatos and could not be arbitrarily imposed by a central authority. Each sindicato, each district, and each regional was autonomous. No sindicato could be ordered to do anything to which it had not previously agreed. Although this hampered the power of their officials, it is doubtful whether the organization could have survived without this liberty, given the nature of anarchism and the ideals and character of the membership. This right of independence had helped to contain within the movement such diverse groups as urban workers in Catalonia, miners in Asturias, rural field laborers in Andalusia, and small landowners and renters in a number of other provinces.

In the interest of bringing off the revolution, the national committee now insisted that the regionals surrender their independence to choose whether to participate in a strike. The ruling, however, tried to avoid the concentration of decision-making power. In place of a central authority, the national committee surrendered executive power to whichever regional branch chose to exercise it. In a letter to the regional confederations on December 29, 1932, the national committee directed that "whichever region raises the flag of revolt, all other regions must follow in line and commit themselves equally to the revolt." The impetus for relinquishing independence appeared to be a brutal confrontation with reality, but in fact the new ruling simply made it possible for a small number of faístas in a single regional to initiate actions that would engulf the entire CNT and its membership.

At the end of December, a new threat to the proposed insurrection appeared. The explosion of a detonator in a garage beneath a small house in Barcelona led a pair of civil guards to the location of an anarchist arsenal of rifles, bombs, and dynamite. The two young men who had rented the garage explained that they were making Japanese toys, and they escaped in an automobile before the suspicious guards returned and the arsenal was discovered. That night the police brought into court five persons who had been held in custody for several days for the possession of bombs and weapons. One had been found with a suitcase filled with twenty bombs under his bed. Information uncovered pointed to a revolutionary movement in the immediate future that would be coordinated with the railway strike. Also found were lists of names of soldiers in regiments throughout Spain with whom the revolutionaries were in correspondence.[4] The police were apparently well informed about anarchist plans and membership: on December 30, the day following the garage explosion, the two men who had escaped were arrested, together with the compañera of one of them. Additional bombs and weapons were found at her apartment.

The *CNT* treated the arrests and the accusations contemptuously. They were described as customary false police accusations to justify repression of the anarchosyndicalist movement.[5] In reality the organization was seriously concerned. On January 3 the civil guard located another, still larger arsenal of arms, substantiating the fear that well-placed informants, or the documents discovered earlier, were helping the police locate the CNT's secret stores of weapons.

The confiscation of their stock of arms added to the dilemma of the national committee. If there were further delays, few weapons would remain for the battle. Yet it was evident that railway workers and their leaders lacked the will to strike. Without their strike, the strategically necessary impetus for the insurrection no longer existed. But there remained the tantalizing possibility that railway workers affiliated with the FNIF would go out. The FNIF leadership had finally fixed a date. They promised to serve notice of the railway strike on January 9, and they agreed to strike on the day determined by the national committee of the CNT, even if the date fell before the ten-day waiting period required by law. Given this information, the national committee decided that any action must wait for the railway strike.[6]

4. *El Sol*, December 30, 1932.
5. *CNT*, January 2, 1933.
6. "Actas del pleno de regionales celebrado los días 30 y 31 de enero y 1 y 2 de febrero," *Boletín de la Confederación Nacional del Trabajo* 2, no. 15 (March 1933): 14; see also Schapiro, pp. 8–9.

The organization of the CNT now proved unequal to the task of controlling its multilayered committee structure and the factionalism that existed. Power had passed from the national and regional level to the local defense units, which were now armed and tempted to act independently. In addition, the chain of authority leading from the national committee had been disrupted by the ruling of December 29, which called on all regionals to follow the lead of whichever regional went out first. There was, moreover, a confusing overlapping of authority: the same person could initiate action as a member of a committee and then pass judgment on his own decisions in another position of national responsibility. Such was the situation of Manuel Rivas, a faísta who was secretary of the national defense committee but had also taken Angel Pestaña's central position as national secretary of the CNT. The fate of the organization and the lives of many of its faithful followers were now in jeopardy.

## Preparations in Casas Viejas

At the close of 1932, the centro of Casas Viejas held new elections for officers. José Monroy was happy to retire as president, and Francisco Gutiérrez Rodríguez, a campesino nicknamed Currestaca, was named to succeed him.

*José Monroy:* Currestaca was very unpolished. He wanted me to continue as president. I had finished my mission of six months, and I had to make a living. Sindicato business took place at night, and at night I had to walk my goats. I had no land, and I had to sneak my goats to graze on other people's lands. So I told him, "I'll advise you, and you represent us; but I can't do it, because I have to earn a living."

The events of January 1933, however, moved so quickly that Monroy found himself forced to remain leader of the sindicato.

As the year ended, the delegate to the national defense committee from the district defense committee of Jerez brought news of the plans for the uprising.

*José Monroy:* We had a defense committee of four members: myself; Currestaca, the president; Juan Sopas; and Antonio Durán. It was for secret matters. Our defense committee was made up of those who had an affinity for each other—those who got along with each other.

We received word to send a representative on the second or third of January to a secret meeting in Jerez—a trustworthy person. We chose to send Sopas, and he agreed.

Other towns in the province were also informed. The representative from Medina Sidonia was Manuel Llamas, the militant faísta. Vejer de la Frontera sent two of their number to attend, Nicolás Braza and José García Pérez. These two were well matched: Braza was a careful man, inclined to see all the negative possibilities, while García Pérez was an enthusiastic obrero consciente widely known by the name he had adopted—Germinal ("Germination"). To avoid being observed, Braza and Germinal did not take the bus but instead walked the twenty-seven kilometers from Vejer to Medina Sidonia. There they met Manuel Llamas and Juan Sopas. The following dawn the four walked another fifteen kilometers to Paterna de Rivera, where they took a bus to Jerez.

The representatives from throughout the region met in the office of *La Voz del Campesino,* which was still directed by the moderate Sebastián Oliva. Germinal recalls that Miguel García, secretary general of the anarchist groups of Jerez and the district, addressed the members present: García said, "we are going to take to the streets to see if it is possible to attain what we have desired, to realize once and for all the libertarian social revolution. The movement will begin on the eighth of this month."[7]

Zurita, the district representative to the national Defense Committee, assured the delegates of their strength: "Valencia is armed to the teeth, and the same is true of Barcelona and other capitals. We consider that the triumph will be absolute, uncontainable, overwhelming."[8]

The need for coordinated attacks and the promise of violence created some apprehension. Germinal pointed out the doubtful contribution of his own sindicato:

> We don't doubt what compañeros have previously stated in their long and optimistic declarations. We don't doubt that there are places such as Casas Viejas whose militancy was such they have taken from the marqués's wire fences the lead that binds the wires to make shot for their shotguns. But in Vejer not only are we without pistols and revolvers; we don't have shotguns, either. As you know, in Vejer there were never any anarchists or anarchosindicalists. For this reason there haven't been the same preparations as in Medina, Paterna, Jerez, and other areas. And so our group of young compañeros have taken the first step and organized the sindicato. We now have enough work to do organizing some workers who had never attained this objective. I think it would be convenient if the com-

7. Personal communication from Germinal, September 7, 1979.

8. The account of the district meeting in Jerez was written by Germinal for Federica Montseny's *María Silva, La Libertaria*, pp. 13–16. Montseny's work is a fictionalized version. Germinal's account, however, set within quotation marks, is based on his actual experience. His comments on the militancy in Casas Viejas and the uncertainty of his own sindicato are of course after the fact.

pañeros would tell us how we will attack the quarters of the civil guard and the carabineros without any weapons.

Sebastián Oliva, the moderate editor, felt impelled by his loyalty to the movement to join what he considered an ill-advised venture.

I've been listening to everyone; and although the young reaffirm that I am a reformist, because I never liked improvisations, I will say that although I know that this boat will not arrive at a good port, I will come on board, compañeros. And as the days remaining are so few, you will all remember well that I was right about what I have said.

According to Germinal, these cautionary remarks were not given any respect.

The compañeros Miguel Llama[s] and Juan Rodíguez [Sopas] of Medina Sidonia and Casas Viejas objected to what was said by the delegation of Vejer as well as what was said by compañero Sebastián Oliva. These compañeros, especially referring to García Pérez [Germinal], asked, "He's afraid, isn't he?"

Juan Sopas, however, recalled his attitude at the meeting somewhat differently: "At the meeting I opposed the use of violence. I have always opposed violence. I did not agree with it. I knew that it would fail. I was against the violence. I disagreed with them. Nothing could result from it."

But the argument was moot since, as Zurita pointed out, agreements had been made on the national level. He went on to explain the signal for the attack.

All the sindicatos of Spain, as well as the anarchist groups, should understand the following: don't launch your attacks until you've definitely heard on Radio Nacional that the battle has been won in Barcelona. That means that that regional will hit the streets on the night of the eighth. And if we are defeated, no one should do anything. So all compañeros should be waiting for this signal.

While the radio news would inform the men in the cities when to strike, those of the smaller towns, with less access to electricity, would rely on visual evidence, as they had in earlier generations. On a clear Andalusian night the cities and towns of the southern part of the province, set on hilltops and along the coast, are as visible as distant stars. The lights would be the signal to rise. Manuel Llamas said, "The plan was that the high tension wires in Jerez would be cut. When the lights went out, we would know that the movement was successful, and we would begin in Medina." With the lights of the cities darkened, the men of Medina Sidonia would then signal the men of Casas Viejas by lighting a fire atop the ruined castle on the heights of Medina Sidonia.

As it developed, the plan became more than a mere diversion to prevent troops from reinforcing Barcelona. The anarchosyndicalists envisioned a short battle before they began the reorganization of town and countryside.

*Germinal:* We would take possession of cortijos, cattle, workshops, factories, and so on. Simultaneously, we would begin the march to Jerez de la Frontera, where the worst Andalusian feudalism reigned.

Once we controlled this reactionary center, the capital [Cádiz] would not be long in surrendering, having counted on the defeat of the people by the army and the navy at San Fernando.

A form of blockade was studied. Cádiz and San Fernando depend on water pumped in from Tempu. The electricity comes from Guadiaro. Meat, bread, vegetables, and fruits are brought in each day from the outlying towns.

With very little work, we would be able to halt their provision. The same could happen to communications by telephone, telegraph, train, and road. The only ones who would be able to leave would be the big fish, who would go to Morocco or the Canary Islands.

The meeting ended with the forecast of heroic triumph.

*Germinal:* The delegates left that meeting with the absolute conviction of winning one of the most brilliant battles against the monsters of all discord—the state and the bourgeoisie. We were also convinced we would lose our lives. And since life is painful indeed in the false society that we must endure, it was worth it, and it still is, to die battling courageously against the enemy.

*Manuel Llamas:* We knew it would be difficult, but if one didn't protest, one would be an animal—some species other than man. We did it not for one locale but for all humanity—to create Socialism throughout the world. Under capitalism the world would never attain happiness. There was no difference between us and the masses other than that of comprehension. There was always censorship, and we could not propagate the *idea*.

Returning to their towns the delegates took various roundabout routes to avoid being noticed by the civil guard. Braza and Germinal took the train to San Fernando but hurriedly left their coach on the side away from the station platform when they spied civil guards checking the front cars. Sopas went by bus to Cádiz and then returned to Casas Viejas. He reported the results of the meeting to the other members of the local defense committee.

*José Monroy:* Sopas brought back instructions that the revolution was about to begin. He told me the orders: when they signaled the light in Medina, we were to begin the revolution. We knew of it at least four days in advance, but we did nothing to prepare for it. There was nothing to prepare. All the men had shotguns, because we lived by hunting. We were waiting only for the final date. Tentatively, on the eleventh, we were to go out on the street.

I'm not for violence. But if someone's choking you, you have to use force to stop him. If one has to do it, one does it. But I was never a lover of violence.

The other members of the sindicato knew nothing of the plans. The defense committee was particularly careful to keep silent about these matters in the presence of the headstrong Gallinito. From José Monroy's point of view, "he didn't know anything. He didn't deserve our confidence. He could do some foolishness and cause our downfall."

## The insurrection in the north

On the evening of January 7, at a special meeting of the CNT national committee in Barcelona, it became apparent that the chain of authority had crumbled. At that time the national defense committee asked the national committee for instructions, warning that the Catalonian defense committee intended to initiate the revolution. The Catalonians argued that any delay meant the destruction of their plans and loss of their arsenal of weapons.[9] In view of the railway workers' strike notice promised for the ninth of the month, the national committee told the Catalonian defense committee not to take any action that would begin the insurrection prematurely. But without even obtaining the approval of the regional committee of the confederation, which held the decision-making authority for the region, the Catalonian defense committee announced their intention to begin the insurrection at 8:00 P.M. on January 8, in the hope that the railway workers would follow them out the next day.[10]

Manuel Rivas, general secretary of the CNT national committee, expressed his opposition to the decision, but he declared himself in sympathy with their desire to fight. Under the impression that the decision had been approved by the regional committee of Catalonia, and in accordance with the December 29 ruling (that all regionals were to go out if one went out), Rivas, in his

9. Schapiro, p. 8. For a general summary of events, see Joaquín Arrarás, *Historia de la Segunda República Española*, 2:78 ff.; and José Peirats, *La CNT*, 1:53–55.

10. *Boletín de la Confederación*, pp. 9–10. Representatives of the following committees participated in the discussion: the national committee, the regional committees of Catalonia and the Levante, the national defense committee, the regional defense committee of Catalonia, the local defense committee of Barcelona, and the national committee of the FNIF.

other capacity as secretary of the national defense committee, cabled the various regional committees that Catalonia had revolted. The regional organizations that received the telegram, however, assumed that it had been sent in Rivas's position as CNT general secretary. The message therefore had much greater authority. The insurrection was set in motion.[11]

The forces of the Republic were alerted as well. On the morning of January 8, Prime Minister Azaña wrote in his diary,

> At 11:00 this morning, Casares [Quiroga, minister of the interior] telephoned me that according to all indications, the anarchist movement that we were waiting for would be launched today, late in the afternoon. Their plans are to assault the military barracks of Barcelona, Zaragoza, Seville, Bilbao, and other points. Something is also expected in Madrid, but of less importance. I am sending instructions to division generals.[12]

The attacks began as planned, on Sunday evening, January 8. Military headquarters and civil guard posts were fired on in Barcelona and other towns in Catalonia. A bomb was detonated in front of the police station in Barcelona. In response to Rivas's telegram, there were similar attacks in Madrid and Lérida. There were uprisings in outlying towns as well. A train was derailed in Valencia. In the Valencian town of Ribarroja, the anarchosyndicalists had a small success: they cut the lines of communication, and an anarchist force took over the town hall and burned the archives in the plaza. A barricade was raised before the civil guard post, and the two forces exchanged fire.

The government declared a state of war in the areas affected by the rebellion, and the anarchists captured were treated as military prisoners under the army's jurisdiction. The sindicatos were ordered closed.

In Madrid, on the night of the eighth, Arturo Menéndez, director general of security, held a meeting of the chiefs of security forces in the city and issued severe orders.

> A revolutionary movement of an anarchist and extraordinarily violent nature has just broken out, one that could endanger the security of the nation, which compels the security forces to use the greatest energy against any rebellious act that might be encountered. As a consequence, firearms are to be used without hesitation against those among the rebels who might use similar weapons against our force, and this rigor should be greatest with regard to those who might make attempts with explosive

11. Schapiro, p. 9.

12. "Papeles inéditos de Azaña, 8 de enero de 1933," cited by Arrarás, 2:79.

weapons or materials against the representatives of authority, or those who might carry out acts of sabotage on public utilities.[13]

The orders were unusual, because the security forces were customarily advised to avoid using their weapons in putting down public outbreaks, except in extreme cases. They had been consistently ordered never to use weapons against crowds. The new orders were passed orally down the chain of command.

No government instructions were necessary to take charge of the railways. The FNIF never declared a strike. The railway workers had settled for a pay raise of fifty céntimos a day.

The anarchist attacks were a failure from their inception. Though the skirmishes were bloody, they fell far short of a revolutionary movement. The general populace, instead of responding to the call to revolt, locked their doors. The barracks gates did not swing open in invitation; no soldiers switched their allegiance. Army posts had been on the alert since the early afternoon; and soldiers, civil guards, and special police squads were stationed at strategic locations in the cities. Cars were stopped at roadblocks, and any suspicious action touched off gunfire. Some prisoners were taken and were badly beaten. The leaders of the movement, including Juan García Oliver, were arrested by chance at the very outset of the revolt, when their car was halted at a checkpoint.

Although the attacks made on the evening of the eighth failed, the revolutionary movement became a wave carried to other anarchist strongholds in Valencia, Zaragoza, Cuenca, and Oviedo. Everywhere it touched there were sporadic outbursts of violence. General strikes were declared in Barcelona, Valencia, Játiva, and Seville. By the evening of the ninth, the initial uprising had been broken, but on the tenth the new wave of violence reached the province of Cádiz. There were anarchist outbreaks in Jerez, Cádiz, Alcalá de los Gazules, Paterna de Rivera, Los Barrios, and Sanlúcar.

In response to these new threats, on January 10 the government shifted some forces south. Captain Manuel Rojas Feijespán was ordered to proceed with his company of assault guards from Madrid to Jerez de la Frontera to put down anarchist violence. There had been no railway strike, and the trains were still running. Captain Rojas and his troops set out on the all-night ride to Jerez.

13. *Diario de sesiones de las Cortes Españolas*, March 15, 1933, No. 311, pp. 118–27. The exact wording of these orders came under close scrutiny, as we shall see. Some critics contended that the verbal commands contained much harsher language.

## The first hours in Casas Viejas

Since the plans for the uprising had been kept from the general membership, when the insurrection began in Barcelona on January 8, the members of the sindicato of Casas Viejas had other matters on their minds. The sindicato's committee for political prisoners addressed a letter to the *CNT* in support of workers striking in a distant town in Asturias. Included in the letter were thirty-five pesetas, collected during that week.[14]

Throughout the province there was peace and quiet on the first morning of the insurrection in the north. While anarchists in Barcelona began their attack to overturn society, in Jerez de la Frontera it was calm. *El Guadalete,* the conservative newspaper in Jerez, reported on efforts to provide aid to the less fortunate. It asked for charitable contributions to the poor to help alleviate the rigors of winter. There were also modest signs of the government's progam of land reform: the director general of the Instituto de Reforma Agraria was scheduled to arrive in Jerez the following day to visit various cortijos.

On the ninth, as on every Monday, most newspaper presses were still. *La Tierra,* an anarchist-oriented periodical, was one of the very few to publish an edition that day. Its stark headlines proclaimed, "A Social Revolutionary Movement."

> In Madrid, Barcelona, Lérida, Sallent, Zaragoza, and other cities, violent clashes are taking place between police and workers.
>
> There are a large number of injured and dead. In Madrid an attempt was made to take over the Carabanchel barracks, and in Barcelona a similar attempt [was] made at the Atarazanas barracks. Comunismo libertario has been proclaimed in Sallent. Bombs and other explosives [have been] discovered. [There has been] a dramatic episode in the struggle in Lérida. In Valencia the strike has begun, and it is believed that it will become a general strike this afternoon. Until now the movement has not affected the railways. The list of casualties will be made available tonight. Precautions continue.

It was not until Tuesday, January 10, that the major newspapers provided their readers with accounts of the events; but by then it was clear that the danger to the Republic had passed. In the nation's most prestigious newspaper, *El Sol* of Madrid, banner headlines reported the attacks on the barracks in Catalonia and Valencia. Set in boldface above the headlines however, was the news that the rebellion had been capped: "ANOTHER ANARCHOSYNDICALIST ATTEMPT FAILS."

14. This note was not published in *CNT* until February 7, 1933.

The major attacks, confined to a few points, were rapidly brought under control by the armed forces. Nonetheless, sporadic skirmishes continued to break out in new areas. Throughout the day of the tenth, Arturo Menéndez, director general of security in Madrid, received telephone calls from the mayors of towns in the province of Cádiz informing him of anarchist strikes or violence of varying degrees in Jerez, Cádiz, Sanlúcar, San Fernando, Chiclana, Algeciras, Alcalá de los Gazules, and Arcos de la Frontera. These outbreaks, however, failed to reach significant proportions. As Pelele explained, "they failed to blow up the generators in Cádiz, because an army group had infiltrated the ranks and had learned of the plans." As the major strikes died down, towns waiting to go out called off their participation. In Vejer de la Frontera, the town made preparations to rise and then drew back.

*Germinal:* January 10, 1933. It must have been around 8:00 in the morning. People were gathering in our center at an unusual hour. It was more common for us to be busy in the afternoon.

N. Braza, pessimistic as ever, uttered in a loud voice, "This large assembly is going to give us away. It isn't the appropriate time for large meetings."

More than ninety men had assembled. The attack against the barracks of the civil guard was to be first, and then the assault on the troop of the carabineros. There were plans to seize the post office and the telephone and telegraph communications, which operated separately. We were going to seize the municipal building and the court house.

We would try to avoid any killings. To cause anyone's death is always terrible. We wanted to see our enemies working beside us in the fields. We wanted all men—laymen, carabineros, and priests—to dress in manly clothes. We were hopeful of convincing them of the nobility of a lofty ideal: anarchy.

I was explaining these ideas to those workers who were only too eager to begin the struggle on the streets.

But suddenly the president arrived, looking quite upset, and addressed us in this way:

"Compañeros, last night I tuned in my radio for the news. I have just heard the latest news. The revolutionary movement has failed. Only skirmishes were reported in Barcelona. The same is true for Valencia. The same is reported for Zaragoza, Seville, and the rest of Spain. If we launch a battle here, it will be like deliberately committing suicide."

The unanimous answer from about 100 men was, "There's still time to reflect. Let's act with calm and serenity. These are not children's games."

On the night of the ninth, our compañero the president had slept very little. He had remained as alert as a brave pilot in high seas during a stormy night.

After a serious examination of the situation at the local, regional, and national levels, we discussed the information that he had brought us.

We contemplated our defeat with true sorrow. Our "forces" were insignificant in comparison with the enormous force that the enemies of the people had organized so well.

True, we had agreed to some actions together with men with whom we had common feelings—aside from sharing the same determination.

"What should we do?" we asked ourselves. We decided to honor the resolution adopted in Jerez de la Frontera to abide strictly by the orders originating in the peninsular committee of the confederate FAI and the defense committee—and also, needless to say, to keep in mind the warnings voiced by the president of our sindicato.

The decision was taken in time. However, we all suffered great disappointment during those bitter hours. But for the time being, we spared the noble campesinos of Vejer from a horrible slaughter such as occurred in Casas Viejas.

After the initial attacks, there was little communication among the sindicatos, the FAI, or the defense committees. *La Tierra,* which had been published on Monday the ninth, carried the information that the struggle had begun but that the railways had not yet struck. It was still only a possibility. Subsequently, two messengers arrived in Casas Viejas from Jerez to confirm that there was no railway strike. Their compañeros in the north were at battle, but the outcome was in doubt. The news was vague and inconclusive.

On the morning of January 10 in Medina Sidonia, Manuel Llamas, the local faísta leader, became impatient about the lack of information and the absence of a direct order to join the revolt.

*Manuel Llamas:* I went to Jerez to see if there was going to be a general strike. I couldn't reach the organization headquarters because of the police. I met an associate in the street who gave me a note. The message itself did not have the organization stamp or seal in order to protect the organization. The note read, "At 10:00 at night, no matter what the consequences."

I carried the note from Jerez to Medina. I turned over the same paper to Osorio and told him to take it to Casas Viejas and hand it over to those responsible there. The note was carried by Osorio to Casas Viejas. Osorio was also in the FAI, in the same group I was.

*Pelele:* Since one of us, Osorio, had a novia in Casas Viejas, Manuel sent him. I was there when he told him "If the civil guards stop and ask you why you're going there, say you have a novia there."

Early on the evening of the tenth, Osorio arrived at Casas Viejas with the message given to him by Manuel Llamas. He turned the note over to Juan Sopas.

*Juan Sopas:* Osorio was looking for Gallinito, but he met me and, because we were all together, turned the note over to me. The note read, "The strike begins at 10:00."

After receiving the note, I held it for two hours. I read it. A strike! What for? They didn't have a plan about what to do afterward. They didn't have a plan, nor did I. If I didn't have one, they surely didn't have one. So I thought, What for? Why strike? I received the message around 7:00 P.M., and I held it in my pocket until about 9:00 P.M. I didn't want to hand it over.

But Gallinito and his group knew something was up. The note was sent to him but had been given to me. Then Gallinito threatened me: "Traitors have to be taken care of." After that I gave [the note] to him. I didn't hand it over right away. I thought, and then I said, "OK, here it is."

In the early evening, Villarubia, the young secretary of the sindicato of Casas Viejas, returned from work in the campo. He went to the centro and read the contradictory reports on the progress of the strike:

First of all *La Tierra* came, announcing the revolutionary strike on the part of the railway workers in Zaragoza. Then two men sent from the comarcal in Jerez walked all night to carry a circular that said the revolutionary strike by the railway workers of Zaragoza should be considered fictitious. We had read the newspaper in the morning. When I arrived back at night, we had a contradictory notice. I didn't see any note from Osorio.

None of the syndicalists owned a radio to hear the latest news; however, there was access to at least one radio in town. In the evening, the schoolteacher, Manuel Sánchez (who was now also part owner of the mill that provided electricity during the evening hours), would bring his radio to the schoolroom, where everyone could listen.

*Andrés Vera:* I remember the night before I was with the schoolteacher, and he had a radio, and it said that the movement had failed. The schoolroom was just opposite the sindicato, and I remember that one of the leaders came over to listen. He heard it. But they didn't believe the reports. They thought they were being tricked.

During the evening, the centro was crowded with excited campesinos waiting to learn the progress of the revolution. The fighting had now spread to Andalusia. In Jerez and other towns the workers had gone out. Now it was their turn.

*Villarubia:* The discussion began around 9:00 at night. I was behind the table with Monroy and Juan Estudillo. I was in the center, and Monroy was on my left and Estudillo on my right. The other committee members were with the group. The place was filled. There were some eighty or ninety inside the centro, and others were outside on the street. There were 300 members in the sindicato, and almost all of them were there.

I read the notice [brought by the messengers from Jerez] at the meeting. I read it, because it was my duty. It was my obligation. I read it to everyone. "This contradicts the newspaper. This says the latest news is that the railway strike in Zaragoza is fictitious. Should we be going out on a revolutionary strike, a strike here, that has failed at the start in Zaragoza? That doesn't seem right to me."

Monroy was in agreement. He had a balanced temperament. He didn't agree with the strike either, and Juan Estudillo even less so. He had little spirit. Two of the other three committee members wanted it. I read the notice at the meeting. The message was understood. I explained it, and good heavens, as the saying goes, one began to incite the other. They responded that we had to join with our compañeros in Jerez.

Gallinito urged the men to join the revolution. Pepe Pilar recalled that "Gallinito did influence people on that night. He said, 'Let's go out! Let's go out!' " And Manuel Legupín confirmed: "Gallinito said, 'I prefer to die fighting than to die of hunger.' "

Villarubia, however, spoke out strongly.

I said, "Do you want to become martyrs? Don't you understand that the strike in Zaragoza is over, and we're going to raise an armed revolution here? Don't you realize that it's impossible?"

One began to incite the other. They began to collect explosives that were stored, hatchets, and shot for every caliber of gun. When I saw the attitude that existed, I took a sheet of paper and I wrote, "I do not accept the attitude of the workers of the centro. I resign as secretary, and I resign as a member."

And Monroy began to say, "Look what you've signed. You've signed it in spite of your compañeros."

And I said, "I won't accept responsibility for the consequences. You may sign it or not, as you like. It's the same to me. It won't make any difference to the commander of the garrison." And Monroy and Juan Estudillo signed.

The treasurer of the sindicato, Juan Estudillo, had remained quiet before the passionate voices raised in the centro.

*Pedro:* Someone told Juan Estudillo, "Stop all this nonsense. The movement has failed."

And Juan answered, "I lack the words to convince the youth. We can't hold them back."

When the meeting broke up, the men gathered above the town on the lip of the mesa to wait for the signal light.

In Medina Sidonia, a similar scene was taking place. There, eyes were also turned to the north, toward Jerez. The signal to attack in Medina would be the destruction of the generators in Jerez and the blackout of the city. The campesinos had broken up into small groups stationed in strategic locations on the outskirts of town. One group was by the castle tower, another was on the opposite side. When the lights of Jerez would be cut the men would simultaneously enter the town from several directions. As the men waited impatiently, however, a detachment of civil guards on their way to Jerez entered Medina and spent several hours there. Their presence panicked the campesinos. The attack was hastily aborted and the campesinos fled into the surrounding countryside. In the confusion and sudden flight, their obligations to Casas Viejas were forgotten.

*Manuel Llamas:* The people in Casas Viejas couldn't see the entrance of the civil guards. They were waiting for a torch to be lit, but of course no torch was lit. When the guards came, we went into the mountains. We were there for two days. No one thought to go to Casas Veijas. It was so far away.

At night the campo is as dark as the sea, and the wind is wet. The men stared into the darkness in the direction of Medina Sidonia. As José Monroy recalled, "it was winter, and the night was obscure. Sometimes the light seemed to be out, and then it seemed on again. In winter one can't see very well."

In Casas Viejas the impulse to join their compañeros at the barricades was irresistible. José Monroy issued instructions to his compañeros to begin the takeover of the town:

I couldn't tell them anything else but what I was told—that comunismo libertario would come tomorrow. I told them to go here or there. I said that no one was to go to work in the campo. We were on strike. I sent men to tell those outside the village to return. I sent men to strategic spots, where people pass when leaving town, to tell them not to go to the campo. I told them we were going to win the movement. We were prepared to do it. "Grab your arms and do what you have to do."

Juan Sopas also spoke. He advised them, "Don't abuse people. Behave yourselves. Don't molest anyone. If you enter stores, don't touch anything. It's not necessary." I suppose Currestaca and others spoke too, but I don't recall. Gallinito's responsibility was to see that everyone was in his assigned place.

The first action was to seal off the town. Telephone wires between the town and Medina and Alcalá were cut. At the same time, some men were sent above to dig a ditch to prevent cars from entering the town. Others were sent to guard the crossroads and the paths leading to Casas Viejas. Another group was assigned to surround the civil guard barracks. Others fanned out to alert the remainder of the townspeople. Pepe Pilar said, "We went about spreading the word to the youth to gather whatever weapons they had, that comunismo libertario had been established, and we had to defend ourselves."

To supplement their homemade lead shot, the campesinos broke into the shop of Alfonso Jiménez Lago and stole 3,000 shotgun cartridges, ten kilos of black powder, shot, and percussion caps.[15] A few weapons had also been collected by Pepe Pilar in earlier years in preparation for the revolution:

I had a pistol and two shotguns. I gave the pistol to La Libertaria, and she carried it around the street. I loaned out the other gun. We brought the pistols in around 1920—those of us of the committee of Juventud Libertaria of the FAI. We got the pistols from Juventud Libertaria in Cádiz. I paid for mine.

Since this was an insurrection, the risks were much greater than if it had been merely a strike. One's loyalty to the sindicato was severely tested. The choice was relatively simple for the obrero consciente. Some acted to fulfill their ideals; others were prompted by their sense of duty toward fellow workers.

*José Monroy:* If I hadn't believed that comunismo libertario would come the next day, I would have stayed with my goats instead of spending three years in prison, instead of being beaten. Sure, you can save yourself, but if you believe in something, you go out.

Events had taken place so swiftly that the decision to participate had to be instantaneous.

*Pepe Pareja:* I was out by Cantarrana with another fellow, setting traps for birds. There was no work, and one had to eat. By the time we returned at night, the town was already aroused. Everyone was out, and since I was a member of the sindicato, I had to go out too. I couldn't say, "Not me." My brothers all had shotguns, but I never went hunting, and I had only a pistol. I was sent out with a group toward the new cemetery to defend the road.

For many members of the sindicato who responded to the summons, the purpose of the sudden uprising was uncertain. Miguel Pavón had been preparing charcoal in the campo and was awakened by a committee at one in the morning. "The town is up in arms! Let's go!"

15. Archivos de la Audiencia Provincial de Cádiz, sumario 6, no. vii, 14 de marzo 1933.

I thought the rich would have to distribute their money, their wealth, their land to everyone. The land that all of us work belongs to all of us. But I didn't understand much of that stuff. I was always in the fields.

To others the revolution promised not cooperative effort but immediate individual rewards, a reparto—a division of the lands.

*Leñador:* the night before the uprising, a neighbor came to my mother and told her, "Tomorrow we're going to be rich."

For every enthusiast dreaming good dreams of the morrow, there were others who were frightened, unenthusiastic, or cynical about the prospects of an insurrection in their town.

*Venta:* The day of the uprising, two men came down and said to me and my father, "All the animals have been left unguarded. There's a strike. Let yours loose too. Take your shotgun and come up and join us."

We said, "No, we're not going."

They said, "If you don't join, you won't share with us later."

During the preparations for the rising in Casas Viejas, Anónimo, who was working as a laborer on a finca nearby, unaware of the impending insurrection, had walked to town to spend the evening in conversation at the sindicato. Now he found himself an unwilling observer of the events:

At once everybody went to the outskirts of the village to forbid any exit by means of the country roads leading in and out of the village.

After midnight and after the street unrest had subsided, work for its defense was started. Campesinos who were active in poaching proceeded to arm themselves with their shotguns, and each one took up the place assigned to him by the revolutionary committee; some opened up ditches in all access roads, others kept guard at strategic points, and spread the road with small nails. . . .

On the highest point of the sindicato, the red and black flag was waving, and thus they made ready for the defense of the revolution.

The masses' jubilant mood was spectacular; enthusiasm was indescribable; cries for the revolution were shouted endlessly; they thought that the time had come for them to obtain their liberties—and yet, how distant they were from them! Who could have told them what was yet to happen!

I, faced with the sudden and unforeseen situation in which I was involved, had no alternative but to await patiently the unfolding of events, of whose impropriety I had no doubt and which were happening with strange rapidity, and so I killed time there the whole night. During my stay, I was advised not to leave the sindicato, this being a village I did not know well, so I could not be informed of the places where the reactionary elements were, which meant I could be a victim of one of their shots in any attempt to get out. Thus I remained, for what seemed like hours, with a heavy heart and full of worrisome thoughts, for I could foresee the grave incidents that might follow, as was the case, when the most horrible events in modern history took place.

During the late hours that evening, the men spread through the town to enlist every able man and assign him to a post. The town marksmen were especially needed.

*Encarnación Ruiz:* Gallinito and another came to my house at 11:00 at night to ask for Pinto's gun and for Pinto. Pinto had been out hunting the day before and had loaned his gun to Miguel Pavón. I was pregnant at the time, and I begged him not to go. He went down below with them but then returned and stayed home. He wasn't involved. Just before, when he returned from hunting, he had stopped to talk with the guards down below. He didn't know anything was happening.

*Juan Pinto:* At midnight Perico, Seisdedos's son, and Manuel Quijada came to me and said, "The hour has arrived to defend ourselves."

I said, "Look, this is a very small town, and there's no need to get involved in this." They wanted to cut the road, and I didn't see the point of it. I would have had to cover my face to go. I wanted to work. They didn't say anything.

I had an old gun, and I went down in the street. But a gun is no gun if it doesn't fire. I went to my uncle, who had two shotguns, but he had already given the other one away. I went to the sindicato and said, "It's useless for me to be here without a gun. I'm going home."

Men with military experience were quickly sought out, but former soldiers who had seen war at first hand were not the most eager recruits:

*Salvador:* They wanted me to be head of the group to take the civil guard post, because I had been in the war and had military experience. But I declined. I would fight if I had to, but I wasn't going to look for it. I had been in the army in Africa in the disaster of 1921. Thousands and thousands of men had been slaughtered. Hardly more than 100 were left of my regiment. I bowed out. It seemed impossible to me. How could men armed with hoes and pruning hooks fight against rifles?

The sergeant of the civil guard, Manuel Álvarez García, was informed of what was taking place. Villarubia had carried out his threat and gone to the civil guards to absolve himself of any blame for what would take place:

I went with the signed paper to the civil guard barracks, and I presented it to the sergeant. And I said, "Look at what this says. From this moment I am no longer the secretary or even a member of the centro."

The sergeant asked me about the workers' attitude, and I told him more or less that they were furious, and I wasn't in agreement with them.

"And since I didn't want to take responsibility for their actions, I've come to tell you about it." He was a good man. He knew what the situation was in the pueblo. They were prepared.

Currestaca, the president of the sindicato, now also had second thoughts about the impending uprising. During the night it seemed confirmed that the revolution had collapsed elsewhere. He made a circuit of the posts where the campesinos were stationed to argue that their action had become hopeless.

"Let's pull back. They haven't contacted us. The hour has passed and the movement has failed. Let's stop this nonsense because we'll get nowhere."

But the men with whom he spoke insisted that they were going ahead. Unable to convince his compañeros, Currestaca decided to abandon the revolution. He slipped away and made his way out of town toward the campo.

The revolutionaries surrounding the two-story barracks of the civil guard were in the most dangerous position. Four civil guards, including the sergeant, were posted inside. There was one door and an upper window in the front, and one upper window in the rear. The anarchosyndicalists, however, had sufficient cover to begin a siege. Opposite the front of the barracks was the site of the new house being constructed by the Espinas. Work had just begun on the newly raised walls, which were then only two meters high. There was an opening for a door and two post holes, which could be used as firing positions. Behind the barracks was another wall which was head high. It provided cover for a second group assigned to watch the rear window of the barracks.

The campesinos needed as much protection as possible to compensate for the discrepancy in fire power. The civil guards carried rifles that were deadly at long range. From their windows on the second story, they could dominate the street. The campesinos had shotguns with a range of fifty meters. If the weapons were loaded with bird shot, they were not likely to do any serious damage, even if their aim were true; however, cartridges loaded with buckshot were prepared. The range was still short, but these large pellets could be deadly if they struck a vital area.

The campesinos sent to cover the barracks were the best sharpshooters in the area—men who spent much of their time hunting.

*Cristóbal:* I had been working on a cortijo outside of town, and they came to tell me to come in, that something was going to happen. When we first entered, the road had already been cut. We went up above, where there were six or seven men. The others had been sent to various places. Monroy, Sopas, and Durán were there—all of the leaders. We were given just general instructions. We were told to fire if anyone left the barracks.

Sebastián [Pavón] and I and Zorrito [Jerónimo Silva] and Manuel [Quijada] were among the best shots in the village. They could all shoot well, and I was not bad myself. I didn't know Zorrito very well, because he was always in the campo making charcoal. He was a heavy-set fellow. There were three of us sent down opposite the barracks' door, and there were two or three others facing the barracks on the other side. We were crouched down behind the wall that was being constructed. We went there in the middle of the night.

There were three men hidden by the half-finished wall of the Espina house: Cristóbal; Jerónimo Silva (Zorrito), Seisdedos's son-in-law; and Sebastián Pavón. Four other men were posted behind the wall in the rear: Manuel Quijada; Perico Cruz, Seisdedos's son; Miguel Pavón; and Pepe Pilar, who found himself there because of his sense of duty rather than his skill with guns.

*Pepe Pilar:* I was up above on the mesa, guarding the road, and Antonio Durán came to me and asked me to loan my shotgun to one of the men stationed by the barracks. I said, "No, that's a lot of responsibility. I'll go myself." That was the most dangerous spot, but we thought that the guards wouldn't come out.

Miguel Pavón found himself together with Pepe Pilar for equally personal reasons. After arriving in town in the early hours he was given an allotment of shotgun shells and sent to the barracks. Miguel was known as a hunter, someone who rarely missed with his shotgun, but he was not active in sindicato affairs and could have refused this dangerous assignment.

If someone had a good shotgun and did not want to go and take the barracks, then he had to give up the shotgun. I was one of the better marksmen, and I had a good weapon. I would have regarded myself as a coward had I given up my shotgun. If it came to giving it up, I'd rather go to the barracks.

If the insurrection failed, those men posted to exchange gunfire with the civil guards would be the most severely punished. Two members of Seisdedos's family, his son and son-in-law, were thus in the most exposed and dangerous position in the uprising. Seisdedos, the old charcoal burner, was then almost seventy-three and took no part in the insurrection. As Juan Pinto said, "Seisdedos was not in the street. He was in his house during the uprising."

The men at the barracks blackened their faces to diguise their identity. Then they waited in the cold for dawn. Cristóbal was not worried about being recognized: "They couldn't see us. The sun was behind us. We were well positioned."

# Thirteen

# The Uprising at Casas Viejas

## The attack on the barracks

In early January dawn comes late, around 7:00, and the excited campesinos were parading on the street before light. It was Wednesday morning, the eleventh of the month. During the night, while preparations to take over the town were underway, the sindicato leaders had tried to avoid alerting the civil guards in the barracks. Now there was no masking the noise of insurrection. María Silva, La Libertaria; her friend Manuela Lago; and Gallinito took the red and black flag that hung in the centro and paraded through the town.

*Antonia Márquez Mateo:* On the morning of the uprising, all the people were out on the street. The men were going down below with shotguns, and those who didn't have shotguns took hoes and pruning axes. I went outside. "What's going on?"

"It's a revolution. The civil guard is surrounded."

*Juan Moreno:* Everybody marched behind each other in columns of one or two. They had armbands, shotguns, pistols, and flags. They all marched around the town—all the workers.

The marchers first sought some official target. There was no town hall to seize; the town records and land registry were in Medina Sidonia. Instead, the campesinos ransacked the room containing the receipts of the *arbitrios*, the petty tax records on goods entering the town. The records were of no significance, but they were a symbol of government, and the campesinos threw the papers outside and set fire to them.

Before the sunrise, the deputy mayor of the town, Juan Bascuñana Tudillo, was visited by the revolutionaries. Bascuñana, a shoemaker, was a member of the Radical party, but his brother was affiliated with the CNT. Of course he knew the men who came to his door.

*José Monroy:* I said, "Comunismo libertario is declared here. Tell the civil guards not to leave the barracks, because they're surrounded. If the guards don't leave the barracks, nothing will happen."
I didn't ask for their arms or anything.

Monroy was the official spokesman for the sindicato, but he found that Gallinito, in his exuberance for revolution, had preceded him to the mayor's house:[1]

*José Monroy:* Gallinito spoke to the mayor before I did and told him to go to the barracks, but the mayor hadn't paid any attention to him. The mayor knew that Gallinito didn't have any authority or experience, and he didn't listen to him. He told me that Gallinito had been there, but that he hadn't gone to the civil guards.

Bascuñana delivered the message to remain inside the barracks, but the anarchosyndicalists quickly realized that the sergeant was not about to abandon his honor.[2]

*Pepe Pilar:* The sergeant tells Bascuñana, "We not go out? I've gone out in Cádiz. Am I not going to go out here?"

As soon as the mayor left, Sergeant Álvarez tried to telephone Medina, but he found that the line had been cut. To determine the seriousness of the situation, the sergeant and two guards made a reconnoiter around the rear

1. The report of the parliamentary commission states that at 6:00 A.M., a group led by Gallinito went to the mayor and told him that comunismo libertario had been proclaimed and that authorities were no longer in control. They told him to advise the civil guard that if they surrendered, nothing would happen. The report does not mention Monroy's visit to the mayor (*Diario de sesiones,* March 10, 1933, 309, p. 11750). The message the mayor conveyed to the civil guard may have been a composite of what various persons had told him. His statement to parliamentary investigators reports the following: "Between 6:00 and 7:00 A.M. on the eleventh, a group of workers went to his house and told him libertarian communism had been proclaimed in Spain, that they didn't want to take any action but were commissioning him to go to the headquarters of the civil guard and tell them to surrender their weapons, for now we were all equal in Spain" (ibid., February 23, 1933, 300, p. 11406).

2. According to both the mayor's account and the summary of the parliamentary commission, the sergeant was reported to have said he would die defending the Republic rather than surrender (*Diario de sesiones,* February 23, 1933, 300, p. 11406, and March 10, 1933, 309, pp. 11750 f.; see also *El Sol,* May 23, 1934). José Monroy insists, however, that he asked only that the guards remain inside: "I did not tell him that they had to surrender. If they hadn't gone outside, nothing would have happened."

of the barracks, where Pepe Pilar was at his post with Manuel Quijada, Perico Cruz, and Miguel Pavón.

*Pepe Pilar:* He went out and around the barracks in his cap and cape. Our shotguns were pointed at him but no one fired. Then he went to the front and there was a loud report and he ran inside. Those in front of the barracks had fired on him.

The men stationed behind the wall of the Espina house had taken the armed patrol as a challenge.

*Cristóbal:* When the guards García and Salvo left the barracks, they had their rifles in their hands. Sebastián and I shot at them but missed. I missed because I had mistakenly loaded my shotgun with a cartridge of birdshot that I had in my pocket. I fired the right barrel and missed. I don't know why Sebastián missed.

In fact the campesinos had hit their targets. The small shot, however, could not penetrate the guards' heavy capes. Guard Pedro Salvo was slightly wounded, but the campesinos, seeing that their shot had had no apparent effect, thought that their aim had been bad.[3] The guards quickly retreated inside the barracks and moved to the second floor, where they could command a view of the street. Sergeant García presented himself at the front window with his rifle, and Guard Román García Chuesca peered over his shoulder, searching for the men hidden behind the half-constructed wall who had fired at them. It proved to be a fatal error for both men.

*Cristóbal:* They went in, and immediately the sergeant opened the window. He didn't say anything, and we didn't say anything to him. Zorrito fired and hit the sergeant and the guard with the same round. The cartridge had two or three buckshot, and one hit the sergeant and the other the guard.[4] Then Zorrito turned to me and said, "Take my place here and keep your eye on the window." I took his place. When I poked my head

3. José Monroy gave the following account: "Three of the guards went out into the street. They were armed, but they wore their capes, and their guns were slung over their shoulders. The men fired on them, but they had small shot in their guns, and nothing happened." The parliamentary report notes that Guard Pedro Salvo was wounded by the first shots (*Diario de sesiones,* March 10, 1933, No. 309, p. 11750).

4. In some second-hand accounts, it is asserted that the sergeant shot first from the window. Cristóbal, however, clearly states that the campesinos shot first on two occasions—at the guards reconnoitering the street and at the sergeant when he appeared at the window. There is no certainty that Jerónimo Silva fired the fatal shot. He was in position to do so, but so were Sebastián Pavón and Cristóbal. At the time Cristóbal was considered a prime suspect for the deed (see *Diario de Cádiz,* January 16, 1933). Most verbal descriptions support Cristóbal's account that both men were killed by a single round. A few believe that two or three campesinos fired simultaneously.

out a bit, the peak of my cap showed first. [Guard Manuel García] shot at me, and the bullet struck close by. It whizzed by my face and hit the wall next to me. I was hit by the fragments from the wall.

Both guards had received mortal head wounds. The sergeant fell unconscious and was to die the following day. Guard García Chuesca, hit in the eye, would die several days later following surgery.

The noise of the shotgun blasts echoed in the streets. Juan Pérez Blanco, the storekeeper who lived above his store close to the barracks, leaned out of his window to see what was going on, and a ball just missed his head.

None of the town authorities came out to investigate the results of the firing. Don Federico Ortiz Villaumbrales, the town doctor, had heard the shots.

He looked out from the terrace of his house and verified that they were coming from the civil guard barracks. Signals were exchanged, and he saw a civil guard, with a handkerchief red with blood, indicating to him that there were wounded men inside the building. But he did not go out because it was extremely dangerous then, and nobody called him.[5]

The priest was advised to remain inside:

*Andrés Vera:* I lived in a small inn near the plaza. Early in the morning, I heard what sounded like shots, but I thought it was a truck backfiring. When I came down to ask what it was, the innkeeper said, "There's been an uprising. It doesn't concern you. Go back upstairs to bed." So I went to bed. It wasn't until later in the morning that the barber, who realized that I was hungry, came and brought me coffee and told me what had happened.

Other town leaders who feared they would be attacked also shut their doors.

*José Suárez:* The night before, the anarchists were out in the street having drinks with the priest and the Velas. They were angry only with the Socialists. I stayed in my house and put sacks against the door.

Nor did Villarubia, former secretary of the centro, venture out: "The day of the uprising I remained in the house and didn't leave it for anything."

Juan Estudillo had not taken part in the parading or in the attack. He waited anxiously in another shoemaker's home.

5. *Diario de sesiones,* February 23, 1933, No. 300, p. 11406.

*Juan Moreno:* He had nothing to do with it. He didn't have any weapons. He was in my house when they killed the guards. He knew that everything was lost. He was very frightened, because he saw that things were muddled. He said, "Within an hour we'll see what happens."

## The retaking of the town

After the first exchange of shots, there was silence. The two remaining guards, Pedro Salvo and Manuel García Rodríguez, retreated from the window. They could not call for reinforcements, since the telephone line to Medina had been cut. At this time, however, the actions taken earlier by the anarchists began to break down.

At 8:00 A.M., while the barracks were under siege, the telephone operator in Medina Sidonia reported that service to Casas Viejas had been cut. The mail truck, scheduled to leave from Casas Viejas but unable to cross the newly dug ditch, had not arrived in Medina either. At about 10:00 a telephone repairman, accompanied by three civil guards, was sent to investigate. Just outside of Casas Viejas, the repairman spied the place where the wire was broken. As the car stopped, four men hidden by some cactus attempted to run off but were taken prisoner by the civil guards. The repairman quickly reestablished communication with Medina: "Advise Medina to send additional guards to Casas Viejas, as something unfortunate has taken place."[6]

Below, in the town, after waiting through the long morning, the men who had surrounded the barracks were finally relieved. The town was still on alert, and Pepe Pilar elected to go above to defend the road. Manuel Quijada lived near the barracks, and he returned home. Perico Cruz and his brother Paco walked up the hill to the choza where their father, Seisdedos, was waiting. Zorrito, their brother-in-law, accompanied them there.

A few of the men in the street decided to pay a call on the priest.

*Andrés Vera:* At 11:00 they came to the house asking for me, and the woman of the house became very nervous and said I was probably at the church. But they said no. They didn't bother her further, perhaps just out of pity for the poor woman's distress. I didn't come out until the guards came at 2:00 in the afternoon.

A group of men stood warming themselves around a fire in Calle San Juan, and Cristóbal stood with them for a while waiting for news:

I walked up the hill to the main street. Some men had a fire going, since it was a brisk morning. Then someone, maybe Sopas or someone else, said

6. Declaración de Francisco Muñoz Rivera, Medina Sidonia, March 21, 1933, Archivos de la Audiencia Provincial de Cádiz.

that the three men posted above had been captured by the civil guards and taken to Medina.

When news of the capture spread, Juan Sopas, frightened and realizing that the end was near, set out to escape by walking the fifty kilometers to Cádiz. Currestaca, who had spent the night about a kilometer from the town, was already well on his way to La Zarzuela, twenty kilometers south, where his in-laws lived on a finca called El Conejo (The Rabbit).

The town was quiet until almost 2:00 in the afternoon. At that time, a squad of a dozen civil guards from Alcalá, under the command of a Sergeant Anarte, arrived on the outskirts of town. They left their truck above on the mesa and entered Casas Viejas at a dead run, firing their rifles into the air.[7]

*Juan Pinto:* When the sergeant and eight guards or so from Alcalá entered the village, the sindicato was filled with men, and the sergeant came down running, shouting: "Eight here!" and "Eight there!" as if he had a large force. All the men ran.

The campesinos scattered along pathways leading out of town. Some raced home, pausing there only long enough to gather provisions before fleeing to more distant hiding places to avoid being taken prisoner. Two civil guards had been mortally wounded, and their comrades would take out their fury on anyone who fell into their hands.

*Pepe Pareja:* When they came in trucks, everything fell apart. We all fled. I went up to my house, and then Antonia and I and another went to my father's house in the campo. Then I left for the mountains.

Some, foolishly as it turned out, sought security in their homes rather than in flight to the mountains. Manuel Quijada, Miguel and Sebastián Pavón, and the family of Seisdedos returned to their chozas and remained there. Once the guards commandeered the streets, escape became more difficult.

The campesinos defending the roads and paths were cut off from the center of town.

*Pepe Pilar:* At 10:00 A.M. we were relieved by others, and I went above to guard the road. When the force from Alcalá entered, they came in shooting. They killed two in their doorways. When they entered the town with such a large force, truckloads of soldiers, we couldn't get back in. The others down below fled.

7. The sergeant was later commended by Andrés Vera, the priest, and by law student José Vela for the minimal force he had employed in retaking the town. Since the campesinos had been bunched up in the street, there would have been many more casualties if the guards had sought targets when they first entered the town (testimony of Andrés Vera and José Vela Barca, *Diario de sesiones,* February 23, 1933, No. 300, pp. 11405, 11407).

Pepe Pilar and some others chose not to run, and they remained close by on the outskirts of town.

The beleaguered civil guards at the barracks were relieved, and an ambulance was summoned from Cádiz. Sergeant Anarte stationed his men at the main cross streets and posted two or three men below in the plaza. There was no resistance; however, the guards were nervous and fired at any suspicious movement.

*Perico:* My cousin could not hear or see very well. He couldn't hear the orders of the guards. He was thirty years old. He was in the house and had to urinate. Since there was a young girl in the house, he went outside to the corral. The guard stationed at the plaza fired at him and killed him. Manuel Mañez went to his aid, and he was wounded in the shoulder.

There were no further incidents, and for three hours the town was quiet. With his small force, Sergeant Anarte had complete command of Casas Viejas.

At about 5:00 P.M., a force of twelve assault guards and four civil guards arrived from San Fernando under the command of Lieutenant Gregorio Fernández Artal. The lieutenant, who only the day before had reached San Fernando from Seville, had received his orders at 3:00 in the afternoon to proceed to Casas Viejas and bring it under control. They moved into the town cautiously to avoid being surprised, but they found the streets quiet, with the houses and windows closed. The men were armed only with pistols, and they held their fire on orders of the lieutenant, who reminded them that they each had only twelve bullets and would need them if attacked.

Lieutenant Artal's force joined that of Sergeant Anarte. They took down the anarchist flag hanging by the sindicato and raised the national flag provided them by the schoolteacher. The lieutenant ordered that villagers open their doors and normal activities resume. With the aid of the two surviving civil guards, Pedro Salvo and Manuel García, Lieutenant Artal began to seek out the insurrectionists who remained hidden in town. He was tense and suspicious and treated the campesinos roughly.

While making a search in one house where the women present denied that any man was taking refuge there, he saw four or five men in a dark room, and then he lashed the women several times with his short whip. But when the [local] civil guard told him that they were good people, he set them free, advising them to let what had happened serve as a lesson so that no other occasion would arise when the civil guard would be attacked.[8]

8. Report of the commission, *Diario de sesiones,* March 10, 1933, No. 309, p. 11751.

From the two surviving local civil guards, Lieutenant Artal learned the name of one of the insurrectionists, Manuel Quijada, who had been seen positioned behind the barracks.

*Antonia Márquez:* Manuel was hidden behind the wall in the back. He tried to disguise his face, but he was short and had to pop his head over the wall. The guards saw him and recognized him. Later they went to his house.

Manuel was seized at his home. The guards also took his brother-in-law prisoner for having a loaded shotgun in his possession. Both men were beaten in order to learn the names of others involved. Who had surrounded the barracks? Who had fired the fatal round that mortally wounded two civil guards?

*Ana:* Manuel Quijada was very small and light. They played with Manuel as if he were a ball. There was blood coming from his ears, nose, eyes, and mouth.

Manuel fell down, and the guards kicked him until he struggled to his feet. Manuel's wife, pregnant with their first child, pleaded with them to leave him alone, and the guards struck her with their clubs.[9] One or both of the captured men identified some of those who had surrounded the barracks.

The family of Seisdedos was now seriously implicated. Perico Cruz had been behind the barracks with Quijada. Jerónimo Silva had been stationed in front of the barracks in position to fire the fatal shots. Paco Cruz may have been identified as well.[10] The surviving local guards knew that Perico and Paco Cruz lived with their father and that Jerónimo Silva lived close by. The three men were likely to be together at Seisdedos's choza. The guards led the lieutenant and his men to Calle Nueva.

## The siege

Seisdedos's choza was situated in a small corral that dipped below Calle Nueva. The choza's roof of thatch and cane rested on mud walls strengthened with bits of stone. A single door faced the street. It was the main source of light inside the choza, and so it was usually open; the only other light came from a tiny window in the back. Next to the choza was a stall for the burra

9. *Diario de sesiones*, February 23, 1933, No. 300, p. 11410.

10. A month after the uprising, María Silva, La Libertaria, told Antonia Márquez Mateo that Paco had also been at the barracks.

that the men used to carry charcoal. In the rear of the corral was a stone oven for baking bread.

The small choza housed six people: there were Seisdedos and his two sons, Perico, aged thirty-nine, and Paco, aged thirty-six, both of whom were unmarried; also living in the choza were Josefa ("Pepa") Franca Moya (the widow of Seisdedos's stepson) and her two sons: Francisco, then eighteen years old, and Manolo, almost thirteen.[11]

*Manolo García:* The three of us [my mother, older brother, and I] slept in the rear of the choza, separated from the rest by a mud wall that went part way up. My two uncles and my grandfather slept in the front part of the choza—my uncles used the bed, and my grandfather made a place for himself on the floor with straw and a blanket. My grandfather was then over seventy, but he was still agile and often went to the campo.

In the front part of the choza, where Seisdedos and his two sons slept, there was a small stone hearth that served as a stove. Pepa Franca prepared the meals there, using the charcoal that the men brought in from the campo. Pepa Franca's husband had died of the grippe during the epidemic of 1918, leaving his young wife and two small sons. With no one else to care for them, Pepa and her sons had gone to live with her father-in-law.

The Cruz and Silva families lived in close proximity. Jerónimo Silva's choza was just across Calle Nueva, and the choza of Juan Silva, where La Libertaria lived, was a few steps down the street.

On the morning of January 11, after the fighting at the barracks, Perico and Paco Cruz and Jerónimo Silva returned to Seisdedos's choza, where they sat waiting with other members of the family: Seisdedos, Pepa Franca and her elder son Francisco, María Silva (La Libertaria), and María's close friend Manuela Lago. Just a few hours earlier, María and Manuela had marched together exuberantly through town, carrying the red and black banner of anarchism. Now they sat in a worried circle.

No one knows for certain why the men had not fled with the others when the civil guards retook Casas Viejas. José Monroy speculated that "those in the choza undoubtedly believed that everyone was still in town. But everyone had fled when the guards entered."

11. Seisdedos's three stepsons, all of whom had adopted his trade of charcoal burning, perished in the 1918 epidemic of the grippe. Two had died while working the campo, and Seisdedos had carried their bodies back to town on the backs of burros. In the church records the two sons and three daughters of Francisco Cruz Gutiérrez (Seisdedos) were considered illegitimate, born of an unknown mother. All the village knew that their mother was Catalina Jiménez Esquival, Seisdedos's common-law wife. According to law, however, Catalina Jiménez was legally married to José García Guerrero. They had married in 1880, had three children, and then had separated. Catalina had taken her three young sons with her when she went to live with Seisdedos, with whom she began a new family.

It is possible that the men thought that the uprising was still underway. Or they may have felt that running was useless—that their fate was sealed by their role in the attack on the barracks: Jerónimo might have killed the sergeant and the guard.

*Cristóbal:* I suppose that they didn't leave for fear of being shot. The door was shut. And there was no one to tell them if the way was clear or when the guards were out of the way.

Pepa Franca's younger son, Manolo, was playing just outside the choza:

I was kicking a ball on the street. It was after dark. There were few people on the street. The lights were lit. At about 7:00, I went into the house to eat. It was dark inside. I heard one of the brothers say, "There's García and Salvo."

The two local civil guards had led Lieutenant Artal and his men along Calle Nueva to Seisdedos's choza. Although it was now night, there were no lanterns lit inside. They could see a burra tied up in the stall next to the choza. Lieutenant Artal waited in the street while Salvo and some assault guards descended the short decline to the corral to see if the men were inside.

*Juan Pinto:* Civil guard Salvo came to the door and said, "Perico, come out, and nothing will happen." They didn't answer, and he said, "Lieutenant, they're not here." But he winked. He went to the street and he said, "Lieutenant, they're here."

One of the civil guards was ordered to force the door open with his musket. He then stood aside for Assault Guard Martín Díaz.[12] As Díaz stepped into the choza, he was met by a shotgun blast, and he fell dead in the doorway. The blast echoed in the street, and Lieutenant Artal ordered his men to fall back to the knoll overlooking the choza. One assault guard, Fidel Magras Corral, remained in the corral in case those within tried to flee.

Lieutenant Artal shouted to the people in the choza to come out with their hands in the air, assuring them that they would not be harmed. But the men would not surrender. There was an exchange of gunfire, and Assault Guard Magras was wounded and cut off from his companions. They could not reach him to offer aid. They had learned that the campesinos were deadly marksmen, and they did not dare show themselves.

Those inside the choza had no means of escape. The one door facing the street was covered by the guards. The window in the rear was too tiny for

12. Testimony of Lieutenant Artal, in *El Sol*, May 23, 1934.

even a child to crawl through. The choza itself was a feeble fortress. Its mud and stone-chip walls could not stop a rifle bullet, and a single spark could send the straw roof up in flames. Their only protection lay in the position of the hut in the corral. Because the land was set below the street, it was difficult for the guards to fire effectively into the choza. The men crouched in the front room to shoot from the doorway, which was partially blocked by the body of Guard Martín Díaz. The women and the two boys lay on the floor in the back room.

Some of the shot poured at the guards came not from within the choza but from other points nearby. A small number of campesinos had not fled, and now they peppered the guards who tried to move down the street.

*Pepe Pilar:* When they began attacking Seisdedos's choza, we came to protect them. They shot at us, and we shot at them and hit quite a few. We fired at the guards coming by the street. We were hidden in the *chumbas* [cactus], and they came in by the street.

Manuela Lago's father, Fernando Lago Gutiérrez, heard the firing and came to protect his seventeen-year-old daughter, who by chance was inside the choza with her friend. He climbed onto a roof where he had a strategic view of the battlegound. In the darkness, his position was invisible, and he fired at the flashes of the guards' gunfire. With his accurate firing, he helped to shield the choza through the first hours of the night.

*Antonia Márquez:* Some stayed nearby up above, and all night they fought with the guards. All that night there was a battle between workers and guards. It was a war.

Lieutenant Artal did not order an attack in the rear, because there seemed to be gunfire from several points on a nearby knoll as well as from the choza itself. It was dark, and he was unfamiliar with the terrain. The civil guards had rifles, but the assault guards were equipped only with sidearms. Unable to mount a successful assault, Lieutenant Artal decided to try to use his two prisoners (Quijada and his brother-in-law) to coax the revolutionaries into the open. At the very least he could learn their strength if the prisoner returned. He sent in Manuel Quijada, still in handcuffs and badly bruised from the beating he had received.

*Lieutenant Artal:* I gave him twenty-five minutes to try to get them to surrender, with the assurance that if they did so, nothing would happen to them. If, on the contrary, they persisted in their attitude, they would be the first to suffer the consequences. Since I was afraid that those pinned inside would not want to come out of the hut, I sent Quijada inside handcuffed, and entrusted him to observe the weapons of those in the stronghold. The time limit passed, and no one came out—not the prisoner nor those already inside—and they continued attacking our force. The other prisoner was taken to another part of the village.[13]

Seeing Manuel Quijada's bloody condition gave the campesinos a foretaste of what they could expect from the hands of the guards—if they were not immediately shot down as they stepped from the choza. When Quijada was forced to join them, the men learned for certain that almost everyone else had fled and that the town had been retaken.

*Antonia Márquez:* About a month after the uprising, La Libertaria told me what had happened inside: "The night before I had gone in the street with Gallinito, singing songs and carrying the red and black banner. Paco was behind the barracks, and Pedro was in front. I think it was Manuel Quijada who killed the sergeant, because he was the best shot. He was home taking off his shoes, and they took him outside handcuffed, without shoes, and they beat him black and blue. They said to him, 'Take us to Seisdedos's choza.' We never thought they would come to our house, because we were innocent. When one of the guards loooked in, he was shot. We fired back through the door and through the back window, because we were surrounded. We hit a number of guards. Seisdedos was in bed. He was an old man. They threw Manuel inside to tell us to come out, but we couldn't come out, because they would shoot us. We said to Manuel, 'We won't go out, and you won't either. We'll all die here together. Everything is lost.' When they threw Manuel in, we knew all was lost. We freed him from the handcuffs."

Unable to dislodge the men with his small force, Lieutenant Artal determined that he needed additional firepower to clear the choza:

[At 8:00 P.M.] I asked the civil governor to send reinforcements, informing him at the same time that a guard had been killed in the corral and that another was gravely wounded. I added that I did not dare to burn the choza for fear that the whole village would be burned down. I needed hand grenades to gain control of the situation.[14]

At 10:00 P.M. two corporals arrived with hand grenades, rifles, and a machine gun, along with additional assault guards. By now Artal's force had swelled by twenty men under the command of civil guard Lieutenant García Castrillón. The governor's delegate, Don Fernando de Arrigunaga, had also reached Casas Viejas.

13. Testimony of Lieutenant Artal, in *Casas Viejas: un proceso que pertenece a la historia*, pp. 69–70.
14. Ibid.

The assault now intensified. The machine gun could not be made to work, but the guards poured rifle fire into the choza and tossed some grenades. There was little apparent effect. The angle of the slope and their awkward position prevented the guards from raking the choza. The grenades too failed to explode, because the spongy surface of the thatch cushioned their impact. When Lieutenant Artal ordered the guns to fall silent and called on the choza defenders to surrender, the reply was a volley of shotgun pellets, and two troopers next to Artal were slightly wounded. The attack was renewed, but without success. The two lieutenants conferred and decided to hold off an assault until morning. Darkness and the campesinos' accurate marksmanship augured too many casualties. Their decision, however, would soon be countermanded.

## The massacre

In Madrid on January 10, the day before the uprising in Casas Viejas, Captain Manuel Rojas Feijespán and Lieutenant Sancho Álvarez Rubio of the assault guards were ordered to take a company of ninety men to Jerez de la Frontera to suppress anarchist violence there. After an all-night train ride from the capital, the company spent the day of January 11 patrolling the streets of Jerez and helping to close some centros.

At 7:30 in the evening, Captain Rojas received a telephone call from Director General of Security Arturo Menéndez to proceed immediately with his men to Casas Viejas. The orders called for swift and uncompromising action to put down the uprising that was now centered at the choza of Seisdedos.

> Requisition two trucks and leave for Casas Viejas with forty guards. Take all machine guns and war supplies you have. You must take control of the situation and cut the movement within fifteen minutes. If you have to burn Seisdedos's house in order to overcome resistance, burn it. Fire without mercy against all those who may fire against the troops.

Captain Rojas protested that his men had been without rest or sleep for forty-eight hours. They were exhausted from the effects of the train ride from Madrid and from the tension of continuous duty in the streets of Jerez. Director general Menéndez was adamant: "No matter. . . . It is urgent to end it all quickly."[15]

Since the journey from Jerez to Casas Viejas was undertaken at night, Captain Rojas and the assault guards were wary of an attack along the way.

15. Report of the parliamentary commission, *Diario de sesiones*, March 10, 1933, No. 309, p. 11754.

They had heard that 500 anarchists from Medina Sidonia were hiding in the mountains. After they passed Medina Sidonia, the truck headlights were turned off, and they drove slowly in the dark. The ride was uneventful but as they neared Casas Viejas they encountered a corporal and an assault guard who had been wounded in the fighting and were on their way to Medina for treatment. It was an ominous sign.

It was well after midnight when Rojas and his men arrived in Casas Viejas and learned from Lieutenant Artal of the resistance at the choza and of the dead and wounded. The guards could not approach the choza without coming under fire by the campesinos positioned above in the chumbas.

*Pepe Pilar:* The guards entering by the street were shot. We were scattered all around in the chumbas, thirty or forty of us. Fernando Casares was in a good spot and shot at all the guards that were there. One guard came down to Rojas below, and some well-to-do townsmen, not affiliated with our organization and who therefore hadn't run away, heard him say, "Captain, the chumbas are killing all of us. We can't get up close."

Lieutenant Artal informed Rojas that rather than risk more casualities, they had suspended a final assault until morning.

*Lieutenant Artal:* Captain Rojas responded that the hut must be taken that same night, no matter what it took, because he had very severe orders, including the application of the ley de fugas.

"Look, Manolo," I told him, "this can't be done and won't be done." This remark disturbed him greatly, and he told me to follow my superior's orders. To that effect he set up the machine gun brought from Cádiz opposite to the hut. The gun would be fired until he blew a whistle to signal its suspension. The signal would indicate that Rojas was to enter Seisdedos's choza to seize the rebels.

At first we fired with rifles, because the machinegun did not function, but it was soon repaired, and it opened fire. . . .

Rojas called out to the rebels in the choza:

I warned those who occupied it to surrender. We were answered with vile insults and shots, and the resistance and firing against the public force was intensified.[16]

The mud walls and thatch were no protection against bullets from rifles and machine gun. Some of the occupants soon fell.

16. *Casas Viejas,* pp. 70, 33.

*Manolo García:* The machine gun was mounted opposite the front door. Myself, María, Manuela, my brother, and mother huddled in the back room. Manuel Quijada was thrown in, but I don't recall how. We could hear the brothers speaking to each other. One said that Seisdedos was dead. I suppose it was a bullet. Then Perico sin Hueso was killed.

Only the steep angle of the descent saved the choza from being swept with gunfire. "No one inside our back room was hurt. The machine gun was mounted high up and couldn't command a good view of the choza."

Although Seisdedos and Perico were dead, there was still no sign of surrender from the choza.

*Lieutenant Artal:* Captain Rojas blew the whistle, and the firing stopped. A guard going toward the hut fell mortally wounded from a shot by the rebels inside. I then made the captain see that his determination would cost many casualties, but he insisted on the order that he had given, on the premise that he was following what he had been told by his superiors to end the resistance in the least possible time, even to the point of leveling the house.[17]

The machine gun intimidated most the campesinos who had been spraying the guards with buckshot from the chumbas.

*Pepe Pilar:* Since they couldn't approach from the street, they set up a machine gun above to shoot down at the choza. That's when we all fled. We heard the noise of the machine gun.

At about this time, Fernando de Arrigunaga received a telegram from the governor reinforcing Rojas's command. The telegram, carried to Rojas, read, "The minister of the interior strictly orders that the house where the rebels have fortified themselves is to be levelled."[18]

Captain Rojas then ordered the choza to be set on fire. Cotton was soaked in gasoline and wrapped around rocks. Once again, the rebels were invited to surrender, but to no effect. While Rojas waited in the street below, Lieutenants Artal and Sancho lit the swatches of cotton and tossed them. One landed on a neighboring choza. It caught fire, and the dry thatch was immediately swallowed in flames. The blaze leaped to the roof of Seisdedos's choza and it caught instantly. Those within had only moments to decide

17. *Casas Viejas,* pp. 70–71. For contradictory reports concerning the origin of the wounds suffered by one of the guards, see *Diario de sesiones,* February 1, 1933, No. 287, p. 10864.

18. Report of the commission, *Diario de sesiones,* March 10, 1932, No. 309, p. 11752.

whether to run. While the fire raged, the guards continued shooting at the doorway.

*Antonia Márquez:* La Libertaria said, "We hadn't anticipated that they would burn down the choza."

She saw the dead around her. Her grandfather was dead. She knew all was lost. Pepa and her sons were hidden in the corner storage bin under the stove.

She said, "We shouted at them: Criminals! Assassins! Cowards! Jerónimo was the last to die."

The choza was burning. Pepa Franca shouted, "Don't shoot! My children! My children!" While Pepa was shouting La Libertaria grabbed the boy and ran out. When she ran out she cried, "Don't shoot! It's a boy!" They stopped for a moment.

*Manolo García:* It was still dark when they set the choza on fire. As soon as the roof started burning, María ran out, and I ran out. I ran to the side behind the oven, and then I ran down the street.

*Antonia Márquez:* Manuela and Manolo's brother were killed in the doorway. María's hair was scorched. She ran behind the burra and around the oven and then went to her house and knocked at the door. "Mamá, it's me, it's me. Let me in. Don't make any lights."

*Lieutenant Artal:* When we threw the torches, . . . Lieutenant Sancho and I observed two figures coming out of Seisdedos's choza who managed to escape, in spite of the fact that we yelled at them "Halt!" Rojas noticed them at the same time as we did and shouted, "Don't shoot! It's a woman and a child!"

At the time that these two fled, some guards approached the hut with the purpose of entering, but noticing this, another guard, [wounded and] pinned down nearby, warned them not to go in the yard because they would be fired on.

Moments later . . . two other persons attempted to leave the hut but fell, mortally wounded by the guards' shots. We approached and could see that they were a man and a young woman. When the destruction of the hut was completed, the forces returned to the plaza at approximately 3:00 in the morning.[19]

The fire consumed the bodies of the men who had been involved in the attack on the barracks: Jerónimo Silva, Perico and Paco Cruz, and Manuel Quijada. Dead with them were Seisdedos and his daughter-in-law, Pepa Franca. Outside the doorway, killed while trying to escape the flames, were the bodies of Francisco García Franca, Pepa Franca's eighteen-year-old son; and Manuela Lago, the seventeen-year-old friend of La Libertaria. By the

19. *Casas Viejas,* p. 71.

doorway was the charred body of Martín Díaz, the assault guard shot when he had tried to enter the choza. The burra lay dead in the corral, killed in the gunfire aimed at those escaping through the doorway. The wounded assault guard, Fidel Magras Corral, who had remained in the yard all night, was rescued.

When the roof crashed in, the firing suddenly broke off.

*Antonia Márquez:* Manuela's father had been shooting at the guards from a rooftop. Others had been shooting too. When they saw the choza burning, they all ran off. Everyone who was able to left town.

*Pepe Pilar:* I saw the burning of the huts, and my father was crippled and couldn't walk or even move. So I thought to myself, "They've begun to burn down everything around here." Everything here was made of wood and straw. It was about 3:00 in the morning. I told my late wife, my sons, and my father, "Let's get out of here. These people are going to burn everything." I left my house quickly and ran to Seisdedos's choza and I tell you, if the guards had seen me, they would have killed me right then and there. But by the time I got to the hut, it had been burnt down to the ground. Nothing was left, and I returned home and said to my wife, "Come on, let's go. These people are going to burn everything they find." So I got my father and carried him out and I saw a house with a tile roof, and I said to everyone, "If these people burn everything down, we'll be safer in a tile house."

A few moments later I heard shots being fired at the choza, and so I took the entire family and ran to the campo. "These people are assassins," I thought.

All resistance in Casas Viejas had ended. The civil guards and the assault guards moved down below to the plaza before preparing to leave. None of Rojas's company had been wounded, but some found spent birdshot in their capes. The marksmen in the chumbas had been accurate, but their shotguns were inadequate for warfare. Rojas and his fellow officers returned to the tavern across from the plaza. It was close to dawn, January 12.

Rojas sent a telegram to the director general of security, informing him that the choza had been leveled: "Two dead. The rest of the revolutionaries caught in the flames." He added, "I will continue to make prisoners of the leaders of the movement, to which end I will advise you accordingly."[20]

The town now held almost one hundred assault and civil guards. They trooped back to the plaza and sank down to rest. Two hours passed, until 7:00 in the morning, but the tension aroused by the night's fighting, with

20. Report of the commission, *Diario de sesiones*, March 10, 1933, No. 309, p. 11752.

its fearsome conclusion, had not subsided. The guards' emotions "went from fear to depression and then to indignation. . . ."

Rojas said, "A lesson will have to be taught."[21] He ordered three patrols, under the command of Lieutenants Artal and Sancho and a junior officer, to search the houses and round up the most outstanding militants. Anyone found with a gun was to be taken prisoner. The patrols were accompanied by Civil Guards Pedro Salvo and Manuel García, the two surviving guards of the assault on the barracks, and other civil guards. Rojas instructed the men to fire at anyone who resisted or refused to open the door, and to shoot whenever they felt threatened.

Don Fernando de Arrigunaga noted the increasing agitation and excitement on the part of the guards.

I told Captain Rojas that the guards were too excited and that it was possible for an unfortunate incident to occur. He responded that I shouldn't worry about it. The guards' state of excitement was such that I observed one of them take out a pistol and fire at a window until he emptied the magazine. When asked why he did this, he answered that he had seen a curtain move. The lieutenant of the civil guard was also aware of this and observed identical examples of nervousness among the guards. I told him that for my part, I had done everything possible to prevent anything distressing from happening, but I found myself powerless since the mission that took me to the village was purely informative.[22]

The assault guards aimed their rifles at two men who were crossing the street, but they were restrained from firing by a civil guard, Rodríguez, who assured them that these were good people and should not be shot. There was no one, however, to save Antonio Barberán Castellar, a man of seventy-four, when the assault guards pointed their rifles at him in the presence of his thirteen-year-old grandson. He cried out as he closed his door, "Don't shoot! I'm not an anarchist!" Three shots were fired through the door, killing the old man.[23]

Miguel Pavón and his brother Sebastián fled from their house minutes before the guards arrived.

My father and my mother were here, and the guards asked: "And your sons?"

"In the campo," my parents answered.

"In the campo?" Of course they had seen us from the barracks' windows. They said, "They are going to die like rabbits."

21. Ibid.

22. *Casas Viejas*, pp. 87–88.

23. *Diario de sesiones*, February 23, 1933, No. 300, p. 11407.

In their sweep through the town, the patrols took whomever was at hand, receiving guidance from Salvo and García, the two local civil guards. Those taken were at home with their families.

*Pepe Pareja:* They were innocent, and knowing they were innocent, they didn't run away. The guards grabbed whomever they could. The ones who had participated had gotten away.

At 7:00 A.M., a patrol came to the door just as Sebastiana Reyes Estudillo (aged thirty-eight), her husband, Manuel Benítez (forty-six), and their five children were getting up.

Three assault guards came in. When they saw her husband they asked him, "You! What are you doing?" "You can see for yourselves—taking care of my children." They searched the whole house over and took away a very old gun from the time her husband had been a field watchman. They carried him off, and seeing her sons crying, clinging to their father, they told them, "No crying, little ones. Word of honor, we won't do anything to your father."

At dawn one of the patrols came to the choza of María Cruz García, a forty-three-year-old woman with eleven children. They arrested one of her sons, Andrés Montiano Cruz, aged twenty, and his cousin, the son of Isabel Montiano. "At her lamentations, they told her not to be frightened, that it was only to obtain statements from them, and that nothing would happen to them."

Guards arrived at the choza of the widow María Toro Pérez, aged forty, also at about 7:00 in the morning. Her only son, José Utrera Toro, aged twenty-five, suffered from tuberculosis.

At the time, she was preparing a cup of coffee for her son, who was feeling bad and had just gotten up. The guards came in and took him away, throwing her furniture all over in the process, in spite of her crying and showing them, as proof that he had done nothing, that his bed was still warm. They told her they were going to "take down a declaration."

Dolores Benítez had sat up all night with her husband while the fighting was going on. Their choza was close to that of Seisdedos, and they showed no light for fear of being fired at. Dolores was forty-eight, and she had seven children. Her two eldest sons, Juan García, twenty-two, and Manuel, twenty-one, were sleeping in the same bed. When Seisdedos's choza was set on fire, Dolores had them rouse the other children to help prevent their own choza from catching fire.

At 7:30, in bright daylight, she heard a lot of noise, and her daughter looked out the window and saw the whole backyard full of guards. They said, "Men, outside." Seeing her weep, her son told her, "Don't be afraid, because whoever hasn't done anything has nothing to fear." Then they took him away. She went after them, crying, whereupon an assault guard told her, "Walk on ahead, you, too," and then, further down the street near Seisdedos's house, he told her, "Now go back, and don't turn around, or I'll shoot you dead." Then she looked around and heard some-one say, "The captain says there are enough now."

Juan Grimaldi Villanueva, thirty-three, was at home with his mother at around 8:00 A.M. when a group of assault guards arrived and ordered him and his father outside, with their hands up. Juan's mother, María Villanueva, seventy-two, remained in the house with her daughter.

A guard came in and turned her bed over with his gun barrel, and when she complained, he said, "I'm looking for a gun." "There is nothing like that here," she replied. . . . Officer Salvo was standing in front of the door. The assault guard, seeing her cry and embrace her son, pulled her away, saying, "Nothing is going to happen to him. It's just to take down a statement."[24]

Juan Silva, forty-five, the father of seven children (including María, La Libertaria), was taken from his house although he was seriously ill and it was obvious that he could not have taken part in the uprising. He appealed to civil guard Pedro Salvo: "Salvo, you know me. You know that I'm a family man." Lieutenant Artal recognized his condition, and, after hearing a good report on his character, told the guards to return him to his house. As the guards were escorting him home, however, they passed Captain Rojas, who ordered that "no one could be set free, that the judge would do that, and that he should be put back under arrest."[25]

One patrol went to the choza of Fernando Lago, whose daughter Manuela had been shot down, and they took him prisoner. Fernando was the only person arrested who had been involved in the uprising. He had fired on the guards in defense of his daughter, but the guards were not aware of his role; he was taken, as were the others, by chance or by the directions of guards Salvo and García. Rosalía Estudillo Mateos, Fernando's wife, already knew that the guards had killed her daughter Manuela when she had tried to escape.

24. Ibid., pp. 11410, 11406 f., 11410, 11409.

25. *Diario de sesiones*, February 23, 1933, Num. 300, p. 11398; Lieutenant Artal, in *El Sol*, May 23, 1934.

That morning they took her husband out of his house and tied his hands; and since the children were crying, clinging to their father, one of them told her little girl, "Little girl, don't cry. Your father will be right back."[26]

The guards arrested Balbino Zumaquero, twenty-three, the son of Gaspar Zumaquero, who had been the head of the sindicato in 1915. They also took three others: Manuel Pinto González, aged thirty-nine, a bachelor and field worker; Juan Galindo González, thirty-nine, married, with five chldren; and Cristóbal Fernández Espósito, twenty-two, unmarried, also a field worker. In all, twelve men were taken prisoner.

After a half an hour, the whistle called the patrols together.

*Manuel Pérez Blanco:* I was sitting with the assault guards in the cross street, and I saw Rojas sitting in the bar. He broke a bottle of cognac against his heel and drank it. And the guards drank before killing the others. One guard told the guard sitting with me to go up, and he answered, "I'm not going. My head hurts." Then Captain Rojas rose to go above.

Fernando de Arrigunaga accompanied the patrols as they herded the prisoners, some handcuffed, toward Seisdedos's choza:

*Lieutenant de Arrigunaga:* The detainees were taken toward the plaza to bring them together . . . I believe I was at the head, accompanied by the civil guard lieutenant. Upon passing in front of the little corral, we paused, but I continued on toward the plaza with the civil guard officer . . . I don't know if [Rojas] ordered a halt in front of the choza or not. The truth is that I continued on the way because I was almost convinced that something violent or abnormal was going to occur . . . because the guards' state of excitement clearly increased when they saw the corpse of one of their companions in the interior of the choza.[27]

The prisoners were ordered to descend the few paces that led from the street to the choza. In the doorway of the ruins were the bodies of Manuela Lago, her clothes still smoldering; young Francisco García; and Assault Guard Martín Díaz, his body half consumed by the fire.

*Juan Sánchez Gómez, civil guard:* When the detainees arrived at the corral, Rojas told them to go in and see what they had done, asking them if they recognized the corpses.

"This is my daughter," said one of them.

"And that is our brother!" the guards responded, referring to the dead guard.

26. *Diario de sesiones*, February 23, 1933, No. 300, p. 11410.
27. *Casas Viejas*, pp. 85–90.

During this brief dialogue, some cried while others made aggressive gestures toward the captain. A shot from a pistol was heard, and then a volley, but I didn't hear the command to fire.[28]

Nor did he hear the hurrahs for the captain that followed.

According to the testimony of Lieutenant Artal (*El Sol*, May 23, 1934),

. . . He did not notice anything unusual about Rojas when all the arrested men were brought together. He says that when they went by Seisdedos's choza, they saw the body of the assault trooper who had fallen before the door, of which only the upper part, still burning, was left. Captain Rojas then told the arrested men, "Look what you have done with our brother. Walk by and look." When the arrested men started to go down some steps behind a gate, [Artal] heard them say some words, and at that moment Captain Rojas fired twice with the pistol he was carrying; he ordered his men to fire also, whereupon a volley was heard. . . .

He adds that right afterward, they walked to the town plaza. Rojas commented to them about what had occurred and said that it was deplorable but necessary. Artal stated that he disapproved of what had happened.

The medical officer of the civil guards, Don Antonio Verdes de la Villa, ordered an assault guard to finish off the survivors, but the guard, and then another one, did not carry out his orders. Don Antonio then drew his own pistol to give the wounded the coup de gráce.[29]

The families of the detained men, hearing the gunfire, hurried to the choza. An official report states that Isabel Montiano

saw them there, "thrown head down," and that she came back and told [María Cruz], crying "They've killed them . . . they've killed them." They went to the choza, and there was no guard there, but there were "rivers of blood being drunk by the dogs." They had been killed in a criminal fashion. They had taken away her son, the only help of his father. It was a very great crime. She prayed to God to do the same with them as they had done with her own dearest son. They were like little heaps of hay thrown on the ground.

Dolores Benítez went in search of her two sons.

She heard a lot of people's cries and then went over to Seisdedos's choza and found them "already corpses, one bent over the other, the older one's

28. Ibid., p. 107.

29. *Casas Viejas*, pp. 77, 180; *Diario de sesiones*, February 23, 1933, No. 300, p. 11406.

leg over that of the younger." There was an enormous pool of blood, so you couldn't step anywhere." She noticed that one "had had his head blown off, and the other one she could no longer see because she was blinded by pain."

Sebastiana Reyes Estudillo found her husband Manuel Benítez killed by a shot "that had broken off a chunk of his skull." María Toro Pérez went to the corral and saw her only son "dead with a hole in the head, and her hands filled with his blood when she went to kiss his neck."

The elderly María Villanueva went to "the slaughterhouse" in search of her son Juan Grimaldi.

They left him there, dead. She went over there to see him, and a guard pointed his gun at her, threatening to kill her. She fell to the ground with grief, and they picked her up from there."[30]

Pepe Pilar, having settled his family in a safe location, was on his way to a hiding place in the mountains when he heard the new burst of gunfire:

From this side of the river I began to go upstream, and as I approached a barn that was on the other side, I heard some shots fired. I thought to myself, "These poor people are being taken out of their homes and shot to death."

At 9:00 A.M. Don Federico Ortiz Villaumbrales, the doctor of Casas Viejas, returned to the choza to find twelve new bodies, in addition to the two bodies lying in the doorway that he had observed two hours earlier. There were no weapons next to the bodies, and it was thus evident that they had not been killed in battle.[31]

*Manuel Pérez Blanco:* When they came down, a guard was still seated with me; and when they arrived, the other guards said to him, "We made a good find. We've killed a number of them." They had killed the twelve. I was there with some others. When the magistrate and the doctor arrived to take up the dead, the magistrate said, "Let's go up. We all have a duty to aid justice." And I went up with the funeral car. They passed the bodies into the car. I was afraid, and I remained inside.

Then a woman came to Seisdedos's choza weeping because they had killed her son. And a guard raised his rifle: "Get out; otherwise you will have the same luck as those who are dead here." And the woman left.

Later someone peeked in the window, and the guard pointed his rifle at him and said to the magistrate, "I'll shoot him." And the magistrate told him, "No!" "If he looks again, I will."

30. *Diario de sesiones,* February 23, 1933, No. 300, pp. 11406f., 11409, 11410, 11409, 11406.
31. Ibid., p. 11406.

Then I pulled the corpses inside the car. When the car was filled, I had to put the feet of one corpse on top of another in order to fit them in. After the car was loaded, they carried the dead to the cemetery.

Lieutenants Artal and García Castrillón returned to the plaza and made known their distaste for what had taken place. Captain Rojas arrived and said to de Arrigunaga that he was the first to lament what had happened, but orders were orders.[32] Rojas, however, was not finished punishing the town. He handed his cigarette lighter to Lieutenant Artal and ordered him to set fire to other chozas. Artal appealed to de Arrigunaga and asked him to convince Rojas of the uselessness of the act and the grief that would result. Upon de Arrigunaga's pleas, Rojas finally desisted.

The guards regrouped, and de Arrigunaga thanked them and said that they had carried out the governor's orders (which the governor later disowned). There was a minute of silence for the dead, which ended with a hurrah for Spain and another for the Republic.[33] The assault guards, the civil guards, and their officers got into their trucks and drove off. The town was suddenly quiet.

The bodies of those murdered had been taken to the cemetery, where the doctors performed autopsies. The charred bones of those who had perished in the fire lay where they had fallen. The wooden stocks of the shotguns had been consumed by the flames but the barrels protruded among the debris. In the corral nearby lay an unexploded hand grenade. The skull of one of the defenders could be seen in the embers. There remained an overpowering stench of burned flesh.

Juan Pinto learned that his brother Manuel had been one of those shot in front of the choza. Neither Juan nor Manuel had participated in the uprising, but Juan now wondered if his brother had been shot in his stead, because Juan himself had been seen on the street earlier carrying a shotgun:

When they killed my brother, I thought that they had killed him because of me. I went straight away to find the civil guard. I wouldn't have cared if they killed me. Then I said to Salvo, the guard who had survived, "Come out." Then he came to me and gave me his condolences. He greeted me. They had killed my brother. They had killed him, but he wasn't at fault. I said, "Look, this is what I think. You know what my brother was like. He was the sort of man who never bothered anyone or anything. If they wanted to kill those in politics, all right. But my brother was a man who never got involved in anything like that, nor me either. But I came down to see what happened."

32. *Casas Viejas*, pp. 85–90.
33. Report of the commission, *Diario de sesiones*, March 10, 1933, No. 309, p. 11753.

And he said to me, "What happened with your brother is that I could not get there in time. I couldn't be everywhere."

They asked me what I had done with the shotgun. It was a shotgun that I had for hunting rabbits. I said, "Look, I took the shotgun to the sindicato."

And he said, "OK, that's all." And after that, they didn't bother me for anything. Later they really beat many people. Oh, they really beat them. It was a bad thing.

During the next ten days, the village dogs dragged bones out of the ashes of the choza and carried them through the town. Then the remaining bones and ashes were gathered up and buried in unsanctified ground in the cemetery.

# Fourteen

# The Government and the Press

## The first reports

The death toll in the small town of Casas Viejas shocked the nation. Twenty-two campesinos had been killed; three guards were dead and at least four others wounded. All the dead campesinos were believed to have fallen in battle at Seisdedos's choza or in an exchange of gunfire from other points after the choza was destroyed.

The liberal and conservative press, stunned by the casualties and by the ferocity of the fighting, deplored the social conditions that gave rise to actions so destructive and so futile. At the same time, there was a sense that given the nature of revolution, such a high number of deaths was inevitable. In the view of many supporters of a strong central authority, the revolutionaries had received only what could be expected. The monarchist newspaper *ABC* in Madrid approved of the government's swift and decisive action: "The government responds to the rebellion in the only useful adequate form, with the use of force as hard as is necessary to wipe out the disorder and subdue the rebels. We applaud this conduct" (January 13, 1933).

Investigation of the uprising began only hours after the firing had ended. Although Casas Viejas had no newspaper of its own, reports of the intensity of the fighting attracted to the village reporters and photographers from the national and regional press. The first reporter on the scene was V. Gutiérrez de Miguel of *El Sol,* the distinguished liberal newspaper in Madrid. Gutiérrez prided himself on his objectivity and his journalistic ability. His newspaper ranked with the best newspapers in the world, customarily furnishing the most complete record and impartial coverage of events.

When Gutiérrez arrived on the afternoon of January 12, the doctors were doing autopsies on the bodies brought to the cemetery. He observed that the village was quiet but that women were weeping in doorways. He set about to do his work. "I immediately dedicated myself to determine impartially the origin of the events that had developed there, and therefore I went to speak with the doctor, the priest, the schoolteacher, and the deputy mayor" (*El Sol,* January 14, 1933).

In his articles, Gutiérrez described the uprising, the battle, and the number of campesinos dead in the corral, presumably fallen in the fierce battle at Seisdedos's choza. He noted that except for two men who were over forty, the others were boys of less than twenty years of age. Virtually no information was obtained from the silent women who remained in their doorways or from the campesinos who had fled and were subsequently taken prisoner. No one looked for or questioned young Manolo García, the single campesino survivor of the battle at the choza.[1] Neither the doctor, priest, schoolteacher nor mayor explained what had happened. Gutiérrez remained ignorant of the manner in which the men brought to the choza had met their death.

## Official investigations

The government did not name an investigative body to study the incident; but Casares Quiroga, minister of the interior, sent Antonio de la Villa, editor of the Madrid newspaper *La Libertad* and delegate from Cádiz to the Cortes, to investigate the incident on his behalf. On January 15, de la Villa traveled to Casas Viejas, accompanied by a military doctor and five assault guards. He uncovered nothing untoward in the conduct of the troops.

On the same day that de la Villa arrived in Casas Viejas, in Madrid Prime Minister Azaña confided to his diary his deep fears for the Republic:

> Three representatives from different parties have spoken to me today about dictatorship as the only possible solution for anarchist uprisings, if they continue. This is the national inclination, carrying over from previous times and foreign influence. Can Spain in fact live within democracy and under law? Nobody wants to obey, except by force. Friends and foes of the Republic and enemies from both extreme wings are doing everything in their power to express the idea that "things can't go on like this," and minds turn to thoughts of dictatorship. The Republic is caught in a pincer grip. How to escape it? I would prefer not to have to break through it, but I am much afraid that few will aid me in this; and of course, in the parties I will find only suspicion and envy.[2]

1. Forty-eight years passed before he was first interviewed. With the help of Pepe Pareja, I found him living in a settlement not too distant from Cádiz.

2. *Memorias íntimas de Azaña,* January 15, 1933.

Azaña's primary concern was the ability of the government to survive continuing attacks from the left. He and his ministers believed that the government had to be hard on revolutionaries in order to save the Republic. They accepted the loss of life as inevitable consequences of insurrection and hoped that time would diminish the shock of the incident.

Local officials, too, were more concerned with the morale of the forces upholding society than with the excessive repressive zeal that had been employed. On January 17, the civil governor of the province of Cádiz, Pozo de Rodríguez, traveled to Casas Viejas, where he personally congratulated Civil Guards Salvo and García for their heroic conduct and their aid to the assault guards.[3]

## Regional newspapers

The regional press, although closer to the scene, perceived what had happened no more clearly than did the reporters from the distant capital. The first accounts printed in the *Diario de Cádiz* were based on the statements of the civil governor and the observations of Civil Guard Fidel Madras Corral, who lay wounded near the choza throughout the night of fighting and was afterward brought to the hospital in Cádiz. It was not until 7:00 in the evening of January 12 that Federico Joly, director of the *Diario de Cádiz,* and reporter Juan López Estrella began the sixty-four-kilometer drive from Cádiz to Casas Viejas. After passing through Medina Sidonia, however, their car and another carrying reporters and photographers from *ABC* of Seville and *El Liberal* were stopped at the crossroads of Vejer and Casas Viejas by two civil guards, who warned them that it would be unsafe to continue. Communication with the town had been broken off once again, they were told, and the postman and the guards had been fired on. The damage done to the postman's car by unknown assailants was covered extensively by the frustrated newsmen.

The following day, January 13, they reached Casas Viejas at 9:15 A.M. and were directed to the cemetery, where the doctors were still doing autopsies. After speaking to the doctors and to Deputy Mayor Bascuñana, who told them of the first moments of the uprising, the reporters visited the site of the destroyed choza. Accepting the account that there had been a fourteen-hour gun battle in which all of the men had died, they speculated that Manuela Lago, whose body had fallen just beyond the doorway of the choza, had been the gun loader for her father. His body was found in the clump of twelve others. The reporters did not realize that the two had been far apart during the battle. They noted that the body of only one relative of the Cruz family, Juan Silva, could be identified, but again they failed to distinguish

3. *Diario de Cádiz,* January 18, 1933.

between those who had died inside the choza and the victims, like Juan, who had been brought to the corral. The remains inside the choza could not be identified, and so it was not yet certain if Seisdedos and La Libertaria were buried under the remains of the roof or if they had escaped. Since the telephone lines had not yet been reopened, the reporters from Cádiz left at 12:00 noon in order to file their story for the afternoon edition. They had been in town only two hours and forty-five minutes.

In Jerez, after the initial shock had worn off, the regional newspaper *El Guadalete* took a philosophical view of the uprising. They saw society threatened by long standing social problems, but they managed to find hopeful signs in the solutions sought by the Republic and in the spirit of sacrifice and duty exemplified by the civil guards (January 17, 1933). Like the *Diario de Cádiz,* they did not uncover the fact that twelve unarmed men had been brought to the choza of Seisdedos and shot down.

## The anarchist press

The only opposition to the litany of praise for the actions of the guard came from anarchist newspapers. The anarchist press viewed the uprising at Casas Viejas from the campesinos' perspective rather than that of the guards and the government. However, in the first days following the uprising, they too accepted the twenty dead at the choza as a sign of the fierce resistance of the anarchist fighters.[4] *Solidaridad Obrera* described the valor and firmness of the revolutionaries, who fought to win their liberty against an overwhelming force armed with every kind of weapon, including machine guns and incendiary bombs. Casas Viejas was an example of the undying heroism of the revolutionaries and the brutality of the government. The headlines of the *CNT* added Casas Viejas to the list of martyred towns: "Castilblanco, Arnedo, and Casas Viejas" (January 14, 1933).

The first notice that a massacre had taken place appeared in a compelling account of the uprising published in *CNT*. Its correspondent was Miguel Pérez Cordón. Immediately following the uprising, the people of Paterna, where Pérez Cordón lived, had contributed small sums to be given to the victims' families.

*José Vega:* About six or eight days after the uprising, a collection was made by our sindicato to help the poor families who were without means and without protection. We took the money to bring to the families. We stopped at a small store that was there on the right on Calle San Juan, and as we arrived Corporal García saw us: "You! Come here."

4. *Solidaridad Obrera,* January 14, 1933.

We said that we were going to turn in a donation that we had collected for the victims of the past events.

"Come to the barracks." There they interrogated us, an interrogation of "My Lord and Our Father," as we say here in Andalusia. From there they moved us to Medina, where we were detained. For that simple deed, we were detained several days.

It was the first time that I had been in jail. And there I met María Silva and some others from the movement who were already imprisoned there. Coincidentally, we were put in the cell just opposite La Libertaria. Miguel had not known her before.

After eight days they released us—Cordón, myself, Francisco Vega, and two others, who had composed the committee. María was in longer. When Miguel came out, he wrote articles about her.

By virtue of coming in contact with the prisoners from Casas Viejas, Pérez Cordón learned details of the uprising that would have been otherwise sealed off from him. Much of his account, however, was an idealistic rendering of an anarchist revolution:

It was the night of the tenth when a battle began, but it was not aggressive or cruel or inhuman; it was, rather, kind, noble, and dignified. Those "illiterate man-beasts" in the village rapidly made themselves masters of the situation without shooting, without wishing to satiate a hatred accumulated by having always been the object of so much abuse. They disarmed the bourgeoisie. Only one, José Vela, resisted and fired at the rebels from a balcony. Only one pair of civil guards resisted in the middle of the street in order to disrupt the movement. The workers destroyed some useless bundles of papers from the town hall, and they wounded some guards who tenaciously resisted the new form of life of the collectives. They posted sentries at the exits of the town, as well as next to the barracks of the civil guard who did not want to surrender.

The morning of the eleventh was for those workers the annunciation of comunismo libertario not as a utopian theory but as reality, as they demonstrated that same day, although for only a few short hours.

They began the distribution of provisions among all the villagers. No special consideration was given to any individual. Everyone was attended to equally. The revolutionary committee signed some vouchers; these were presented at the storehouses to receive provisions, clothing, and so on. This lasted some three hours—three hours of communist fairness that captured the sympathy of those who still remained resistant to the new social organization. There was happiness on everyone's face. There were hearty hugs and handshakes. There was a completely pure fraternal feeling that spontaneously unified everyone to arrange for the distribution of food. They then began to think how they would organize production. The red and black flag waved in the sindicato, as it had the night before, as a promissory sign that a tyrannical and unjust world had disappeared forever, giving way to a new world of liberty, equality, and love between human beings.

Pérez Cordón then published the first accusation that most of the dead had not been killed in the fighting at all:

> What a show of force to crush a few men almost without arms! Those inside—machine-gunned. Bombs, rifles. Not a cordial word. Not an official to visit the revolutionaries to explain to them why they should not continue their rebellion. They all had to be killed. "They're savages," they said. The guards captured and handcuffed some men. They brought them before the uniformed "victims" [the dead assault guard]. There they were not told, "Look at the victims you have made," but there and then the ley de fugas was applied—or better said, they were put to death.[5]

The new information was ignored, taken to be antigovernment rhetoric. As an established anarchist propagandist, Peréz Cordón's reliability was no doubt open to question. Writing in *CNT* some weeks later (on February 9), he denied that María Silva had even been in her grandfather's choza on the night and morning of the battle.

A more carefully drawn account by Eduardo de Guzmán appeared in *La Tierra* (January 23). Guzmán visited Casas Viejas in the company of Ramón J. Sender, who was writing for *La Libertad*. After seeing the site of the burned choza and talking to the campesinos, Guzmán asked some pointed questions about the size of the choza and the nature of the terrain; and he noted that handcuffs had been seen half-hidden in the refuse.

> How did these men come to die? Where did they come from? Where were they? The official statement, the version of the government newspapers, is simple: they left the burning house, shotguns in hand, firing against the guards, trying to answer shot for shot, wounding whoever wounded them. But opposed to these contentions, I hear the emotional words of some of the survivors of the catastrophe, the burning and active indignation with which they reject this view, and the rage with which someone, hidden, I don't wish to know where, shouts to me.
>
> The statement that nineteen men were hidden in the house is a scheme used to justify what is unjustifiable. It flies in the face of those who try to maintain this lie.
>
> And this view is not only that of the campesinos. The most elementary logic refutes the lie. The very unfolding of the tragic events destroys this absurd hypothesis.
>
> How could they fit into two small rooms? It couldn't be done, even jammed one against the other. And what of the corral? In the corral, they would not have had any defense against the guards who fired from above. They would have died in the first moment. How could policeman Madrás have escaped alive? No. Flatly and definitely not. The thirteen men found dead in the corral were perhaps never in the burned hut, nor in the sur-

5. *CNT*, January 18, 1933.

rounding area during the fighting. Where did they come from? How did they get there? How did one of them especially get there, one who—it is said—was rather seriously ill and who had not been outside his home for many hours; who, moreover, would have to have felt more ill at the horror of the battle? One could make but this reply: no wounded or prisoners. When the shooting is over, there are no wounded left; only heaps of corpses with horrible rips in their noble bodies, which were weakened by hunger. But not a single one who might have been grazed lightly by the bullets, not a single one lightly or seriously wounded by the guns of the guardians of order. All those who faced the public forces were dead.

## The debate in the Cortes

Despite Guzmán's articles, unnoticed or again ignored as propaganda, no official effort was made to uncover the facts. It was not until February 1, more than two weeks after the events, that the Cortes reconvened and the matter could be aired before the national parliamentary body. The coming debate on Casas Viejas could not be disassociated from the larger political picture. Those who opposed the government on other grounds—for its economic, social, military, or religious policies—were eager to use the issue of excessive brutality in Casas Viejas to flay Azaña and his ministers.

Azaña's government was a coalition of Socialists and Left Republicans (composed of Azaña's Republican Action Party and the Radical Socialists). Additional support was given by the small regional parties of the Catalonian Esquerra and the Galician Federal Republicans. The coalition was united by its anticlericalism and its acceptance of regionalism.

Opposition to Azaña's government came from a variety of political parties. The largest group were the Radicals, led by Alejandro Lerroux, who held the center of the political spectrum and were opposed both to the church and the Socialists. Serious dissent was also voiced by a wing of the Radical Socialist party (some of whose members were in Azaña's ministry) which, led by disenchanted intellectuals such as Eduardo Ortega y Gasset (the brother of the philosopher José Ortega y Gasset), sought drastic reform including expropriation of the lands of the nobility and abolition of the civil guard. Attacks from farther to the right stemmed from the Progressive party of Niceto Alcalá-Zamora and the Conservative Republican party of Miguel Maura. Still more intense opposition to Azaña originated with the Agrarian party, which represented the landlords of Andalusia, and from the conservative delegates of two regional parties, the Lliga Catalán and the Catholic Basque Nationalists, who had good reason to fear the antireligious policies of the Azaña government. The anarchists had no elected representatives in the Cortes, but Representative Barriobero often presented their point of view.

The government had overwhelming support in the Cortes; however, a small minority of opposition deputies were critical of the haste taken in burning, bombing, and machine-gunning Andalusian campesinos. There were unanswered questions concerning the conduct of the troops and the severity of the orders they had received.

On February 1, Don Eduardo Ortega y Gasset, the deputy of the Radical Socialist party, asked to address the chamber.

He began with an indictment against the fruitless policies of the government that had failed to resolve agrarian problems.

> A broad examination of the facts shows that in good measure the government bears the blame for the wave of campesino hostility that broke out. After two years of the Republic, the campesinos without land and the day workers without work find themselves in a hungry and desperate situation. Their hopes have been destroyed by promises that failed to materialize. This wave of hostilities then broke out.

He then moved to his startling accusation:

> According to the information that reaches me, burdened by the trouble of having to guard eleven campesinos—who were handcuffed and defenseless, incapable of doing any damage—the guards, in order to rid themselves of this concern, shot them, apparently some of them with eleven bullets.

Equally shocking was the fact that this news had not been revealed either by responsible officials or by the press:

> Tragic details have come to me by chance. Some workers from Seville were traveling in the same train as the assault troops who had participated in the attack at Casas Viejas, an attack in which the people were treated, as was said and must be repeated here, with more violence and cruelty than if they had been African Berbers.

Antonio de la Villa, the delegate from the province of Cádiz who had gone to Casas Viejas on January 15 on behalf of the minister of the interior, was the first to respond.

> The government forces went to bring about the reestablishment of order and, in the face of savage, barbarous, and organized attack, had no other remedy than to defend themselves. It is possible that their later reaction was a violent one, like the attack upon them, and this has of course given rise to those writings in the press that come from we all know where, [and] to those campaigns that come from we also know where.

Parading all the common misconceptions, de la Villa maintained that the uprising was initiated and organized by Seisdedos, who was assisted by Sopas, whom he identified as an expelled civil guard. The 450 workers of the sindicato, he believed, had lived in houses around that of Seisdedos, and at least 300 of them had fired twenty shots for each bullet fired by the guards. In his explanation of the high number of casualties at the choza, he noted that as the firing went on, "then occurred what occurs in all revolutions."[6]

Lerroux had not been present for the debate on February 1, but the following day he pressed the government to answer the charges leveled against it. Prime Minister Azaña undertook the major defense of the government's actions. Azaña assumed a larger role in the debate than he would have ordinarily, since Casares Quiroga, the minister of the interior, was ill in Ronda, barely able to sit up in bed; and Arturo Menéndez, the director general of security, was himself under attack for his part in the incident. Without knowing that innocent men had been shot down, Azaña based his argument on the government's need to respond to aggression. At the time it appeared to him that a partisan attack impugned the honorable motives of the government and himself. He was later to regret the choice of words he used in his defense, for his explanation, like de la Villa's, was ambiguous and would later appear to be deliberately deceptive and callous.

> Fellow Representatives, no matter how much is investigated, not a speck of guilty action will be found against the government. What happened in Casas Viejas is what was bound to happen. An armed rebellious uprising against society and the state having been staged, what took place in Casas Viejas was absolutely unavoidable, and I would like to know the man who, sitting in the ministry of the interior or in the presidency of the council of government or any other place of authority, could have found a way to allow the events in Casas Viejas to take a different turn. I would like the recipe, so I could learn it.

To explain the swift and severe actions, Azaña called on the ghosts that plagued past governments: the weakness of the Kerensky regime, toppled by the Bolsheviks into a dictatorship, and the specter of La Mano Negra. He reminded his audience of great numbers of campesinos, angry and violent, loose in the campo of Jerez.

> If the rebellion at Casas Viejas had lasted one day more, the entire province of Cádiz would have become inflamed. And we would now be saying that, not having been severe, swift, and energetic in ending the uprising at Casas Viejas, we have provoked by our lenience the revolt of all the cam-

6. *Diario de sesiones*, February 1, 1933, No. 287, pp. 10860, 10861, 10862, 10865.

pesinos of the province of Cádiz. [*Noise of approval.*] That is what you would be saying now, and that is the essential reality.

There was no other remedy than to end it. And in what manner? In the only manner possible.[7]

While the government continued to deny that unnecessary violence had occurred in Casas Viejas, it opposed any investigation of the charges. Maintaining, with some justification, that the criticism against them was politically motivated, the government would vigorously defend the conduct of the public forces. It was not yet known that twelve men had been torn from their families and shot. This last terrible episode of the repression at Casas Viejas remained a virtual secret for several more weeks. On February 8 government supporters defeated a call for an official investigation by a vote of 123 to 8. Azaña had argued, "The government and the Cortes know everything that happened." In protest, the indignant minority planned to prepare an unofficial inquiry, which would begin twelve days later.

## The *Diario de Cádiz*

A month had now passed, and despite the attention drawn to the massacre, the liberal and conservative press still failed to investigate the charges raised by Pérez Cordón and Guzmán in their articles and by Ortega y Gasset in the parliament. The regional newspaper closest to the site was the *Diario de Cádiz,* located in the provincial capital, only sixty-four kilometers from Casas Viejas; but the editors ignored the evidence, even when it was written by a guest correspondent in their own newspaper. On February 13, members of the Association of Printing Arts went to Casas Viejas to distribute the pesetas they had collected from a lottery held for the widows of the town. The secretary of the association was José Martínez Regal, whose account of how the funds were distributed described a visit to the grieving mother of Manuel Benítez: " 'From here,' she pointed to an opening in the choza that one could not call a door, 'they took my son, and a few hours later they killed him.' "[8]

The visitors heard from the townspeople that Seisdedos had not been involved in the uprising. When they departed, the association members expressed the wish that the deputies who had voted against an official commission to investigate the incidents could have experienced this visit. They eagerly awaited the inquiry of the unofficial commission, soon to arrive.

Despite this surprising account, on February 16, three days after José Martínez's report, the *Diario* published a front-page article by their reporter

7. *Diario de sesiones*, February 2, 1933, No. 288, pp. 10892, 10893.
8. *Diario de Cádiz*, February 13, 1933.

Juan López Estrella that boasted of the ample coverage by the *Diario* and criticized other papers who had not honored the truth as they had.

> The *Diario de Cádiz* has probably been the newspaper that has given its readers the fullest and most accurate details of the events. This is logical, since its director, Federico Joly, himself went to the scenes of the tragedy, and I had the honor of accompanying him, when there were still echoes of the bombs.

Like government officials and most of the national press, the *Diario* accepted the high casualties as the normal consequence of revolution and did not concede the necessity to look further. López Estrella glossed over questionable details with a certain distaste: "The eternal song took place in Casas Viejas. Innocent people died, induced by those who brought them to suffering for the sake of politics. This is the only truth."

On February 18 the unofficial parliamentary commission arrived in Cádiz to visit Medina Sidonia and Casas Viejas. A photo of the group and an article describing their plans appeared the following day on the front page of the *Diario de Cádiz*. Included in the article, however, was "incredibly interesting" news provided by an anonymous person who had just been in Casas Viejas. The account told of documents discovered showing that if they had been successful, the rebels had intended to hang the daughters of the leading landowners from the lamp posts in the plaza. The anonymous informant assured the *Diario* reporter, "So that you won't doubt it, I can give you not only the names of the landowners but those of the daughters who were to be victims as well." Cited were the landowning families: Don José Espina, José and Juan Vela, and three others.

The story was patterned upon the history of La Mano Negra. Rumors of murder plots had been told about Casas Viejas eighteen years before, concerning the events surrounding the death of Gaspar Zumaquero. Printed on the day of the commission's trip to Casas Viejas, this newly exhumed accusation would make the *Diario* appear either amazingly gullible or party to an attempt to confuse the issues under investigation.

## The unofficial investigation

On February 19, the extraparliamentary committee of the Cortes visited Casas Viejas and gathered evidence that the *Diario* and the national press had ignored for more than five weeks. They interviewed the leading citizens—the priest, the deputy mayor, and landowners—but they also took depositions from the mothers and widows of the victims. In apparent amazement, the *Diario de Cádiz* declared,

The versions collected, they tell us, fully confirm the commission's concept regarding the repression.

The mother of the person nicknamed El Ronquito ("Hoarse voice") confirmed that her son, who was ill, was taken handcuffed from his home to the choza of Seisdedos, from which he never returned.

They tell us there are truly sensational versions that, when they become known, will have a great effect on public opinion. [February 20, 1933]

Also present were reporters from the *CNT, La Nación, La Tierra, ABC,* and other newspapers spanning the political spectrum. They found the villagers eager to make statements about the tragic events in great detail.

"We ask for justice. We want the guilty punished!"

The discussion with the women was truly amazing. While they told of their grief and sadness, they never ceased to weep and lament bitterly.

There was damning testimony too from those of the upper class, including José Vela Barca, the son of Juan Vela.

He saw the assault guards with their guns out, and they didn't know how to disassemble them. . . . He walked along with the assault guards, and they would shoot anybody walking down the street. He was filled with fear, staying clear of the gunfire and getting inside doorways. He saw Quijada taken out of his house with blows from clubs and rifle butts; and saw that they also struck [Quijada's] wife. Indignant, he returned to the plaza, where Guard Salvo said that the rebels had entrenched themselves in Seisdedos's choza. One of his day workers, José Toro, was taken out of his own house, and [Vela Barca] believes, as do all the townspeople, that those whose bodies appeared in the corral were executed. . . . He says the whole town agrees it was a real crime. He believes that most of the dead were innocent. Once the rebels had made their attempt against the barracks, they fled into the countryside.

The depositions not only strengthened the assertion that a massacre had taken place; they also sustained the charge that the cause of the uprising was the government's failure to remedy impoverishment and injustice in the countryside.

Andrés Vera, a priest of Casas Viejas. He has been there seven months. We know he lives in a miserable house, unfit for a human being. At the time of the interview, we saw a great number of women in mourning clothes on their way to request charity, which is given to them in the form of cash and bread.

He says there are two syndicalist groups in Casas Viejas—the UGT and the CNT. The day before the events, he hadn't noticed anything abnormal in the town. He says his community is exceedingly good, bearing their great misery with resignation.

The cause of the events, in his opinion, is hunger, which could not have gone on any longer. He says property is very badly distributed, for there are only four landowners in town, plus a few outsiders. All the rest are day laborers, who earn wages very few days in the year.

He says he had noticed that since August the unemployed workers had been gathering in large groups in the square, and that this misery gave him great sorrow. To alleviate the situation, the city council of Medina, since Casas Viejas is a quarter of that town, was sending about 150 pesetas a day, which was given to the heads of households.

When the commission submitted its report to the Cortes on February 23, Prime Minister Azaña was confronted with the overpowering depositions citing atrocities. General Fanjul of the Agrarian party, and one of the members of the unofficial commission, called the incident the failure of a system and a government. He asserted that "the decisive orders from the prime minister or the minister of the interior, or both, were carried out with complete severity, with accursed severity."

Azaña had to counter the suspicion that the government had deliberately covered up the facts:

We have placed in politics our dedication, our public zeal, our understanding—be it large or small—our speech, our work, every minute of the day; but I, at least, have not placed in politics my inner conscience, and that is not available for anybody to profane. I may err more than anyone else, but no one has a right to place in the innermost center of my conscience such an accusation against my integrity and honesty.

Azaña noted that orders issued called for the public forces "to respond to aggression with force, to repel violence with violence," but he argued that if the government had given especially cruel orders, there would have been extensive losses throughout the country. He then went on to defend his earlier choice of words: "When I said that what happened in Casas Viejas was what had to happen, I was not thinking or aware that something had happened in Casas Viejas which an honorable man could not approve."[9]

In the debate on the following day, February 24, Azaña bemoaned the dilemma of those in high authority who must answer for the actions of those below them:

We have the misfortune of having been in the government when this lamentable event occurred. The public force is the custodian of society. But

9. *Diario de sesiones,* February 23, 1933, No. 300, pp. 11407, 11405, 11418, 11416, 11422, 11423.

who has custody of the custodian? Is it at all possible for a state or a government to be responsible at every moment for the calm and composure and moral strength of its agents?[10]

Azaña now pressed for an official inquiry, and by a vote of 173 to 130, the majority in the Cortes supported him. A group of deputies was named to investigate the circumstances.

In the countryside of Andalusia, the determination of responsibility had already been made. During the last week of February, while Azaña was denying that any atrocities had taken place, the festival of Carnaval was celebrated in the villages of Cádiz. Casas Viejas was in mourning, and there were no local masked singers to mark the festival; but a chorus from nearby Alcalá de los Gazules visited the town with a song composed in honor of the fallen heroes. The verses did not mention Captain Rojas; Azaña and his ministers were depicted as the chief villains.

| | |
|---|---|
| Casas Viejas, el gran día | Casas Viejas: on the great day |
| De su revolución, | Of its revolution |
| —Tará, tará— | —Tará, tará—, |
| Con las armas en las manos | Its weapons in hand, |
| Ya a la burguesía | It overpowered |
| Toda la rindió, | The bourgeoisie |
| Y al grito de "Abajo | At the shout of "Down |
| Con la reacción," | With the forces of reaction." |
| Que ya ha llegado la hora | The day has arrived |
| De que se termine | To put an end |
| Tanta explotación. | To so much exploitation. |
| ¡Qué grande este ejemplo | What a great example |
| Para la nación! | To the nation |
| Que este pueblecito | This little town |
| Ya lo demostró: | Has given! |
| Bajo la bandera | Under the banner |
| De la libertad | Of freedom |
| Lucharon por un ideal | They fought for an ideal |
| Que supieron implantar. | That they knew how to establish. |
| Fueron dominados de nuevo | They were overcome once more |
| Por las muchas fuerzas | By the overwhelming forces |
| De la reacción, | Of reaction |
| (Que) destruyó una choza humilde | That destroyed a humble hut |
| Y a unos cuantos libertarios | And the libertarian people |
| Que se defendían | Who defended themselves |
| Con mucho valor, | With great valor. |

10. *Diario de sesiones*, February 24, 1933, No. 301, p. 11463.

Trató de incendiarlos
—Instinto criminal—,
Y qué más La Libertaria,
Seisdedos, y veinte más,
De ese crimen monstruoso
Nos tenemos que vengar
—Tará, tará—.
Castigando a los culpables,
Y haciendo justicia
A la humanidad,
Porque los tiranos
Han de terminar.
De la justicia del pueblo
Ni Azaña se escapará,
[Ni] Casares Quiroga,
ni Fulano de Tal,
Que fueron los que ocultaron

Esa orden criminal.
Los nombres de esos canallas
No podemos olvidar
—Tará, tará—
Porque todos los sabemos,
Y en el parlamento quieren
Disculparlos bajo un buen
Principio de autoridad.
Si han cometido ese crimen,
Bien duro lo pagarán.

[The reactionaries] burned them—
What a criminal instinct—
—La Libertaria,
Seisdedos, and twenty more.
Such a monstrous crime
We must avenge
—Tará, tará—
By punishing the guilty,
And doing justice
For the sake of humanity,
Because tyrants
Must vanish.
From the people's justice
Azaña will not escape,
nor Casares Quiroga
nor Fulano so-and-so,
Since they were the ones to cover
up
The criminal command.
The scoundrels' names
We cannot forget
—Tará, tará—
Because we all know them,
And though parliament wants
To excuse them under the good
Cover of authority,
Those who committed this crime
Will pay for it.

## The debate continues

Although Azaña continued to defend the actions of the public forces in Casas Viejas, he was beginning to have doubts concerning Rojas's testimony to the effect that nothing unseemly had taken place. At 11:00 at night on March 1, Azaña met Rojas personally for the first time, and he heard the captain deny receiving monstrous orders and then directing a massacre. Although Azaña was not favorably disposed toward Rojas's general demeanor, at the same time, he was impressed by the conciseness of his testimony.

*Azaña:* There were no executions?
*Rojas:* No. We were hard, cruel, if you wish. We fired at those who ran and did not raise their hands when we ordered. We fired at those who looked out of their windows. When they fired at us from the chumbas, we responded with machine guns. But that was all. . . .

*Azaña:* "Isn't it true that you ordered a raid in the village?"
*Rojas:* "It's a lie."[11]

Unknown to Azaña, Captain Rojas was preparing another line of defense. On the same day that he spoke with the prime minister, Rojas drafted a statement accusing Director General of Security Menéndez of giving him the damning orders in Madrid on January 10. Rather than defend the government, he would extricate himself by throwing the blame for the massacre on his superiors:

The orders that he gave me were that as soon as the movement broke out, I should not fear anything or feel burdened by responsibilities of any sort, because there was no other way to act than this: I should take no wounded or prisoners, because they could tell what happened; and in order to avoid this, I should apply the ley de fugas and everything else that was necessary. Everyone with weapons or implicated in the movement should be shot in the head; he said, "not leave a puppet with his head on." If they pulled out white cloths, I should disregard them and answer with fire, because there had already been many similar cases—when we got close, they caused many casualties. In short, I should not have compassion of any kind, because this had to be done for the welfare of the Republic, and it would be good to make an example so that it would not be repeated. I told him that these orders seemed a bit severe to me, but he answered that there was no other remedy than to do it and have a tranquil conscience. Besides, he took responsibility for everything.

Rojas maintained that when the troops were about to depart at the railway station in Madrid, Menéndez gathered the officers together and stated that he did not want wounded or prisoners. Then he reminded Rojas of the specific orders he had given him earlier: "You already know what I told you."

Having blamed Menéndez for the orders that had initiated the massacre, Rojas then charged the director general with insisting on the cover-up as well:

Upon my return to Madrid, I told him all that had happened, and he told me that it wouldn't be good for the government if I told in what manner we had killed the prisoners and that absolutely no one should find out about it, because word would get around. He demanded my word of honor that I would tell absolutely no one, and I gave it to him.[12]

Unaware of Rojas's statement, and reassured by his interview that nothing criminal had taken place and that the government was the victim of partisan

11. Azaña, *Obras*, 4:452.

12. *Diario de sesiones*, March 7, 1933, No. 306, p. 11634; and March 10, 1933, 309, p. 11754.

attacks, Azaña again defended the government and the troops against the charge of unconscionable brutality. He rejected the new evidence and recalled how on January 8, in various localities throughout Spain, members of the public forces had been sacrificed in an effort to avoid acting too severely. In Casas Viejas, he argued, more resistance had come than was possible from a miserable choza containing four men with shotguns. The local civil guards were in a desperate situation, he asserted, on the point of abandoning the town; and when the rescue forces arrived, they were fired on from all the houses in town:

> With the province of Cádiz on the verge of widespread rebellion of the same sort, there was no other remedy than to end the disorder of Casas Viejas immediately. And not that day, nor before, nor later, have orders been given or obeyed to exterminate every living thing or to set such a terrible example as has been described.[13]

Following Azaña's spirited defense, the government beat back a motion of censure, 190 to 128. It was the government's last word on the tragedy; but despite the measure of support demonstrated, the general indignation could not be contained, and continued pressure would soon bring out new and conclusive testimony.

## Gutiérrez de Miguel

During an earlier course in the debate, Azaña had noted a peculiar phenomenon that, politics aside, piqued his curiosity—no questions had been raised for many days after the uprising, despite the fact that visitors to Casas Viejas included newsmen, military officers, a civil and a military judge, and public officials—some of whom had spoken with the villagers themselves. Nor, Azaña noted, did the military officers and men directly involved, including the local guards who had been there throughout the uprising, make the slightest allusion to anything alarming that had occurred.[14]

On March 2, V. Gutiérrez de Miguel, who had boasted of having been the first reporter in Casas Viejas, tried to explain in *El Sol* how evidence of the slaughter had eluded him. Gutiérrez had been a reporter for twenty-two years, and his pride was wounded. He recalled arriving in Casas Viejas when the choza of Seisdedos was still smoldering. The doctors had just concluded the autopsies and were washing their hands in the stream opposite the cemetery. The sight of the corpses, still unburied, profoundly disturbed the newspaperman and he vented his moral passion on the villagers he saw.

13. *Diario de sesiones*, March 2, 1933, No. 304, p. 11573.
14. *Diario de sesiones*, February 24, 1933, No. 301, p. 11464.

My first reaction was anguish, caused by the indifference of the people—to the point that, watching a group of women gossiping, as if unaware of everything, at the corner of the street that climbs up to Seisdedos's house, I blurted out, half astonished and half indignant: "It seems as if the dead men were from Gerona. Seventeen victims should be enough to set the whole town weeping."

Determined to write the full story of the uprising, Gutiérrez sought out the deputy mayor, civil guard Salvo, Don Andrés Vera the priest, the mailman, and the telegraph and telephone personnel. He tried to speak to the few people on the street and to some of the dazed men who had straggled in to surrender to the guards. In the company of the doctor, Gutiérrez went to the charred ruins of the choza where he discovered three more bodies and a pistol beneath the embers.

From all his contacts Gutiérrez learned in great detail about the siege at the choza of Seisdedos, but he now complained that he never heard a single word to indicate that innocent men had been dragged from their homes and shot. He questioned the motives and the morality of those who had kept silent before him, and, despite his apologetic confession, he still maintained some doubt concerning the charges of a massacre.

I will repeat a hundred times, they told me nothing. I stake my professional achievement and my love for the truth in saying so, and in this particular case, something men prize highly: my sympathy with other people's grief. I don't know which has caused me greater amazement—what made them keep silent then . . . or what now moves them to speak so much and to so many. Until an impartial investigation clarifies the events, I will continue to ignore how and when one or the other served the truth better: their silence—I would like to think it was full of emotion, which they maintained before me and kept for many days—or the present declarations, which, even if true, seem less a belated reaction to a grief that begs for justice than an effort to sustain and serve the politics of enmity.

Gutiérrez's account contains the reasons for his failure to uncover what had taken place. He went for information to established authority figures—the priest, the mayor, and the civil guards—all keenly aware of the undesirability of stirring up accusation and recrimination. He also spoke with semi-official personnel such as the mailman and the telephone repairman, both from outside of Casas Viejas, who at best could provide scant information.

The villagers that he should have spoken with seem to have been inaccessible—not because they were not present but because they were beyond his ken. Gutiérrez observed that there were few people in the street, and those who were there did not act according to the standards he considered appropriate to the situation. Instead of interviewing them, he scolded them for their lack of compassion. He knocked on no doors to seek out campesino families, and his attitude and moral posture made him inaccessible. No one lied to him. He had made himself impervious to the truth.

## The official investigation

Until March 2 the government maintained its original position, without vigorously investigating the charges or even questioning the officers and men who had fought in Casas Viejas. The first investigators dispatched from Madrid and Cádiz had returned with self-serving findings: the public forces had met armed resistance with justifiable severity. Obviously many people knew of the massacre; others suspected that something terrible had taken place. Yet none of the officers and officials who had been at the scene came forward. Initially town officials were frozen into silence, while the campesinos were virtually ignored by newsmen and other investigators. The testimony of men taken prisoner too went largely unrecorded, perhaps because, as they were awaiting trial for insurrection, their accounts were considered less than candid.

Now Menéndez was spurred into action. Determined to establish that nothing unwarranted had occurred, he collected pertinent newspaper articles, and had a declaration taken from Juan López Estrella of the *Diario de Cádiz*, who as late as February 16 had published his disbelief that atrocities had taken place. The next step was to take statements from the principal officers involved.

Lieutenant Artal had been pained and depressed by the incident at Casas Viejas; and Rojas, who feared what Artal might do, visited him in Seville to urge him to remain quiet, saying that such was the wish of Director General of Security Menéndez. On March 2, however, Menéndez ordered Artal brought to Madrid, and on the pretext of having him attend the Press ball at the Zarzuela theater, had him escorted instead to the Ministry of Security. Artal, lacking a formal jacket, had been assured that he could dress in black; however, instead of enjoying the alternating performances of the theater's three orchestras, Artal found himself alone in an office with the state's attorney, Señor Franqueira.

*Lt. Artal:* Once the lieutenant colonel had left, Sr. Franqueira approached me reservedly and said, "Look, Artal, we all know what happened at Casas Viejas. It's necessary that no one else should now about it and that none of us should be blamed for it. I have here a statement from López Estrella, in which he says that nothing happened at Casas Viejas, and here also is Rojas's, along the same lines. I have a similar statement prepared for you. All you have to do is sign it. Some copies have been made for a few other guards who were at Casas Viejas, and they can sign in the same manner as you."

I did not give in and sign the statement; I told him, "Sr. Franqueira, this would be very well, except that I must tell the truth and nothing but the truth."

"You leave me speechless," responded Sr. Franqueira. "This is a bombshell! It looks as if you have some political interest in this matter. Do you have something against the security director or against Rojas?"

"On the contrary," I responded, "a close friendship unites me with Captain Rojas; and in reference to Sr. Menéndez, I don't know him personally."

Franqueira reminded Artal of the need to consider his career, and he suggested that Artal claim he had been in bed at the time the events occurred. The interrogation was interrupted several times by Franqueira's visits to the office of the director general, who, he said, demanded a statement that same night. Artal finally complied, but with his own version of what had occurred.[15]

On March 3 Azaña recorded the news in his diary:

At 5:00 in the morning he declared that in Casas Viejas, by orders of Rojas, twelve or fourteen prisoners had been shot, and that Rojas had said that he had orders from Menéndez to apply the ley de fugas. As if this were not enough, Artal adds that Rojas had told him that the minister of the interior and the president of the council [Azaña] were committed to get them off the hook. Artal also asserts that Rojas went to Seville to reassure him and to urge him not to tell the truth.[16]

To Azaña, "it could not be worse." Menéndez offered his resignation, and it was accepted. Azaña entered his own despair in his diary:

I went to the office of the ministers, and there I had a long conversation with Largo, Ríos, Domingo, Prieto, and Albornoz about my repugnance concerning the campaign being mounted against us and the fact that because of their desire to unseat us, they would not give up thinking that we ordered the atrocities of Casas Viejas, or that we covered them up. I told them of my weariness, the breaking of my will, my horror of the calumnious atmosphere in which we move, the uselessness of our efforts to liberate ourselves from the coalition of so many resentments, of so much

15. Testimony of Lieutenant Artal, in *El Sol*, May 23, 1934, and in Casas Viejas, pp. 74–75.

16. Azaña, *Obras*, 4:454.

personal hatred. I declared that I can't go on like this and that I am only too willing to make a disturbance from the government bench. . . .[17]

Despite the evidence accumulating against him, Captain Rojas continued to deny that any massacre had occurred. He accused Artal of personal enmity, because he had been forced to reprimand Artal's poor conduct in Casas Viejas.

Fellow officers of the assault troops came to Rojas's aid with accusations of their own. Five assault captains in Madrid signed a declaration (on February 26) alleging their receipt of verbal orders, originating with the director general of security, to take "neither wounded nor prisoners" any armed rebels.[18] Given the opportunity to add his own signature, however, Rojas declined to do so. Another officer, Captain Bartolomé Barba Hernández, testified that he had received similar orders from the minister of war (Azaña), although he initially declined to make a statement about them unless released from the responsibility of confidentiality. Barba claimed to have been told to accept "neither wounded nor prisoners" and later he was to add, "shoot them in the belly" ("tiros a la barriga").[19]

On March 5, however, close to two months after the uprising, Rojas confessed before a special judge that Artal had told the truth. Twelve helpless prisoners had been murdered. Rojas's statement, written on March 1, added that when Menéndez saw them off at the train station in Madrid, he had given strict instructions to take neither wounded nor prisoners and to apply the ley de fugas or any other means.[20]

Azaña was dumbfounded. "What manner of man is this Rojas, who has been denying all this for two months and continued to deny it until Friday, even when he had signed that new statement?"[21]

Government figures close to the events hastened to protect themselves. Pozo de Rodríguez, civil governor of the province of Cádiz, now maintained that he had been unaware of what had happened throughout January and most of February. According to the governor, he had received no relevant information from his representative, de Arrigunaga. For his part, de Arrigunaga denied having witnessed the executions, although this was disputed by the

17. Ibid., p. 455. Francisco Largo Caballero, Minister of Labor and head of the Socialist trade union, the UGT; Fernando de los Ríos, the Minister of Education; Marcelino Domingo, Minister of Agriculture; Indalecio Prieto, Minister of Finance and Public Works; and Álvaro de Albornoz, Minister of Justice. Largo, Prieto and Ríos were members of the Socialist party; Domingo and Albornoz were co-leaders of the Radical Socialist Party.

18. *Diario de sesiones*, March 7, 1933, No. 306, pp. 11631f.

19. *Diario de sesiones*, March 15, 1933, No. 311, p. 11829f; and *El Sol*, May 24, 1934.

20. *Diario de sesiones*, March 7, 1933, No. 306, p. 11634; and March 10, 1933, No. 309, pp. 11754f.

21. Azaña, *Obras*, 4:459.

military officers present, among them Lieutenant García Castrillón of the civil guard, who maintained that he had appealed to de Arrigunaga to stop the executions.[22]

Events now occurred in rapid succession. The parliamentary commission visited Cádiz for additional testimony on March 6, and four days later they submitted their report to the Cortes. The commission found that the orders issued by Menéndez on the night of January 8, as recalled by the director general himself, were unusually severe. He had described the initial incident at Casas Viejas as a violent revolutionary movement and specifically ordered the use of firearms against armed resisters and saboteurs of public utilities.[23]

Despite the orders, however, the commission found the evidence against Menéndez ambiguous and inconclusive. Two of the senior officers present at the January 8 meeting independently gave accounts virtually identical with that of the director general, and the same version was given by others who had received the verbal orders from those officers. There were some in the same chain of command, however, who recalled being told to "take neither wounded nor prisoners," which matched the accusation of the five captains. But there was nothing in writing. It was argued that an officer given orders that he believed to be illegal could demand a copy in writing; none of Menéndez's accusers had done so. Moreover, as Azaña pointed out in debate, none of the five officers bringing the complaint had followed such orders. Rojas alone had initiated a tragedy. Rojas's disclaimer of responsibility could not be taken seriously, and the other accusers' right-wing allegiance had to be considered motivation for their charges against Menéndez and the government.[24] After examining declarations by witnesses and the texts of various telegrams, the commission specifically absolved the government of blame for the atrocities committed in Casas Viejas.[25]

22. *Diario de sesiones*, March 10, 1933, No. 309, p. 11755.

23. For the text of Menéndez's orders, see pp. 187–88.

24. See Jackson, *The Spanish Republic*, pp. 223, 513 f.

25. "The commission hastens to state that it has found no proof whatsoever that allows even the hint that the public forces carried out the repression under orders from members of the government. The only observation possible in this respect relates to the behavior of the public forces facing the rebels; that is, when they were defending the established social order, limited as they were by the telegram sent by the governor of Cádiz to the government delegate in Casas Viejas, did they enact the order received from the ministry to level Seisdedos's house, or the other one, of dubious interpretation, which Lieutenant Artal maintains he received by telephone from the governor of Cádiz to 'restore order in any way he could, and that if and when he telephoned back it should be to inform him that the people had been brought under control.'

"Captain Rojas, in command of the troops, declares he did not receive any order from the ministry of the interior; and the director general of security throughout the periods in his declaration asserts that he, directly and in person, gave and transmitted orders to his subordinates containing no allusion to directives or hints from his own superior [Azaña]. There is, therefore, no evidence that any member of the government took part in this matter" (*Diario de sesiones*, March 10, 1933, No. 309, p. 11753).

It is still difficult to evaluate the responsibility of the leaders in the Azaña government. Rojas may have lied at every turn: his testimony is uniformly self-serving, and his recollections were used to pardon inexcusable crimes. But the role of Arturo Menéndez remains ambiguous. It is possible that the orders he actually issued were still harsher than the version that he admitted to. If so, they could have been overly suggestive to a weak subordinate eager to curry favor, or to an officer with sadistic inclinations. At best, government instructions primed an already explosive situation. Although Menéndez did not tell Rojas to murder twelve men, his instructions, supported by those from the minister of the interior and the governor of Cádiz, encouraged Rojas to raze the choza, which resulted in the unnecessary deaths of Seisdedos and his family. Indifference to the lives of the campesinos then led to the second tragic phase of the uprising.

In the weeks afterward, perhaps for reasons of state, personal fear, or misguided loyalty to the public forces, Menéndez may have preferred to dampen the controversy rather than face the public storm. He may have learned what took place from Rojas, as the latter claimed. He may have ordered Rojas to Seville to urge Artal to remain silent. And he may have preferred, even at the final hour, that Artal support the government's version rather than reveal what had actually occurred. At the end of the affair, Azaña too wondered when Menéndez had learned the truth.

From comparing Azaña's speeches and his diaries, it is apparent that he knew little of the transactions going on among Rojas, Artal, and Menéndez. It could seem that he did not want to know. He never pursued his own suspicions. Azaña did not meet Rojas until March 1, weeks after he had been defending the captain's actions. He learned of Rojas's puzzling trip to Seville to see Artal, and he considered how that visit might have compromised Menéndez; but again he failed to follow up on his doubts with any zeal. Although aware of Menéndez's extreme loyalty to the military, Azaña never hesitated to accept his subordinate's view of the orders issued.[26]

In the end, Azaña relied too heavily on his powerful rhetoric and on the parliamentary majority he enjoyed. He saw events in terms of the conflict between his coalition and the opposing political parties. Perhaps he can be faulted also for excessive faith in the virtues of government and for justifying repression of the anarchist movement. He was too involved in his government's need to survive to face the tragic fact that he was taking part in the destruction of his own hopes and ideals.

Just as the right-wing revolt of the previous year had served to speed land reform legislation, the insurrection of January 1933 created a brief flurry of activity in the government's agrarian program. The end result of the turmoil,

26. *Obras,* IV, pp. 461, 447 f.

however, was death to land reform. Weakened by the trials of Casas Viejas, government efforts came to a halt. In addition, eroded by plans for religious and educational reform, the coalition of parties that had given Azaña parliamentary majority collapsed. On September 8, 1933, nine months after the uprising, Azaña was forced to resign, and President Alcalá-Zamora asked Alejandro Lerroux, the leader of the Radical party, to form a new government. In the coming months, the government would move inexorably to the right.

The notoriety of Casas Viejas was sustained by pamphlets issued by those from the left and the right who sought to discredit the Republic. On the anarchist side, Miguel Pérez Cordón, Federica Montseny, and others retold the story of the January uprising, painting a portrait of conscious heroic resistance.[27] In 1934, Ramón Sender, who visited the town shortly after the insurrection, published a documentary novel, *Viaje a la aldea del crimen,* portraying Seisdedos and his family and solidifying the old man's position as a revolutionary hero. Like other works of propaganda, *Viaje* attained neither a high level of art nor accuracy. At its core it served only to denigrate the government of Manuel Azaña.

In May 1934, Captain Rojas was tried in Cádiz and the charges against the Azaña regime were aired once more. Azaña, Quiroga, and Menéndez testified, lending the trial greater national significance. As expected, in his defense Rojas repeated the accusation that he had been ordered by the director general of security, Arturo Menéndez, to take no prisoners or wounded. He also claimed to have been offered, through his brother-in-law, Lieutenant Colonel Hernández Saravia, a bribe of one million pesetas to remain silent.[28] Rojas's claims were discounted, and he was sentenced to twenty-one years in prison.

*Colonel Salas, civil guard (retired):* Every day I took him from the prison and brought him to the trial, and then when it was over, I delivered him to Granada. He was a degenerate. When we were on the way to Granada, with his wife waiting in sorrow in Seville, and after such a terrible trial, he said, "Let's go to a cabaret." He wanted to go out to such places—and he was in the uniform of an officer, and I was a civil guard. There was something wrong with him.

27. Miguel Pérez Cordón wrote the section on the province of Cádiz in *España 1933, La barbarie gubernamental* (Barcelona 1933). Cordón's account was included in the publication of the *Comité Nacional* of the *CNT: La Verdad sobre la tragedia de Casas Viejas.* The regional confederation of Andalusia prepared its own pamphlet: *Han pasado los bárbaros, lav verdad sobre Casas Viejas* (Sevilla, 1933). Federica Montseny's narrative of the events appeared in *María Silva, La Libertaria* (Toulouse, 1951).

28. *El Sol,* May 23, 1934; *Casas Viejas,* p. 40.

Captain Bartolomé Barba's testimony, like Rojas's, was unsupported and carried little weight in the court; however, the charge of callous brutality—"neither wounded nor prisoners," and Barba's unforgettable embellishment, "tiros a la barriga"—was stamped on the Azaña regime. Azaña's ministry became known as "the government of Casas Viejas."

Captain Rojas's explanation of what had occurred was included in the report of the parliamentary commission:

> I told those prisoners, upon going down to Seisdedos's house to show them what they had done, to see what had happened because of them and the base act they had committed. Since the situation was of great gravity, I was extremely nervous—because it was not only a matter of Casas Viejas. The whole province had risen, and I had had to go there, leaving behind 500 armed men, the men of Medina Sidonia, the townspeople, and everything in a state of anarchy. I wasn't thinking only of myself, because any sacrifice I may make for the Republic is little, but of my men. If I didn't teach a lesson then, there was a chance anarchy would be rampant, and everything would collapse in the hills, which would be very bad. Given this, the orders I had, the fact that we just had to do it for the sake of the Republic, the government, and my men, when we got to the house . . . when they went down, although what I would rather have done with the prisoners was to use the ley de fugas on the outskirts of the town, one of the prisoners who saw the burned guard in front of the house told another fellow something and then looked at me so . . . that I couldn't contain myself and stand for his insolence, and I shot him, and immediately the others fired also; and those who were there looking at the burned guard also fell; and then we did the same with the rest who hadn't gone down yet, two of them, I think. This is how I carried out my orders and defended Spain and the Republic from the anarchy that was rising everywhere.[29]

29. *Diario de sesiones,* March 10, 1933, No. 309, pp. 11752–53; *Casas Viejas,* pp. 19–20.

# Fifteen

# Responsibility and Punishment

## The military court

Scores of townsmen had fled to the mountains to avoid arrest, but within a few days almost all of them returned. It was mid-winter. They had little food, and shelter was precarious. The civil guard was sweeping the countryside.

The defeated campesinos who returned surrendered at the barracks of the civil guard, as Gutiérrez reported in *El Sol* (March 2, 1933):

> The arrest of these people went like this. We were at the gates of the cemetery; I saw a lean, meager man walking up the center of the road. He walked erect. In his right hand he had a disassembled shotgun, barrels and breech. In his other hand, four shells. When we saw him approach, one of the guards who had gone inside Seisdedos's house went up to him, and the man gave up his shotgun and shells, while the guard Salvo, who stood some distance apart, said, "Put handcuffs on that one, because he is one of the main lawbreakers."
>
> I accompanied the arrested man. I tried to find out what had happened from him and the other seven who were alone in the room where they had taken them; all I heard were statements concerning their miserable life and their struggle to earn a living.
>
> They were as if in a daze. And then, before those handcuffed and defenseless men, about to face the cold interrogations of the law that were in store for them, I experienced a pain as deep as the one I had felt before the bodies of the victims.
>
> The arrested men told me nothing, I repeat, although we were alone. I asked one in particular for news about a brother of his, who they had told me was among the leaders. This man, speaking with a calm that made me shudder, answered: "My brother, with his . . . (here he used a rude and abrupt expression), he must be among the dead."

As soon as the men were identified as revolutionaries, they were handcuffed and sent to Medina for questioning. The guards confiscated all weapons taken from the prisoners or found in a search of the town: recovered were 134 shotguns, all allegedly fired, and five revolvers. Tools identified as weapons included three axes, six pruning axes, twenty-nine sickles, two knives, and seven clubs.[1]

Pepe Pareja took the precaution of surrendering in a town other than Casas Viejas:

> I stayed in the mountains for several days. During the first days I hid at the hut of one of my family, but then they warned me that the guards from Alcalá were looking for me, and I fled again. Then I decided I had better surrender to the guards from Alcalá rather than to those in Benalup [Casas Viejas], since they were so furious here. I went to the lieutenant to give myself up, but he wasn't there. He's the one that they brought here and shot at the start of the war—and so I went to the jail myself. Then I was taken to Medina, where I was tried.

However, the site of one's surrender proved to be little protection. Salvo and García were called from Casas Viejas to identify the most notorious of the revolutionaries.

> *Cristóbal Torres:* The next day someone came to my brother's house and said I should present myself at the barracks. I said I would, but I went instead to Medina, because I knew that here they would beat me. When I arrived in Medina, I met a guard on the road, and I said, "I'm here to be taken to prison."
>
> And he said, "Are you one of those from Casas Viejas?"
>
> I said, "Yes." And he took me in. But from there they called Casas Viejas by telephone and when they were told who I was, they beat me good.

María Silva, La Libertaria, was taken into custody on January 14 and placed in jail in Medina. In newspaper interviews she denied having any part in the uprising.

> "You are a communist?" we asked.
>
> "I don't understand that nor do I concern myself with those things. It's bad enough that I don't know how to read and write."
>
> "But you went out into the street the day of the uprising. You were seen carrying arms by the civil guard."
>
> She answered rapidly: "That's not true. I didn't leave the house. They've arrested me because I live in the house further up from that of

1. Archivos de la Audiencia Provincial de Cádiz, sumario 21, 6, no. XI, 25 de octubre, 1933.

Seisdedos. But soon they'll be convinced of my innocence and will set me free. I'm sure about that" (ABC, January 17, 1933).

María had no visible wounds and she had covered her fire-singed hair with a kerchief. The *Diario de Cádiz* reported that there were bloodstains on her clothing that she could not explain.[2] As no military charges were placed against her, she was soon released, only to be rearrested and returned to jail in Medina and then in Cádiz, where she remained until the following month.

Juan Estudillo had not participated in the uprising but had gone into hiding nonetheless. He surrendered to the civil guard only after receiving assurances that they would not kill him.[3]

Pepe Pilar was not about to help the military authorities assemble evidence against him. He stuck to his story: that he had not participated in the uprising.

After the guards entered, we went to the campo, six of us, and hid out there for a day and a night. I wanted to reach Jerez, but when we got to La Boca de la Puerca in the mountains, where lived a goatherd who was a friend, he told us that the mountains were filled with guards. We hid in the woods. He gave us a sack of charcoal to burn, which wouldn't give off any smoke, and so we kept warm. We had brought some bread. We stayed there that day and night. Word went out that they wanted everybody who had participated to show up. The entire campo was surrounded, and anyone found there would be shot on the spot. Anyway, I turned myself in, because at the time I was with a group of people who all turned themselves in, and I didn't want to remain alone. Three days after the uprising, I came back to town.

We left early in the morning to return to Casas Viejas. I went to the barracks and asked if Salvo, one of the guards, was there. They said no, he was in the street; but as I was going up to my house, I met him, and I said, "Salvo, I'm here."

He said, "You ran away."

I said, "Not ran away. Like everyone else, I left."

He said, "All right. You come down to the barracks tomorrow at 12:00."

They sent a military judge to Casas Viejas. The next day I went down, and the military judge asked me where I was during the uprising. I said, "I had no part in it."

They said, "Can you prove you didn't take part?"

I said, "Look, I was taking care of my sick father, and if you want proof, go to the doctor."

So they sent me with two guards to the doctor to ask him. And the doctor said, "That's true. His father is ill, and I saw him there. But what he did or didn't do, I don't know."

So they sent me to Medina, and there the guards began to question me.

2. *Diario de Cádiz,* January 15, 1933.

3. Ibid.

The Pavón brothers remained in the mountains for eighteen days. Their father was held hostage to ensure their return. At last they too surrendered at Medina Sidonia and were subjected to brutal beatings, their toes battered by repeated blows from the guards' rifle butts.

Currestaca and Juan Sopas were not captured. Currestaca remained hidden in the mountains near La Zarzuela, where he kept in touch with his wife, who came to live with her parents. Rather than try to find sanctuary in the mountains, Juan Sopas had headed for Cádiz, the provincial capital. The city was more hospitable in winter than the campo. Sopas's singular good luck in escaping, however, would later be held against him.

A military judge, Julio Ramos Hermoso, captain of artillery and law, was sent to Casas Viejas to conduct interrogations and trials. He soon learned that the campesinos considered the leaders of the uprising to be Monroy, Sopas, and Gallinito. According to the *Diario de Cádiz*, Gallinito was the soul of the movement, and one published report suspected him of placing a bomb in a government building window in Cádiz (January 21, 1933).

José Monroy, despite his role in the events, appeared to be surprised at the accusations made against him:

After the uprising, when they were questioned, many said they went there because "Monroy sent me"—to avoid assuming responsibility. No. I didn't send anyone. It's everyone's responsibility. Because of those accusations, I spent three years in prison. "Who sent you there?" they were asked. They accused me of everything. It was true that I sent them, but they shouldn't have said so.

The interrogations were simple and brutal.

*Pepe Pilar:* They put me in a small room where there were four beds in which the guards usually slept. They sat me on a chair.

"Tell us where you were. Who was with you?" I said, "I told you what I know. I can repeat the same thing."

One of them, a son of a bitch, hit me and knocked me to the ground. I got up, and they again sat me down in the chair. He told me to tell the truth. I answered, "I've already told you the truth, so don't ask me any more." So he hit me again, and again he knocked me down to the ground. Then a third time.

When he saw me get up, that son of a bitch thought I was going to hit him back, so he stuck his gun right in my chest and said, "I'll kill you."

"Well, kill me," I replied, "but don't you dare hit me again. Either kill me, or we'll kill each other here if you hit me again."

He was afraid of me. So he went to see the judge who was outside. This all occurred, mind you, in a room inside the barracks of the civil guard. They stepped out and told Don Julio, "This fellow says he had no part in it."

He said: "Continue questioning him."

So he got me by the arm and took me to a corner, that son of a bitch. They asked me if I had seen Gallinito. I said, "Yes, he was walking along like me doing nothing."

One of them went to hit me with his rifle butt in the ribs, and I put my hand there to protect myself. As a result my hand was all swollen. But I accused no one. So after he got tired of hitting me, he said, "Well, Don Julio, this guy doesn't want to talk." The judge was in another small room, but you could see him because the door was open. "This fellow says the same thing over and over." So he said, "Take him out."

Salvo and García were the ones who beat me. There were other guards in the room, but they were the ones.

Pepe's silence did him little good. A number of campesinos named him as one of the most active participants in the uprising:

I stuck to my story of carrying my father to the country and not being in the village. The next day, however, they brought me to the court down a long room, and there were eight people who had accused me. And the judge said, "Uh-huh, look at these statements." He read all eight depositions to me.

One said I had given him a shotgun and had said to him, "Today we're going to implant comunismo libertario." Another said I had given him a gun, and a third said he had seen me hand La Libertaria a pistol. It was burned in the choza. Altogether, eight people accused me.

"You've told a different story. Do you now deny what these witnesses have said?"

And I thought, "If I say yes, they're only going to beat me again. Salvo and García are downstairs waiting to beat me." And I said, "No. They said it, and I'm not going to contradict them."

The eight accusations said only that I had gone around getting people in from the fincas. No one said I had been at the barracks.

Pepe, however, was not about to give in without a final word:

When I appeared before the magistrate and they asked me if I had anything to change in my story, I said, "The first version is true. I told the second only because I was afraid of a beating. All the accusations made against me were made because they too were afraid of being beaten."

By January 20 there were sixty-nine campesinos crammed in the Medina jail. At least thirteen others, already heard by the military judge, had been transferred to jail in Cádiz to face serious charges. There were other arrests and transfers still to be made. Pepe Pilar's denials notwithstanding, he and Gallinito were admitted to the jail in Cádiz on June 21, 1933.

*Pepe Pilar:* The military judge in Medina sent us to jail in Cádiz and then to Puerto Real. I spent eighteen months there. When they took me from Medina to Cádiz, one guard wanted to handcuff my swollen hand, but another fixed it for me. So you can see there are all kinds of people.

The tough questioning loosened tongues, but not every painful reply was truthful. Although the campesinos knew that Seisdedos had had nothing to do with the uprising, he and his sons served as convenient scapegoats. In order to avoid incriminating others, the old charcoal maker was often named as the fiery leader of the insurrection. The dead could suffer no damage from the accusations.

*José Monroy:* All those who survived threw the blame on those who were dead. Actually they did nothing, but the blame falls on those who cannot talk. It was our defense. They couldn't do anything to them, and so we threw the blame on them. They beat me up in jail. They wanted me to tell the truth, but it didn't suit me to do so, and so I lied. They had three clubs and went at me for an hour. They hit me with their guns on my foot. They asked me if I had been at the meeting the night before the uprising, and I denied it. Then they brought in a man who said he had seen me there, and I had to admit that I had been there. They asked me what I had done. I said, "Seisdedos ordered me to cut the road, and so I went and did it."

"Why did you do it?"

I said, "Because he said if I didn't do it, he would kill me."[4]

Pepe Pareja also found it convenient to blame the dead rather than inform on living compañeros:

They said that some reported I had a revolver, and they asked me why. I said, "It was given to me in case someone bothered me."

"Who gave it to you?"

"Jerónimo Silva." I gave them the name of someone dead.

"Where's the gun?" I told them, and they got it. They saw that I hadn't used it.

They questioned me. I said, "If I didn't go, Seisdedos would have shot me."

One campesino beaten by the guards, rather than name a fellow townsman, threw blame on an outsider; and so Anónimo, who had found himself in Casas Viejas by chance, was named a conspirator:

4. José Monroy, Sebastián Pavón, and Pepe Pilar showed the unofficial investigating parliamentary commission the terrible bruises they had received from beatings administered by a corporal of the civil guard, by Sergeant Marín, and by Civil Guard García (*Diario de sesiones*, February 28, 1933, No. 300, p. 11408).

I was standing in a bar when Alfonso G. entered and grabbed me by my jacket. "You should be shot!" he said.

"What are you talking about?"

He told me that I had raised Casas Viejas. D. had accused me of coming to the village to arouse it. I went with Alfonso G. to the jail, where D. repeated the charge in front of me. I had nothing to do with it, but as a result I spent nine months in jail. I never wanted to have anything to do with D. after that.

Pepe Pilar, D.'s good friend, was surprised by the charge:

I don't know why D. said that Anónimo was in the movement here. He had no part in it. Perhaps it could have been from the beatings they gave us. But they beat me more than he, and I didn't denounce anyone. Maybe he did. Anónimo said he did. I never spoke to D. about it. Anónimo says he asked D. in front of the judge, "When did you see me there?" And the judge said, "He thinks he's going to evade the responsibility in this way, but he's not going to."

After the investigation, there was a military trial. The prosecution attempted to determine who had fired the shot that killed the sergeant and the civil guard. Cristóbal Torres was a prime suspect and had been named the deadly marksman by the newspapers.[5]

*Pepe Pilar:* In the court [Civil Guard] García accused Cristóbal Torres of shooting the sergeant, and Pavón [the defense attorney] asked how he had seen him. García said he was standing in the window.

"And where was the sergeant?"

"Behind me."

"Then how is it that the sergeant was killed and not you? It's all a pack of lies."

Initially Pepe Pareja was charged only with carrying a weapon, but suddenly another complaint was filed against him:

At the trial, one of the guards accused me of being in front of the barracks. But that was a lie. I was well defended by Pavón. . ., and I was convicted only for carrying arms.

Osorio was tried with me. They made a great deal of the point that he was supposed to have carried the message here, but Pavón defended him and made light of it. "What's the difference if the message came by wire or letter or telephone? It's beside the point."

5. *Diario de Cádiz,* February 16, 1933.

By the time the trials took place, the men had already spent several months in prison; and after the evidence was presented, most were released on probation. Thirteen men received stiffer sentences, among them Gallinito, who was given six years; Cristóbal, five years; and Monroy, three years. Most everyone was relieved to be on probation. Pepe Pareja, however, refused to accept liberty that was conditional in any way. He insisted, "Imprison me, or set me free without conditions." As a result, he spent a year in jail; he was then freed unconditionally.

Bickering and resentment were inevitable in the prison cells. Cristóbal Torres, who had only the vaguest ideas about politics, had been badly beaten by the civil guards and faced a long prison term for his part in the attack on the barracks. Considered a dangerous anarchist by the authorities but regarded as a naive campesino by his compañeros, Cristóbal now felt he had been used and then abandoned:

I was sentenced to five years in prison, but it was later reduced to two years. When I was in prison, the others, the leaders of the movement who had directed the whole business, said to me, "You're guiltier than we are, because you were with the ones there firing on the barracks."

## The town

The activists and those who had helped them were now in prison. While court procedures went forward, the townspeople began to sort through their own observations and opinions. The uprising had decimated families and shattered the town. Why had Casas Viejas, the townspeople asked, among all the towns of the province and the country, been singled out for such suffering? Who was responsible?

Townsmen of *categoría* (the upper class) assigned the cause—ignorance.

*Andrés Vera:* They didn't have any education. What could they want? There was no education at all in the village. How could they have a revolution the way they were? They didn't even have decent arms: old shotguns tied with wire. How could they fight a public force? They wanted to divide the land. They were anarchist communists, the same as the Russians. They were against the Republic and the Socialists.

The campesinos could agree that they were uneducated, but they saw their ignorance as the means by which they had been manipulated and driven to be slaughtered. They believed that they had been aroused as part of a capitalistic plot to discredit the Republic. Just as rich landlords had not sown their lands and thus had created unemployment and unrest, so they had conspired to use the misery of the campesinos to wreak havoc and destroy the credibility of the government.

Before the uprising, anarchist orators had come to town and had aroused the campesinos to a fever pitch. But who, it was asked, had paid them to incite the people? The campesinos believed that the señoritos were responsible. The capitalists were behind it. They also implicated the church, their ancient oppressor. In fact the orators were rumored actually to have been priests disguised as anarchists.

Capitalist conspirators were also alleged to have paid some renegades to burn the crops standing in the fields. According to Juan Pinto, "there were many fields burned before the uprising. The capitalists would start the fires. They would do this to blame the workers, in order to make them do what they did."

Although civil and assault guards, led by Captain Rojas, had fired the fatal shots, the townspeople did not view the troops or their superiors in the government as the true perpetrators of the massacre. Rojas and his men were strangers to the town. There were no past ties of intimacy or antagonism. As for Azaña and his ministers, they were hundreds of kilometers away, too remote for an exchange of hatred or sorrow.

*Juan Pinto:* They wanted to place the responsibility on the government. Captain Rojas had to go on trial. When Azaña came before the president of the court, where one has to name a lawyer, the president said to Azaña that he could have a defense attorney. And he answered, "I don't need a defense attorney. I can defend myself. I did not order anyone to shoot anyone in the belly." If he had ordered anyone to be executed, he would have had to sign the order; and since he did not sign, he did not have any responsibility. Had he given such a command, where was his signature?

In the confined universe of peasant society, the possible causes and likely actors were limited to established relationships where there was a history of animosity. It was not difficult for townspeople to agree on the identity of the local señorito responsible. José Vela, El Tuerto, was the most despised landowner in the area. He was said to have little sympathy for others' needs. On his own lands and on rented pastures, José Vela raised crops and fattened cattle for slaughter. Rude in manner and hard in business, he soaked the small renters when he subleased to them a few hectares of land. It was now alleged that he had encouraged the slaughter of the innocent campesinos.

*José Suárez:* After Seisdedos's death—and before—Captain Rojas spent the whole night in the bar drinking wine with the Velas. Everything was over. The soldiers were in the truck ready to leave when El Tuerto said, "If you leave without giving them an example, the same thing will happen again."

No such charge was ever made in the hearings following the uprising. Nor did Captain Rojas or anyone else testify that José Vela had made such a suggestion. But in the town the accusation was commonplace.

It was inconceivable to townspeople that El Tuerto had acted alone. Separated from the workers by class, it was said he had needed an accomplice among the campesinos to incite them. Someone had been a traitor to his class. The townspeople searched among the leaders of the uprising—Monroy? Gallinito? Badly beaten and sentenced to long prison terms, they had harvested no benefits from the disaster. They had suffered with the others.

*Juan Pinto:* Monroy was not a traitor. He was a truer man than the others. He held his position without ulterior motives. This came from his soul. Back then he had forty or fifty goats, and he earned his living this way without bothering anyone.

Who among the leaders had not suffered in the repression? Some of the leaders of the sindicato were said to have escaped punishment. Were Currestaca, the new president, and Durán in prison with the others? Where was Juan Sopas, the smartest of the bunch?

*Salvador:* There wasn't one head of the sindicato—there were several: Durán, Sopas, and the others. And they let the ignorant go in front and take the blows, like Pepe Pilar and Pepe Pareja. The ignorant went into the fire. The leaders left.

Monroy and Miguel Pavón, among others, recalled that Durán served time in prison, and the parliamentary record confirms that Durán was one of the detainees.[6] But local gossip paid little attention to details. The people felt betrayed by the sindicato leaders.

*Juan Pinto:* When the civil guards were killed here, Currestaca, Durán, and Sopas did not suffer any consequences. The three of them left for Cádiz, dressed as priests. They were safe there, without any of them being grabbed by the civil guard. While the others in town had to go to jail, they remained in Cádiz. They were traitors, because they were protected by the capitalists; otherwise, they would have had to go to jail, because

6. *Diario de Sesiones,* February 23, 1933, No. 300, p. 11408. In the Cortes, Balbontín stated that the government held fifty-nine prisoners (*Diario de Sesiones,* March 10, 1933, No. 309, p. 11759). There is no way to verify that figure as records have been destroyed. A larger number were imprisoned initially, and some were released, rearrested, and then sentenced during the course of the investigations. After the trials the men were sent to three different prisons: a few were sent to the provincial jail in Cádiz; a larger number were sent to El Penal del Puerto de Santa María, where they were divided into two groups—those placed in a common cell and a lesser number kept in separate cells; a few who received longer sentences were remanded to Ocaña (Toledo), close to Madrid.

they were responsible for the death of the sergeant and the guard. Those traitors had convinced the people, the most ignorant among them, that they had to kill the civil guard. Since these people had no education, and this was repeated over and over again, they did what they were told. A man who has a little bit of sense first of all will not go. And then he will hold back to see what direction the affair will take.

My brother was killed, and they are responsible. If they had not taken the town along with them, the town would not have moved. The most innocent were killed—the ones who did not do anything at all.

Everyone hated them. Everyone was against them. Anyone who was not dumb knew that they were the guilty ones.

Those who had fled and were believed to have remained free were accused of being in league with the capitalists and the church. The capitalists had paid them to arouse the campesinos to revolt, and the church had shielded them afterward.

Most eyes focused on Juan Sopas. Everyone considered him to be the most astute and capable of the lot, and at least in retrospect, some thought he was a cynic and opportunist. According to Villarubia, "Sopas was never an anarchist or Socialist. He was for himself. He never went to the centro. He was a leader in the street."

Sopas's recent change of trade sharpened suspicions concerning him. He had been a field worker and then, fired by ambition, had opened a small grocery. Where had the money come from to enable him to improve his station? Traits once seen as virtues—his intelligence and generosity—were now considered part of the plot to subvert the people. Why had Sopas extended credit to the poor? It was alleged that this all too clever campesino had been paid off by El Tuerto to betray the town.

*Nicolás:* El Tuerto sold out the village. He set up a store for Sopas, who sold bread for two reales a kilo. He put Sopas in a good spot and paid him to incite the people. Sopas was more intelligent than the rest.

A host of details seemed to fall into place for the bereaved townspeople.

*Juan Pinto:* Sopas was paid off. He wasn't an anarchist or anything. He was just a bandit. He was close to the capitalists. He used to work with me reaping wheat, and we earned twenty-two reales. And he said to me once, "I'm not working any more. I'm going to find another way of earning a living." The year that he said this to me, he opened a grocery store. And the whole town went there to shop. He would say to them, "Don't hurry. If you can't pay today, you can pay tomorrow." What he had belonged to the capitalists. They were behind him so he would lead the town to do what it did. He started to bring food and guns for the attack on the barracks. He got the town into such a state and stirred them up so much that the men attacked the barracks like obedient dogs. He tried to overthrow the government. That's what the capitalists were looking for. And that's where everything started. Sopas was a traitor against everyone.

It was recalled that Sopas had been a Socialist and then an anarchist. He had presented the false candidacy of Ramón Franco to the town. José Suárez, the first socialist mayor, had had bitter contacts with both José Vela and Sopas. It seemed natural to him and to others to tie the two together.

*José Suárez:* José Vela was hated, and after the uprising, someone in Cádiz fired a shot at him and tried to kill him. He had promoted everything. He defended the monarchy against the Republic.

José Vela paid Juan Sopas. Sopas was in with Tuerto Vela. He didn't work. Sopas gave away wheat, he gave away bread, and he said you don't ever have to pay. It was a bribe for the elections. The ballots were a fraud. When the elections were over, he gave them nothing. The slaughter was his fault. He couldn't return. The fathers of the dead wanted to kill him.

Sopas became the last victim of the uprising—treated as a pariah in the town. His life was cursed by his successful escape.

## The prisoners

While in prison the anarchosyndicalists from Casas Viejas and Medina Sidonia tried to assign blame for the tragedy.

*Anónimo:* The failure of the uprising falls on the FAI and on the violent members in the movement, the young people of the FAI. All they wanted was revolution, revolution. All they knew was violence.

Manuel Llamas bore a special burden, because he had brought the message to rise from Jerez to Medina. He had sent the signal on to Casas Viejas and then had forgotten them. Though a friend of Manuel's, Pepe Pilar considered the militants' role to be fatal to Casas Viejas:

If there is any fault, it must lie with Medina, who sent us word to go out, and with the militants who urged us on. Medina had no right to tell us. We often spoke about it in prison. After the fact we considered what we should have done. We said that the militants should not have urged us out. A revolution takes time. The people have to be educated and uplifted.

Manuel Llamas believed that the cause of the tragedy lay in their innocence and lack of preparation:

We thought that making a revolution was easy. We were young. We were still walking on all fours, like a child. We did not have the capacity for revolution. We were ignorant. But in spite of this, we were like caged birds who have no other mission in life than to see if the master will leave the cage door open.

On reflection, Pepe Pilar could not single out any single person for condemnation.

The blame was ours, shared among us. This was not a strike. It was a revolutionary movement that began in Barcelona. We had been prepared in the spirit of revolution because of our misery, our suffering, and the tyranny of capital and the state.

No one is guilty for what happened. The guilt was in the faith we had. We couldn't wait, and so we went out. We were mistaken. We were innocent; we had no education. The meetings that we had here had aroused us. Outsiders came here to tell us that we must prepare ourselves for the revolution, and they told us how to do it—to collect guns and ammunition. "The revolution is at the door! Come into the street!" It was not the orators' fault. They wanted to call on the youth and create unity. But when the enthusiasm was created, we couldn't wait.

Our lack of education was partly to blame for the uprising. What did we know at that time? A man who cannot read lacks experience. Reading adds experience. I had ten children. But what did we know? If we had been educated, we would have waited. But we had faith we would win. We couldn't go on living the way we were. Calling this one a traitor or that one a traitor is wrong. The blame was shared among us.

Pepe Pareja considered the temper of the time.

Since this town was aroused to revolutionary fervor, it can be said that the villagers believed that everyone else was also alerted. And that being the case, the government could not repress the entire nation. For if an alert like this had taken place throughout the whole country, what would have happened? The forces stationed in each town would not have been enough to suppress a general movement. Don't you think so? That is what happened here. And here this little corner of the world remained with its belief. And here there was a massacre.

As for Sopas, the men in prison continued to regard him as a good compañero who had the bad luck to make good his escape. Nor did the imprisoned anarchosyndicalists consider Sopas part of a carefully designed capitalist-clerical plot. They knew that the orders to rise had originated in Barcelona; they realized that the orators who had visited the town were true anarchists and that the ideas they had expressed were not false. Sopas had not been paid by a señorito to draw them into the streets.

*Anónimo:* If Sopas had served his time in prison, nothing would have been said. No one would have held him responsible. But now he can't go back to Casas Viejas.

Juan Sopas, who settled in Jerez and Seville, regarded the charges against him as ridiculous. "The people don't know who their friends are," he said.

I walked to Cádiz, but not in the clothes of a priest. I never entered a church more than twice in my life—to marry and to baptize my children.

I hid in Cádiz in the hotel of a friend who was a Socialist representative in the Cortes. The writer Eduardo de Guzmán came to see me. He wrote down everything I told him.

I was in contact with the CNT. They found work for me. The committee for prisoners in Cádiz put me on a boat to La Gudina in Galicia. I was protected by them. I was there a year working as a waiter in a bar. From there I went to Badajoz, where I worked as a road contractor. I had various jobs in Zaragoza, Bilbao—all over Spain.

I can explain it in two words. All that took place was due to ignorance and want. The people didn't have enough to eat, and 99 percent of the people couldn't read or write. This was true all over Spain. They wanted to have another way of life, but how? They knew how to destroy, but not how to build. It takes time to build. In Madrid in 1934 I said to La Libertaria, when she came there with Cordón, "Where are you going with your revolution? With those who can't read and write?"

In Zaragoza I said not to go out, it would be another Casas Viejas, but they went out. In Zaragoza among some compañeros, I said, "There's not one region or one town in Spain prepared to make a revolution, and I know all the towns, because I've seen them. The only thing that can happen is a massacre, as in Casas Viejas."

When I said that, they fell silent as though a ton of snow had fallen on them. They knew I was from Casas Viejas and that I was right. They took me to the railroad station and put me on a train. "Get going. Don't talk about such things here." They were afraid, since they knew it would fall badly on others' ears.

The Republic was an opportunity to do something good, but it was lost. They were good people, but they didn't know what to do. Without eyes, where can a blind man go? Without eyes one cannot see. They didn't accomplish anything for the people. I was in favor of a republic, but one that insisted that management provide work. We needed a stronger republic. The workers have to earn and buy in stores. If they had had enough to eat, nothing would have happened. When the Republic came in, the rich were terribly afraid; but when they saw that the Republic didn't do anything, they lost their fear. They threw the workers into the street. They wanted to create conflict to discredit the government. Then the people had no alternative but to protest against the regime. For this reason Casas Viejas occurred, and Castilblanco. What was needed was bread in one hand and a club in the other—for the same worker. He had to have respect. I did not have the same beliefs that they did. I was for a republic, but a strong republic.

## CNT and FAI

The national and regional anarchosyndicalist organizations had to take their own reckoning of the revolutionary debacle. The failure of the January uprising had left the anarchosyndicalist movement in disarray, with its propagandists floundering in disclaimers. In the first days following the uprising, the national committee of the CNT found itself in a contradictory role—in favor of the spirit of revolution but unable to declare support for the ill-timed faísta-inspired revolt. The pronouncements of the organization were at cross purposes, damning the barbarism of the government and proclaiming new martyrs, while at the same time withholding official approval of the insurrection.

With the collapse of the insurrection at its inception in Barcelona, the CNT took up a defensive posture. On January 9, the day following the first outbreak in urban centers, the newspaper *CNT,* the official voice of the syndicalist organization, denied responsibility for the events then taking place. The headline read, "This is not our revolution. Is a trap being prepared for us?" The newspaper then condemned the naive conspiracies of the FAI:

> Our revolution is not a mere plot; we do not arrive at our ends through conspiracy. [Our revolution] concerns the elevation of the proletarian conscience. It involves the organization of workers in large central sindicatos who will join the revolution when their potential reaches its maximum, and when the central organization—not the [local] committees—determine it. Our revolution is not a game for big kids; it is something too serious, too profound, too transcendent to be reduced to the insignificant posturing that the authorities assume belongs to us.
>
> Our revolution does not consist of an assault on a civil guard barracks or army post. That is not revolutionary. We will declare a general strike when we can count on the greatest possibility of success; when we can take over factories, mines, electrical centers, transportation, all the means of production, everything that is vital. That cannot be done secretly. The preparation must be done publicly, in the light of day.
>
> The surprise blow, the rash attempt, are already out of date. Such maneuvers can be blamed, we think, on certain factions that are very interested in carrying out a repression against the CNT.

While the *CNT* chided the FAI for its recklessness and immaturity, its primary concern appeared to be fear of government retaliation. In a bold display of accusatory tactics, startling in the light of its inflammatory headlines prior to the uprising, the newspaper accused the government and the Socialists of initiating the movement in order to repress the CNT and to hunt down its militants.

On January 10, the day following the *CNT*'s disavowal of responsibility, the *Solidaridad Obrera* in Barcelona expressed equal bewilderment:

> We cannot condemn the movement of Sunday. On the other hand, we cannot accept it as an act of the Confederación Nacional del Trabajo, because the organization was not aware of the events.

They too accused the government of abuses that had brought about the disastrous insurrection.

No one stepped forward to accept responsibility for the ill-fated revolt and its terrible consequences. Denial and attack were customary dodges in politics and revolution, and the protestations sought to avoid not only internal criticism but also possible incrimination and indictment by government authorities. The counteraccusations also sought to salvage some ideological advantage from the defeat. In any event, the effort to shift responsibility was not convincing. During the months preceding the January insurrection, the anarchist press had intensified its propaganda for revolution. While it could accuse the government of perpetuating such causes of unrest as poverty and injustice, it bore the responsibility for arousing the membership at an ill-advised moment and for leading them into a futile battle. Having helped to build the bomb and set the fuse, the press now seemed to disclaim responsibility for striking the match.

In great measure, the January uprising signified complete defeat for the moderate wing of the CNT. The treintistas, the thirty moderates of the CNT who had lost power in the struggle with the FAI militants, saw their worst fears realized: the national confederation and the regionals had been manipulated by a small group of militants who had committed the entire membership to precipitous and dangerous action. The membership had been badly mauled in street fighting, the leaders arrested and beaten, and the sindicatos closed. The insurrection had only provided the cause with new martyrs , the campesinos of Casas Viejas.

The failure of the revolt, however, gave moderates the opportunity to voice their criticism and regain some ground, and they now attacked the FAI in their own publication, *Cultura Libertaria* (January 19, 1933).

> The law, being harsh and cruel, will throw all its weight on our fallen comrades. However, no mistake could be greater than that. With only a few exceptions, the men who were defeated, the hundreds of comrades who lie behind bars and can expect the inflexible weight of the law, not only are not responsible for what happened but are also the first and most pitiable victims. The men in jail, the dead, and those who will have to flee in order to avoid persecution by the authorities—these are the only ones

who have a right to demand that those responsible for the fight step forward. Who are they? Who are the ones whom everyone points to? They are the ones whom every generous conscience and every faithful and truly revolutionary spirit point to with disgust, contempt, and horror.

The men to blame are the ones who, from the podium, in the press, and in public as well as private conversations, have constantly instigated the workers to engage in acts of violence and senseless barbarism, hence mistaking disgusting actions for what the social revolution ought to be and what the working class ought rightfully to claim.

The FAI could not avoid criticism for having touched off the ill-fated insurrection, and the CNT could not deny that it had failed to control the various elements of the anarchosyndicalist organization. At a meeting of the regionals held in Madrid from January 30 to February 2, the assembly censured the national committee of the FNIF (the railway workers affiliated with the CNT). The national committee of the CNT, however, was found innocent. It was the sort of whitewash of which only the government seemed capable. The finding was not unanimous, however. The Valencia regional refused to attend the meetings. Having gone out in support of Barcelona on January 8, Valencian anarchosyndicalists protested against the CNT's evasiveness in assigning responsibility for the fiasco.

Let everyone who engages in revolutionary "games" know that when we are treated like foot soldiers and told to "strike" or to "revolt," we shall demand some explanation at the end; and if this explanation is denied us, we shall tell them all to go take a walk.[7]

Alexander Schapiro, the incisive Russian anarchist who was visiting Spain for the International, observed the widespread efforts to shift blame to those outside the organization. In a report to the International Association of Workers covering the period December 16, 1932 to February 26, 1933, Schapiro cut through the rhetoric and evasiveness. He cited three groups who could not avoid their measure of responsibility: first, the national committee of the Federation of Railway Workers (FNIF), for not carrying out the general strike voted by their congress in Madrid, and for not informing the government of their intent to strike on January 9; second, the national committee of the CNT, for showing weakness before the defense committees, for ignoring the organization's interests in favor of personal friends, and for not heading off precipitous action; and third, the faístas, for disregarding the best interests of the CNT and for acting selfishly and naively.[8]

7. Domingo Torres, in *Sindicalismo*, February 14, 1933.
8. Schapiro, pp. 14–15.

In his letter to the national committee, Schapiro urged the CNT to make clear that it alone had the duty and the right to organize the revolution and to choose the most propitious moment to initiate it. A coup by a small group would inevitably lead to a concentration of power. While the question of overlapping responsibilities had been resolved by the resignation of Manuel Rivas from the national defense committee, Schapiro considered this insufficient and urged that the defense committees be dissolved so that the confederation could reestablish its authority over a new, more closely coordinated committee structure.

Confronted with mounting criticism, the peninsular committee of the FAI declared proudly that they bore full responsibility for the events that had taken place.

> We say loud and clear, we affirm it absolutely, that we take responsibility for all that occurred on the eighth and on the following days as a violent protest against arbitrary acts. We are sick and tired of so much government crime. It is natural that we should appeal to methods that will make us heard, and reasonable that we should not cease until the insults, the sarcasm, the jeers, and the violent acts against anguished and hungry people are ended.

The statement was an affirmation of the FAI's independence, but it also tacitly acknowledged its failure to arouse the general membership and the populace.

> We want all the responsibility for ourselves, since we have not asked for the collaboration of anyone or for the support of the working people, or even the CNT; and we did not even advise our best friends of what we intended to carry out; and we will continue this course in the future, in order to be the only ones with the responsibility that derives from an attitude of straightforward rebellion and protest.
>
> We know the tactics of the enemy from experience, and for that reason we have preferred not to call on the organized workers to second and maintain the protest. We are ourselves strong enough to act on our own, assuming all responsibility.

The statement ended in a vision of triumph to come:

> The social revolution will take place soon. We have the sympathy of the revolutionary people and the indestructible weapon of reason. Let government oppressors and their accomplices tremble. Forward, comrades! Everyone at his post, and wait for the moment. On the red and black banner we have written the words "Love and Justice." We are invincible.
>
> Long live the free workers of the city and the campo!
>
> Long live comunismo libertario!

Long live the Federación Anarquista Ibérica![9]

The enthusiasm of the militants in Barcelona had not been diminished by the defeat of the uprising and its tragedy. The faístas had claimed responsibility for initiating the insurrection, but they now challenged their critics with plans for further disorder. The general membership too appeared as buoyant as ever. The defeat had generated a clamor for a forty-eight-hour strike to protest the arbitrary imprisonments, the closing of the sindicatos, and the dictatorial powers of the government.[10] A new campaign of agitation was launched to prepare the membership. The spearhead of the propaganda was provided by the heroic martyrs of Casas Viejas.

On March 1, 1933, the headlines of the *CNT* read, "Workers! The slain in Casas Viejas were our brothers; our protest must be made evident by means of the general strike." Those who had suffered through the January uprising could feel a cynical edge to the propaganda campaign, as the new martyrs of Casas Viejas were used to draw in other innocents.

## Hobsbawm's version

The contradictory reports of the uprising at Casas Viejas did not end with the investigations and trials of 1933–34. Inevitably, subsequent historical interpretations viewed the events from still other perspectives, in some instances advancing a theoretical framework for conceptualizing revolutionary activity. The most influential of these later accounts is that of Eric Hobsbawm, who described rural Spanish anarchists in the context of groups he termed "pre-political"—"primitive rebels."[11]

Although Hobsbawm writes that he visited Casas Viejas in 1956 and spoke with townspeople, his account is based primarily on a preconceived evolutionary model of political development rather than on data gathered in field research. The model scales labor movements in accord with their progress toward mass parties and central authority. In short, he explains how anarchosyndicalists were presumed to act rather than what actually took place, and the uprising at Casas Viejas was used to prove an already established point of view. Unfortunately, his evolutionary model misled him on virtually every point.[12]

9. *CNT,* February 11, 1933.

10. Schapiro noted that it was the first time the organization acknowledged a prerevolutionary goal (pp. 21, 23).

11. E. Hobsbawm, pp. 1–6.

12. While Hobsbawm's theoretical model is evolutionary, in his own treatment anarchism is often regarded as unchanging from one decade to the other. In his text, attitudes and beliefs of 1903–5, 1918–20, 1933, and 1936 are lumped together or considered interchangeable. Of course during those decades the anarchosyndicalists had developed their programs, and the individuals involved had become more experienced. See, e.g., p. 90, where Hobsbawm offers

Hobsbawm believed that Casas Viejas was the classic anarchist uprising: "utopian, millenarian, apocalyptic, as all witnesses agree it to have been" (p. 90). But the facts prove otherwise. Casas Viejas rose not in a frenzy of blind millenarianism but in response to a call for a nationwide revolutionary strike. The insurrection of January 1933 was hatched by faístas in Barcelona and was to be fought primarily there and in other urban centers. The uprisings in the countryside would be diversionary and designed to keep the civil guard from shifting reinforcements. The faísta plot was then fed by intensive newspaper propaganda, by traveling orators, and by actions undertaken by the defense committees. Representatives of the defense committees from Casas Viejas and Medina Sidonia had received instructions at a regional meeting held days before. On January 11, the anarchosyndicalists of Casas Viejas believed that they were joining their compañeros who had already been at the barricades since January 8.

Prior to the insurrection, was Casas Viejas a town noted for its militancy and millenarian fervor? Quite the contrary. Just one year earlier, both Casas Viejas and Medina Sidonia were regarded in the anarchist organization as towns "where the people are desensitized with regard to politics" and where greater efforts were required to organize the workers.[13] The sindicato, slow to recover from the events of 1915 (the suicide of its president, and its closure by the governor), was only newly organized.

The membership of the sindicato spanned a great range of belief and commitment. Not all were revolutionaries; some believed in a moderate union working for social progress. While almost all the workers were affiliated, many were members simply out of necessity. During the uprising, some of these found reasons to remain in their homes, or they ignored the duties assigned to them. Others were swept along as passive observers. The small core of obreros conscientes were themselves divided by generation and conviction. Only a handful of the younger members, enlisted in the Juventud Libertaria of the FAI, were impatient militants.

Hobsbawm argues that the uprising at Casas Viejas occurred in accordance with an established economic pattern:

> Economic conditions naturally determined the timing and periodicity of the revolutionary outbreaks—for instance, social movements tended to reach peak intensity during the worst months of the year—January to March, when farm labourers have least work (the march on Jerez in 1892

---

examples from 1936 and 1903–05 in the same paragraph; and pp. 86–87, where he lumps experiences from 1932–33 together with the illuminations of 1918.

13. *Memoria del primer congreso*, p. 9.

and the rising of Casas Viejas in 1933 both occurred early in January), March–July, when the preceding harvest has been exhausted and times are leanest. [P. 79]

In reality, most agricultural strikes took place in May and June, the period of the harvest and the only time of the year when the campesinos had any leverage against the landowners.[14] The uprising at Casas Viejas occurred in January precisely because it was *not* an agricultural strike. The timing of the insurrection, hurriedly called to coincide with a planned railway strike that would make it difficult for the government to shift its forces, was determined by strategic rather than economic considerations.

Observers have pointed out that revolutionary activity usually diminishes in periods of economic decline. What de Tocqueville noted concerning rising expectations preceding the French Revolution ("the evils that were endured with patience as long as they were inevitable") was also observed in Spain. Writing on the agitation in Córdoba, Díaz del Moral commented,

> Social quacks have always attributed Andalusian uprisings to hunger, when the truth is precisely the opposite. The movements always burst out during periods of relative prosperity: if collective hunger appears, the movements are arrested or die out. . . . At the time of the 1919 uprisings, there were landowners who ardently wished for a bad year in order to put an end to them.[15]

Both workers and landowners, as Díaz del Moral pointed out, recognized that hunger simply undermined the workers' power to resist.

Since kinship is a key feature in "primitive" societies, according to Hobsbawm, it was a major factor in the leadership of the sindicato in Casas Viejas.

> In the nature of things the small band of the elect drew together. The case of Casas Viejas, where personal and family relationships linked the leading anarchist cadre, is probably typical: Curro Cruz's granddaughter María ("La Libertaria") was engaged to José Cabañas Silva ("The Little Chicken"), the chief of the younger militants, another Silva was secretary to the labourers' union, and the Cruz and Silva families were decimated in the subsequent repression. The *obreros conscientes* provided leadership and continuity. [P. 86]

14. Little is known concerning the origin of the march on Jerez in January 1892. Kaplan writes that it might have been planned as a widespread insurrection, since several other towns rose that night and there were disturbances in still other towns a few days after; or, she suggests, it might have been an effort to free political prisoners or to assert their right to protest (p. 172).

15. *Historia,* p. 219, n. 1. Hobsbawm acknowledged the same simple observation: "Anyway, famine normally had its result of inhibiting rather than stimulating social movements when it came, though its approach sharpened unrest. When people are really hungry they are too busy seeking food to do much else; or else they die" (p. 79).

There is no evidence that kinship had anything to do with leadership in the anarchist movement in Casas Viejas or anywhere else. The reverse would be closer to the truth. Since the anarchists expressed belief in universal brotherhood, kinship ties were often undermined. In times of strike or in carrying out any decision of the collective membership, obreros conscientes sometimes had to act counter to kinship demands in order to keep faith with the movement and with their compañeros.[16]

Hobsbawm's specific examples are unfortunately based in part on errors of fact. He erred in noting Gallinito's full name, which was Antonio Cabañas Salvador, not José Cabañas Silva. Gallinito was not related to the Silva family.[17]

Hobsbawm's report on the sequence of events in the uprising contains other erroneous information: "Secure from the outside world, [the men] put up the red and black flag of anarchy and set about dividing the land. They made no attempt to spread the movement or kill anyone" (p. 89).

As is already evident, rather than securing themselves from the rest of the world, the uprising at Casas Viejas was a pathetic attempt to join in an ill-fated national insurrection. With regard to his second point, there was neither the time nor the opportunity to "set about dividing the land." The men were scattered in various locations guarding the roads and paths leading to the town. There were no meetings or discussions during this brief period of control. Only a few hours separated the shooting at the barracks and the entrance of the small rescue force from Alcalá. Contrary to Hobsbawm's description of peaceful enterprise, at the outset the anarchists surrounding the barracks had fired on the civil guards, mortally wounding two men.

Hobsbawm's model requires a charismatic leader. Accordingly, the inspired leader of the uprising is said to be "old Curro Cruz ('Six Fingers') who issued the call for revolution and was killed after a twelve hours' gunfight with the troops."[18]

This assertion would appear to be Hobsbawm's least vulnerable argument, since he can find support in every historical account of the past forty-nine years. The emphasis differs, of course, depending on the different authors'

16. As we have seen, e.g., during the strike of 1932 Pepe Pareja and his brothers refused to carry out their filial obligation to reap the wheat sown by their father, because it would have been a betrayal of their fellow workers.

17. Hobsbawm's error concerning kinship has been compounded in works that rely on his study of Casas Viejas. James Joll writes that "there seems to have been a kind of anarchist dynasty in which young revolutionaries married into the families of old anarchist leaders" (*The Anarchists*, p. 249). Less significant is Hobsbawm's error that a Silva was secretary of the union: Villarubia was secretary of the sindicato; Jerónimo Silva held the less critical post of secretary of the committee to free political prisoners. In any event, none of the Silvas were considered to be leaders of the sindicato.

18. P. 86. Hobsbawm's views concerning charismatic leadership depend in some measure on the perceptions of Díaz del Moral; see *Historia*, p. 23.

underlying views and styles: Hugh Thomas's narrative of the uprising is painted in heroic colors, with Seisdedos refusing to surrender and La Libertaria acting as his gun loader, until they both died in the flames when an airplane reportedly dropped bombs on the choza.[19] Gerald Brenan's rendition is based on his image of a religious revival, with Seisdedos acting "in one of those bursts of millenarian fervour that are so typical of Andalusia" (p. 247).

This celebration of Seisdedos's role, however, ignores the unanimous view of townspeople of every class and political persuasion, who assert that the old man was apolitical and had nothing to do with the uprising. This was true of those giving depositions in 1933,[20] and it is true today, as testified to by my interviews, in which every observer and participant in the uprising agreed that Seisdedos was not the leader and was never anything other than a virtuous charcoal burner with but slight interest in anarchosyndicalism.[21]

Nonetheless, the myth of Seisdedos persists, and at first glance it seems to be supported by the apparent logic of the situation. If Seisdedos was not the leader of the uprising, why had the civil guards singled out his choza? Why was the assault guard who came to the door shot down? Why did those trapped inside resist so fiercely?

The answer lies not with Seisdedos's own role but with the parts played by his son and son-in-law during the uprising. Once the men who participated in the assault on the barracks are identified, the reason for the guards' attention is clear: Jerónimo Silva, Seisdedos's son-in-law, had been stationed in front of the barracks and may have fired the round that killed the sergeant

19. Hugh Thomas, *The Spanish Civil War*, p. 65. In the second edition, Thomas substituted Pepa Franca as gunloader.

20. See, e.g., the statements of the priest and the deputy mayor (*Diario de sesiones*, February 23, 1933, 300, pp. 11405ff.)

21. During 1977 and 1978 there were rumors that a Spanish film was to be made of the uprising, and one of the participants in the events, Francisco Estudillo, wrote a letter (for which no date is available) to the *Diario de Cádiz* voicing opposition to the project on moral and political grounds. He says in part, "I have read that in the script of the above-mentioned production, Seisdedos is treated as a leader of the peasants. Nothing is further from the truth. Seisdedos was an older man who did not participate in the events, either as an initiator or an actor. He was worn out from his life as a charcoal worker. In the long nights in the mountains, he would read whatever fell into the hands of his large family. It is true that his preferred literature was *La novela ideal* by Federica Montseny, *El Luchador*, and *La Revista Blanca*. I would like to affirm that what happened in Seisdedos's hut was the result of the lack of imagination of his sons, Pedro and Paco, who . . . took refuge in the house . . . and drew the attention of the assault guards there. A movie that depicts Seisdedos as a leader should not be made. It would be fraudulent to the truth and to history."

Several scenarios were prepared but none reached production. In 1981, however, a thirty-six-year-old fledgling film director, José Luis López del Río, wrote a screenplay and began a low-budget film production, relying on a cameraman and actors to lend their services without pay in hopes of a later return. López del Río characterized the film as "a historical chronicle with poetic elements." Estudillo, the letter writer, declined to take a small role in the film, and he continued his argument, pointing out various inaccuracies in the production.

and the guard; Pedro Cruz, Seisdedos's son, was hidden with the men behind the barracks or was posted nearby. As early as January 15, 1933, the *Diario de Cádiz* had identified Perico sin Hueso as having been in front of the barracks; but since only his nickname was used, no one unfamiliar with the townspeople would realize that this was Pedro Cruz, Seisdedos's son.

Should the accolade of charismatic leader be given to someone else in the town? This was not a case of mistaken identity. No single person in Casas Viejas could lay claim to dominating the hearts and minds of the men. As we have seen, in this second generation of anarchosyndicalist development in the town, no one had the oratorical and organizational gifts of José Olmo, the founder of the sindicato a generation earlier. Throughout the anarchosyndicalist movement, organization was slack. The sindicato was loosely governed by a junta. Among the cast of characters there is no sign of charismatic leadership: José Monroy directed the uprising, but he never pretended to be heroic, and he initiated no independent actions; the sindicato's treasurer, Juan Estudillo, was quiet, apprehensive, and opposed to violence; the secretary, Villarubia, was not even a confirmed syndicalist, and he was not only opposed to the uprising but reported the plan to the civil guard; the president of the sindicato, Currestaca, quickly realized that the revolution had no chance for success and left town before it got underway; Sopas was respected for his intelligence, but his views were idiosyncratic; Gallinito sought to be an inspiring leader, but he was scorned by the older obreros conscientes as overexcited and a pedant.

The crucial act of the uprising was set in motion when Manuel Quijada was captured after having been seen at the barracks, and he and his brother-in-law were beaten until one of them revealed the names of those who had fired at the civil guard and mortally wounded two men. It then became known that Seisdedos's family was implicated in the attack. When the guards arrived at the choza to arrest the men, one or all three men inside believed their fate to be sealed. The assault guard who forced open the door was gunned down, possibly by the same marksman who had shot the sergeant and the civil guard. The remainder of the tragic history then unfolded. Hobsbawm's adherence to a model, and the accumulation of misinformation, led him away from the essential conflicts underlying the tragedy and from the reality of the people who participated in it.

# Part Three

# Sixteen
# Aftermath

## La Reforma Agraria

The insurrection of January 1933 momentarily spurred the government's agrarian reform program. The efforts were short-lived and the end results minimal. The complex legislative web, landowners' opposition, and the government's lack of energy delayed implementation of the program. Initial hopes of settling 60,000–75,000 families a year and resolving the land problems in little more than a decade were scaled down sharply. By the end of 1934, only 12,260 families had been placed on agrarian reform settlements throughout Spain, and in the intervening period the mandate of the Republic had eroded.

In western Andalusia, the agrarian reform program failed to satisfy the deepest aspirations of either the anarchosyndicalists or those independent campesinos who preferred a reparto and their own portion of land. Independent campesinos could not be lured to work for wages on land they could never own. Anarchosyndicalists, who sought to create a new way of life, saw that the agrarian reform cooperatives were not independent free units and that the land and the authority for its governance would always remain with the central government. Although worker committees would help to organize cooperative labor, the management of the settlements was under the supervision of the Instituto de la Reforma Agraria. Money, to anarchists a source of evil, remained the means for commercial transactions. Rather than exchanging labor and goods according to need, workers were paid in advance a daily wage against the settlement's future earnings from its crops and herds. There was no system of exchange with other settlements. Nor was there a sense of forging links with the working classes of the world or of transforming personal attitudes and beliefs.

The agrarian reform cooperatives put into operation did help to reduce some unemployment and want in specific localities. Those who had suffered from a lifetime of privation found that these were not unsubstantial goals.

*Juan Pinto:* They were good lands [at Charco Dulce], and they gave a good yield. We had enough to eat, and every fifteen days they gave us one fanega of wheat. We had food for our children. We felt secure, because every day we had a place to work. The other way, you work today and you don't work tomorrow. I had to go with a burlap sack to try to gather wild asparagus, and I could not provide enough for my family. I saw that it was much better whenever one has work every day and one's children have enough to eat.

Some twenty agrarian cooperatives were started in the province of Cádiz, the heart of the latifundio region. Three of the cooperatives were in the township of Medina Sidonia: San José de Malcocinado (Las Yeguadas) in 1934, with forty families; Pedrocile in the same year, with twenty families; and Charco Dulce (Freshwater Pond) in 1935, with eighty families, forty from Casas Viejas and forty from Medina Sidonia. In all, a total of 140 families were involved in the township, just a small fraction of the landless laborers in the area.

The first of the cooperatives, San José de Malcocinado, covered an area of 3,000 fanegas located just four kilometers from Casas Viejas. Two years earlier, in 1932, the Instituto engineer for the area and José Suárez had petitioned the minister of agriculture to create the settlement. Expropriation was unnecessary here, since the land belonged to the government (purchased earlier from the marqués of Negrón) and had been used by the army to breed mares. After a two-year delay, the necessary authorization was granted. Many of those who had originally agreed to join had changed their minds, and José Suárez had to submit names without permission in order to make the deadline. On January 1, 1934, the lands were turned over to the members of the new agrarian cooperative. A government loan enabled the cooperative to purchase 120 cows, 46 sows, 15 mares, and a variety of seed for planting. Although it was late, they immediately began sowing wheat and chickpeas. By this time one of the forty had dropped out. To avert the Instituto engineer's forecast that the cooperative would fail, Suárez agreed to live there and serve as director. The new settlement required someone with a knowledge of agriculture and a strong hand.

*José Suárez:* I was in charge of everything—selling, buying, building the school. The men knew how to work in the campo, but they didn't know how to direct the work—how much a pig weighed, how to organize the tasks. I bought orange trees for the huerta and planted them so that they would have food, and I organized the cooperative commissary so that they could buy cheaply.

The settlement of San José had a promising beginning. A garden, a commissary and a bakery were started. A great variety of fruit trees were planted, including orange, pomegranate, pear, apple, fig, quince, lemon, and plum. Artichokes were sown. Strands of pine trees were in place for future harvesting and sale. A modest medical plan covered their health needs, and a burial program was arranged as well. A school was established for the children. Labor on the land was done cooperatively. An organizing committee met five nights a week to divide the work for the following week, and a general assembly was held each month to consider long-range plans and problems. In the first two years, the number of yearlings doubled the cow herd, and the pigs increased twelvefold. The settlement had successful harvests of wheat, lima beans, barley, chickpeas, and millet.[1]

While the cooperative slowly expanded its herds and crops, social development took a different course. The workers were unprepared for the conflicts that arose.

*José Suárez:* The fear of being cheated and deceived made the workers afraid and created problems. The smallest problems caused the most trouble—who had the most sons, who was working hard, and who was shirking. One would say that another was not doing his share. There was jealousy. Or one was older than another. It was ignorance and lack of confidence.

At that time the sons were too small to work, and so the only workers were the *colonos*. We were planning to put in industry when the children grew up. But the colonos were afraid and ignorant. We paid insurance to have a doctor, and each paid so much. And the ones who were healthy would complain that they were paying for the sick. They didn't understand.

At San José the discontent and the potential for disorganization were kept under control. At six of the twenty other agrarian cooperatives begun in the province, however, misunderstandings, confusion, and poor leadership led to failure. At harvest time, when they should have reaped their crop to pay off their debts, the workers went on strike, demanding higher pay. It was impossible for officials to explain that the harvest was the workers' own, and that they were doing injury only to themselves. The cooperatives were in shambles. Seed and fertilizer putrified. Mules and other animals were sold. Tools were broken or confiscated by the workers. In one a shoemaker and a barber had been placed in charge of agricultural production, with predictable results. After visiting the six cooperatives for the Instituto de la Reforma

1. Francisco Retamero, *¡Colectivización! La explotación colectiva de "Malcocinado."*

Agraria, José Suárez recommended that these be shut down and a smaller number, better run, be developed as examples to the surrounding communities.

The land reform program of the Republic soon stagnated from legal snarls, landlord protest, and lack of energy and initiative. In July 1935, new legislation undid major provisions in the agrarian reform law. Large estates were made virtually invulnerable to expropriation. Land reform came to a standstill.

## Civil War

On July 17, 1936, three and a half years after the uprising at Casas Viejas, the garrisons in Spanish Morocco were taken by the troops of General Francisco Franco; the following day, July 18, in Andalusia, forces loyal to Franco were successful in Cádiz, Seville, Jerez, Algeciras, and La Línea. Moorish troops were flown across to the mainland and solidified the rebels' hold on Andalusia.

Immediately a purge began of those identified with the Republic and the left. The most prominent victims in the towns were local officials, Socialists, and Republicans who held public office: mayors, deputy mayors, and managers of cooperative agrarian farms, as well as officers of the civil guard loyal to the Republic. The blood bath quickly reached out to include all those "with ideas"—Socialists, Republicans, and anarchists who were known for their strong opinions and their actions. To avoid being taken and executed, many hid in the countryside or fled to join the forces of the Republic. Some were forced to serve with Franco.

In Casas Viejas there was a small group of men, twenty or so, who enlisted in the Falange. Most were members of the middle class, but there were a few skilled workers and even two or three campesinos among the new converts. To judge by reports, the motives of the membership, as in every organization, were mixed: some joined for power and prestige, some for profit, and some for excitement and a chance to be on the winning side. It is impossible to learn with certainty what actions, if any, they participated in.

The following accounts tell what happened to some of the major figures in this history from the start of the Civil War in 1936 to 1974, the year before Franco's death. In the initial account, Pepe Pareja relates the events of the first days. In the concluding statement, he tells a parable of reform and revolution.

## Pepe Pareja

When the war began, I had gone to the campo to collect palmitos, and while I was working I pinched a nerve or pulled a muscle in my back, and I had to return to the village. All that day I saw planes flying back and forth in the sky. They were carrying troops—Moors from Africa to La Vega Caulina near Jerez. I heard some gunfire from one place. When I returned, I learned that a plane had banked over Alcalá and dropped a bomb, killing some people.

That night, at 11:00 or 12:00, they brought some people here from Alcalá and shot them in the crossroads above. They had taken Antonio Gallego, who was the deputy mayor, Domingo Sánchez, and La Paradera. (A couple of days later they brought another group from Alcalá and shot them below by the Suerte del Pollo, where the road marker says "11 kilometers." But I was not here then. I had left before.)

The next day I didn't go out. The second or third day a group of Falangists [from Medina] came here. Some who saw them enter left running, and the Falangists who were above on the heights started shooting at them with rifles. Some of the people had been slaughtering a pig, and they left with the leather chaps on their sleeves. From my doorway I saw them moving just above. When they passed, I cut out behind them, and I went to the far side of the pueblo. With my blood rushing and adrenaline pumping, the pain in my back left me instantly. Antonia knew where I was, and when they left she came and told me, and I returned.

*Antonia Márquez:* There were five Falangists posted above, and Pepe was below, without his jacket; and I thought, "The poor man, he doesn't have his jacket, and he's ill." I tied his jacket around my waist under my skirts, and I went out carrying my daughter, who had a cold. I called up to one of them, "Look at my sick daughter. I have to go for medicine for her." And he said: "You can pass." So I went below looking for him, and I found him on his nephew's land up in a tree.

*Pepe Pareja:* I was up in a *chaparro* [scrub oak], because from there I could see in all directions. That night I left the town. I heard that they were going to kill this one and that one, and that night I left for Jimena. I told myself that they weren't going to kill me. I thought, "I'll die, but not at their hands." That night I left, and I reached the mountains. The day before I had heard it announced that the navy was going to fire their cannons and destroy the wharf at Barbate. The next day I was in the mountains, and I heard the first cannons of the bombardment. Hearing those explosions, I continued my journey until I arrived at Jimena. I stayed there until it was about to be taken by the *requetes* [Carlists] and the Falangists, and then I went to Estepona, the shore. The front was formed there from Casares to Málaga. Then I went to Almería, where I worked for some time in the construction industry, because everything was destroyed there. While I was working on the wharf, I slept on a boat that was from Barbate.

## Pelele

Manuel [Llamas] and I went to all the cortijos to inform the workers. We walked all night. By dawn we were back at the pueblo [Medina Sidonia], and we went to the town hall to see what was happening. The mayor, the lieutenant mayor, and the lieutenant of the civil guard were there listening to the Voice of the Republic on the radio. They put some local Fascists in jail. This was on July 19.

When I went out of the house again, the Fascists were out in the street, and the mayor was in jail. I decided to leave then, dressed just as I was. I was on the other side of the street and my mother was in the doorway of her house watching me to see what I was going to do. We looked at each other. I waited until she turned her head for a moment, and I slipped away.

I hid out during the day, and that night I left for Boca de la Pila, the closest mountain to Medina. Forty workers gathered there, each deciding what to do. Then Manuel Llamas said, "I'm leaving, because I don't know what's going to happen."

I said: "I'm going with you." Manuel, without depreciating anyone, was the best fighter there was, a great compañero, and we were very close.

Four of us went looking for a way out to Gibraltar. When we reached Los Barrios, we saw we couldn't make it, and we returned to tell the others that the way was closed.

When we four came back, the others had returned to their places, to town and to the cortijos where they worked. Some twenty workers, mostly anarchists but many Republicans—about half and half—were taken and shot at the cemetery.

We left for Jimena, and we stopped in Estepona, and there in Estepona there was more resistance. We then went to Jimena, and there we organized. We got some arms, shotguns and rifles, to put up some resistance.

*Manuel (Pelele's brother):* We heard that there was comunismo libertario already in Jimena. We heard it from a *contrabandista* (smuggler). Three of us brothers went, and we met Pelele there—the four of us together.

Algeciras remained free, but the campo was in Fascist hands. We couldn't reach Algeciras. There was a ship in the harbor with the words "The Republic Lives!" painted on it, but we couldn't reach it.

We spent three days in Jimena, and then we left and went to Ronda. We three brothers enlisted in an army brigade.

*Pelele:* I went to a collective, the cortijo Santerje, in the township of Huelva in the province of Jaén.

## The repression

*José Monroy and Pepe Pareja:* They brought ten people here from Alcalá and killed them down below at the curve in the road, number 11 on the road, at a place called La Suerte del Pollo.

Outsiders came here to do the killing. They killed three men from here—all Socialists. They weren't in the CNT. One was in Las Yeguadas. His mother had been of the nobility, but she didn't have a title. She owned a drugstore, and they called her La Droguera. She had two children, and he was her son. He was a Socialist with Pepe Suárez and served in the junta with him in Las Yeguadas.

They killed Benio. He had a tavern opposite the administration office. He was a Socialist. He was in his bar talking to another Socialist. They grabbed them both. They shot Benio. They questioned the other, and he said they didn't want him, they were making a mistake; they really meant his brother, who was in Las Yeguadas, and so they left him and went for his brother.

He was a Socialist, but they really wanted his brother. Or so we suppose. This is what we believe happened, but we are not certain.

*José Suárez:* When the war started, they came to San José looking for me. I had left for the Republican zone. They broke down the door, and they destroyed my furniture and books.

The mayor of Medina, who was killed in 1936, was a real Republican. He and the lieutenant mayor were killed. He was a good man. He had been a schoolteacher and was mayor for one year. He was shot in Medina in the street, and later his body was dragged through the streets tied to a car.

*Juan Pinto:* The mayor of Medina was a Socialist and they killed him. His body lay in the street for two days like a dog. A señorito came along and kicked him, and a short time afterward, his leg dried up. There's no one above, but somehow he lost his leg, the leg with which he kicked the dead Socialist mayor. They killed the mayor, they shot him, and he didn't suffer any more. But the one who kicked him and whose leg dried up continued to suffer. That's what I believe.

Here, Manuel Sánchez was the schoolteacher and a supporter of the Republic. They were looking for him to shoot him. They shot the schoolteacher in Medina, who was also the mayor, and left his body in the street. They were looking to shoot Manuel Sánchez too.

The priest from Medina was his *padrino* (godfather). He was the one who saved him. Juan Pérez-Blanco was of the right, but he was a friend of his. He and the priest saved him. The priest intervened and had him drafted into the army. After the war, when he came out, he stayed close to the priest. He went to mass much more than before and then went right into his house. He was rarely seen on the street, whereas before he had always walked around. He would look over his shoulder fearfully.

When they killed the men [brought to Casas Viejas] from Alcalá, a few Falangists went out to meet them, to see what was there. They found three out of four men dead and a trail of blood where one had left the road wounded. They found him about twenty steps away, and he was still alive. Then they finished him off. One of them began to search his pockets, and he found some crackers and other things. Then he said, "Here! Have some crackers." That's what a Falangist did to a dead man. "Eat your crackers now," he said.

*Manolo:* It's good to have a house on the outskirts. Then you aren't in the center of the town. Twice people have had to flee for their lives from here—once during the uprising, and then when the war broke out and the Falangists came here from Medina.

The mayor came down to call my father. The mayor was Baltazar. He told my father to come up above. My father thought he was going to be shot. The mayor led him and some others up to the crossroads. There were the bodies of those who had been shot. Their faces had been disfigured to make them unrecognizable. They had been smashed in with a rifle butt. He said, "Load them in the truck."

They had to put the bodies in the truck. My father couldn't eat for eight or ten days. He could take only a little sip of coffee.

*Antonio:* Three days after the movement began, there were twenty to thirty in the Falange here. They were workers and members of the middle class. Two were campesinos, one was a carpenter, two were bricklayers. In Casas Viejas the head of the Falange during the war was the schoolteacher Sergio, who came from Madrid and who still lives there now, and his brother Julio, who has died. Sergio was a Socialist of the left. On July 17 he was talking with workers in the bar. On the nineteenth, the day after the revolution, he had changed his shirt. He hung up the emblem of Franco. He was a good person. He was a leftist, but life is sweet.

Two men who were born here and one who lived here for several years were shot. The two were in San José de Malcocinado: Francisco Guerra, who had a fabric and food shop in San José and Francisco Guiena Pérez. Both were Socialists. Benio, who had come to live here, was also a Socialist. He had a bar. It was said that someone came up to him and said, "You had a pistol. Come on." This was in August 1936, in the first days after the movement. No one knows where they were shot or where they were buried. It is believed that they were shot near Puerto Real. Twenty-two others from Alcalá and Paterna, including Antonio Gallego, the deputy mayor, and Domingo the tailor were killed at the crossroads at Benalup. Antonio Gallego and Domingo had gone to Cádiz in 1932 to petition for an agrarian reform settlement. Eleven thousand were shot at the gateway to Cádiz in the gully. Gypsies had lived there. It looks pretty now. There's an official building and a little park.

There were about twenty to thirty Falangists here. Two reported Ricardo for listening to the radio. One died later in Seville. The other is still here. There was another Falangist said to have killed people in Arcos.

In the time of the Civil War, it was reported that one talked to this one or that one. Friends that one had did this—not here, but elsewhere.

As a defense, one talks to people of different classes. If you talk to me, you also talk to another. If I am seen talking to you, I'm also seen talking to José Vela. This is the best defense a person can have.

Some asked me to join them and go over to the other side. But not me. A rifle bullet is nonpolitical. One shot from either side can kill you. One fellow left, and they took his mother and made her drink castor oil.

*Antonia Márquez:* The Falangists came here various times, and there were some Falangists here as well. They took several women whose husbands or sons had fled. After asking where the men were they took the women instead. They held them for twenty-four hours in the Falangist quarters here, and then they took them to Medina. They took the wife of Durán, the mother of the Pavones, and Manuela "Clavejo," whose son Joaquín Gómez had fled to the other zone, and the gypsy Joaquina, whose son had left. They gave the mother of the Pavones and the gypsy Joaquina a purgative to drink. The mother of the Pavones was a very outspoken woman, and they took her because she had three sons who had shot too well during the uprising. Afterward, from the purgative and the fright, she became ill and died.

## Captain Manuel Rojas Feijespán

[*At the outbreak of the war Rojas was released from prison and readmitted to the army with the rank of artillery captain.*]

*Anonymous high-ranking officer:* Rojas returned to Cádiz in July 1936, when the war began and he started looking for the man who had been the prosecuting attorney at his trial. At the time the man was in prison in Cádiz, and Rojas said to me, "Let's go down to the prison tomorrow morning and shoot him." I reported what he said, and Rojas was ordered to leave Cádiz.

[*During the war Rojas added to his reputation for cruelty.*]

*Ramón Salas Larrazábal, Secretary of Civil Aviation (personal letter):* Rojas was in Granada on July 19, and he showed once again his personal character during the repression, which was particularly harsh, thereby putting an end to what little prestige he had left.[2]

## Lieutenant Gregorio Fernández Artal

[*Lieutenant Fernández Artal served with the Republic, and he did not survive the war.*]

*Ramón Salas Larrazábal:* Gregorio Fernández Artal was assigned to Barcelona in the nineteenth division of the civil guard, and he enlisted in the People's Army. He was promoted to captain for his loyalty to the Republic. He was active along the battle lines of Aragón, in the Trueba del Barrio battalion, called the Karl Marx battalion. Apparently, although I cannot state it categorically, he was captured and executed by the National forces.

2. Gabriel Jackson reports on other well-known persons: "Captain Barba was one of the founders of the UME [Unión Militar Española]. He went on to purge Saragossa in the first weeks of the Civil War and to earn there a reputation even among reactionaries as a bloodthirsty criminal. . . .Arturo Menéndez was taken off the Barcelona-Madrid express at Saragossa on July 18 and shot by the Nationalists" (*The Spanish Republic*, p. 514). Manuel Azaña again became prime minister in February 1936, following the victory of the Popular Front; and in May 1936 he was elected president of the Second Republic, a less politically combative post, which he held throughout almost the entirety of the Civil War. After the defeat of the Republic, Azaña escaped to France, where he died in November 1940.

## In the campo

*Rosario:* There was no fighting here [in Casas Viejas] or in Alcalá, but many people were carried off in trucks and shot. I don't like to talk about it, because I lived through it, but the priest of Alcalá, Father Manuel, took confession from those whom they shot in Alcalá. They took a gypsy, a good man who sold cloth in the mountains, to be shot in the cemetery with others. And at the cemetery he fell on his knees and cried out, "Madre mía de los santos, sálvame!" ("Mother of the saints, save me!"). Then they shot him.

After that Don Manuel would not confess those to be shot any more. He said, "When a person in time of death calls on his Heavenly Mother to save him, one must heed him." He moved to La Línea and wouldn't take any more confessions from those to be shot.

They took the doctor of Alcalá, Don Franco, to Medina and shot him. Some people say he was a Freemason. Who knows why they shot people? For some small thing—for saying one didn't believe in the saints, for saying something against the saints. One had to be very careful about what one said. They were shot to cleanse Spain to make a great and glorious nation.

*Monte:* We were working in the campo, and it was lunch time. We were eating a stew of chickpeas. Three men came—a civil guard, a Falangist, and a soldier. They asked for José Camacho, whose nickname was "Reberte," because when he had been young he had liked the bullfights, and Reberte was a famous toreador. They asked where he was.

I said: "He's over there eating. I'll call him over."

"No. Wait till he's finished."

When he was finished, they called him over. He had been eating a melon, cutting it with his knife, and they asked to see his knife.

"Let me see it. Oh, this is nothing." It was a pocket knife. "Put it in your pocket. Come to the truck."

He said: "Let me get my jacket."

They said: "No. Don't bother. Leave it there."

But he said, "No, I'll get it." He hung the jacket over his shoulder and got in the truck.

That was the last we saw of him. They shot him. Before working in the campo, he had had a bar where people talked about politics. José could not read or write, but he had ideas.

Manuel Lago and Juan "Mentira" were harvesting cork in Ahijón in 1936. They were eating when they came for them and told them to get in the truck. Manuel was about fifty or fifty-five then. He could read and write well. He had been one of the leaders of the sindicato. Juan could read and write well too.

They came to the cortijo and asked for Pedro Jaén. They were mistaken. They were looking for another Pedro Jaén, but there were many with this name, and they had been sent to him. He was a peaceful man. He and three or four others were told to dig their graves, and then they shot them.

Before they shot him he took what he had in his pocket and gave it to "Paso Largo," a Falangist who was his friend but who had come with the others. He could do nothing against the majority. He said nothing. He gave him five duros, his tobacco pouch, and his knife, and said to give them to his wife. So later "Paso Largo" gave them to her. Pedro Jaén had been a guard for "Leggings."

*Anónimo:* Sebastián Oliva, the director of *La Voz del Campesino,* was shot during the war. Diego Martínez of Jerez and Baistero were shot too.

*Juan Moreno:* They killed everyone who had any brains. They killed all the shepherds, and without a shepherd, where can the flock go?

## Juan Estudillo

*Juan Pinto:* I was in my house, and Juan [Estudillo] was up the street. Someone said, "The Moors are coming!" When he heard this, he went to pieces. And so did I. As he ran from his house, he fell and hurt himself. I also ran in the direction where he was going. We went up an alleyway and reached the heights of the mesa. I said to Juan, "Let's stop. Perhaps no one's coming." Someone had said, "Here come the Moors!" and a whole crowd started running. There was an uproar. The Moors didn't come. Nobody came.

Juan remained very pensive, and the next day he went to the well and threw himself in. He thought they were going to kill him: "Before these people kill me, I'll kill myself."

*Pepe Pilar:* I had told him, "Juan, when I leave you're going with me." I told him two or three times I wanted to take him with us.

That evening I came home and suddenly people said, "The Falangists are here!" We had to run, because when they came here, it was to get whomever they could. I fled down toward El Chorro, and I hid in Juan Luna's mill. Poor Juan was at home, in that choza beside María Toro's. [*Juan Estudillo began a common-law marriage in 1935, the year before his death, with María Toro. María Toro had three children from an earlier marriage, but none had survived to the time of the war. A daughter had died of tuberculosis; a son, José Utrera Toro, aged twenty-five, was one of the twelve men taken from their homes and shot during the uprising.*]

Well, the poor fellow, when they made that riot, "The Falangists are coming!" he also ran, and as he thought about it, he threw himself into the well. He was a good and noble person. He would sacrifice himself in the matter of printing pamphlets and books and all that. Whatever he earned as a shoemaker he divided with compañeros. Some paid him, and others didn't.

*Pepe Pareja:* I left before Juan killed himself. If I had said to Juan, "Come with me," this suicide wouldn't have occurred. One left from fear. The rabbit thinks the warren is his salvation from pursuers, the hunter and his dogs. But the hunter has been more astute and has blocked the entrance holes. The rabbit can't enter his shelter. He is caught.

*Isabel Vidal:* Juan Estudillo took the shoelaces from his shoes and tied them around his feet and jumped into the well. He was a saintly man who liked to read.

## María Silva, La Libertaria

*Antonia Márquez:* La Libertaria went with Gallinito for about six months. She was his novia. They went out carrying the black and red flag with Manuela Lago. After the uprising, Gallinito was put in prison. La Libertaria's mother took her six children and went to live in Cádiz. La Libertaria went with her.

Miguel Cordón began to court her there, and after about two months of seeing each other they went off to Madrid. They lived together in free union. But first she asked her mother's permission.[3]

*José Vega:* María Silva was like a symbol. In reality María Silva was a good girl and even more, but they made her into an idol. She had ideas, but actually the only thing she had done was to save her own life.

*Antonia Márquez:* La Libertaria named her son Sidonio. He was small, still at her breast when they killed her.

## Juan Pinto

In the first days of the war, I was in an agrarian reform cooperative, Charco Dulce, about two leagues (ten kilometers) from here. When the movement broke out, the Fascists showed up—with the original owners of the land. We thought they were going to kill us, and we started to scatter like birds.

One day when the men were returning, a squad of Fascists came—carabineros, civil guards, Fascists. A squad of them came and they said to some of us, "Do you see that guy's face? He has the face of a criminal. You! Do you have a knife in your hands? Come on. Hands up." And the Fascists poked their guns at two or three who were there. They were pale. When the Fascists left, they told us what had happened.

They said: "I'm leaving. I'm not working any more. If not, they're going to kill us right here."

The foreman said, "If they haven't killed you by now, they won't kill you. There's no reason to run." He didn't want any of us to leave. What was for one should be for all. And they didn't kill anyone. There were two

3. Lois Iturbe relates, "A year after the tragedy of Casas Viejas, María Silva united with the militant Miguel Cordón and moved to Madrid with him. Later they both returned to Andalusia. In July of 1936 the couple lived in Ronda. When the Fascists occupied this area, Miguel Cordón took refuge in the mountains. María Silva remained at home with her son, who was a few months old. The civil guard went to her house to arrest her. As a mother, she must have suffered the worst of all tortures. Her little child was snatched violently from her arms, and they took her away under arrest. Upon reaching the road outside of the town, she was assassinated by the guards" (*La Mujer en la lucha social y en la Guerra Civil de España*, p. 97); a more impassioned account can be read in Montseny, pp. 46–51.

agrarian reform farms: one in Medina and another one here. They killed only the foreman from Medina. I was pretty frightened there. We slept out in the mountains.

In short, they came one day, and they grabbed two or three of our group, and the foreman told us, "It's nothing. Don't run. You gather all the grain that there is in the field. No one will bother you." And no one did. But no one paid us, either. We received wages until the movement began. After the movement broke out we didn't collect a penny. The foreman told us to continue working in order to gather the harvest. And we did, and he didn't say anything. Then the foreman told us, "My friends, go wherever you can." And each one of us went home. We didn't get paid anything, and I worked for them for two months.

Each one went home, and around here nothing happened. The owner came in again and took charge of everything—the wheat, the cows, and the tools. He took everything and did not pay us anything. That's the way things are in this world. We were so scared that what we wanted to do was go to the red zone where the government was. The country was divided into two bands. Málaga was in the red zone.

## Pepe Pilar

When the war started, they came shooting and everyone fled. I was hiding with Alfonso Osorio on the mesa. Osorio's father was a cowherd on a finca where the priest's uncle was a guard. His father said, "Stay here. This is a safe place."

His father brought us food, and we were there for several months, until we saw things calm down. We had planned to join up with the forces at Málaga. I had never been there and didn't know anything about it. We thought that the forces were going to march down to Algeciras, and we would join up with them there. But before we knew it, Málaga was lost to the Nationalists, and our plan fell through. [Málaga fell on February 8, 1937.]

I said, "Málaga is lost. We've no place to run to."

Alfonso said: "I'm not leaving." We hid for three months.

I had told my compañera to send someone down to let me know if the Falangists came looking for me. She knew where I was. When she appeared that morning before sunrise, I said to Osorio, "Look, here comes my wife. Now we'll have to go."

My wife said, "Last night after 1:00, three Falangists came to the house asking for you. I said you weren't here. You were in the campo. They told me, 'The Falange chief says you have to present yourself at headquarters.' Then he said: 'Get up, and have your daughters get up also.' "

They had to get up, and the Falangists searched the house. When they had finished investigating, they saw there was nothing, because there was nothing to find there, and they left. They told her that I was to present myself.

After she told us this, I said to Alfonso, "Well, Alfonso, we can bypass Algeciras to look for our forces."

He replied, "I'm not leaving here. I'm not leaving."

And I told him, "I haven't left before, because we agreed to leave together, and now you're staying here."

He said, "My father is alone, and he told me not to leave. I can't go."

So I was alone. "Well, I'm going to see what happens. They won't tie me up. That I can definitely say."

I left and went down to the headquarters of the Falange, which was in the bar opposite the town office. There was Antonio, and I said, "Listen, Antonio, is Andrés Muñón in?"

"Yes, he's here. He's in there."

"Tell him I'm here."

He shouts toward the door, "Andrés, Pepe is here."

"Tell him to come in."

"He says for you to go in."

"You tell him to come out."

"Andrés, he says for you to come out. He won't go in."

Then he comes out with a big smile. But I don't smile. He was killed soon after in Seville by a blow on the head with a bottle.

"*Hombre,* what's going on?"

I tell him, "That's what I would like to know. Why have I been asked to come here?"

He replies, "Look, the chief said that you're hiding, that you haven't presented yourself." The head of the Falange was Sergio from Alcalá. He was here in town.

"Look, you tell him that I'm not hiding. You know that you've been in hiding with me. In the first days of the movement, you were in hiding. Why did you run?"

"Because I was afraid of what was happening."

"Well, I was with you in hiding. Now you have no reason to hide, and now you come after us, eh? Before you ran from them, and now you come after us."

He says nothing.

"You tell the Falange that I'm not running away, but that I don't stay at my house either. I go to my house to eat, and after I finish eating I leave. I don't stay there."

Then he tells me, "Sergio is the head Falangist, and you have to present yourself to him."

"And where is Sergio?"

He says, "He's at Ricardo's [bar]."

I reply, "I won't go to Ricardo's. I won't go any further down into town than here."

Then Eugenio, who had come to the door, asks me, "What are you doing there, Pepe?"

"Look, they say Sergio wants to see me, and he is at Ricardo's, and I won't go to Ricardo's."

"Stay there." And he goes and calls this Sergio.

Sergio arrives like a captain. And I recall that he also was a Socialist and had been in hiding with me together with Andrés during the first days. Then Sergio says out there on the street, "Let's go into my house." We go into his house, and he puts out a glass of wine for each one and then he asks me, "Well, what's going on? What do you say? You're in hiding, eh?"

I say, "Not me, hombre. I'm not running away. Who told you that I'm running away? I'm hiding as I did when I was with you. That time you were hidden, you and Andrés. Why did you hide? Because you were afraid. Well, I'm still doing the same, since my fear hasn't gone away. I don't stay at home, but I go there every day. You tell the chief of the Falange that I'm not running away."

Then my old pal tells me, "Well, look, I'm going to tell you something. You know the six who were killed at Piebajo? I was convinced that one of the corpses I was going to pick up was my brother." Because in Alcalá they caught Sergio's brother and were taking him to be killed with the other six, but when Sergio found out that the boy was with them and was going to be killed, he took a car and caught them half-way there, and he stopped them and put the boy in his car and took him away.

And I ask him, "What do you mean? If you were going so calmly to pick up your brother's corpse, what aren't you capable of?" And I tell him, "I have but one life to lose. If you take it from me, you can add one more to your account of the many that are murdered. Better to die than be responsible for what you're doing. Better to lose my life than to have your job. So now you know it all. You tell the Falange that I haven't fled. I haven't stayed at home, nor do I stay there. And I haven't done harm to anyone."

He tells me, "From now on I am responsible here. I don't have any orders to detain you, but if I receive them, I'll come for you."

"Well, you don't know where I stay anyway. If you find anything out about me, you're going to have to search for me like a rabbit in the hills, because you won't catch me here."

He says, "Well, that's what I have to say to you."

I said, "I'm in the campo, but I come home every day to my house to eat. I'll be here." But of course I stayed in the campo for months.

The chief of the Falange was one of his uncles from Madrid. They had been Socialists, and they were the biggest Falangists there were in Madrid.

We were afraid not of the local Falange but of those from Alcalá and Medina, because the local group didn't kill anyone from the pueblo. They went to another pueblo. Those from Alcalá went to Medina, and those from Medina went to Alcalá.

There was one member of the Falange, José Guién, who was our friend. He wore the clothes of the Falange, but he would warn us if something was up, if they were going to get someone. He had a bar, and one day I went to his bar in order to find out if I should flee or not. I peeked in the back, and there was Don José talking to three of his cowherds, and he said, "We've killed 3,000 in Arcos, Sanlúcar, and Jerez. We'll get on top, and the police will step in, and there won't be a communist left alive." I left.

Another day our friend in the Falange showed me a list with eighteen names of people here. Pepe's name was on it, Juan Sopas, Monroy, Juan Román, to be shot.

Those who joined the Falange were those who had a few glasses of wine and believed anything. Some were thieves who stole chickens to sell them.

In Medina they shot some Falangists because they were thieves. There were perhaps thirty or forty Falangists here. They signed up to protect themselves. Before, some had belonged to the Socialists or even the CNT but were not convinced of anything.

Andrés Muñón was a Falangist. He had capital. He had land and 100 cows. Serjando was a worker. He was from Alcalá, and he married a girl from here. Once five or six cars came from Medina. I looked out the door and said, "Where are they from?" And someone said, "They've brought people to shoot them here." And that's what it was. They shot them at the crossroads below.

The first shot were those from Alcalá. There were six. One was shot in the leg and was still alive, and they finished him off. One of the Falangists had cookies in his pocket he had taken with him, and he said, "Here, eat a cookie." The man who did that is still alive. He's paying for it, though. He has passed through more calamities than anyone.

Once they took off Ricardo, of the bar, to Cádiz to be shot. He was listening to National Radio, but someone put on a foreign station. Someone entered and heard it and denounced him: "You're listening to the red radio." The very one who put on the station denounced him. They took him to Cádiz to shoot him, and if it hadn't been for the intercession of Juan Pérez-Blanco, Don Manuel the schoolteacher, and the priest, he would have been shot. And A. was to blame—because he owed Ricardo seventy duros, he denounced him.

## Juan Vidal Benítez

*Isabel Vidal:* First my father burned all his books for fear of reprisal. He kept only the dictionary, geography, and the like.

It was hot out. He had bronchitis. The doctor said he must have caught a draft. I said to a neighbor, "How could he catch a draft? He sleeps in such a nice warm bed with blankets."

She said: "Fool, don't you know that for the past month your father has been going down below to sleep on the ground, because he's afraid they'll come for him?"

One day my father made a statement to the barber that the uprising was due to the señoritos. Later, when the war started, he became fearful that it would be repeated. He slept out every night under a tree on a friend's huerta, so that he wouldn't be at home if they knocked on the door for him.

He died shortly thereafter. He died at seventy-five [July 6, 1937], with all his teeth in. They never did come for him.

## Anónimo

During the Civil War, I was very lucky. The religious teachings I told you about are always helpful. That was very valuable to me.

This is a secret, but I've told it to a few since so much time has passed. At first I was in hiding. I did not leave with the others from Medina because of a difference of opinion, and that is what saved me. To remain here was very difficult, very difficult. But I didn't go through anything, in the sense that I had influence [through a close relative]. For another thing, a civil guard was always watching my back, so that I would not be hurt.

And then, at 1:00 in the morning, I was called to the barracks. I said, "Jesus!" And I looked at the civil guard. "What is this?"

And he said, "Don't worry. I swear to you by my children and whatever else you want."

I trusted him, and I finally got up the necessary courage, and I went there. They locked me up with him [the commander of the post]. I wept with emotion.

At that time many commanders were not too sure of the movement. This fellow took the opportunity to take someone into his confidence, and that person was me. He says to me, "This is the way it is. I think that you are a man, and as a man I trust you. You are the only man here. You can go on the street, anywhere, and nobody is going to bother you, eh? Don't leave for anything. I guarantee your safety. Don't leave."

This was the point. The commander said that I would serve as his witness, that he was a decent person if things should go the other way and the Republicans should win. And then I went home.

When the war broke out, I was secretary of the CNT. Some Falangists came once and wanted to make me secretary of their union, and I told them no. And the commander called me in. "Don't you want to be secretary of the Falange?"

"Look, I'm leaving. I can't resist this. I won't be secretary for those people even if ——"

He said, "Don't worry; they wouldn't dare do anything."

This was the way I survived here. Of course I've had to keep it a secret, because one doesn't mention such things.

You cannot speak, even jokingly, to a civil guard about those who died or were killed during the war. They say simply that they disappeared. I said to one, "Oh, so and so was killed at the beginning of the war."

He said, "Oh, no. He disappeared in the war." They don't like it, even as a joke.

## Palmiro Olmo

They executed my brother Germinal, whose name was Mateo, in Puerto Real. He was twenty-four. He was more involved in politics than I was. He was involved in the sindicato. In reality he was like my father; he was a good man. Not me. I said, "I want to be a white-collar worker." But I was becoming aware of things as I went to the meetings of the CNT. I didn't want to get into those things, but I signed up. And they came to look for me twenty-four times. Twenty-four times they came for me—just because I belonged to Juventud Libertaria. They shot a boy just for putting on a priest's hat and selling workers' newspapers. I hadn't done anything—nothing more than signing my name there, nothing else.

I managed to keep my freedom, because I was warned ahead of time. I was working in Calle Ancha, at the Casa de Arena, as a laboratory technician in a photography studio. And the woman said, "Get out right away, because they are looking for you." I jumped into a ditch, and I came here. What could I do? One day they found me. I hadn't done anything wrong. I was twenty-seven at the time.

They took me to San Fernando, then to Burgos, from Burgos to Victoria and to Huesca. I thought they were going to execute me, but they put me in the trenches—all because I belonged to Juventud Libertaria. I couldn't desert to the other side. The fact was my mother was still alive, and I had married during the war. If I deserted, they would shoot them.

When I came back from the war, they gave me a certificate. I served six months at the front, having demonstrated great bravery, subordination, and loyalty to the Caudillo [Franco], and therefore I deserved the protection of my country and the respect of its citizens. You see that's how I saved myself. That's how I saved myself.

### Villarubia

During the war I was at the front—from Montilla [Córdoba] to Alcalá la Real, in the province of Jaén. I was there two and a half years.

[*What did you think when you had to fight against your friends?*]

I thought the same as always. You have to obey the one who commands.

[*Did you want to join the other side?*]

Me? What for? If I had wanted to pass over, I would have done so at the start. Paco went over at the start.

[*You didn't want to go?*]

It's not that I didn't want to go. I didn't go over to the other side, because the force here was superior. So it seemed to me. I was better off here.

[*But Paco wanted to go over to the other side because of their ideas. You didn't have any ideas?*]

Not me. I was named secretary of the sindicato. Well, I was named. What could I do? It was not for ideological reasons.

## The red zone

### Cristóbal

When the war started, a notice came saying that all those who had been in prison for the uprising should present themselves at the barracks in Medina. Instead, I went to the other side. I was in Málaga working on a cortijo, raising food. After Málaga was taken, I returned, and I was sent to prison for three years, first in Medina and then in Cádiz.

### José Vega

In the Republican zone the Socialists, the communists, and the cenetistas each had an organization independent of the other. They had land and industries, because the owners had been killed or had fled or had been driven out. Each organization formed communes or collectives. A finca was expropriated. The quickest group grabbed it and sent twenty workers there. Each organization had its own system. The communists called them *comunidades*. The anarchists called them *colectividades* (collectives). They were federated sindicatos affiliated with the CNT.

We produced wheat and oil. What was needed for the collective was put in the storehouse. The excess was turned over to the provincial federation. We in turn received the extra that came from other collectives. Here are so many liters of oil. They gave us rice and clothing that we needed. They guarded the excess and regulated it. We developed the system ourselves.

Each worker received ten pesetas a day. They did not pay for things raised there, nor did they pay for things that were sent in by the federation, such as rice and oil. They did not pay for whatever the federation could gather. A worker in the collective took what was necessary that wasn't produced there—cloth, rice. Each one used what he wished to in the way of wine, coffee, tobacco. It was an individual question. There were few ideas and little education. There was little time to think of such things. There were few obreros conscientes.

There were about twenty workers and families there in the collective. This was only ten kilometers from Málaga. Almost all those in the collective were from elsewhere, although some were local. There was one manager. He supervised and organized the work and did what was necessary. If someone was good at this, he was sent here; if he was better at another task, he was sent there. For all important decisions, a meeting of all the workers was called. The headquarters, the group in charge, was the provincial federation in Málaga. The regional federation was there too, because Seville had been taken by Franco.

I was in Málaga from July 1936 until it fell in February 1937. Then I went to Almería through the mountains. It took twenty-six days to reach Almería, hiding. Many walked barefoot or with their feet wrapped in rags. Leaving this zone for the other gave one courage.

## Gallinito

[*Gallinito, Antonio Cabañas Salvador, became the political officer of his regiment. He was killed in action. Monroy's brief account is typical of what is told about Gallinito during the war. Sopas's version has an edge honed by his own bitter fate.*]

*José Monroy:* Gallinito kept going out of the trench to show that he was more valiant than the rest. They warned him he was going to get killed, and it happened.

*Juan Sopas:* Gallinito was a man filled with rage. At that time, after the uprising, La Libertaria left him for Cordón. She had been his novia, and he didn't know what to do.

During the war, Gallinito was with me in Málaga. When Málaga was lost, we went to Almería, the capital.

Gallinito died in 1937, in November, in the front lines at Pozoblanco. We were in the same brigade. After eight or ten days, they transferred me to the rear guard.

Gallinito was more cowardly than a chicken. He could have died of fright, he was so scared. When we arrived at Almería from Málaga, he told me, since I was the agricultural delegate, to use my influence to get him into the rear guard. He said, "You're going to the rear guard. Take me with you, because I'm afraid I'm going to die here."

I said to him: "The war needs men, and you are a great warrior, and your place is in front. There you have it. Why run from it?" He didn't say anything. They organized a brigade, and he was sent to Pozoblanco.

We were advancing through an olive grove. The Moors were attacking, and we left the trench to throw them back. He was shot in the temple. I looked at him and saw that he was shot square in the forehead. I kept going forward. When I returned; his body had been taken back.

If I knew then what I know now, nothing would have happened [at the uprising]. I would have punched Gallinito in the jaw when he threatened me, and nothing would have occurred.

## Pepe Pareja

I worked in various cooperatives run by the CNT. In Málaga I was with Manuel Llamas in Guaro de los Cesperones, which is arable land, and after that I was in Almería, and then in 1937 in Jaén, again with Manuel and with Juan Martínez, who was at the storehouse. In Jaén I was in Solera, by the boundary of Granada, near the town of Guadahortuna near the Sierra Nevada.

At a meeting I was asked to be in charge of one place, but I declined. They asked me at a second meeting, and so I had to accept. Some people there knew me, and knew I could plow the land. I had to accept the responsibility. I was put in charge of the Cortijo de la Huerta near the capital. The land lay alongside the road that goes to Jaén. There was one other family and a guard for the animals there. I organized things and also plowed with a team of mules. When I arrived there, they had many chickens, but there were no locks on any of the doors, and so whoever wanted to could go and help himself to eggs. I arranged a lock so that every morning I could go and collect the eggs. Then if someone wanted an egg, or two, or five, or ten, he could come to me and get them. And I marked down on a sheet what each took. It was a control. At the end of the month, when they were paid, I deducted what they took from their pay. They were paid in paper. If they said, "I didn't take that," I would say, "Well, here it is on the list." I had to administer the rations of the people there. I stayed there until the end of the war.

## Juan Sopas

When the war started I went to the other side [the Republic]. I was put in charge of the men working on several farms. I was agricultural delegate in Málaga. Pepe Pareja was with me, and a daughter of Monroy.

In Alicante I left for the rear guard. They needed men to organize, and so they picked me. I was in the town of Almoradi, in Alicante. I was the delegate of food and transport for six collectivized towns. Each town consumed what it raised, and then it asked the delegate what extra was needed [which was deposited in a common warehouse]. The fincas were collectivized by the CNT and the UGT.

Some did not agree. They had had land before and wanted to be free. So we gave them land to be free—1,000 meters and a little bit more to each one.

The factories of Alcoy were collectivized: shoe factories, a brick factory. We lacked a great deal, but it was just a beginning.

## Miguel Pérez Cordón

*José Vega:* Miguel worked in the campo, or in construction, or building roads. He didn't earn money from his writing. It was only during the war that he did nothing but write and edit and earn his way from it.

During the Civil War we went together to Ronda, Málaga, and then to Cartagena, where he died. In Ronda, in September, for a few months, he was the director of *La Nueva.* It was only two pages.

María Silva was shot while Miguel was still in Ronda, the last of August or the first days of September in 1936. They put her in jail in Paterna, and then some days later they took her to Cañuela, between Medina and Jerez, near the lagoon, and shot her there with several others. Some said they insulted her and abused her sexually. The same men who did it boasted of it. Miguel learned of it by word of mouth as people drifted across to the other side.

Before her death María gave birth to a baby, who was subsequently raised by her sister-in-law.

We passed through Málaga but spent only one or two days there and went on to Cartagena, where Miguel stayed until March 1939. Some compañeros put him in as director of the newspaper *Cartagena Nueva,* a four-page paper.

The masses exalted him, and he then believed himself more than what he was. Even if a man is the most important and the most intelligent, I believe that he should not think himself above other men. His education shouldn't set him above, but, on the contrary, he should always act with equality toward those with whom he is identified—with his class, with what he defends. He should not believe himself superior.

This was especially true during the war. I had seen other occasions when he was influenced in this way by egoism. He had already been in Ronda. He had been in Málaga. He had already been in Cartagena. Then all these small fragile towns were being occupied. The sindicatos had few men, because among the mass of workers there is always little intelligence. In Spain they have never had the means to educate themselves in order to elevate themselves morally, and a man stands out because of his intelligence or because of his sacrifices. Cordón was one of those men.

There was a counterrevolution when Negrín was the prime minister. This was when the communists were in power. The sindicatos arose against the counterrevolution, and Cordón died in this movement.

Cartagena is a military town, a naval base. There are capitalists and military people. The military people took advantage of the time to unite with the communists. They were Fascists masquerading as communists. They dominated the situation.

Many compañeros took refuge in a flour factory that had been collectivized. They couldn't attack Cordón there. They called him, and he went to keep the appointment. He thought the caller was a person of good faith. According to what I was told by those there, he was killed by the forces of order, the police. He was killed in the street. They said he died with his pistol in his hand. Many of us carried pistols then.

## Miguel Pavón

I was in prison from 1933 to 1935. In 1936 I again had to run, this time to the red zone. Sebastián and I were on one side and three other brothers were on the other side. Antonio, Manolo, and José were shooting at us, and we at them. My mother died of the insults she suffered.

I saw Sopas in Alicante, where he was the leader of a collective and had young men working under him. He had food delivered to the workers with trucks. And he saw me and said, "Look, there's no work here. Go to Churra in Murcia and there you'll find Currestaca. And we were with Currestaca until I went to the front lines in León to fight.

I went to the front—to Estepona and then to Córdoba, then to Pozoblanco, then to Zaragoza, and then I deserted, because I didn't feel like fighting in the war. I had requested a transfer to the rear, but they didn't want to approve my request, and so I just deserted. Then when the war reached me again, I re-enlisted in fortifications.

## Juan Moreno

It scared me to kill anyone. I hated it, because we were all Spaniards. We fired at all our brothers, and brother was killing brother. I could kill someone without knowing if it was my brother I was killing. I was being fired at, and I didn't know if it was my brother who was shooting.

When we saw that the enemy were Moors and Italians, then we really hit them. Then we were all vigilant. We would kill as many as possible.

We were in the trenches, and since we talked at night, we knew they were Spaniards, and they said, "Well, look, we aren't going to fire any more!" And we didn't fire any more. They were in trenches, and we were in other trenches, and we didn't fire at each other. When we engaged in combat or an attack had to be made, we had to fire, but meanwhile we didn't fire at each other. We didn't fire even if we saw each other. During the daytime we agreed we would fire no shots. They were on top of the trenches, and we would see them, and we were also in front of the trenches smoking, and they would see us. And they didn't fire at us, and we didn't fire at them. We exchanged tobacco and paper. Usually six or seven of us would go down. Sometimes as many as forty would go down.

I went down one day, but without a hat and without a shirt [because I was an officer]. It was so calm, chatting and chatting. There was nothing else to do. Where are you from? Where are you not from? You are from such a place, and I from such a place. I have so many brothers, and another so many. I have a sweetheart. I don't have a sweetheart. That's what we talked about—not about the war. This took place in the middle. When we finished talking, they would go over there to their trenches, and we to ours.

Once I was shaved between the lines. One of them was a barber. I yelled over to them, "Tomorrow I'll bring tobacco, and you shave me!" and he agreed. And the next day we met. I brought the tobacco, and he shaved me.

This [ceasefire] happened to me three or four times. It would last about fifteen days. The bad thing was when they changed troops. When they did, that was the worst, because the new men didn't know about the truce, and they did fire.

But one felt much worse after such meetings. Afterward, probably within the hour, we would be firing. Or the next day we would be in combat. I was afraid to kill. I didn't like it. But one had to shoot. I have killed a man, and he could have been my brother.

When I left training school, I was transferred to the tanks. When Teruel was taken, I was in a tank. Before entering Teruel, we had to cross a bridge called the Bridge of the Viaduct, because there was an arch. There was a kiosk there. Our soldiers had no tobacco. The infantry coming up behind the tank saw the kiosk, and one of them went over to it. They fired on him from the seminary of Teruel and killed him. We advanced, and we had to go over the body of the dead man with our tanks. I was very frightened, because we had to cross the bridge, and I feared that the bridge was mined. Another tank was ahead of us, and when I reached the other side I felt a great relief that the danger was over. Then we entered Teruel. They fired on our tanks with rifles. We felt the bullets on the armor of the tank, but they didn't do any damage. We fired at the windows with our cannon, and everything was over.

It was a Russian tank, and the machine gun was Russian. We liked the tanks, because in a tank one is more protected. We weren't very concerned, because in Teruel at that time there were no anti-tank cannons; when they have anti-tank guns, it's the worst thing possible. It's certain death. One cannon shot hits the tank, and bang! All the ammunition explodes, and everyone dies.

We were in defensive positions at Chelva around Teruel. The enemy attacked our position on July 2, 1938. I thought it was the last day of my life. It was hand-to-hand combat from 6:00 in the morning until 7:00 in the evening. Only myself and ten others survived from our company. Everyone else was killed or wounded. Only ten survived from a company of 120.

I thought it was the end of the world because of the intense fire of the enemy—the artillery, mortar, and bombs from the air falling on our position. The afternoon came, and the position was not taken, and at 6:30 we received the order to retreat. The captain had been killed and the lieutenant, who had been beside me. I had to take charge of the company. We retreated as best we could, while the enemy fired on us from our flank, from right to left. They fired on us. Those of us who were left had the good fortune to reach another position without any casualties, in spite of the heavy fire.

We were disillusioned, because for each cannon that we had fired, they fired ten. For each one of our planes, they had ten. For each one of our tanks, they had ten. It was impossible to fight against such overwhelming odds. They had so much material that it was impossible to resist an attack like that. Our soldiers believed in the Republic at first, but as the war advanced, they became disillusioned, for a very good reason. Instead of winning, we were losing. We didn't have sufficient men or materials.

Some months before the end of the war, it happened that I was in Valencia on leave, and on that date La Pasionaria was giving a speech. I don't remember all the speech, because it has been a long time, but I can recall some of the words she said on the Plaza de Emilio Castelar. She spoke this way: "Spaniards! In these historic and happy moments that our beloved people live, I carry in my soul the memory of my comrades fallen in battle and the mothers and children destroyed by the Fascist barbarism. . . . I say to you it is better to die standing on one's feet than to kneel and be shot like sheep."

[*Franco's troops entered Madrid on March 28, 1939. The surrender of the Republican forces ended on April 1.*]

## The war ends

### Pelele

In Huelma, in the province of Jaén, we had a federation of collectives. It was administered by the workers according to agreements made in meetings that were held every fifteen days. There was no chief, no mayor. It was true federalism. We interchanged articles with Murcia, Valencia, and Madrid. We produced cereals, potatoes, wheat, chickpeas, and lentils.

When the Fascists won, we were returning to the town of Huelma. I said, "Let's wait a moment and listen to what's happening in the town." I was cleverer then than I am now. And we listened and heard "Viva!" People were shouting cheers after a talk by a Fascist. We took advantage of the fact that the streets were empty, and we went to the house of a friend, Juan Navarro.

A few days later, he said that in such-and-such a house one could get good conduct passes in order to travel. I investigated and found it to be true. When we left there, we came to Jerez and returned to Medina.

I thought it best for my brothers and me to go to the mountains, but we were caught by the civil guard. We had just arrived and were sitting down to a meal of green broad beans from the garden, prepared by our mother. A number of women were there greeting us, welcoming us, and one was the wife of a guard. She must have reported us. We were just sitting down to eat when a guard came to the door and said we were to report to the barracks. We said we were going to but had just arrived and wanted to eat first. He said, "Right now." And so we had to leave right then. When we got to the barracks we said, "We haven't eaten yet." And the sergeant said: "It's not important to me." Our mother hadn't seen us through the war years.

We went before a court martial. We were each sentenced to six years and one day.

*Manuel:* I served five and a half months.

*Pelele:* I served two years, because I was better known. Almost everyone in Medina was put at liberty, because we were simply defending our right to live. We weren't criminals. But the court martial board met with the landowners here and were told who were the most outstanding workers. And so I was sentenced to six years and served two. Most were let out after three or four years.

I served ten months in Medina and ten in Jerez. There were 900 prisoners there. Every day six or seven died of hunger. Some died of hunger; some went crazy. If I had not been let out then, if I had served one more month, I would have been dead of hunger.

## Juan Moreno

At the end of the war we were cut off, and I couldn't escape to France. I was twelve months in jail waiting for trial, and then I served thirteen more months. At the trial they sentenced me to to twelve years and one day.

There were eighteen men in our cell. It was five feet wide and twelve feet long. There were no beds, and we slept on the floor. During the day we remained seated, because it was too small to walk around. We had nothing to eat but lentils at noon and lentils at night. We went outside for an hour each day to exercise.

We spent the time sitting there, talking, chatting. We talked about nothing, because we were very hungry and really didn't feel like talking. We spoke very little since we were many, and we did not know each other. We didn't trust one another.

There were small rooms, many doors. Behind each door there were sixteen or seventeen men. They would take one or two from there, from behind one door, and then open another door and take another. They took whomever they wished to. From Castellón we could hear the discharge of the guns. They shot them near Castellón.

The men they killed were politicians or had been accused of something, or had burned convents, or had intervened in shootings, or had been denounced in their towns. They had something on them. Some were killed, and everyone was afraid of that. Some preferred to kill themselves rather than be killed. The fellow sleeping next to me cut his veins before they could kill him. Everyone was very frightened.

I was freed early, because Franco's decrees covered me. I was given provisional liberty. I remember the day they gave me my freedom. A jail guard came, very serious. I was in the yard, and he says to me, "Juan

Moreno." He had the papers behind him. He had them behind him like this. He says, "Where are you from?"

I say, "From the province of Cádiz."

"What town are you from?"

I say, "From Casas Viejas."

"And how long have you been here?"

I say, "Eleven months."

"And how long since you have seen your family?"

I say, "It's been three years and a half."

"And what cell are you in?"

I say, "In number 11."

"Do you have belongings?"

I say, "Yes sir."

"Well, take your papers and leave." And I left in freedom.

When I returned here, it was bad, bad, bad, very bad. I thought of my friends, my companions who were left in jail. I used to think of what might have happened and what might not have happened, and it would turn my head around. I wondered whether the Germans, if they came to the frontier, would come here. What I thought didn't happen. It was worthless.

## Juan Sopas

When the war was lost, the others fled. I didn't run. What for? I had done nothing. When they came with the civil guard to take over, I gave them the keys. They gave me a safe-conduct pass, and I returned to Casas Viejas. But when I returned in 1940, someone denounced me to the civil guard, and I was arrested. I spent three years in jail.

Suárez, who had returned to town, was also arrested, and we were sent from Casas Viejas to the court handcuffed together: the two mortal enemies handcuffed together. But enemies, no. I told him, "The enemy is in front of us." Some people had denounced me—Suárez, maybe, and others—and sent in accusations. I wasn't allowed to write anyone. Finally I was given permission, and I wrote six cards explaining exactly what I had done all those years. But when we were brought before the court, one of the officers had been a guard at Casas Viejas at the time of the uprising, and now he was a lieutenant colonel. Suárez was set free, but I was given twelve years. I served three.

*José Vega:* I was very close to Juan Sopas in Málaga. In Málaga he was responsible for an agricultural community. He was in charge of the community where we were. Here was an individual who was at the service of the community.

After the war I saw him in Jerez, and I found him very cold. I did not like his attitude. I no longer saw in him the same friendship, the same ease. It was psychological. It was as if he were a different person. He was already someone else—because of age, because of fatigue, because of a change of concept. Who knows what it was? But I considered him to be another person. It's not that he was afraid. No, it's that, like all things, lack of enthusiasm is followed by discouragement. After the battle, after the Civil War, there was great loss of faith and spirit.

## José Súarez

Toward the end of the war, the Instituto de Reforma Agraria sent me to Valencia, and I was taken prisoner there. I was judged before a military court and sentenced to twelve years and a day. I was in a concentration camp for the first forty days. Each day we had a can of sardines for two people. There were six sardines in the can—three for each one. That was at 12:00. Every four or five days we received a loaf of bread for five men. We went days without water. Then they brought in a trough of salty water, enough for perhaps 2,000 men—but there were 18,000 men there. The ones who got there first got the water, for whatever good it did them. There were Moorish guards with clubs who beat the men to keep them in line. After twenty-five days we received good water, and more of it. After forty days they gave us lentils, half-cooked, with hot pepper, hot enough to burn your tongue. Those who ate it the first day got diarrhea and died. The stomach couldn't take it after so many days of hunger. Those who ate a little bread and little of the soup without lentils got through. They said to the others, "Don't eat, or you'll get sick." But when you're hungry, you can't stop yourself. They began to give us lentils every day. We ate a few lentils every day until we were accustomed to them. Then they gave us a little roll of bread every day and water. We slept on the ground. Eighteen thousand men. About half survived.

Every day they would call out names and take them away to be shot. In October they sent us to a building that had been an infirmary, and there were many floors and rooms, and we had a roof over our heads. They had good water. When someone left, he would give another his blanket. Then the priest found out and took the blanket. If your family sent food, you would go to the office, where they would open it and check to see if it was complete. Then they wouldn't give it to us. The priest would say, "It's all there. Good. You don't want for anything here. Go." And he would give it to someone else who would sell it. We couldn't say anything, because the priest censored our letters.

They put in Spanish guards in place of the Moors, and they were worse than the Moors. The commander was a royalist, a Basque, and the priest was a Basque. We were divided into groups of forty men with a sergeant in command. The young men among us were sent out to work. The rest remained quiet. They put in spies.

After fourteen months I was set free. I had a second trial but was paroled.

## Pepe Pareja

At the close of the war I was in Jaén. I heard that there was a decree that those who had no blood on their hands could return to their native lands. I went to Almería by train. There were many control points then on the roads, and so I walked at night. I wanted to reach Málaga, because Málaga is our neighboring province. There are good communications, and they could telephone to ask if such a person lived in Benalup. I intended to turn myself over to the authorities. Once I was spotted by a troop of soldiers, but they thought I was dead. Another time at night a carabinero fell in step with me, but all he said was "Be careful of your answers." So I knew he wasn't one of them.

I met some Falangists who asked me how things were in Almería, but I said I knew nothing. They invited me for a drink, and I accepted. Then they offered me a second, but I said, "Gentlemen, I don't drink. I accepted the first only out of a sense of fellowship." They gave me some pesetas when I said I was going to Málaga and told me a coach passed by, but I saved the money for food and continued walking. On the way I asked directions, and the woman to whom I spoke said, "Wait a minute," and she returned with some figs, which are very nutritious.

When I reached Málaga, I went to see the governor, but they said he was out and would be gone until 10:00 the next day. So I went to a pensión to eat, and there a fellow invited me to eat, and so I was lucky that day. When I returned the next day, they gave me a safe-conduct pass to return to Benalup.

A few days after I arrived here, I went to Medina to report to the civil guard. I was in prison in Medina for five months. Finally two members of the military court came, and there was a hearing.

They asked me, "Why did you go?"

I said, "I left for fear."

"Fear of what?"

"I heard that the Moors that came to Vejer killed people, and I became frightened and I left."

"Yes," they said, "the Moors are very ferocious."

I couldn't tell them, "I fled from you, criminals." I had to defend myself and tell them that I was afraid of the Moors.

"Did you ever have a gun in your hand?"

"No!" I answered. I had had more than one, but what was I going to tell them?

"Why didn't you come from there to this side?"

"Many times I wanted to, but there was a great deal of vigilance, and I couldn't."

They were killing people with their hands tied, for all sorts of personal vendettas, and I had had a dispute with a señorito [José Vela] here about rent for land, and I didn't know if he was intimate in the movement or not. I had planted fourteen fanegas of wheat in 1935, but only seven came up. Bad weather killed the other seven when the wheat began to flower. He wanted me to pay the complete rent. I said I'd pay from what I reaped. I said, "José" (I called him "tú" because we were the same age), "the weather did not help me to reap the wheat." I sowed with borrowed seed which I had to repay. He wanted to incite me to say something. I said, "If I become aggravated with you, it will be bad, and if you become angry with me, it will also be bad. We need an intermediary. Let's go to court, and I'll pay you whatever is decided."

"Pay me what you want," he said. This was in the time of the Republic, and he knew I would win. Since he was rich, I didn't know if he was part of the movement and would point me out and have me killed.

In 1935 when I was renting from El Tuerto Vela, he came by. At that time there was war in Abyssinia, and there were workers unemployed; and I said, "Do you know how to avoid these antihuman acts? It is better to kill the sperm beforehand than to harm so many people." And he replied, "women like it naked."

To avoid all these things, one must study. The rich, in ignorance, live in a grand orgy, with all their comforts, taking all the young girls.

After the war when I was imprisoned [for three months], they told me that the wife of a prisoner was entitled to receive so much money to live on, but that this applied only to legally married couples. It was the art of political deception. In this way they force a person to do things and take away his freedom. They asked me if I would marry my compañera. I told them: "Well, if she wishes it, I accept."

*Antonia Márquez:* When they asked me, I said, "No. My father was angry with me then, and I'm not going to wed now."

And the jailer said: "If you don't marry, your husband will be behind bars all his life." Then I said yes.

After the ceremony the women went out to a big room to eat, to celebrate. I went with my mother-in-law and sister-in-law to eat. All the wives of the prisoners went.

*Pepe Pareja:* And we went back to jail.

## Captain Manuel Rojas Feijespán

*Ramón Salas Larrazábal:* After the war Rojas's situation became very uncomfortable, and General Queipo de Llano used the opportunity provided by an incident that would have had no importance in the case of anyone else in order to put him on trial and to have him expelled from the army.

The incident occurred on March 1, 1938, when Rojas, at the time acting *comandante* although he had not yet been promoted, was enjoying temporary leave, and decided to go have a good time. He had the bright idea to do so using the car assigned to the overseer of military transport, a move aggravated by the company of a young lady of ill repute.

As I have said, General Queipo used this opportunity, and instead of being reprimanded, as would have been the case in dealing with someone else, Rojas was condemned for theft to eight months and twenty-one days in jail, with simultaneous expulsion from the army. This was an unusual sentence, for in Spanish military tradition, expulsion is never accompanied by a sentence of less than three years and one day. The court martial took place in Seville on April 4, 1939.

[According to another report, Rojas avoided prison by running away to South America.]

## Manuel Llamas

*Pepe Pareja:* During the war Manuel was in the rear guard in Málaga, working on the land to produce wheat. When Málaga was lost, he went to Almería, and from Almería he went to the province of Jaén, where he was located in the commissary of a workers' collective of the CNT. At the end of the war, the victors persecuted the most intelligent and became masters of the most ignorant. If he had been found, he would have been killed, because he was one of the most important leaders in the district, the representative of Medina in Jerez. Because of this fear, he did not return to his native village. He hid for seven years in a choza about fourteen kilometers from Medina, not far from where his brother guarded goats. He never ventured out during the day, and a few close friends brought him what he needed. At the end of this time, a relative spoke for him to the police, and he was able to return.

*Pepe Pilar:* Manuel went to the house of a friend and then went with his brother, who was a goatherd. Between his brother and his uncle, who was also a shepherd, he survived. His uncle told me that Manuel is in a *chabola* (choza) in such-and-such a place. When I reached there, I had made noise walking through the woods, and he had heard me and left. I found a stew of mashed wheat. I called out his name, and he recognized me, and came out and we had a good talk.

I used to go every eight or nine days to carry supplies to Manuel in the mountains. A compañero had to do these things, had to help his fellows. I carried messages in wartime. If I had been caught I would have been shot immediately. It's a chance one takes. It's not important.

*Manuel Llamas:* Once while I was in hiding, I ventured out at night as usual to get water. I went to the well, and as I poked the cows with my stick to get through I saw a guard seated with his rifle across his knees. I wasn't frightened of him, but I was worried about where his companion might be. He could be watching how I conducted myself and could put a bullet in me. I pulled up the water can from the well, and the guard said, "Who's there?"

I replied, "Oh, I didn't know you were there."

"Who are you?"

"I'm a charcoal burner from down below."

"Oh, fine."

And I knew I was safe.

[The two presidents of the sindicato, José Monroy and Currestaca, survived the war. Monroy had remained in hiding at the outset but then returned to guard his flock of goats and was not troubled further. Currestaca, who had been in the mountains since the uprising, fled in 1936 to the Republican zone. He worked on a collective in Murcia and was given a post of responsibility there. After the war he returned to Casas Viejas and resumed work as a campesino.]

## Juan Pinto

In 1940 there was a terrible hunger. There was nothing to eat. There was no bread, no oil, no bacon. It was incredible. Many people died from hunger. One who was called Cultebarra died from eating the fruit of the wild olive tree. It was the worst period that Spaniards have ever known. The hunger that came was a bad thing. Terrible. I used to go to Algeciras with fig bread. It was seven or eight leagues, and I went on foot to bring a few things to sell here. All the way I was close to fainting. It was a bad thing. I also brought tobacco back from Algeciras.

I've never had any land. In the winter one worked at plowing, because back then the earth had to be broken. There were no tractors, as there are today. It was done with an ox team. And when the summer came, one had to reap what had grown and pick the beans and the chickpeas. That was the work of the country. 1946 was the most difficult time of all, because there was nothing to eat. One day at 2:00 in the afternoon, no one had had any breakfast yet. Then a hortelano came bringing two or three cauliflowers. He got six pesetas for them. My children grabbed them as if they were gifts.

"Look," I told my children, "I'm going out to the mills." Back then many people used to come with contraband to the mill of Benalup to grind their wheat. They wouldn't sell it, because the civil guard was watching the bakers to fine them. Some of them sold it illegally. The government had taken all the wheat, but some poor people hid some. If they hadn't, they would have died also. In short, I arrived one afternoon at the mill, and there were a few there waiting to mill their wheat. I said, "You'd better sell me a couple of kilos of flour, because things are very bad." Then they sold me two kilos. That night at least we ate bread soaked in water. In all my life I've never experienced anything like that.

My mother would tell me that she had to eat some gazpacho in the morning and more in the evening, because she couldn't afford anything else. At first, when my mother got married, my father earned two reales. Back then it was the worst misery that there was. My father knew the worst misery of all.

In those times when we had nothing to eat, in 1941, after the war, the government controlled everything, and we had no bread. I had seven children. I wasn't going to let my children starve. Every so often I would go out to the fields and shoot a pig. We could live on that for quite a while, the fat and the meat. Every month or so I would go out and shoot a pig. I wasn't worried about being caught, because it is only right and natural to feed one's family. Every so often they would catch someone and take them to Medina, but they would be back by afternoon. Once another fellow and I drove two pigs here and shot them down below. It's only natural to feed one's family.

In those days there was no bread or oil or anything. My wife had made me sell the huerto for 1,000 pesetas. It sold last year for twenty times that price. If we had kept the huerto, we could have grown vegetables.

I worked for three or four years on a finca for a landowner, and there, whenever an animal died, we ate meat—when something died because it had to die. We desired meat so we ate it even though it was dead. The fire, they say, takes care of everything. We were just like buzzards. We ate it, and it tasted good to us, because there was no other meat. I was there at least five or six years. My children were small then, and I had no alternative but to stay there permanently, whether things were good or bad. I worked to earn bread for my children. This is the life of the poor here.

I don't understand these things of Socialism or communism, because I have no education. I'm not going to fight for comunismo libertario, because I don't understand it. Besides, if Socialism comes, or comunismo libertario, I have to keep on doing the same things—working. How can I pretend to know anything if I'm illiterate?

## The cooperatives of the Republic

[*San José de Malcocinado (Las Yeguadas) was the only agrarian reform settlement near Casas Viejas that survived the death of the Republic. There, since San José had been government land, no landlords returned to reclaim the property and the stock. In 1949 the new Instituto Nacional de Reforma y Desarrollo Agrario gave the forty families the opportunity to decide if they wanted to continue working in common and to share a common herd, or if they wished the lands and goods to be divided (with the government remaining as landlord). The cooperative had just suffered the worst of times. The future seemed to offer little hope of change. To have a cow and a sow of one's own, and a hold on a small piece of land were great temptations. The majority voted to divide. The break-up of the cooperative of San José Malcocinado was the final dismantling of the changes made in the area during the Republic. The event was recorded in "coplas" by Esteban Moreno Caro, the shoemaker and poet of Casas Viejas, who lived close to the settlement. Esteban Moreno was a son of Casas Viejas and had been sentenced for carrying arms during the uprising. He composed his wry and ribald songs while stitching and nailing shoes. He never wrote the words down.*]

| | |
|---|---|
| ¡Qué grande fue aquel día<br>Que repartieron los cochinos<br>En Las Yeguadas!<br>Hubo quien no cogió el sueño<br>En por lo menos una semana.<br>Tan grande fue la sorpresa<br>Que él dijo en aquella hora,<br>"Soy propietario de un cerdo<br>Con tope de siete arrobas." | What a great day it was<br>When they divided up the pigs<br>In Las Yeguadas!<br>There was one who didn't sleep<br>for at least a week.<br>So great was his surprise<br>That he said at that time,<br>"I'm the owner of a pig<br>With a weight of seven arrobas"<br>(175 lbs.) |
| Siempre lo tendré presente<br>El día en que se repartió,<br>Que aquello fue un caso de risa<br>Para todo el que lo presenció.<br>Todos los agrarios corriendo | I'll always remember<br>The day of the division,<br>For it was a comical affair<br>For all those who were there.<br>All the agrarians were running, |

Buscando soga y tornillos,
Y otros gritaban muy fuerte:
"¡Cógeme uno, chiquillo!"
Los niños también corrían
A presenciar el reparto,
Y de cuando en cuando decían,
"Viva el Instituto Agrario!"

Looking for ropes and screws,
And others cried out very loudly,
"Grab one for me, little boy!"
The children also ran
To witness the division,
And now and then some would say,
"Long live the Agrarian Institute!"

Las mujeres medias locas
Abrían puertas y ventanas
Y una vieja de la alegría
Hasta se cagó en la cama.

The women were half-crazed
Opening doors and windows,
And one old lady was so overjoyed
That she crapped in her bed.

Aquella noche en su casa
Un matrimonio decía:
"Vamos a tener una vejez
Mejor de lo que yo creía
Porque cuando ya nos pongan
A todos iguales
Harán un nuevo reparto
Para poder continuar.
Nos darán tierra y ganado,
Grano para sembrar,
Y unas cuantas pesetillas
Para podernos manejar.

That night in their house
A couple said:
"Our old age will be
Better than I thought
Because when they make us
All equal
They will have another distribution
So that we can go on.
They will give us land and cattle
And grain to sow
And a few little pesetas
So we can manage.

Si las cosas vienen bien
Y el tiempo nos favorece
Para el año venidero
Podremos respirar fuerte.
Entonces podré decir:
Por la salud de mis hijos,
Entré aquí de jornalero
Y gracias a Dios todo es mío.

If things go well
And the times favor us
For the coming year
We can breathe heartily.
Then I will be able to say:
For the health of my children,
With my labor
Everything is mine, thank God.

Si viniera lo contrario,
Le diré a mi compañera:
"A mí me ahogan las trampas.
¡Que se joda el que le debo!"

And if things turn out otherwise,
I shall tell my companion:
"I'm smothered by debts
So screw whomever I owe."

"No te hagas ilusiones,"
Le dijo la mujer a su esposo,
"Que aquí el final de nosotros
Será tirarnos a un pozo."

"Don't kid yourself,"
Said the woman to her husband,
"Because here our end
Will be when we throw ourselves
down a well."

## Under the dictatorship

### Pepe Pilar

My father was a fighter all his life, and I had faith in him, because what he was fighting for seemed right to me, and I fought also. I received my ideas from my father, and I will keep them until I die—without offending anyone, but just defending my rights. No more. Let what you have be yours, but what is mine is mine because I worked for it. That I will defend if they let me. Not now, you see, not now [1970]. I don't want to die without knowing, without seeing something happen after all that we've suffered.

Twelve years ago, I was working in Las Lomas, weeding cotton. It was May, and there was a missionary in Las Lomas, and he said mass for several days, one hour a day, and work was stopped so that we could go to hear him. We were paid for the time to go to listen to him. I stayed in our sleeping quarters, and there was other fellow with me. And he said to me, "They're going to tell the señorito that we're in here and not there. Let's go there this afternoon." So we went.

When I entered the room, he was giving a sermon, and he stopped his sermon and said, "There was once an anarchist in a town, and he had a little girl. And this girl joined together with others, and the others were saying the catechism, and this little girl learned the catechism from her friends. And when the father heard her saying the catechism, he said, 'You know that I don't want you to learn the catechism.'

" 'Oh father,' said the little girl, 'it's so beautiful and good.'

" 'No, I don't want you to learn it.' But she convinced her father, and he became more convinced than she was, and he told her, 'You must go to mass every day!' "

That's what the son of a whore said—directly to me.

I have five children here and five there in Valencia. When I'm here I miss them, but when I go there I want to come back. I don't like it there. I was raised here. I like the campo. There, there is a better ambience, but it doesn't have any interest for me. I don't want to go to the movies. It's for the new generation, but not for me. And the food here is much better. There everything is artificial. Everything is poisoned, because the magnates are interested in production. The health of human beings no longer counts. All that poison poured on the plants goes into our systems.

When they arrested me in the 1950s, I was in a bar, and there was a procession outside. I was seated just inside the door, and I saw the sergeant go by, but he didn't see me. Later a guard came to get me. He poked me on the shoulder. "Come with me."

"All right."

"To the barracks." We went to the barracks. They accused me of another matter, and the sergeant said, "When the procession came by, you ducked into the bar."

"No, that's a lie. Whoever told you that is telling a lie against me without cause. I was already seated in the bar when the procession went by."

I was taken into custody in the 1950s when I was accused of being a contact for *los rojos* (the reds).

[*Those who fled to the mountains at the start of the Civil War and remained there in hiding were called "los rojos." Almost all of these men returned to their towns after the war. Subsequently, the mountains became the refuge of bandits who had no political ideas. They were also called "los rojos" (and later "los secuestradores," the kidnapers). During the 1950s fear of robberies and kidnappings forced many of those living on isolated cortijos to return to the towns for protection.*

*It was assumed by the civil guard that the bandits had contacts in town. Those who traveled the mountains at that time fell under the suspicion of both bandits and the civil guard, as being spies for one or the other side. Pepe Pilar was picked up as a suspect and terribly beaten. He could never speak of those events without trembling with fear and rage.*]

Then in Alcalá, the judge said to me, "You'll spend the rest of your life in the prison of Puerto."

I said, "We'll see. I've been in Puerto before, but then there was cause. This is different."

When they freed me he called me over. "What happened? Who defended you?"

"I defended myself. There was no proof against me."

"Well," he said, "watch your step from now on, because if you slip just once, it won't happen like this again."

The one who had accused me disappeared and was not seen again. He had been an informer for them. He had accused me to defend himself. They did away with him.

## Germinal

[*At the end of the war Germinal García Pérez escaped to Venezuela. He later secretly returned in order to rescue his novia.*]

Venezuela
June 4, 1961

My dear friend Rodríguez [Pepe Pareja],

I wish you good health in the company of your compañera, the rest of your family, and your friends in general.

Today I have in my possession a letter from my parents that refers to you, for I have never forgotten you, as it is the case with all the others, either dead or alive. I have not written to anybody, for I'm afraid they would not answer me, a thing that has been happening to me with others from Medina, Barbate, and even Vejer.

I really would like from now on, even though it would be only once every two months, to receive some correspondence from you, counting, of course, on your desiring it and being able to do it. You should know that I am the same type of person as I was when we met nearly thirty years ago.

Perhaps I am heavier, a bit grayer, with all my teeth in place, and as strong as a lion, a few wrinkles on my face, and with ideas as firm as when I had the pleasure of knowing that old generation of the Curro Cruz family. . . . As a good vegetarian as you were, you can appreciate what I am saying—and above all, the eternal love for that sublime idea that ennobles the heart, a heart always youthful.

When I received that letter with your name and address, pleasant memories of that distant past came to my mind—beautiful dreams that were never realized, to the misfortune of all the children of Casas Viejas, of Vejer, of Medina, of all Spain, and of the world. To my mind come memories of fresh and pleasant nights, when during the springtime I enjoyed strolling through the plaza of that town . . . by the side of some young girls who have passed away and others whose addresses I do not know. I also remember the glasses of *mostelle* that I used to drink next to the Casa Grande, in the tavern of our friend. . . .

My mind is always filled with the same illusions, a memory as permanent as the warmth of the tropics. I see the tortuous streets of Casas Viejas; and the chumbas between the chozas; the abundant, clear waters always running down the streets . . . lost waters that are still being wasted on those lands without giving the fruits for the good of the campesino and of the nation that saw us born.

I remember the natural beauty of the place—the Celemín and Barbate [rivers] running the length of the lands, fertile and uncultivated—for in a structured Spain, in a well-organized Spain, those waters now wasted in the sea could give fruits in great quantity and feed a considerable number of all kinds of domestic animals. Laguna Janda, today the home of mosquitos, carriers and propagators of yellow fever, could be an incalculable fountain of riches. Cotton, potatoes, corn, wheat, sugar beets, and so on would result from the efforts of the campesinos. With the aid of agricultural experts, they could realize the crops in these lands, rich today as yesterday, for many others. There also comes to mind the abundance of rabbits, hares, quail, and many other animals that I have never seen here. This too constitutes a great wealth that one can appreciate only from afar.

About my life I could tell many things. I am working here as a miner; in other words, in a mill where they cast iron from the rich zone of Venezuelan Guyana. The dust one inhales is beyond description. And even though the pay is not bad (thirty-two *bolívares* per day), forty-four hours of work a week, for which they pay a rate of fifty-six hours per week, it isn't enough to save for retirement before silicosis penetrates your lungs. I don't want to die here. [I prefer to die] there, even if it would be with my boots on. In spite of our pessimism, we shall see. As long as there is life, there is hope.

I see that you keep moving to increase your living, making bread, with material that we are not sure is flour. It may be anything else, but it's not wheat. The salaries that you enjoy in Spain today are not what a small newspaper says, that the phonies of Rentería [San Sebastián] sent me. According to these pictures and articles, everything in Spain is flowers and violets. The title of that newspaper is *Spain Today*. What a disgrace!

I must tell you that I have two magnificent lads. One is called Floreal and the other Germinal. Let's see if they turn out like the first one, Manuel, who until he was seventeen was my compañero. But when he turned eighteen, because he was studying in a public school in Bolívar City, the *politicos* from Acción Democrática in the country were able to conquer him. In essence, another traitor to the ideas of his father, to his father and the cenetista movement. He turned out to be unfaithful, like his mother. This is as much as I can tell you of the unpleasant things with respect to my life.

Our friends from France seem to have been reconciled. But here in Caracas things are tangled. There are those who want to have managers and workers together in the same group. A hell of a mess has evolved, and the result is divisiveness. It is natural. There are guys who became contractors when they arrived in America. They exploit their compañeros as they do others, and therein lie our great differences. This I tell you so that you know about matters here.

So today I won't bother you further. Through the distance that separates us, receive this strong and cordial embrace that you should extend to as many good friends as you may see there.

Germinal García Pérez

## José Suárez

After the war I didn't want to return to Casas Viejas. It was awkward. People would come to talk to me, ask me to do things, and I would be in trouble. They would arrest me. So I went to Los Barrios, and I had a little bar there.

I was watched by the civil guard. If I talked to people, people coming to consult me, the civil guard was waiting. They were going to arrest me again. I went to Seville. Here one is more independent. If you do not go to church, no one knows. One can talk of social matters here. The other day we had a conversation about Socialism.

The monarchy lasted for 300 years and ruined the country. The Republic couldn't erase in five years the harm that had been done in 300 years. It needed the work of a generation. Everyone must be educated.

In the fifteenth, sixteenth, and seventeenth centuries, the Inquisition killed or forced out nine million people—Moors, Jews, and others. Today [1970] the Inquisition is more refined. After thirty years, you still have to look behind you.

## Juan Pinto

One of the two guards who was here at the time of the uprising lives in J. His leg has withered. It's a punishment for what he did here.

## Anónimo

My generation made a great change. They inherited the misery of the past and wanted to change it. We are the most martyred of generations.

## Pelele

One can't ever leave the road to liberty. There's a new generation now to continue to struggle. Man was born not to be a beast but a man. When he has had enough, then he will enter the life of federalism. This must be spoken about, and thought about.

## Manuel Llamas

In the name of ignorance, they put in a dictatorship. They say it is because we are too ignorant to govern ourselves. Then they deprive us of education, and in this way they keep us subjugated. How can we become free if we're not educated?

When I left, they put my three daughters in the convent, teaching them ideas contrary to mine. I was supposed to be dead. My wife couldn't take care of them and was serving as a maid in San Fernando. When I returned ten years later, we took them out. When I left, the smallest was fourteen months old. She was put in a convent after the war. She got out, and she wanted to go to mass. I let her. After the age of fifteen, she stopped going. I never said anything. None of the three have religious ideas now.

It's more than thirty years since I could express myself. Now I lack the words. And I have a great deal to express.

I don't regret trying to change the system. My life is short and will end before the change. There's going to be change. But I can't see the light coming within the seventy years alloted to me. Everyone is anxious for education, but there is little education to help us. I'll die before the revolution. But I'm not worried that it hasn't occurred yet. It will occur. We are just a species of animal, but we have a distinct intelligence. We're always fighting for man's well-being. One must fight for a better existence. You cannot live according to the system. We are fighting, but it is very hard. Liberty still has many enemies. The youth is better than before. They're coming out of the universities. They're better educated. There are slaves all over the world. We must fight for change.

Where are the results of the French Revolution? Where are the results of the Russian Revolution? They were not worldwide revolutions. Each had its limits. If you look at this situation, there is no light. But our task is to open a road. We must look for an opening. If we do not look, we will never find it.

## José Vega

I used to live in the campo, but after the war I came to town. I could have gone to France, to another country. But the moral circumstances that encircled me then made me skeptical, so much so that death was almost appetizing. And I came back to town precisely for that. That is why I left, and that is why I returned—to seek it. But they let me live, and so here I am, wagging my tail, as we say in Andalusia.

## Pepe Pareja

To live is to struggle. The youth today are struggling and are better than we were, because they're better educated. All the world is struggling for revolution.

A campesino was eagerly trimming some ripe branches and cutting off the fruits. Another worker who was passing by asked him, "Why such a radical pruning?"

The first campesino said, "All the fruit from these trees are spoiled."

The second man said, "The fruit does not go to waste from the branch but from the roots. Apply the blows of your ax there."

The campesino took the advice, dug in the ground, and discovered many worms at the roots.

For fifty years we have been trimming the branches of the social tree whose fruits grow poisoned, and we have not achieved any improvement. On the contrary, every spring we see the tree becoming yellow at the time when the fruit is about to sprout. And it isn't that we lack diligence. Hourly we invent new tools and new products to deal with the disease, with no results. We're working for a better world. We have pensions, cheap houses, salaries adjusted to family size, but it is all in vain, all vacuous. We trim the limbs, when the problem is in the roots.

# Glossary

| | |
|---|---|
| **amo** | The owner of an estate (lit., master). |
| **aparcería** | Sharecropping arrangement in which the landowner customarily supplied the land and the seed, and the worker contributed the team and the labor. |
| **aranzada** | An ancient land measure of approximately five hectares. |
| **arbitrios** | Taxes on merchandise entering a town. |
| **arroba** | Measure of dry weight (25 pounds) and liquids (varying from 2.6 to 3.6 gallons). |
| **bandurria** | Bandore; a small, guitar-like instrument with six double strings. |
| **barrio** | A district, quarter, neighborhood, or ward of a town. |
| **boyero mayor** | Chief ox drover on a cortijo. |
| **cabrero** | Goatherd. |
| **cacique** | Political boss; influential landowner, politician, or administrative leader in a given town or region. |
| **calle** | Street. |
| **campesino** | Countryman, peasant, rural worker. |
| **campo** | Countryside. |
| **capataz** | Foreman, overseer. |
| **carabinero** | Excise officer detailed to collect taxes and pursue smugglers. |
| **categoría** | Upper class. |

| | |
|---|---|
| **casino** | Casino, club, clubhouse of a town's influential and affluent citizens. |
| **cenetistas** | Members of the CNT. |
| **céntimo** | One cent; one-hundredth part of a peseta. |
| **centro** | Workers' meeting and educational center. |
| **chipionero** | Resident of Chipiona. |
| **choza** | Thatched cottage or hut. |
| **chumba** | Prickly pear type of cactus. |
| **CNT** | Confederación Nacional del Trabajo (the anarchosyndicalist revolutionary trade union founded in 1910). |
| **colono** | Settler. |
| **comadre** | The relationship between the mother and the godmother of a child. |
| **comarca** | Canton, district, region. (*Comarcal,* pertaining to a district.) |
| **compadre** | The relationship between the father and the godfather of a child. |
| **compañero compañera** | Lit., companion. The term is used to signify the brotherhood existing among workers as well as the relationship established by a couple united in free love. |
| **comunales** | The common land belonging to the township and its citizens. |
| **comunismo libertario** | Anarchist communism, the system of socialism without government, as opposed to state communism. |
| **confianza** | Confidence, trust. |
| **corral** | Yard. |
| **cortijo** | Grange. An outlying farm or country estate, or, more particularly, the housing compound on the estate consisting of the housing area, the kitchen, and the barns and storage rooms. |
| **cuadrilla** | Gang or crew of workers. |
| **a destajo** | Piece work; contract labor as opposed to hourly wages. |

| | |
|---|---|
| **don, doña** | Title of respect prefixed to a given name. It is used to address those with advanced degrees or titles or those who hold positions of power and authority. |
| **duro** | Coin worth five pesetas. |
| **egoísmo** | Egoism, selfishness. |
| **encargado** | Foreman, manager. |
| **era** | Threshing floor. |
| **ermita** | Hermitage. |
| **eventuales** | Day workers. |
| **FAI** | Federación Anarquista Ibérica (a clandestine group within the CNT, founded in 1927). |
| **faístas** | Members of the FAI. |
| **Falange** | Spanish Fascists who supported Franco's revolt. |
| **fanega** | Land measure of 5,480 meters, the equivalent of a little more than half a hectare, or 1.6 acres. (The measurement for a fanega may vary from one township to another, so that a fanega in Alcalá is 400 meters larger than a fanega in Medina Sidonia.) The fanega is also a measure of capacity equivalent to 1.6 bushels and a measure of weight (about 116 pounds). |
| **Federación de la Juventud Libertaria** | Federation of Libertarian Youth. The youth group of the FAI. |
| **fijo** | Permanent (fixed) worker on an estate employed on a yearly verbal contract. This contrasts with the temporary work arrangements made by the eventuales, the day workers. |
| **finca** | Country estate, farm. |
| **FNIF** | Federación Nacional de la Industria Ferroviaria, the railway workers union affiliated with the CNT. |
| **formal** | Serious, reliable, and punctual (adj.). |
| **ganadero** | Cattle worker, cowboy. |
| **gañán (pl. gañanes)** | Farm laborer. |
| **gañanía** | Living quarters of the farm laborers. |

**gazpachero** The worker who prepared and carried the gazpacho to the workers.

**gorda** Twenty céntimos, one-fifth of a peseta.

**hectárea** Hectare; 10,000 square meters—the equivalent of 2.471 acres, or 1.750 fanegas.

**hortelano** Gardener, orchard worker.

**huerta** Vegetable garden; orchard; cultivated and irrigated land.

**inconsciente** Unaware, uninformed, without ideas.

**jornalero** Day laborer hired for a season of work.

**jota** Spanish folk dance originating in the region of Aragón.

**Juventud Libertaria** *See* Federación de la Juventud Libertaria.

**latifundio** Large landed estate.

**latifundista** Owner of a latifundio.

**ley de fugas** "Shot while trying to escape" (often used as a cover for atrocities).

**madrileño** Resident of Madrid.

**marqués, marquesa** Marquis, marchioness.

**mentira** Lie.

**moro** Moorish, (colloquial, unbaptized).

**mosto** Unfermented grape juice.

**murga** Chorus of masked singers during Carnaval.

**novio, novia** Fiancé(e); boyfriend, girlfriend.

**obrero consciente** Dedicated anarchist (lit., informed, aware, or conscious worker).

**padrino** Godfather.

**palomo** Permanent worker contracted to work through the year for the added reward of the yield from a half-fanega of land (approximately ten fanegas, or sixteen bushels) (lit., dove).

**pastor** Shepherd.

**patrón** Landlord, employer, patron.

**pegujaleros** Renters of small amounts of land to sow a crop.

| | |
|---|---|
| **pelantrín** | Small farmer. |
| **peonista** | Day laborer hired for the day or for a fixed task; his tenure is even shorter than that of the jornalero. |
| **perra chica** | Five céntimos; one-twentieth of a peseta. |
| **peseta** | Spanish monetary unit. It equals 4 reales or 100 céntimos. In 1914 the peseta equaled 18 U.S. cents; in 1933 it equaled 8 cents. |
| **pistolero** | Gunman, hired gangster. |
| **pitón** | Agare americana; a common straight-shafted plant that grows to a height of approximately twelve feet. Pitones are often used as cross-beams in the construction of a choza. |
| **pueblo** | Village, town. |
| **rancho** | Small house or small holding in the campo. |
| **real** | Antique monetary unit; four reales equaled one peseta. |
| **reparto** | Division of the lands into small holdings. |
| **salud** | Health; used as a salute—"To your health." |
| **a seco** | Lit., dry; the arrangement between landlord and workers whereby the workers brought their own food, as opposed to *a mojado* (wet), in which food was supplied by the landowner. |
| **señorito** | Well-to-do landowner who does not work but lives from the rental of his property or by the effort of his foremen and workers. |
| **simpático** | Congenial, friendly, well liked. |
| **sindicato** | Trade union. |
| **tuerto, tuerta** | Blind in one eye. |
| **UGT** | Unión General de Trabajadores (the national trade union of the Socialists). |

# Selected Bibliography

Abad de Santillán, Diego. *Contribución a la historia del movimiento, desde sus orígenes hasta 1905*. Editorial Cajica, Puebla, México, 1962.

*Actas de los Consejos y Comisión Federal de la Región Española (1870–1874)*. 3 vols. Edited by Carlos Seco Serrano. Colección de documentos para el estudio de los movimientos obreros en España en la época contemporánea. Barcelona, Universidad de Barcelona, 1969.

Álvarez Junco, José. *La ideología política del anarquismo español (1868–1910)*. Madrid, 1976.

Arbelo, Antonio. *La mortalidad de la infancia en España, 1901–1950*. Consejo Superior de Investigaciones Científicas. Madrid, 1962.

Arrarás, Joaquín. *Historia de la Segunda República Española*. 4 vols. Editora Nacional, Madrid, 1964.

Azaña, Manuel. *Memorias íntimas de Azaña*. Edited by Joaquín Arrarás. Ediciones Españolas, Madrid, 1939.

———. *Obras completas*. 4 vols. Edited by Juan Marichal. Ediciones Oasis, Mexico City, 1966–68.

Bakunin, Michael. *Bakunin on Anarchy*. Edited by Sam Dolgoff. Vintage, New York, 1972.

———. *Michael Bakunin, Selected Writings*. Edited by Arthur Lehning. Grove Press, New York, 1974.

Bernaldo de Quirós, Constancio. "Bandolerismo y delincuencia subversiva en la baja Andalucía." In *Junta para la ampliación de estudios científicos. Anales* 9 (1913): 33–55.

———. *El espartaquismo agrario andaluz*. Edited, with an introduction, by Luis Jiménez Asúa. Ediciones Torner, Madrid, 1974.

Blasco Ibáñez, V. *La bodega*. Sempere, Valencia, 1905.

Bookchin, Murray. *The Spanish Anarchists: The Heroic Years, 1868–1936*. Free Life Editions, New York, 1977.

Borkenau, Franz. *The Spanish Cockpit*. University of Michigan, Ann Arbor, Mich., 1963. First published in 1937.

Borrow, George. *The Bible in Spain*. George Routledge, London, 1842.

Brademas, John. *Anarcosindicalismo y revolución en España (1930–37)*. Ariel, Barcelona, 1974.

Brenan, Gerald. *The Spanish Labyrinth: An Account of the Social and Political Background of the Civil War*. 2d ed. Cambridge University Press, Cambridge, 1950.

Brey, Gerard. "Socialistas, anarco-sindicalistas y anarquistas en la provincia de Cádiz en 1932–33." In *Sociedad, política y cultura en la España de los siglos XIX y XX*. Edicusa, Madrid, 1973.

Brey, Gerard, and Jacques Maurice. *Historia y leyenda de Casas Viejas*. Edita Zero, Bilbao, 1976.

———. "Reformismo y anarquismo en Andalucía (1870–1933)." In *El movimiento libertario español: pasado, presente y futuro*. Ruedo ibérico, París, 1974.

Buenacasa, Manuel. *El movimiento obrero español; historia y crítica, 1886–1926*. Impresos Costa, Barcelona, 1928.

Carr, Raymond. "All or Nothing." *New York Review of Books*, October 13, 1977.

———, ed. *The Republic and the Civil War in Spain*. Macmillan, London, 1971.

———. *Spain, 1808–1939*. Clarendon Press, Oxford, 1966.

Carrión, Pascual. *Los latifundios en España*. Gráficas Reunidas, Madrid, 1932.

*Cartilla filológica española: primer libro de lectura*. 10th ed. Barcelona, 1907. Pamphlet.

*Casas Viejas: un proceso que pertenece a la historia*. Edited by Manuel García Ceballos. Fermín Uriarte, Madrid, 1965.

Chomsky, Noam. "Objectivity and Liberal Scholarship, II." In *American Power and the New Mandarins*. Harmondsworth, England: Penguin, 1969.

Christian, William A., Jr. *Person and God in a Spanish Valley*. Seminar Press, New York, 1972.

Clissold, Stephen. *Spain*. London, Thaimes and Hudson, 1969.

Costa Martínez, Joaquín. *Colectivismo agrario en España*. Imp. de San Francisco de Sales, Madrid, 1898.

———. *Oligarquía y caciquismo como la forma actual de gobierno en España*. Editorial V. Campo, Huesca, 1927.

*Diario de sesiones de las Cortes Españolas. 1932–1934*. Madrid.

Díaz del Moral, Juan. *Historia de las agitaciones campesinas andaluzas—Córdoba*. Antecedentes para una reforma agraria. Revista de Derecho Privado, Madrid, 1929.

———. *Las reformas agrarias europeas de la posguerra, 1918–1929*. Alianza Editorial, Madrid, 1967.

Dolgoff, Sam, ed. *The Anarchist Collectives: Workers' Self-Management in the Spanish Revolution, 1936–1939*. Free Life Editions, New York, 1974.

*España, 1933: la barbarie gubernamental*. Barcelona, 1933. Pamphlet.

Gilabert, A. G. *Un héroe del pueblo: Durruti*. Editorial C.G.T., Valparaíso, 1938.

Gilmore, David. "Class, Cognition, and Space in a Spanish Town." *American Ethnologist 4, no. 3 (August 1977): 437–51.*

*Giner, Salvador. "Continuity and Change: The Social Stratification of Spain."* Occasional Publication No. 1 of the University of Reading Graduate School of Contemporary European Studies. Reading, 1968.

Gori, Pedro. *Ciencia y religión. Las bases sociológicas de la anarquía*. Biblioteca Tierra y Libertad. Barcelona, n.d. Pamphlet.

*Han pasado los bárbaros: la verdad sobre Casas Viejas*. Seville, 1933. Pamphlet.

Hobsbawm, E. J. *Primitive Rebels: Studies in Archaic Forms of Social Movements in the 19th and 20th Centuries*. 2d ed. W. W. Norton and Co., New York, 1965.

Iturbe, Lola. *La mujer en la lucha social y en la Guerra Civil de España*. Editores Mexicanos Unidos, Mexico City, 1974.

Jackson, Gabriel. "The Origins of Spanish Anarchism." *Southwestern Social Science Quarterly* 36 (1955): 135–47.

———. *The Spanish Republic and the Civil War, 1931–1939*. Princeton University Press, Princeton, N.J., 1965.

Joll, James. *The Anarchists*. Grosset and Dunlap, New York, 1966.

Kaplan, Temma. *Anarchists of Andalusia, 1868–1903*. Princeton University Press, Princeton, N.J., 1977.

Kenny, Michael. *A Spanish Tapestry*. Harper and Row, New York, 1962.

Kern, Robert W. *Red Years, Black Years: A Political History of Spanish Anarchism*. ISHI, Philadelphia, 1978.

Kropotkin, Peter. "Anarchist Communism: Its Basis and Principles." In *Kropotkin's Revolutionary Pamphlets*, edited by Roger N. Baldwin. Benjamin Blom, New York, 1968. First published in 1927.

———. *The Conquest of Bread*. Benjamin Blom, New York, 1968. First published in 1913.

———. *Fields, Factories and Workshops Tomorrow*. Edited by Colin Ward. George Allen and Unwin, London, 1974. First published in 1898.

———. *The Great French Revolution, 1789–1793*. Translated by N. F. Dryhurst. Schocken, New York, 1971. First published in 1909.

———. *Mutual Aid: A Factor of Evolution*. Extending Horizons Books, Boston, 1955. First published in 1902.

Lacomba Avellán, Juan Antonio. *La crisis española de 1917*. Ciencia Nueva, Madrid, 1970.

Langdon-Davies, John. *Behind the Spanish Barricades*. M. Secker and Warburgh, London, 1936.

Leval, Gaston. *Collectives in the Spanish Revolution*. Freedom Press, London, 1975.

Lida, Clara E. "Agrarian Anarchism in Andalusia: Documents on the Mano Negra." *International Review of Social History* 14 (1969): 315–52.

———. *Anarquismo y revolución en la España del XIX*. Siglo veintiuno de España, Madrid, 1972.

———. *Antecedentes y desarrollo del movimiento obrero español (1835–1888): textos y documentos*. Siglo veintiuno de España, Madrid, 1973.

López Montenegro, José. *El botón de fuego*. Barcelona, 1902.

Lorenzo, Anselmo. *El proletariado militante*. Edited by José Álvarez Junco. Alianza Editorial, Madrid, 1974.

Lorenzo, César M. *Los anarquistas españoles y el poder*. Ruedo ibérico, Paris, 1972.

Malefakis, Edward E. *Agrarian Reform and Peasant Revolution in Spain: Origins of the Civil War*. Yale University Press, New Haven, Conn., 1970.

Martínez y Delgado, Francisco. *Historia de la ciudad de Medina Sidonia*. Notes by Joaquín María Enrille. Impr. y Litografía de la Revista Médica, Cadiz, 1875.

Martínez-Alier, Juan. *Labourers and Landowners in Southern Spain*. St. Anthony's Publications, no. 4. George Allen and Unwin, London, 1971.

Marvaud, Ángel. *La question sociale en Espagne*. F. Alcan, Paris, 1910.

Maurice, Jacques. "Problemas de la reforma agraria en la Segunda República (1931–1936)." In *Sociedad, política y cultura en la España de los siglos XIX–XX*. Edicusa, Madrid, 1973.

Meaker, Gerald H. *The Revolutionary Left in Spain, 1914–1923*. Stanford University Press, Stanford, Calif., 1974.

*Memoria del congreso extraordinario celebrado en Madrid los días 11 al 16 de junio de 1931*. Confederación Nacional del Trabajo, Barcelona, 1932.

*Memoria del primer congreso comarcal celebrado por la Federación de Trabajadores Agrícolas de la comarca de Cádiz, en los días 17 y 18 de enero de 1932, en Jerez de la Frontera.* Jerez, 1932.

Mintz, Jerome R. "Comfortable Old Shrines, Divisive New Visions." *Natural History* 83, no. 4 (April 1974): 40–47, 85.

———. "Trouble in Andalusia." *Natural History* 81, no. 5 (May 1972): 54–63.

Montseny, Federica. *María Silva, La Libertaria.* Toulouse, 1951. Pamphlet.

Morillo Crespo, Antonio. *Vejer de la Frontera y su comarca, aportaciones a su historia.* Edita: Instituto de Estudios Gaditanos. Excma. Diputación Provincial de Cádiz, Cádiz, 1974.

Nettlau, Max. *Impresiones sobre el desarrollo del socialismo en España.* Zero-ZYX, Algorta-Madrid, 1971.

———. *La Première Internationale en Espagne, 1868–1888.* 2 vols. Edited by Renée Lamberet. D. Reidel, Dordrecht, 1969.

Peers, E. Allison. *The Spanish Tragedy, 1930–1936.* 3d ed. Methuen, London, 1936.

Peirats, José. *Los anarquistas en la crisis política española.* Editorial Alfa, Buenos Aires, 1964.

———. *La CNT en la revolución española.* 3 vols. Ediciones CNT, Toulouse, 1951.

Peiro, Juan. *Problemas del sindicalismo y del anarquismo.* Ediciones Movimiento Libertario Español, Toulouse, 1945.

Peiró, P. Francisco. *El problema religioso-social de España.* Editorial "Razón y Fe," Madrid, 1936.

Pennock, J. Roland, and John W. Chapman. *Anarchism.* New York University Press, 1978.

Peñuelas, Marcelino C. *Conversaciones con R. J. Sender.* Editorial Magisterio Español, Madrid, 1970.

Pérez Cordón, Miguel. *Amor y tragedia. La novela ideal,* no. 330, November 30, 1932.

———. "Como las águilas." *La Voz del Campesino,* October 29, 1932.

Pestaña, Ángel. *Lo que aprendí en la vida.* 2 vols. 2d ed. Zero, S. A. Telleche, Algorta (Vizcaya), 1972. First published in 1933.

Pitt-Rivers, J. A. *The People of the Sierra.* 2d ed. University of Chicago Press, Chicago, 1961.

Pritchett, V. S. *The Spanish Temper.* Chatto and Windus, London, 1954.

Retamero, Francisco. ¡ *Colectivización! La explotación colectiva de "Malcocinado."* Madrid, 1935. Pamphlet.

Rocker, Rudolf. *Anarcho-Syndicalism.* Seeker and Warburg, London, 1938.

Sánchez Jiménez, José. *El movimiento obrero y sus orígenes en Andalucía.* 2d ed. Zero-ZYX, Algorta-Madrid, 1969.

Sánchez Rosa, José. *Diálogo: el obrero sindicalista y su patrono.* Seville, 1911. Pamphlet.

———. En el campo: diálogo. Seville, 1911. Pamphlet.

Schapiro, Alexander. *Rapport sur l'activité de la Confederation Nationale du Travail d'Espagne, 16 décembre 1921–26 février 1933.* Association Internationale des Travailleurs. Unpublished ms.

Seco Serrano, Carlos. *Colección de documentos para el estudio de los movimientos obreros en España en la época contemporánea.* Vol. 1. Universidad de Barcelona, Barcelona, 1969.

Sedwick, Frank. *The Tragedy of Manuel Azaña.* Ohio State University Press, Columbus, Ohio, 1963.

Sender, Ramón José. *Casas Viejas.* Editorial Cenit, Madrid, 1933.

Silverio de Santa Teresa, P., O.C.D. *Historia del Carmen Descalzo en España, Portugal y América*. Vols. 11, 12. Tipografía Burgalesa (El Monte Carmelo), Burgos, 1943.

Simón, Segura, F. *La desamortización española del siglo XIX*. Instituto de Estudios Fiscales, Madrid, 1973.

Taster Díaz, Antonio. "Semblanza sobre la vida y obra de Don Juan Díaz del Moral." *Revista de estudios regionales*, no. 4 (1979): 1–31.

Termes, Josep. *Anarquismo y sindicalismo en España: la Primera Internacional (1864–1881)*. Ediciones Ariel, Esplugues de Llobregat, Barcelona, 1972.

Termes Ardévol, José. *El movimiento obrero en España: la Primera Internacional (1864–1881)*. Publicaciones de la Cátedra de Historia General de España, Barcelona, 1965.

Thomas, Hugh. *The Spanish Civil War*. 2d ed. Harper and Row, New York, 1977.

Tuñón de Lara, Manuel. *Introducción a la historia del movimiento obrero*. Editorial Nova Terra, Barcelona, 1966.

———. *Historia y realidad del poder*. Editorial Cuadernos para el Diálogo, Madrid, 1967.

Ullman, Joan Connelly. *The Tragic Week: A Study of Anticlericalism in Spain, 1875–1912*. Harvard University Press, Cambridge, Mass., 1968.

Urales, Federico [Juan Montseny y Carret] *La evolución de la filosofía en España*. La Revista Blanca, Barcelona, 1934.

*La verdad sobre la tragedia de Casas Viejas*. Madrid, n.d. Pamphlet.

Vicens Vives, Jaime. *Approaches to the History of Spain*. Translated by Joan Connelly Ullman. University of California Press, Berkeley, 1967.

Waggoner, Glen A. "The Black Hand Mystery: Rural Unrest and Social Violence in Southern Spain, 1881–1883." In *Modern European Social History*, edited by Robert J. Bezucha. D. C. Heath and Co., Lexington, Mass., 1972.

Wallace, Anthony F. C. "Revitalization Movements." *American Anthropologist* 58 (1956): 264–281.

Woodcock, George. *Anarchism: A History of Libertarian Ideas and Movements*. Harmondsworth, England: Penguin, 1963.

———. "Anarchism Revisited." *Commentary* 46, no. 2 (August 1968): 54–59.

## Newspapers Cited

*ABC*
*Ahora*
*CNT*
*Cultura Hispánica*
*Diario de Cádiz*
*El Guadalete*
*La Internacional*
*El Productor*
*El Proletario*
*La Revista Blanca*
*Sindicalismo*
*El Sol*
*Solidaridad Obrera*
*La Tierra*
*Tierra y Libertad*
*La Tribuna Obrera*
*La Voz del Campesino*

# Index

Jerome R. Mintz is Professor of Anthropology at Indiana University. He is the author of several books, including *Legends of the Hasidim and Hasidic People*, and the prizewinning filmmaker of a series on tradition and change in Andalusia.